T0051799

MITCH, PLEASE!

How Mitch McConnell Sold Out Kentucky (and America, Too)

Matt Jones with Chris Tomlin

Simon & Schuster Paperbacks
NEW YORK LONDON TORONTO SYDNEY NEW DELHI

Simon & Schuster Paperbacks
An Imprint of Simon & Schuster, Inc.
1230 Avenue of the Americas
New York, NY 10020

First Simon & Schuster trade paperback edition October 2020

SIMON & SCHUSTER PAPERBACKS and colophon are registered trademarks of Simon & Schuster, Inc.

For information about special discounts for bulk purchases, please contact Simon & Schuster Special Sales at 1-866-506-1949 or business@simonandschuster.com.

The Simon & Schuster Speakers Bureau can bring authors to your live event. For more information or to book an event, contact the Simon & Schuster Speakers Bureau at 1-866-248-3049 or visit our website at www.simonspeakers.com.

Interior design by Paul Dippolito

Manufactured in the United States of America

1 3 5 7 9 10 8 6 4 2

Library of Congress Cataloging-in-Publication Data has been applied for.

ISBN 978-1-9821-4204-9
ISBN 978-1-9821-6416-4 (pbk)
ISBN 978-1-9821-4205-6 (ebook)

To the people of Kentucky, who opened
their doors and hearts to us, and who showed
us kindness every step of the way

NOTE ON INTERVIEWS

We traveled to all 120 of these counties, and our descriptions of each are based upon these travels. Most of our interviews were done collectively, but some were done by each of us individually. For purposes of narration, we will speak about all of the interviews in one voice.

CONTENTS

MITCH, PLEASE!

Introduction

Powell County (August 24, 2019)

Rallying 'Round the Rooster

"If Mitch McConnell were a hound dog, even the fleas would stay away from him."

It's a hot, sticky summer day in a city park in Stanton, Kentucky, and an elderly man in a flannel shirt and jeans is giving me the what for on all things Mitch McConnell. "I don't like Mitch and I don't know how anyone could. He's a weasel and we gotta get him out of there."

We are at the Powell County Democratic "Rally 'Round the Rooster"* event, a yearly celebration for local Democrats. The event is filled with a disappearing breed, rural blue-collar Democrats, a group that once dominated Kentucky politics that now see their ranks thinning with each passing year. These folks are in desperate need of good news and have come for a sweaty mix of politickin', hot dogs, and homemade potato salad.

The Kentucky governor's election is just a few months away, and this large crowd is ready for change—not just in that race but also another a little more than a year away. The man continues, "Here's the thing, Matt, we can beat Mitch. We can. But we can't be running these

---

* I looked for the rooster to rally 'round; never found it. Roosters are fast.

people from the big cities like Louisville and expect them to come and be able to talk to people out here in the country. We tried that. It don't work. Everybody in this state knows McConnell is awful. But they ain't gonna just vote for anybody. They might vote for you, though!"

I am here, in part, because I am considering a run against Senator Mitch McConnell in 2020. It's admittedly a ridiculous notion. McConnell is the second most powerful man in the country, spending his days ruining America's democracy. I am a forty-one-year-old sports radio host who spends his days entertaining tens of thousands of Kentuckians by debating whether John Wall or Kyle Macy was the better former University of Kentucky (UK) basketball point guard. It isn't the normal biography of a United States Senate candidate, but defeating McConnell in this deep-red state is going to take something out of the ordinary.

I came to Powell County to give my first political speech as a potential candidate. All the big Democrats in Kentucky are here, each trying to energize the crowd. As I await my turn to speak, a line of locals comes over to say hello. They all tell me they love my show, are huge fans of UK basketball, and "hate Mitch worse than anything." They aren't alone.

In fact, if you are reading this sentence, there is a very good chance that *you* hate Mitch McConnell. I can say that in part because the type of person who picks up a book with the title *Mitch, Please!* and a cartoon rendering of America's most reptilian politician on its cover is likely also someone who isn't a fan of the Senate majority leader. And why would you be? Mitch McConnell is the worst. If you are a rational human being with some degree of care for your fellow man, then you have to dislike Mitch McConnell and everything he represents.

Thankfully, most people do. McConnell is not only the least popular senator in America, he is uniquely disliked in his (and my) home state of Kentucky. In the survey research company Morning Consult's quarterly measurement of popularity in a senator's home state, McConnell's Kentucky approval rating nearly always comes in last in the entire nation. His approval rating has been as low as 18 percent and never reaches higher than the mid-30s.

In Kentucky, finding a true Mitch McConnell fan is like finding a fan of our archrival, the Tennessee Vols: one might exist, but that person would be looked upon with a hearty mixture of scorn and pity.

I was quite nervous as I walked up to give my speech to the crowd. The candidates for governor and attorney general had just spoken, and the crowd of a couple hundred people were in a mood to cheer. I had a set of talking points, but they were on a crumpled sheet of paper and hard to read. So I tossed them aside as I got onstage and decided to speak from my heart.

"Mitch McConnell is the single most destructive force to Kentucky and America of my lifetime, and it's time we make it priority number one to send his ass out of Washington once and for all!"

The crowd burst into cheers.

Whatever it is that you hate about politics the most, chances are Mitch McConnell is largely responsible for its existence. The massive amounts of money that have flooded our political elections? Mitch McConnell is responsible. The political divide that seems to be tearing our country apart at the seams? Thank you, Mitch. The gridlock that keeps Congress from passing any meaningful legislation? Three for three. The fact that Congress is full of career politicians who stay in office for way too long? Mitch again. The personal nastiness that is part of every political campaign? You get the picture. Mitch McConnell is quite simply everything wrong with American politics in 2020.

So how did McConnell get to this level of power and destruction? And more important, why does he keep winning? The voters of Kentucky continue to reelect a senator they despise—often by wide margins. In 2014, McConnell's race with challenger Alison Lundergan Grimes was supposed to be a close one. She was a well-funded, relatively popular secretary of state, a young, fresh face that looked to be a perfect contrast to the old, stodgy curmudgeon from Louisville. Some early polls even showed Grimes leading, and national coverage painted the picture that Mitch could be on the brink. Then on Election Day, reality hit: McConnell won by an overwhelming sixteen-point margin, a result not even his most optimistic supporters would have imagined.

The voters of Kentucky may hate him, but each election they look him in the eye and say, "Thanks, Mother, may I have another?"

Mitch is Kentucky's political cockroach, unable to be destroyed, no matter how gross his transgressions. Even though he is so unlikable that he makes Texas senator Ted Cruz look like Tom Hanks, Kentuckians keep choosing his obnoxious leadership while simultaneously honoring him as the least popular politician in America. How does this happen? It is a question that perplexes outsiders and depresses Kentuckians across the Bluegrass. I decided I had to find out the answer.

I was raised in the small town of Middlesboro, deep in the heart of coal country in the Appalachian Mountains. Except for my years at Duke University Law School and clerking on the District of Columbia and Fourth Circuits, I have spent my entire life in Kentucky. I have what my friend University of Louisville (UL) African American Studies professor Ricky Jones calls "an unnatural love affair" with my state. I don't think he meant it as a compliment, but it is correct. I love my home state and consider its people the best you will find.

So it's particularly appalling to me that a man who does such immense damage to our state and country is the face of the commonwealth to the world.* It's important for you folks outside Kentucky to understand, we aren't all like Mitch McConnell. In fact, none of us are like him. This state is unique and full of people for whom being a true Kentuckian really means something. We love the mountains, bourbon, basketball, bluegrass music, hunting, fishing, horse racing, preaching, singing, picking, and grinning—all the staples of Kentucky life. We embrace those with whom we share a common culture and heritage.

Mitch McConnell shares none of these traits with us. He exists as Kentucky's permanent hall monitor, looking over our shoulders with a scowl on his face, ready to perpetually kill our buzz. Mitch McConnell

---

* Kentucky is one of four states (Virginia, Pennsylvania, and Massachusetts are the others) that are technically commonwealths and not states. This difference is nothing important, except it proves we are better than you.

is as much a true Kentuckian as I am a true ballerina, and to have you believe he "represents" us is depressing. I am here to dispel that notion.

I am the founder and host of *Kentucky Sports Radio* (*KSR*), the largest media outlet in Kentucky, with forty-five radio affiliates around the state and a website that gets as many as two hundred thousand visitors a day. Every day on Kentucky's airwaves, my crew (cohosts Ryan Lemond and Drew Franklin, and our producer, Shannon the Dude—yes, he goes by Shannon the Dude) and I talk not only about the latest in UK sports, but also the most important topics of daily life in Kentucky. We spend the day discussing and making jokes about Kentucky's latest news, sports, gossip, small-town strange stories, and whatever else is on people's minds. It's a call-in show and as such, our focus can differ wildly from segment to segment. One segment we might discuss how hundreds of schoolteachers are marching on our state capital to protest the governor's cuts to public education, while another deals with the scourge of a rumored werewolf murdering cattle in Waddy, Kentucky. Our goal is to reflect the conversations that are going on in any McDonald's at eight in the morning anywhere in the state. (If you don't know that all across America, the major small-town conversations occur at McDonald's over morning coffee, then you are officially part of the cultural elite.) It is Kentucky's radio town square, and for hundreds of thousands across the state, we are a part of their daily routines.

As part of this job, I interact with Kentuckians of all types, from every corner of the state. For many of you reading this, you may have some vague understanding that the University of Kentucky is good at basketball and that college athletics are important in this part of the country. But that minimizes what UK (and to a lesser extent UL) sports mean to this state. In Kentucky, college sports, particularly college basketball, is life. There is literally no event that brings the state together like a Kentucky Wildcats basketball game, and my life's work is sharing the obsession of the Blue and White with my fellow Kentuckians. It's a truly unique platform.

And from that platform, *KSR* has become a place where, yes, we talk politics occasionally. While it has been fashionable in recent years for critics to say that sports media should "stick to sports," I have never followed that mantra. Politics is life, and no topic can truly be detached from it. In 2014, the last time Mitch McConnell was up for reelection, I interviewed both him and his opponent, Alison Lundergan Grimes, separately on our show. The interviews were tense (and available on YouTube if you are so inclined). McConnell became very frustrated with my questioning, cutting me off repeatedly and reacting with anger as I challenged him on issues.

During one exchange, I asked the senator if he believed in climate change. McConnell proceeded to produce a long-winded response that answered nothing and ended with him saying "I am not a scientist." When I pressed him on what his not being a scientist had to do with anything and asked for a simple yes or no on the existence of climate change, he barked at me and told me to move on. Mitch became so frustrated that many in the national media ran stories about our verbal joust. Longtime McConnell media followers told me privately I had rattled him, an uncharacteristic response from a man who prides himself on keeping his cool.

The subsequent publicity and interest from our listeners convinced me that politics could be a reasonable, relevant topic on *KSR*. We dabbled in the 2015 governor's race and had an outlandish idea to invite all GOP primary candidates on the air for a debate. To my shock, they all agreed. What followed was the most listened-to show in *KSR* history. Many in the news media believe that surprise primary winner Matt Bevin won the election due to his strong showing in that debate. I hosted a similar debate during the general election campaign, and *KSR* established itself as a regular player in the state's political scene.

Still, I considered politics only a diversionary topic until a surprise moment in July 2015. While watching an episode of *BoJack Horseman*,* I received a call from an unknown DC phone number. Upon answering, I heard, verbatim, "Hi, is this Matt Jones? My name is Steven,† from the

---

* A criminally underrated show.

† Name changed to protect his credibility.

Democratic Congressional Campaign Committee, and I was wondering if you have ever thought about running for Congress?"

After making sure I wasn't being pranked, I asked, "Why in the world are you calling me?" How many hundreds of people must have turned him down before he decided the best bet was a local sports radio host? Steven told me that the DCCC had been polling for the last couple of months, and the numbers indicated that I had the best chance of any Democrat to be elected congressman from the Sixth District of Kentucky. They were hoping I might have interest in running against Republican incumbent Andy Barr and invited me to discuss the possibility with them in Washington, DC.

What followed was the greatest lesson in the reality of American politics that I will ever learn. I went through the process of being recruited to run for Congress by attending a Democratic congressional "Boot Camp." The experience was eye opening and it became clear to me very quickly that there may be few jobs less fulfilling than a congressman in the US House of Representatives. In today's tumultuous, hyper-partisan political landscape, being a House member is akin to being a background hype man for the world's dorkiest rap group. You get none of the acclaim for any of the music, and regardless of what you might really think about any song or the lead singer, you are along for the ride, for better or worse.

The Senate, however, is different. Obviously, there is the practical consideration of only 100 members as opposed to 435. But in addition, the Senate rules actually make being an individual and bucking your party's orthodoxy much easier. In the Senate, the late John McCain can walk on the floor, give a thumbs-down, and literally save health care for millions of Americans, as he did in 2017 when he cast the deciding vote to save the Affordable Care Act from being repealed. In the House, however, the vast majority of members could walk out of the building for a year, and no one would know they were gone. The Senate is a place I could make a difference and fight for the people, the forgotten working class and poor citizens of this state who make me want to passionately pursue public service in the first place. It is not only a better job, it is also one I could justify giving up my life's work for.

So, I set my sights on McConnell. Potentially trying to end his long-term stranglehold on the Kentucky Senate seat and American democracy was an audacious idea. A sports radio show host is probably not most people's Aaron Sorkin–esque dream of the perfect person to try taking on the most powerful force in American government. But these aren't normal times. We elected the host of *The Apprentice* president. It may be absurd to think of a sports radio show host as a senator, but it would be only the tenth most ridiculous news story in the news on any given day.

Over the last two years, I became focused on the race as well as on learning everything I could about McConnell and my beloved home state. I read every biography ever written about the man and studied his thirty-six-year record. I focused on national political policy in a way I had never done before, to understand not only the issues but also how they impacted average Kentuckians and the state as a whole. I researched all 120 counties—learning about their histories, economies, and people—to get a sense of a state that is much more diverse than folks realize. Basically, I did my homework. I tried to discover the full extent of the power of Darth Vader, and what it would mean to try to fight him across the Bluegrass State.

However, others were contemplating taking on McConnell, too. A number of Democrats had already entered the 2020 Kentucky Senate race, the most prominent of which was US Marines veteran Amy McGrath. The first female Marine Corps pilot to fly the F/A-18 Hornet on a combat mission, McGrath was a candidate out of central casting. Her military record made her a hero, and this would not be her first foray into running for office. She had attempted to win a Kentucky congressional seat in 2018, and, based on an unbelievably strong opening video, she went viral and became the hero of liberals across America looking for an ex–military member they could call their own. McGrath's loss in a very winnable 2018 race did little to slow her momentum, and she became the choice of the national Democratic Party to take on Mitch McConnell. With the national party's backing, she raised nearly $11 million in the first quarter of fund-raising, surpassing all Senate and most presidential candidates in the country. She was the establishment pick and the early heavy favorite for the nomination.

There was only one problem. I believed Amy McGrath had little chance of beating Mitch McConnell. After losing a congressional race in a district much more favorable to Democrats than Kentucky as a whole, the idea of her then being able to extend out statewide and defeat Mitch seemed like a long shot. However, she had the money and the backing of the establishment, meaning that if I entered the race, I would have to knock out the mainstream Democratic Party before even getting my shot at McConnell. A difficult task became even harder.

All of which brings me to this book. As I was determining my path, it became clear to me three questions needed to be answered:

1. What has Mitch McConnell's effect on Kentucky actually been?
2. Why has he consistently been reelected, and how can he be defeated?
3. Does it make sense for me to be the one to try?

The answers to these questions lay in the roads of Kentucky. While I had already studied each of Kentucky's counties, I needed to visit them (and their citizens) myself.

Thus, the idea of the 120-county road trip was born. I needed to get in a car and actually ask people directly how (and why) we've let this senator we all dislike wield power for thirty-six years. If I wanted to see what impact his policies and leadership have had on my state, for good and bad, I needed to go to the people affected by them. The people of Kentucky dislike Mitch McConnell, but it isn't necessarily for the reasons the rest of America does. Kentucky's specific issues with Mitch were worth exploring. And if I wanted to see if there was any room for me to try taking on the Democratic establishment and Darth Vader, well, what better way than going and speaking with voters.

So, I created a schedule: 120 counties in 10 weeks. I divided the state into 10 regions and set out to visit them on a massive road trip across the commonwealth. Undertaking this journey by myself was a nonstarter. Road trips are only fun if you have a companion, and my choice was simple. My coauthor, Chris Tomlin, has been my close friend since college. He's a terrific writer and the funniest human being I've ever met. Every footnote you'll read is written by him.* He'll give you his insights as we hit every corner of the state.

What follows is the travelogue of our 120-county journey. Along the way, it confirmed my love for Kentucky and its people. There is no better place in the world, and I hope this book proudly portrays my love for it. In addition, it's a study of Mitch McConnell, the most destructive force in American democracy, and how he maintains power. But it is also a look into how the establishment of both parties maintains control in America, and the consequences of our broken political system.

Is it a lot to cover? Sure. But the goal is to try to identify what's happened to my beloved Kentucky, to its people and our political identity over the last thirty-six years. Oh, and to have some fun along the way. It's time to show Kentucky to the world. And it's time to show who Mitch McConnell really is.

Let's go for a ride.

---

* Even though Mitch McConnell gives me the creeps, I'm not the political animal Matt is. So I will be commenting on the nonpolitical quirks of this trip, so that you will be a hit at your next "Celebrating Kentucky's 120 Counties" party.

CHAPTER 1

The Rise of Mitch

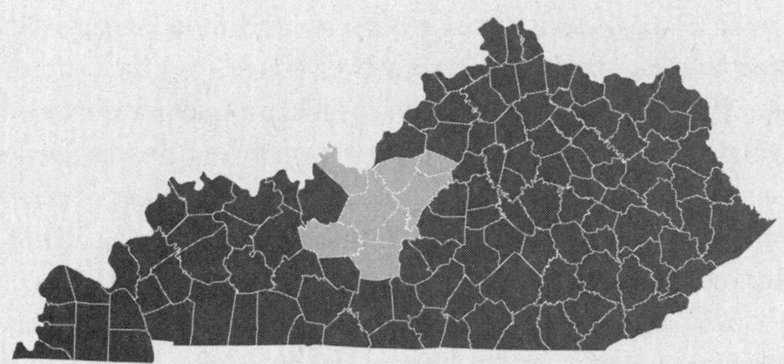

Hardin County

Mitch and the Hounds

When we began our 120-county tour on September 2, 2019, we wanted to visit Mitch McConnell's birthplace, but, unfortunately for us, that sacred site is in Sheffield, Alabama. We thought about hitting Augusta, Georgia, the city where he was raised, but I have a policy against going there unless it's the second weekend in April. Another option was the basement museum of the Mitch McConnell Center in Louisville (where you apparently can learn the most intimate details of the senator's life), but it's so depressing that children begin crying at its mere mention.

So, instead, we made our way to Elizabethtown, one of the most beautiful small towns in America (and the titular site of director Cameron Crowe's worst movie). Elizabethtown is the county seat of Hardin County, accessible by State Route 86, winding north from Breckenridge

County through Garfield and ending just before Cecilia. The elementary school in E-town (as the locals call it) is nearly as big as the town. Churches dot the landscape around every bend, and a fertilizer store's reader board announces terrifyingly, "IT'S TIME TO CREEP FEED"* in blocky, black capital letters.

Our goal was to find the home of Walter "Dee" Huddleston, a man you may have never heard of, but who has had a profound impact on this country. Huddleston was the Democratic senator of Kentucky from 1973 until 1985. His legislative career was fairly mundane, and finding noteworthy accomplishments of his twelve years in office is, unfortunately, difficult. In fact, Huddleston is best known not for what he did in office but rather for how he was booted from it. Yes, he was the person whose loss gave us Senator Mitch McConnell.

Huddleston was a tank gunner in the US Army during World War II. After returning from Europe, he set up shop as a sports radio broadcaster down the road in Bowling Green. After a few years, he was promoted to general manager in E-town and eventually became involved in local politics. Elected as a state senator in 1965, Huddleston found himself a successful legislator, later running for and winning a US Senate seat in 1972. In 1984 he ran for a third term against fellow Democrat (and beloved former governor) John Y. Brown Jr. and a Republican upstart county judge-executive from Louisville named Mitch McConnell. Huddleston took the Democrat far more seriously, as Brown already had household name status, but he breathed easier when Brown withdrew his candidacy due to illness.† Most political observers believed the incumbent was certain to win reelection. McConnell didn't look or act the part of a Kentucky politician. Most believed Huddleston would make short work of him.

Huddleston thought little of the quiet, awkward forty-two-year-old

---

* Otherwise known as the slogan when Rick Pitino and Rudy Giuliani meet for dinner.

† John Y. Brown once owned KFC, Kenny Rogers Roasters, the Kentucky Colonels of the American Basketball Association, the Boston Celtics, and was married to a former Miss America, Phyllis George. He is still alive today at age eighty six, so don't feel too bad about the illness.

local official seeking to upset him. He did little campaigning and spent not even $1 million on the campaign—a very small amount even for the time. He assumed the entire state would see McConnell for what he was: a second-rate local politician whose biggest claim to fame was knowing a former US senator from Kentucky, John Sherman Cooper.

However, Mitch saw an opportunity. At a time when Kentucky politics was a more genteel pursuit, he decided to go hard at his opponent from the outset. In May 1984 McConnell announced a series of weekly press conferences he called "Dope on Dee," at which he'd attack his opponent's record, specifically his propensity for taking money for speeches and missing votes.* The strategy was the brainchild of a McConnell political consultant by the name of Roger Ailes. (Yes, *that* Roger Ailes.) The rise of Ailes coincided with the rise of McConnell, and his suggestion to create an ad campaign taking on Huddleston's voting record led to one of the most effective television attack ads in political history.

Ailes's bloodhound spot was simple: a plaid-flanneled hunter with a pack of leashed hound dogs searches everywhere for Huddleston, who'd been alleged to have been absent from key Senate votes. The dogs drag the frustrated hunter from the front lawn of the US Capitol Building, through the fields of Kentucky, and eventually through Los Angeles and Puerto Rico—two places where the senator was said to have visited when he should have been casting votes. It was theatrical. It was over the top. It was ridiculous. It was questionably truthful at best.

It worked like a charm.

Kentuckians took notice and began asking questions about their senator. Huddleston grew concerned. He began campaigning harder against McConnell in October, but the damage had been done. Huddleston's name was mud.† By the time President Ronald Reagan en-

---

* It's worth noting that McConnell was also taking money for giving speeches at the time as well. Local business leaders paid him for a series of speeches that nearly added up to an amount equivalent to his judge-executive salary. It didn't stop Mitch from his hypocritical attacks.

† Muddleston.

dorsed McConnell in an ad just before the election, Kentuckians had already made up their minds. McConnell took the 1984 Senate election by around five thousand votes—an upset that many still cite as the moment the tide turned from Democratic to Republican in the state of Kentucky. Ailes took credit for the upset for years to come, cementing his status as a conservative political kingmaker.

In the years following the loss, Huddleston admitted privately that he hadn't taken McConnell seriously; that he never even saw him coming. And how could he have known that the political neophyte from Jefferson County would go so . . . so . . . *dirty*? The five thousand votes Huddleston took for granted fueled the rise of the most destructive figure in modern American politics.

In an age where public service has become too often the play toy of the insanely wealthy, Huddleston's old house on Seminole Lane is notable today for its normalcy. The two-toned, brick building looks like any number of homes of the era, sitting in the middle of a quiet middle-class neighborhood, the average product of the subdivision boom of the late 1970s and early 1980s. Its paint is currently chipped and the outside slightly worn, but in its prime, it would have represented the middle-class American dream. Nothing about it screams US senator. It is the gateway to a time in the not too distant past when politicians weren't a distinct class from average citizens.

As I stand in front of Huddleston's former Elizabethtown home and consider the damage that has occurred to America because one sports radio host got a little too cocky about his bespectacled challenger, I can't help but think about the symmetry of the moment. If one sports radio host's mistaken campaign strategy gave the world Mitch McConnell, what if another's decision thirty-six years later could correct it? Only this time, the underdog is not the villain. It has all the makings of an inspirational movie.*

These delusions of grandeur were interrupted by a slam of the door to the house directly to the left. There, the result of McConnell's and Ailes's hound dogs becomes crystal clear. A man walks from his house,

---

* In the movie version, Matt wants to be played by Matt Damon. I prefer to be played by the Rock.

smoking a cigarette, and stands beneath a massive, garish flag bearing the eloquent words "Trump 2020: No More Bullshit." He barks with disdain in our direction, "Can I help you boys?"

We wave, shake our heads, and walk back to the car. Probably time to hit the road.

Grayson County

Guns and Babies

In order to understand Kentucky, you need to realize that we define ourselves by two things: (1) the region of the state we are from and (2) our particular county. This is especially true in rural Kentucky. If you ask people here where they are from, the vast majority will tell you their county rather than their hometown. This phenomenon, unique to Kentucky, is one of the reasons we have so many counties for a state our size.

For example, Leitchfield is the county seat of Grayson County, but most everyone there will simply say they are from Grayson County. And that means they are from one of the world's greatest suppliers of beekeeping equipment. If you are like me, you probably know nothing about the practice of beekeeping, but if you want to learn, Clarkson, Kentucky, is where you should go.

It is the home of Kelley Beekeeping, where beekeepers from all over the continental United States come to restock on equipment. It's very bright, clean, and sterile; it feels like a beekeeping Walgreens. Here you can stock up on all the Bee-Pro (high-protein pollen supplements) and Honey B Healthy (feeding stimulants) you could ever want. An employee explains to me that beekeeping is rapidly on the rise,* and that Kelley Beekeeping's eighty-two-thousand-square-foot facility has been in Grayson County since 1952. It's not the type of industry you would ever envision running across in the quiet, small county.

* I question this, but I can say beekeeping fervor is off the charts here.

We walked into Kelley Beekeeping and had our first taste of a lesson we learned repeatedly on this trip. Most people are very hesitant to talk about politics in public. That hesitancy grows even greater when the topic is Kentucky's senior senator. Time and time again, when we asked people "What do you think about Mitch McConnell?" their first reaction was to jerk their head around and see who might be looking. It was as if citizens in Kentucky naturally believed that Mitch or his cronies were waiting around the corner to potentially take them to Guantánamo for daring to speak a word against him.* In Kelley Beekeeping, the employees and customers were glad to tell us about all the latest products for your home apiary (that's fancy talk for where beehives are kept), but mentioning Mitch led to nervous smiles and a quick change of subject.

We left and drove through Grayson County, passing some amazing local business names. Our favorites:

5. Smokin Rednecks (barbeque)
4. Priority Hair (salon)
3. Whoop-De-Do Design (women's clothing, accessories)
2. Caught Ya Lookin' (handbags, gifts)
1. Farmer's Feed Mill (restaurant)

Because I like to eat—and my hair already looks great—we stopped at Farmer's Feed Mill. It was lunch hour, so the place was extra crowded, meaning it's good. Farmer's is the kind of restaurant where customers call dinner "supper" and framed copies of the Constitution and Declaration of Independence hang on the wall. The chalkboard out front lists the daily specials as meatloaf and "coonhunters' cake."

Here I met Becky and Harold Miller of Leitchfield. Becky is a retired assistant principal; Harold, a Leitchfield city councilman and manager at a nearby electric co-op. Together they are the quintessential southern couple of a certain age, friendly and welcoming, the embodiment of the best stereotypes of Kentuckians. As we sit, Harold runs his

* Their worry was even greater when we asked, "Can we say exactly how you feel about him and put it in a book for eternity?"

fingers over his moustache, and laughing friends come over for a quick handshake just to say hello. Becky spots a former student who drops by to catch up. He's just inherited his grandfather's piano, and they chat about how tough it is to move a piano. As he smiles and leaves, Becky leans in to tell me what a gifted musician he is.

Life is easy for the Millers in Leitchfield because they're good people in a town that appreciates them. However, one thing sets them apart from most of their fellow Feed Mill patrons. They are Democrats in a very Republican county, a facet of life that can occasionally make things difficult. "We may not be the buckle of the Bible Belt, but we're pretty close," Harold says.

Becky shakes her head and notes there are more registered Democrats in the county than Republicans, but in elections it goes Republican nearly every time. They fear that despite a current governor, Matt Bevin, who has been unpopular on issues concerning teachers, the upcoming governor's race will see her county vote Republican once again. "The problem is that no matter what the issues are we can agree on, there are single-issue voters," she tells me. "Guns and babies."

Guns and babies. It's a refrain I have heard for years all across the state, and Mitch McConnell seizes on both in every campaign. *Babies*, of course, means abortion. For many in Kentucky, the issue of abortion isn't just an important issue, it's the only issue. They see the desire to protect the life of the unborn as the primary litmus test that every elected official must pass. You can agree with them on every issue ranging from health care, to unions, to education. But if you are pro-choice, for some that is a level too far.

On the issue of guns, rural America's support is even more unanimous. While some citizens may acknowledge that women should have some say regarding their own bodies, taking away guns is akin to removing a way of life. In rural Kentucky, guns aren't seen as a problem to be solved, but rather a connection to local culture. Guns represent families across the state spending time together hunting deer, memories that span generations. Guns also provide a means of protection for people that may live hundreds of yards away from the nearest neighbor, and the idea of removing them is seen as an attack on their family's safety. Owning guns in Kentucky is simply something that everyone does, and the threat of losing them (which is of course manufactured and exploited by the Right for political gain) can easily sway a hunter to vote in the opposite direction.

While the Millers understand that these issues are critical to many in their county, they sometimes feel it blinds their friends to seeing the greater importance of other topics. While they've never had political disputes with those in their community, Becky does recall an encounter with a Republican door knocker that particularly riled her. "I explained that I was a Democrat, and he told me—can you believe this?—he told me he'd pray for me."

She laughs. "I didn't know what to say, so I just told him I'd pray for him too.* I was so mad. I came in and told Harold, 'Now I have to pray for him because I told him I was going to, but I can't do it right now because I'm too upset.' It just ran all over me because someone was trying to tell me what to believe."

The Millers handle such differences with humor, because in a small town coexistence is a necessity, and at the end of the day these party line differences with their neighbors don't calculate to radically different lives. Becky's religious; Harold's a hunter. In small towns like Leitchfield, the day-to-day differences between parties isn't a demonizing fistfight, it's a generally undetectable dissimilarity between two friendly city councilmen at a town meeting or two parents in the stands of a Grayson County football game. But when it's time to vote, two hard-line issues remain immovable obstacles for Democratic candidates—and not just in Grayson County.

To understand Kentucky—heck, to understand rural America in general—you have to understand guns and babies.

* When Democrats and Republicans pray against each other in Kentucky, the Lord determines the winner via instant replay.

Breckenridge County

"He Doesn't Even Know Who I Am to Look at Me"

Driving into Breckenridge County, it would be easy to miss Jim Bob Mattingly Road. It looks more like a driveway, but in this neck of the woods, most roads look like driveways. I am not familiar with Jim Bob Mattingly except to note that he must have been important enough to have an official roadway named after him on the way into Hardinsburg, the county's largest town. In most other parts of America, the name Jim Bob might sound strange. In Kentucky, I know *three* of them.

Breckenridge County is a peaceful place where, if you stay for more than an hour, someone will remind you that they won the state basketball championship in 1995, led by not one but two Mattinglys. (I attended that tournament as a high school junior and remember being struck by how friendly their fans were. I assumed it was a nice place to live.)

When I arrived, I found it just as I imagined. Turning off Jim Bob Mattingly's road, the county's rolling green hills take us to a billboard-sized sign that reads "Welcome to Hardinsburg" in small letters and, just below it, in large letters, "HOME OF LARRY'S BARBERSHOP."* A car passed me with dark-tinted windows and a white silhouette of a handgun alongside the adage "I Study Triggernometry." I'll take his word for it.

I decided to go for a quick bite at the Brak Restaurant and Meeting House, where, it being four thirty in the afternoon, many of the county's citizens are already sitting down to dinner. There is a direct correlation between the population of a town and the time of day meals are eaten. If it's 7 p.m. in a small town, chances are high most restaurants are packing up for the night. The talk at the Brak is tonight's middle school football game, with some side chatter on Ray's turnips.† As a server

---

* Larry clearly has pull in these parts.

† Coming in nicely, thanks for asking.

brings our check, he tells me, "That elderly couple over there paid for your appetizer and said to write it up as a campaign donation." The couple smile and wave, and I glance around quickly to see if a McConnell spy may be recording their contribution.

This idyllic small town appears, at first glance, charming and pleasant, but Mitch McConnell's slimy, ruinous hands leave no stone unturned. Dean Schamore, the Tenth District state representative for the area, is a Democrat Gulf War veteran who has served in the Kentucky state legislature for six years. He has the look of an everyman: sturdy, with a conventional haircut and a face that suggests "computer programmer who works out on the weekends."

What makes Dean's situation unique is that in the midterm election of 2018, he and three other Kentucky state reps were targeted by Mitch McConnell for a takedown. Well, not by Mitch specifically, but by the Kentuckians for Strong Leadership political action committee (PAC). Kentuckians for Strong Leadership is one of a host of PACs set up to infiltrate elections with millions of dollars in advertising that is unregulated and uncapped, flooding the airwaves with nonsense until Election Day. In the "About" section of its website, Kentuckians for Strong Leadership says it existed in 2014 to "ensure the reelection of Mitch McConnell," but now it was turning its attention to races in the Kentucky State House of Representatives to bring its national nastiness to local small-town politics.

Dean Schamore would be one of its primary targets. Schamore was one of a handful of Democratic legislators who had survived the 2016 Trump wave in Kentucky—one that gave the Kentucky House to the GOP for the first time in nearly a century. He had won by a relatively safe two thousand votes but with a district that was rapidly changing, Mitch was determined to avenge one of his few losses. In 2014, Breckenridge County was soundly Democratic, thanks in large part to its blue-collar worker base, but by 2018, Republicans outnumbered Democrats by 1,400 voters. Seeing this as an opportunity for a Republican to overtake the county, McConnell—I'm sorry, the *Kentuckians for Strong Leadership*—descended upon Schamore's race with a smear campaign targeted to undermine faith in the candidate.

The McConnell PAC sent out mail to all the voters in Breckenridge

County with the words CHEAT and LIAR in bold letters next to Schamore's face. The goal was to target Dean's personal life and make him the focus of small-town gossip. "I was going through a difficult time in my life," explains Schamore, "and all of a sudden there are all these mailers going out calling me a liar and a cheater, saying I lied to the people in my counties. They didn't specifically call out my divorce, but for the people in the community who knew me and knew of my divorce, clearly they knew what the ads were trying to say." The mailers trumpeting "Liberal Dean Schamore Is a Cheat!!!" got traction in the community, and the Democrat's failed marriage became the talk of the town.

Dean was mad but not surprised, and had no doubt who was to blame. "I was upset, but I knew that was Mitch's MO. I'd heard that it's how he does things. That's his style." But while Schamore wasn't shocked at McConnell's actions, he was surprised that the second most powerful man in America even cared about his local race. "I pose no harm to Mitch McConnell. Why target me? I'm a United States veteran," Schamore said. The reason was simple: "I had been one of the few to beat him in 2016. He didn't want it to happen again." Schamore recounts the story almost in disbelief. The race became solely about the PAC's smear campaign, and a two-thousand-vote lead evaporated. On election night, Schamore squeezed out a win with a much tighter margin of less than a hundred votes in his native county. He had weathered the McConnell storm, barely.

Yet as I talked to him in Hardinsburg, he had the look of a man who didn't feel he'd won much of anything. He spoke of being weary of the personal fights and then looked me directly in the eye. "Matt, I won't tell you what to do and whether you should run against him or not. But know this: he will try to destroy you. He did it to me, and I don't even matter to him. It will be worse with you."

After all that, I ask Schamore if he hates McConnell or holds resentment toward him. "I see him at every University of Louisville football game, we sit in the same section, and he doesn't even know who I am," says Schamore, shaking his head. "I mean, here's this guy who spent all this money attacking me, and he doesn't even know who I am to look at me."

Destroying people for sport even though they are so insignificant to you that you wouldn't recognize them seated next to you at a football game. The McConnell political way.

Meade County

"Surely People Aren't Buying This; They Know Me"

As I embarked on this journey around the state, I still had to continue my day job hosting *Kentucky Sports Radio*. So, every morning on the road, I got up and did my show before beginning our daily travels. On this particular morning in Meade County, I'm doing the show on a remote transmitter from the lobby of the brand-new Education and Career Center at Meade County High School. It's sharp, bright, and clean, and except for four mulleted Meade County football players* gawking at this loud man yelling about University of Kentucky football coach Mark Stoops in the lobby, Chris and I are basically alone. Halfway through the show, a young man, clearly not a student, shows up and sits in a chair across from the table where I'm broadcasting. He fits the normal demographic: jeans, sneakers, gray T-shirt, and a ratty ball cap pulled down over his head. He's just a regular twentysomething who likes listening to the radio show.

Only he's not a regular twentysomething who likes listening to the radio show.

He's my Tracker,† sent by Mitch McConnell's people to keep tabs on my travels and follow my every move. For people who don't know, trackers are now a regular part of modern political campaigns. Candidates (or their accompanying SuperPACs) hire kids, usually just out of college, to shadow candidates and film their every move, trying to catch them screwing up. I'd seen him a number of times previously:

---

* Collectively, Meade County produced the best mullets in Kentucky.

† We aren't using his name because it is irrelevant. He is one of the myriad worker-bee warriors McConnell sends out to try to destroy people's lives. We won't do to him what Mitch does to others.

filming my live radio broadcasts, sitting in my restaurant on trivia night* (where he introduced himself to one of our staff members as working for Mitch), and in Grayson County, where he hid quietly in a booth against the back wall as I ate my burger. Sometimes he videos me on his cell phone, sometimes not, and whenever I approach him about it, he doesn't deny what he's doing. He tells me that every morning he gets a text message from the mysterious people who employ him telling him where to go based on my radio conversation and social media accounts. He's surprisingly forthcoming. He says he is recently out of college, working on his master's degree, and using this job as a way to make money and figure out if a career in politics is for him.

It is a bizarre relationship we have. In many settings, the only people there are me, Chris, and my Tracker. I am not sure what exactly he is supposed to be taping, since everything I say is on the radio and available for the state as a whole. He is not intimidating really, just a skinny kid who looks straight out of a frat house, smiling and following my every move. But his presence is a bit menacing, not unlike the federal agents sitting outside the Sherwood diner in *Goodfellas*, waiting for De Niro to move to his next location. He is a consistent presence throughout our 120-county tour, and, when spotted, his appearance changes the vibe of the room for me.

After the show, we head to Little Dave's Roadhouse, where I meet former Democratic state representative Jeff Greer. At six foot three, Greer is a presence: bald, with deep-set, concerned eyes and a bear-paw handshake. He's been at Little Dave's for fifteen minutes, wandering from table to table to speak to everyone he knows, which seems to be most people in the restaurant. As we approach the hostess stand, Greer greets the woman, laughing that "If you think I'm not coming around there to give you a hug, you're crazy." His affection for these people is real and seems to be reciprocated. Greer isn't a point-and-wave politician; he stays to chat and press the flesh.

Like Dean Schamore, Greer once was a target of McConnell's

* KSBar and Grille, where we combine the best in sports talk with chicken wings.

wrath—but with a different outcome. Greer was, until recently, the state representative of Kentucky's Twenty-Seventh District, which includes all of Meade County and parts of Hardin County. He'd been reelected every two years since 2006 and claims the revitalization of Brandenberg's downtown district as the proudest achievement of his tenure. When he talks about Meade County, he does so as a man with a deep pride for his home.

"When I first ran, I didn't run because of Democrats or Republicans," he tells me earnestly. "I ran because I just love this county. This county's been good to me. I've been able to build a business. I got to live my dreams. I wanted to contribute to this community. I knew nothing about politics when I ran in 2006. I just knew that I was willing to find a way to make our community better and more competitive. So that was my driving force. And I'm glad I did."

But in 2018 Greer—like Schamore—was targeted by the patented McConnell attack machine for the unforgivable sin of being a Democrat.

As the chairman of the House Banking and Insurance Committee for eight years, a role that required him to travel to national conferences to keep Kentucky statutes current with those of other states, Jeff ended up on a lot of state-sponsored trips. The travel gave McConnell's PAC an opening.

"They got me, man," Greer conceded. "They called me 'Greedy Greer' and 'Jet Set Jeff,' and I probably didn't defend myself as well as I should have. I thought, 'Surely people aren't buying this; they know me.' But they *did* buy it."

Even though Greer had lived in the county his entire life, he watched as people he had known for a lifetime became persuaded by the bombardment of ads that he was galavanting across America on the taxpayer's dime. Most of the attacks occurred via donations from donors with no ties to Kentucky, and the influx of money was unlike anything anyone had seen in a local race in Meade County. Greer decided not to go negative. "I promised my mom I wouldn't," he explains. Jeff thought he could withstand the bombardment, but in November 2018 he lost his state representative seat to Republican Nancy Tate by only *six* votes.

Greer's home county had broken his heart, and he became distraught at how the county he loved had rejected him. The public perception of the man everyone called "Frog Greer" turned based on the lies of an outsider no one even liked.

"The most disappointing thing to me is that the Democrats that knew me, they just didn't get out and vote," he says. "I sure could've used them."

Greer now smiles and says he had moved on from public service and is happy with his current life. And although he laughed, joked, and paid for our lunch, you couldn't help but notice that, as with Schamore, the experience had left him scarred.

"Mitch is brilliant in ways, I think, but he's the dirtiest player in the game," sighs Greer. "I don't care for the guy."

Bullitt County

When We Walked in Fields of Gold

In J. R. R. Tolkien's *The Hobbit*, the fearsome dragon named Smaug is wrinkly, 171 years old, and lives at the top of Lonely Mountain. He's very smart, he's red, he has an old crust of treasure stuck to his belly, and vehemently hates and wishes to destroy anyone who wants to take anything from him. He is, as described by Tolkien, "specially strong, greedy, and wicked," and he sleeps on a mountain of gold. I am not sure why I thought of Smaug driving into Fort Knox, Kentucky. Probably no reason.

Fort Knox is huge. So huge, in fact, that it covers parts of three separate counties: Hardin, Meade, and Bullitt. We enter from the Bullitt side, stopping at my radio cohost Shannon the Dude's house and picking up a Mountain Dew for the road.* Fort Knox is where the nation stores its resources of gold, and was the setting for part of the James Bond classic *Goldfinger*.† The actual value of the gold in Fort Knox is

* Soda is big here. Many of the kitchen sinks in Bullitt County homes have three settings for the tap: "hot," "cold," and "Mountain Dew: Code Red."

† Fort Knox also doubled as the fictitious Fort Arnold in *Stripes*. That's a fact, Jack.

subject to the daily market, but it generally sits at well over $200 billion. Rather than hide that fact, though, we in America flaunt it. The street address of Fort Knox is literally 127 Gold Vault Road. To get there, you take a left off Bullion Boulevard. Fort Knox is so bombastic about its resources that it's as if Donald Trump himself had a hand in naming the place.

Bullitt County's segment of Fort Knox lies in the southwest area of the county and at its height housed and accommodated a massive amount of soldiers and their families, including those of the First Army Division East and the 194th Armored Brigade. This prior heyday of the base still has relics littered around Fort Knox's borders: large neighborhoods of uniform, family-friendly tract housing, gold-named businesses such as the Gold Vault Inn and Gold City Towing, and more lascivious establishments, including a disproportionate share of strip clubs. (In my previous legal career, I was asked to represent the owner of one such establishment in an environmental action brought by the state because his club was literally falling into the river. He wanted to allow the joint to fall in rather than fix the problem. I looked at the issue, researched the facts, and decided to become a sports radio host.)

For most of the twentieth century, thanks to the housing of gold, Fort Knox was likely the best-known military base in America. However, in 2005 President George W. Bush's Base Realignment and Closure program (known as BRAC) targeted the area. BRAC considered most of Fort Knox's nongold sections expendable and transferred the armored infantry division, by then the trademark of the base itself, to Fort Benning, Georgia. Along with the transfer came a future promise of new troops to replace the population, but it was a promise never met.

Almost immediately, the dynamics of the area surrounding Fort Knox dramatically changed. The federal government had, in one decision, decimated the area's economy, and locals immediately began to ask questions. Mitch McConnell promised repeatedly that he'd do what he could to protect Fort Knox and save the area. However, even with a president from his own party and his standing as a supposedly powerful Senate leader, in the end, all those troops that had once been the lifeblood of the local economy were replaced mostly by US Army human resource personnel and pencil pushers. Because these employees tended to be more white-collar, career personnel, they chose to live closer to the outskirts of Louisville rather than in the immediate area surrounding Fort Knox. The communities around Fort Knox became shells of their former selves.

Understanding it was a meager exchange, McConnell immediately went on the public relations offensive. He loudly took credit for "saving" Fort Knox and noting that without him, the base may have had an even more dire future. His political sycophants lauded the achievement, with Hardin County's GOP committee spokesman crowing that the base might have closed without the intervention of McConnell the white knight. He never showed any proof of his work to save Fort Knox and, further, never addressed the elephant in the room: mainly, how could a senator with so much supposed power lose his military base to Georgia in the first place? A similar move had nearly occurred in 1989, but Kentucky's senior senator at the time, Democrat Wendell Ford, was able to prevent the move as a requirement for his support of the annual defense authorization bill. Ford was not in a position of leadership nor a member of the president's party. (George W.'s father, George H. W. Bush, was then in the White House.) McConnell was both, but he failed where Ford succeeded.

In early 2014, while McConnell was facing Democratic challenger Alison Lundergan Grimes, Fort Knox took another massive hit: three thousand soldiers in the Third Brigade Combat Team—better known as the Duke Brigade—were reassigned and the brigade was inactivated. The reassignment forced thousands of families to leave the area, eventually prompting four Fort Knox area schools to close, with many teachers losing jobs soon after. Even in his role as then Senate minority leader, McConnell had no answer for this second major Fort Knox loss on his watch. All he did was publicly blame President Barack Obama. When it came to tax cuts for the rich, stripping regulations on business, or advancing corporate interests, McConnell always seemed to find a way to succeed. But when it came to protecting the economic viability of these three rural counties in his state, Mitch's power was apparently quite limited. Fort Knox and Bullitt County continue to suffer the consequences.

LaRue County

Oral Reports About Lincoln Are Off-limits

Everyone—except Nazis, segregationists, and Tucker Carlson—loves Abraham Lincoln. The adoration for the sixteenth president, who guided our fractured nation through the Civil War, is ubiquitous across America and leads to states fighting for their own little piece of Honest Abe. Because he served four terms in the Illinois General Assembly and spent his adult life in the state, Illinois is often seen as his true home. Its official state slogan is "Land of Lincoln," and Abe's grizzled face adorns every license plate.

Any true student of history, however, knows that the birthplace and rightful home of Abraham Lincoln is Kentucky. Honest Abe was born in and grew up among the streams and fields of northern LaRue County, Kentucky, a part of his life that Lincoln would often recall fondly years later. And because of that fact, no place celebrates Lincoln and his humble beginnings more vociferously than LaRue County and its county seat, Hodgenville.

Lincoln's Kentucky legacy is so ingrained locally that LaRue County High School English teacher Katy Cecil tells me that "oral reports about Abraham Lincoln are off-limits, because around here we all know everything about him already, and that's too easy."

And why wouldn't they? LaRue County is home to a national park celebrating Lincoln's birth and a near-identical replica of the Lincoln Memorial in Washington, DC. In fact, the monument in LaRue County, complete with the famous pillars and marble features, was actually built before the DC model, making the federal version somewhat of a copycat.* The Memorial Building at the Abraham Lincoln Birthplace National Historical Park in Hodgenville looks nearly identical with

* Shame on you, New York architect Henry Bacon. You could have come up with your own idea.

one noticeable exception: instead of Lincoln sitting in a chair there is a replica of the cabin in which he was born.*

It's quite an impressive sight, one made even more exciting by the dry-erase board with the question "What book would you recommend to Abraham Lincoln?" Visitors all add to the list when they visit, and the day we were there, the top choice was the science-fiction novel *The Martian*—a book I think we can all agree would be very confusing to an eight-year-old Abraham Lincoln. (Seeking to be part of the historical process, I add *Mitch, Please!* to the bottom of the list. I think he would approve.)

It can be argued that since Lincoln, no politician from Kentucky has had a greater impact on the nation than Mitch McConnell. Even though it seems absurd to compare the two men,† they do share some similarities. Both had difficult childhoods, with Lincoln living in a small shack and losing his mother at age nine, while McConnell was diagnosed with polio at the age of two. Both pursued law degrees, Lincoln being self-taught, and McConnell attending the University of Kentucky. (Go Cats!) Plus, both had long electoral win streaks. Lincoln won election to the Illinois House four straight times and McConnell to the US Senate six times.

McConnell likes to quote Lincoln frequently and would probably enjoy any historical comparison to our country's greatest president. So, while visiting LaRue County, I thought I would stack the two men up against each other and see who comes out on top:

CONSENSUS BUILDING

Abe: In a 2013 poll, the *Atlantic* and the Aspen Institute voted him the most unifying president in history. (Reagan came in second.) In his

---

* I would note that it is a replica and in small print at the memorial there is a sign that notes it isn't (a) the real cabin or (b) even the location where the cabin existed (it's a few miles away). Both seem like important points but a woman became angry when I asked about them and just walked away.

† One kept the country together, one falls asleep at night cackling with joy that he is breaking it apart.

second inaugural address, in 1865, with the end of the Civil War on the horizon, Lincoln presented his vision for healing the country: "With malice toward none, with charity for all, with firmness in the right, as God gives us to see the right, let us strive on to finish the work we are in, to bind up the nation's wounds." Also, he *literally* ended slavery.

Mitch: On January 4, 2019, he refused to allow a vote that would have ended a two-week government shutdown affecting eight hundred thousand government workers. This caused them to lose their jobs temporarily—*at Christmas.**

EFFECT ON DEMOCRACY

Abe: Revered by historians for helping facilitate the events that would lead to a blooming of American democracy. As lawyer Nathan William MacChesney wrote in his 1910 book *Abraham Lincoln: The Tribute of a Century, 1809–1909*, "Lincoln did more for democracy than to save the union. The union was not enough. There must be freedom as well."

Mitch: Likely to be less fondly remembered. As author and leading Holocaust historian Christopher Browning wrote in a 2018 essay in the *New York Review of Books*, "If the U.S. has someone whom historians will look back on as the gravedigger of American democracy, it is Mitch McConnell."

SENSE OF HUMOR

Abe: Known to be gregarious and disarming to those around him. British journalist William Howard Russell wrote about a White House state dinner in 1861 at which Lincoln "raises a laugh by some bold west-country anecdote, and then moves off in the cloud of merriment produced by this joke."

Mitch: Calls himself "the Grim Reaper" and sells "Cocaine Mitch" shirts. Fewer clouds of merriment produced.

---

* That night the majority leader was visited by three ghosts: Strom Thurmond, Robert Byrd, and Jesse Helms.

POLITICAL PHILOSOPHY

Abe: Preserve the union and democracy.

Mitch: Win.

FASHION

Abe: Kept his most important documents in his famous top hat.

Mitch: Keeps his most important documents in the deep expanse where his soul once resided.

CUNNING ACHIEVEMENT

Abe: Grave robbers were foiled in 1876 when they tried to steal Lincoln's body.

Mitch: Grave robbers were foiled in 2019 when they realized McConnell was still alive.

PETS

Abe: Had a loving dog named Fido who was tragically killed by a drunken assailant a year after Lincoln's assassination.

Mitch: Got drunk, killed Fido.

Advantage: Lincoln.

Nelson County

"Screw Your Tourism Business, I Want Answers"

If you are not a true Kentuckian but want to feel like one, I'd suggest having a Very Old Barton at a table in Bardstown's Old Talbott Tavern. First, I should note, if you are not familiar with bourbon, Very Old Barton is both a descriptor *and* an actual name of a bourbon distilled right there in Bardstown in Nelson County, the bourbon capital of the only state where real bourbon is actually produced.* Based on my travels, I've discovered that many people have an iconic mental image of themselves drinking a bourbon in an old, rustic environment, and I can assure you there are none better than Old Talbott Tavern. If you're a cool twentysomething in Brooklyn, there's a good chance that when you drink bourbon, *this* is the very place you imagine drinking it in. I am here to tell you it exists.

The Old Talbott Tavern (and its accompanying inn) was built in 1779 and has seen visitors both rough and esteemed: from burly explorers heading west to conquer a new world, to countrymen holding court for the betterment of the nation. President Andrew Jackson is said to have enjoyed the central room's warm hearth, while an upstairs bedroom bears bullet holes from outlaw Jesse James, who is said to have fired his gun at a painting when he drunkenly swore he saw birds moving within it.

Each year, the Kentucky Bourbon Festival draws aficionados to the town from around the world, including regular appearances by celebrities like Bill Murray.† Every small town in Kentucky wishes it had a downtown like Bardstown's, a district where out-of-towners come for bourbon tours and stay for quaint bed-and-breakfasts, cute festivals, and an adorable and upkept main strip of locally owned shops. It calls itself "the Most Beautiful Small Town in America," and you know what? It is. It's a place so fantastic that Stephen Foster wrote our state song, "My Old Kentucky Home," right here. Lively and colorful, the kind of place where you could spend an entire weekend.

But recently, the small town that is the envy of all of Kentucky has been hit with national publicity of a different sort. Since 2013, a straight-out-of-*Dateline* series of tragedies has befallen the community. In the

---

* Technically only whiskeys made in Kentucky are allowed to call themselves bourbon. Some aren't following the rules. If Matt is elected to the Senate, they will pay.

† Half of Bardstown's thirteen thousand residents will claim to have seen Bill Murray sing karaoke in a local bar. Bear in mind that everyone has been drinking bourbon.

early hours of May 25, 2013, Bardstown police officer Jason Ellis was ambushed and shot on an exit ramp at exit 34 of the Bluegrass Parkway. Six years later, the murder has yet to be solved. In 2014, a retired special education teacher named Kathy Netherland and her teenage daughter, Samantha, were violently murdered in their home. Their assailant was never found. Then in 2015 Crystal Rogers, a thirty-five-year-old mother of five who was dating the brother of a Bardstown police officer, disappeared over Fourth of July weekend. Her car was discovered along the Bluegrass Parkway with her purse, keys, and cell phone inside—and more than a year later, her father, Tommy Ballard, who'd been tirelessly searching for his daughter for months, was shot to death on his property. All the murders remain unsolved. Crystal Rogers, after four years missing, is presumed dead.

These "Bardstown Murders" shocked the city to its core. After all, it's nearly impossible to lose five members of a community this size in the span of four years and not have at least one of the crimes affect every person in town. The situation spawned a docuseries on the television channel Oxygen and inspired a massively successful podcast called *Bardstown,* which looked deeper into the murders and Rogers's disappearance. The podcast has risen to the top of the national charts, and the stories continue to generate press. People continue to theorize whether the murders were connected and wonder aloud how it is possible that none have been solved. The Most Beautiful Small Town in America has begun to look like the setting for something much darker and more dangerous.

As I walk through downtown Bardstown's busy, bright business district, I ask some citizens about the murders and their effect on the town. My assumption is that everyone will have a theory they are eager to share.

Instead, I'm met mostly with silence. No one wants to speak with me on the record, and the few who do have little to say. One shopkeeper waves me away, telling me that the murders were simply all random; there's no connection among them. A waitress leans in close and tells me she knew Crystal, and that she happens to believe that the murderer thought the woman knew something she shouldn't have. Three vendors chatting at a local flea market seem to know everyone in town and talk my ear off about what and where to visit next; when I ask about the murders, they all claim not to know anything, never having heard of them. I smile, knowing they aren't telling me the truth, but I understand. Don't engage the tourist about the murders, it seems.

When I finally find someone to talk to me extensively, it's not an opinion on the crimes he shares, but an indictment of dollars over justice. A small business owner tells me, out of earshot of customers, that he believes the city has no answers and is playing down the situation to protect Bardstown's tourism business. "I understand that you may not want to go someplace with a half dozen unsolved murders for your family vacation," the shopkeeper tells me, "but at the same time, there's a real insensitivity to sweeping it under the rug. Shouldn't we be supporting the people in our community? These are somebody's loved ones, friends, and family."

The business owner is even more incensed about the actions in the days leading up to this year's Bourbon Festival, Bardstown's biggest annual tourist showcase. In the days prior to its start, a large number of signs with supportive slogans such as "Prayers for Crystal's Safe Return" and "Justice for Crystal and Tommy" were removed from yards and parks—a move the shopkeeper believes was purposefully meant to keep the pall of the murders from affecting the proceedings.

"If someone was murdered in my family, I think I'd say, 'Screw your tourism business, I want answers,'" he tells me. "The signs were removed so visitors wouldn't see any signs of the murders, because they didn't want that image of the city. It just seems a little icky to me."

Sadly, a similar reality exists in politics as well. Working to hide the truth in order to project a pristine image to the public has become a cottage industry in politics. It's a business Mitch McConnell has mastered. He has continuously flipped on key conservative issues since he began his forty years of political service to the point that the Mitch of today would be unrecognizable to his former self. Abortion, civil rights, campaign finance, unions, China, Russia—Mitch has flipped on nearly all of his original core principles. Anyone who works to expose the truth repeatedly faces McConnell's wrath. Mitch's goal is to obfuscate, obscure, and obliterate the truth about his record because the reality is too damaging to him: that he will say anything, do anything, or take any position if it means helping him gain more political power. Dirty truths are hard to accept, whether in the most beautiful small town in America or the lowest depths of American politics.

Hart County

"You Ready for a Gun, Fella?"

Circling back south toward Munfordville in Hart County, we realize we are low on gas and need a fill-up. We stop at the Green River Hill Grocery on North Jackson Highway, the only business within miles. An old man stares me down as we walk in, flashes a tobacco-stained grin, and says, "Go, Cats," letting me know I am in friendly territory. The store has a great selection of sodas, chips, and other snacks, perfect for tiding us over until dinner. It is also stocked with a large selection of firearms for sale, including a Ruger American 243 rifle with a Tasco 3-9x40 world-class illuminated reticle scope—you know, for the road.

To some of you in other parts of the country, "grocery store weaponry" might seem bizarre. But it's not that crazy here. We in Kentucky can combine the purchase of firearms with most any act.* As I approach the counter, I'm clearly staring behind the cash register at the large assortment of pistols and semiautomatic weapons mounted on the wall, their price tags dangling.

"You ready for a gun, fella?" the grocery owner asks cheerily.

Oddly, this is a question I get asked a lot in Kentucky—I am one of the few eastern Kentuckians I know who doesn't own a gun—but it's not something I normally hear while picking up Honey Nut Cheerios. I ask him what I'd need to do to get one, and he tells me that I'll need a valid Kentucky driver's license, as "even though it don't look like it," he does conduct background checks. I tell him I think I'll pass today but know where to find him if I should change my mind. (I won't change my mind.)

---

* On this trip alone, we encountered a deli in Owenton, a western-wear store in London, and a Radio Shack in Salyersville that all doubled as gun stores.

Feeling sufficiently armed, we head down the more rural, scenic backroads of Hart County to the home of Nichole Nimmo and Jordan Shirley. Their redbrick house is spotted by the sign stuck in the grass at the foot of the driveway that reads "Just Be Kind." Nichole and Jordan meet us out front and are instantly welcoming, showing us around their unique country residence, complete with vegetables, farm animals, and curious cats emerging to inspect the new visitors. The green and red tomato gardens that surround their home are lush and well maintained, the sign of a household that cares and provides for itself.

Nichole and Jordan have been together for eighteen years, married for the last eleven, and look much younger than their life experiences. He is quieter than she, relaxed and easygoing on one sofa, while Nichole brushes her wavy hair from her eyes and talks to us from the other. She is an avid Hart County Democrat, having hit the pavement to talk to prospective voters during past elections, most recently knocking on upward of 1,500 doors to stump for current secretary of state Alison Grimes against Mitch McConnell. She is passionate, as you would have to be to do that amount of knocking in a county that Donald Trump won with 74 percent of the vote in 2016.

Nichole is a produce farmer now, spending most of her days in the garden picking tomatoes, strawberries, and greens, but it's been a long trajectory to this point. At thirteen, she was diagnosed with juvenile rheumatoid arthritis; the condition ended her basketball career and instead led to a more intensive focus on her studies. She eventually graduated from the University of Louisville with a degree in chemistry and landed a job at a Dow Corning laboratory in Elizabethtown. After three years, though, her condition came out of remission and, due to joint problems and associated difficulties related to the disease, Nichole was unable to keep her job. For two years, she had to relearn how to walk, first with a walker, then with a cane.

On top of her chronic struggle, two years later Nichole discovered a suspicious lump, which turned out to be Hodgkin's lymphoma. Already dealing with an expensive regimen of injectable medicines for her crippling arthritis, she began cancer treatment under the coverage of her COBRA insurance plan, which quickly drained the entirety of the couple's savings. Unable to procure new insurance with two serious preexisting conditions, Nichole was forced to move to the only health coverage available to her, through the Affordable Care Act (ACA), or "Obamacare."

"If it didn't completely save my life, the Affordable Care Act was the start we needed," Nichole tells me.

Kentucky has had more success with the Patient Protection and Affordable Care Act (ACA), signed into law in 2010, than virtually any other state. In 2013 Governor Steve Beshear implemented the ACA's Medicaid expansion provision to allow Kentucky's poorest citizens access to health care coverage for the first time. It was a controversial decision for a red-state Democrat, as President Obama was deeply unpopular. But it was undoubtedly successful: within five years, the uninsured rate in Kentucky plummeted from 20 percent to 5 percent, the second highest percentage drop in America. The state's overall health improved dramatically. Gradually Obamacare became a relatively popular policy in Kentucky. So much so that when the next governor, Republican Matt Bevin, attempted unsuccessfully to take away the expansion, the political uproar that followed only cemented his universal unpopularity.

From moment one, Mitch McConnell had opposed the Affordable Care Act, which he helped dub "Obamacare" during 2009 and 2010 in an effort to raise its unpopularity. He believed a willingness to work with the Democratic chief executive would denote a bipartisanship that McConnell wanted absent from Obama's presidency. He set out to repeal the act at the first possible opportunity. That moment came in 2017 when Republicans called a vote to repeal the public health care initiative—a tense moment of truth for the young couple. They were in the same boat as many other Americans on that early morning of July 27, as Senator John McCain delivered his now-iconic thumbs-down deciding vote against the repeal. It would be McCain's last great political move, choosing to save health care for millions of Americans over the intense pressure to follow his party. The Arizona senator would pass away a little more than a year later. Nichole and Jordan shed tears of joy at their blessing. They speak of McCain with fondness to this day.

When I ask Nichole about McConnell, she says, "It would be nice" if Kentucky's leaders would help solidify the policy that has given her a new lease on life. But being nice isn't McConnell's forte. Mitch has vowed if he gets another chance, he will try and take out the ACA "root and branch." Hundreds of thousands of Kentuckians like Nichole and Jordan hope he will continue to be foiled at every attempt.

Spencer County

"I Don't Watch the News. . . . I Have Enough Issues in My Life"

Taylorsville, in Spencer County, is a place I know mostly as a name on a sign I pass on my way to other places. But now on this final stop of Week One, I realize it looks like the set of a movie. And that movie is one where a harried big-city television reporter comes to town to report begrudgingly on some obscure small-town festival (in Taylorsville, it's the Spencer County Gourd Festival), has car trouble and is stranded there for several weeks while it's being repaired, meets all the colorful locals, falls in love with a quirky local doctor or farmer, returns home, decides the big city is terrible, and returns in the final scene to live in the town forever. You've seen it before, I'm sure. It's an age-old tale.*

Taylorsville is that charming community. The buildings are picturesque, the streets are clean, and the birds are chirping. But, there are no people. In fact, it's almost disconcerting how little traffic there is on Main Street. As in, "Where *is* everyone? Have I wandered onto the set of *The Truman Show*?"

Apparently we aren't the only ones who've noticed things are unusually quiet.

"I'd certainly like to see more going on in terms of tourism," says Sharon Whitworth from behind the counter at the Red Scooter, the charming antique shop at the top of the street filled with older teacups,

* Probably starring Katherine Heigl and Gerard Butler and headed straight to TNT.

dark-wood curio cabinets, and, of course, a healthy number of vintage red scooters.*

Pete Rendon, a gray-haired man with a corresponding moustache, lives in Taylorsville and is just hanging out in the store listening to the conversation. He interjects, "I think the city has a problem with allowing infrastructure to come into town. I sometimes think there's very much a mind-set of just having a town that's nice and quaint instead of bringing in a factory for our kids to work in."

By kids, Rendon doesn't mean children. He's referring to a problem increasingly faced by small rural counties in Kentucky: their youth grow up thinking there's nothing there for them, so after high school or college, they migrate to urban areas with better jobs or younger-skewing demographics. In nearly every rural county we visited, locals speak with pride of the young people produced by the area public schools, but they lament that it's unlikely any of them will stay to live and work in their community. And why would they? Without more economic opportunities coming to these areas, young people don't see the appealing future that is offered to them elsewhere.

Without young people to revitalize them, these downtowns dry up, especially when bypass roads are built around them. It's a reality we see all across Kentucky. In Taylorsville, nearby Highway 44 added a four-lane segment that directed more traffic toward the recreation-friendly Taylorsville Lake and made it easier for visitors from Louisville to get to the lake directly. Developments like these are great for commuters, but they crush small-town business.

"There's just no main artery in and out anymore," says Courtney Humes, who owns the Main Street gifts and home décor shop the Sassy Bunny,† which she says has been in the spot for three years and has yet to turn a profit. It's the kind of shop that would kill in nearby Bardstown, twenty-two miles away and, conservatively, a ten thousand times hotter hub for tourism.

---

* If you are currently missing your red scooter, check here.

† Fun fact: Sassy Bunny is Mitch McConnell's CIA code name.

Yet for Humes, who supplements for a lack of foot traffic at the Sassy Bunny with real-time sales via Facebook Live, the loss in revenue for her business is balanced by having a safer community for her three children, two of whom have special needs. With no major inroads funneling people into downtown Taylorsville, the town also—for Humes, at least—offers sanctuary from the modern political nastiness that Mitch McConnell has helped to overtake our political dialogue.

"I like to live in my own world; it's called Taylorsville, and it's here," Humes says. "I don't watch the news, I don't watch TV. Unless it affects me or my family, I have enough issues in my life."

If Courtney knew the reality of how the political sausage is made, she might want to detach even more. In 2015, I saw the sausage close up when the national Democratic Party tried to woo me into running for Congress. As I stated earlier, I was invited to the DCCC political boot camp: a gathering in Washington, DC, for the sixty or so candidates who will be running in the tightest races in America. Actually, I take that back. It is for the sixty or so congressional candidates who will be running in the only *true* races in America. The House of Representatives has 435 members, but thanks to extreme gerrymandering, the power of incumbency, and the natural grouping of humans to live in areas with those with similar political leanings, there really are only about sixty races that decide who will control the US Congress. We are taught that everyone in the House is up for reelection every two years, and if we don't like what they do, we can vote them out. But it's nonsense—375 members won't be voted out without a revolution and are essentially elected for life.

One of those sixty races is the Sixth District of Kentucky, and apparently I was the best the Democrats could do there. When I showed up in DC, I met with the other sixty recruits, and they were all very impressive. Chosen by the DCCC as those most likely to win their respective districts, they made up a refreshingly diverse group. Yes, like all politics, it was disproportionately filled with white males, but compared with the actual membership of Congress (and certainly the GOP*), it

* GOP members of the House of Representatives are 87 percent white male. Think about that for a minute. The only thing whiter and more male than the GOP is a Nebraska Fantasy Football Convention.

was younger and slightly more representative of America in terms of gender, race, and ethnicity.

Over the next forty-eight hours, I met everyone who was anyone in the Democratic Party in the House of Representatives, and they all tried to relate to me. Minority Whip Steny Hoyer of Maryland (upon whom I made quite the impression by continually calling him "Stoney") talked to me one-on-one about how much he loved the horse farms of Kentucky. New Orleans congressman Cedric Richmond was assigned to show me around due to our mutual love of NBA all-star and former Kentucky Wildcat Anthony Davis (I was, however, skeptical when Richmond said he had never noticed Davis's unibrow). Even California representative Nancy Pelosi, then between stints as Speaker of the House, joined the party, coming up to me and saying she enjoyed listening to me and Shannon the Dude* on my radio show. I don't believe Nancy Pelosi has ever listened to *KSR*, but I admit to being charmed at the idea that she would care enough to lie. It was an effective recruitment. People in power telling you how good you are and how great it would be if you joined their club. Yes, it was a dorky club, and one that accomplishes almost nothing. But for whatever reason, they wanted me as a member and were gradually sweeping me off my feet. It's like the first few weeks of dating someone, when they're lovely and you don't worry about your problems in the future, like when the relationship crumbles as she keeps coming home late at night after hanging out with her "work friend" Lamar Alexander.

However, reality soon hit me right in the face, when Congresswoman Cheri Bustos of Illinois addressed the group. Now, let me preface this by saying I am sure she is a nice person, with only the best intentions. But in two minutes, she crushed my illusion that running for Congress would be a good decision. She said to the group (I am paraphrasing), "I want you to know that most everything people tell you is important in campaigning is not. Doing town halls isn't the most important. Traveling and shaking hands is nice but isn't the most important. Knocking on doors isn't the most important.

"The three most important things are money, money, and money."

---

* Again, that's his real name. He is also a professional wrestler.

"Money, money, and money." Her words still ring in my head to this day, because at that moment, thirty-seven years of political naivete came shattering down. I falsely believed that the one campaign I knew, in which my mother ran for county prosecutor and became one of two women to become the first elected to the position in all of Kentucky, was illustrative of campaigns as a whole. My mom went to every community function, visited every Bell County holler, and knocked on every door she could find to convey the message of why she was the better candidate. But here was a congresswoman imploring us to understand the reality that campaigning like that no longer worked. Only money mattered, and winning required lots of it.

As she spoke those words, no one in the room dissented. She noted that in House races, most people don't take the time to learn about the candidate as they do for president, governor, or senator. It is all about name recognition and to have it, you need money. Raising money meant four to six hours a day on the phone, doing "call time" and begging strangers for dollars. I could think of nothing more miserable. Listening to her describe such a demeaning lifestyle, I knew my interest in a potential candidacy for Congress was over. If I ever decided to run for public office in the future, it certainly wouldn't be for this one.

Four years later, it's clear I made the right decision. Trump won the 2016 election with a Kentucky wave, carrying the state by twenty points. The "money, money, money" message did nothing for the boot camp Democrats, most of whom lost in the process. I almost certainly would have lost too. It was the wrong time and the wrong office. Whether this is the right of either remains to be seen.

CHAPTER 2

The Western Front

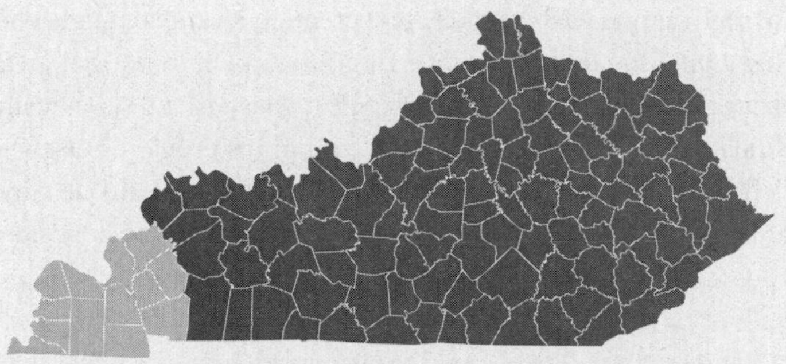

It's time to head west to the part of the state least familiar to me: the farms and plains of western Kentucky. For most of my adult life, the area west of Lake Barkley was a mystery, crossed only for an occasional trip to Paducah or a Murray State University basketball game. (Point guard Ja Morant, now in the pros, is the real deal and was worth the long drive.) The area is somewhat detached from the rest of the state, as most of its media outlets originate from Nashville, Tennessee; Evansville, Indiana; and Cape Girardeau, Missouri. The existence is peaceful enough that western Kentucky rarely makes national news. With little background knowledge, it's the area where I had the most to learn—particularly why Mitch McConnell is so popular here.

Outside of the annual meeting of the world's global, political, and economic elite in Davos, Switzerland,* this area is the closest thing

* I am not a conspiracy theorist, nor a believer in the Illuminati, but the more I read about this event, the more I channel my inner Jesse Ventura.

Mitch has to a home base. While McConnell finds himself immensely unpopular in virtually every other region of the state, far western Kentucky is the one place where you can actually run into people who say, without embarrassment, that they are "Team Mitch." McConnell has cultivated this area since his first election. Knowing that this region of Kentucky was filled with rural conservatives who were registered Democrats but open to voting Republican, Mitch saw an opening. In his first campaign, in 1984, he worked the region extensively, cutting Democratic margins substantially and creating a dent complete enough to bring home his first win. Since then, he has built on that success, nurturing a base of support through cultural issues and specifically targeted policies that would help him withstand his problems elsewhere.

It's a strategy that has worked electorally. To find out why, we headed out to the west side, which you and I know is the best side.

Graves County

99 Problems, but a Mitch Ain't One

Driving to western Kentucky takes forever. So after a long journey, Chris and I stop for a nice lunch in Mayfield. We choose Wilma's Kountry Kitchen, a roadside diner that looks like it might have once been a quaint house. It is filled with a lunchtime rush of the quickest-eating human beings I have ever seen. These folks get in and out of here like an assembly line, and expected us to as well. After receiving our food and being given a good five minutes to eat it, those standing at the door waiting for a table in the tiny dining area fix us with a "Hey, boys, you have already eaten, don't you have somewhere to be?" expression that sends us on our way. The total bill for our two tasty sandwiches, sides, and drinks is (and I am not making this up) eight dollars. We almost paid more money just to feel good about ourselves. Wilma, if you are reading, you are worth so much more.

We left nourished and headed to Fancy Farm, the spot in Graves County that best exemplifies the modern Mitch McConnell. It would be an exaggeration to say Fancy Farm made McConnell, but there is no place where he is more in his comfort zone. Fancy Farm is tiny, but still home to the best event in Kentucky politics—heck, I would argue it's one of the best events in politics period—the annual Fancy Farm Picnic. Fancy Farm is a political spectacle like no other. In 1881 the St. Jerome Catholic Church in Fancy Farm began a local picnic and fundraiser in which the community got together for an annual celebration with numerous events, including speeches by local politicians. It was relatively quiet until 1931, when a Democratic state senator named Albert Benjamin "Happy" Chandler began coming to the event to start "politicking." (Later that year, Chandler moved up to the state's lieutenant governorship, to be followed by one term as governor and one term as US senator. As if his résumé wasn't sufficiently varied, Happy also served as the second commissioner of Major League Baseball from 1945 to 1951. Then it was back to politicking for another four years in the Governor's Mansion.)

Chandler realized there were very few occasions to go to events in the western part of the state that drew such large crowds, and he took advantage. He would show up, get on stage, and entertain the masses by taking clever shots at his political rivals* and firing up the crowd with his intense rhetoric. When it was over, Happy would barrel into the crowd and celebrate, even allegedly dancing with all the women in attendance.† He always exited to a loud ovation, a spectacle not to be missed.

Building on Happy's raucous past, the event has become basically a sporting event, with attendees of either party divided into two sections, each cheering on their representatives as heroes and booing vociferously at those on the other side. While the picnic usually remains civil, the goal is always to be the speaker who can grab the loudest cheers and throw the harshest zingers at the other side. The event is aired across the state on public television, and it is the summer kickoff to every political campaign season.

---

* Think the *Comedy Central Roast* of late 1920s Kentucky governor Flem D. Sampson.

† It was a tactic that worked well for Happy, not so much seventy years later for Anthony Weiner.

Mitch McConnell loves Fancy Farm. Looking out at the crowd on any given year, you can see why. Fancy Farm represents America as McConnell sees it, neatly divided into two groups, one for you and one against you. When the senator gets up and speaks, he plays to his side of the crowd, making them cheer by throwing (usually horribly lame) barbs at the other side.* And when the other side chants and yells at him, he smirks, basking in the glow of their hate. Whereas this event was once good-natured and fun, like national politics itself, it has occasionally in recent years grown nastier and more personal. The Fancy Farm organizers, like Americans as a whole, would like to see the tone settle down. But Mitch McConnell seems to embrace the viciousness.

My mom watched Fancy Farm religiously every year, so I was aware of it but had never attended. While the idea of it appealed to me, watching political figures try to be funny usually made me cringe,† and the oppressive heat that it was known for (the temperature nearly every year hovers above ninety degrees, with high humidity) made the long drive to the event a nonstarter. But then in 2015 the picnic organizers asked me if I wanted to be the emcee. Historically, that task had gone to some local politician, but now they wanted to spice it up and attract a somewhat different, younger audience. I said I was interested only if they would let me do a comedic roast of all the politicians on stage. To my surprise they said yes.

What followed was one of the proudest speeches of my life. For ten minutes, I stood in front of the heckling crowd and made jokes about Mitch McConnell, our other senator, Rand Paul, the sitting governor, Steve Beshear, and everyone else there running for office. The jokes weren't overly harsh, but they were more heated than the norm. The reaction was mixed. While the crowd laughed and cheered me on, the glares from the politicians behind me were menacing; none more so than from McConnell. During a prepared bit about the difference

---

* An example of the tragic nature of his comedy is this gem from 2019: "Washington liberals responded by targeting me. They picked Amy McGaffe . . . Oh, I mean Amy McGrath!" And that was the best one.

† Think of the worst dad joke you know and assume it was delivered by Mike Huckabee. That's Fancy Farm comedy.

between fans of the University of Kentucky Wildcats and fans of the University of Louisville Cardinals, I noted that even though he tried to hide it in a state full of UK supporters, Mitch was a proud Louisville fan and had season tickets to their games. The crowd "oooohhhhed" at me for saying out loud what everyone knew and what Mitch always tried to hide. He is a UL fan and the baring of that truth made McConnell very agitated.*

"Tell them I like UK! Tell them I went to UK Law School! Tell them! Tell them!" he began barking at me from behind the podium, attempting to drown out the laughter. Anger seethed from his face. When I remarked later that because he always leaves the picnic early, Republican gubernatorial candidate Matt Bevin (who had an acrimonious relationship with McConnell due to a past election) wouldn't have to worry, because Bevin may "have ninety-nine problems, but a Mitch ain't one," McConnell became livid. I could feel his stare burning a hole in my back for the rest of the event.†

I am certain that McConnell didn't understand my Jay-Z reference or have any idea why people were laughing. But he did know that the crowd was laughing at *him*, in *his* part of the state, at an event that had *always* been a mini-homecoming for him. And they were laughing because of this young, punk sports radio host who had embarrassed him a year earlier in an interview during the 2014 election. After the event, the Fancy Farm organizers praised me for the spice I'd added to the festivities. But it wasn't a sentiment McConnell shared. He told organizers that if I was ever asked to emcee again, he wouldn't return. As John Cougar Mellencamp once put it, I fight authority, authority always wins.

Driving by the site of the picnic today, it seems much quieter.‡ Un-

---

* I helped write most of Matt's material for this event, and I will just say this: If Mitch was mad about this one, he should have seen what we cut. Had Matt said those, both of us would have ended up in Guantánamo Bay—where we still might end up after this book is published.

† You really have to see this to appreciate the tension. It's on YouTube. If you dislike McConnell, watch it, as you will never see him more uncomfortable.

‡ For old times' sake, Matt did pull over and yell insults at the cows. It wasn't the same.

like on those July Fancy Farm afternoons, the sides of the road aren't filled with cars and vendors. Yard signs do dot the landscape, but the only ones visible are "Jon Hayden for Sheriff." (They are literally everywhere. It was no surprise that he ended up defeating the poor soul who ran against him.) It is bizarre on days like today to think that this tiny town, with a population of less than five hundred, annually becomes the center of the political universe in this state.

As we are about to leave the county, I run into a man on the street who recognizes me and says excitedly, "Matt, you writing about Fancy Farm for your book?"

I answer yes, excited that my forthcoming political book seems to be getting buzz even with a sports audience.

He responds, "Well, that's cool. I wish it were about the Cats, though. Do you think we will beat Florida next week?"

We all have our priorities.

McCracken County

"I Guess It Was at Least Better Than a Poke in the Eye"

Sometimes you can live in a state your entire life, visit its cities multiple times, and still not actually know them. Such was the case with me and Paducah, in McCracken County. Paducah is a major population center of the region, and one of the hidden gems of Kentucky. It's settled on the Ohio River, with a surprisingly vibrant downtown and restaurant scene. When I bring *KSR* to town for live radio shows, we draw huge crowds, and the community is always electric. I always liked the place, but I didn't know it well until this trip.

Paducah's Riverwalk downtown includes a floodwall with vintage postcard-esque images, one of which reads "Welcome to Atomic City." It's a point of city pride, symbolizing the key relationship between the city and America's quest for nuclear power. The Paducah Gaseous Diffusion Plant, often referred to simply as the PGDP, was built here in 1952. It enriched uranium for military reactors and weapons, and, later in its life, for nuclear power plants. The plant transformed a small town in western Kentucky into a booming Cold War hub overnight. Local papers at the time reported chicken coops being rented out as temporary housing due to the influx of workers at the massive new 3,500-acre facility.

When PGDP was built, and for several decades thereafter, many people were unaware of the dangers of nuclear radiation. For workers at the plant, there was no reason to think anything was suspicious. They were paid well to do valuable work; strengthening the United States' nuclear capabilities made them soldiers in the Cold War, helping to defeat the Communist threat. Even though they were wading through ankle-deep sludge, wiping green salt off their lunch tables before eating, and breathing heavily polluted air, employees had no reason to think they were being poisoned. They were unaware of the danger around them until illnesses started to pile up.

No story was more disturbing than that of Joe Harding, who worked at the plant for two decades before he died in 1980. Harding knew something was wrong at the plant. When he began to get sick, he decided to keep a handwritten log of the impacts on his and other workers' health. The log was crucial, eventually turning his case into a high-profile tragedy that shook public opinion.

Harding raised concerns about his health often but was repeatedly told that everything was safe; his health issues had nothing to do with the plant. "Today we know the truth about those promises. I can feel it in my body," Harding wrote before his death. "I spent all those years breathing uranium hexafluoride gas so thick and heavy that you could see the haze in the air. You could taste it coated on your teeth and in your throat and lungs. . . . Powder on the floor was thick enough that you would leave tracks."

After years of this exposure, his skin developed cancerous growths that were clearly visible. He described the effect in morbid detail:

"I have toenails under arches of feet, on top of arches of feet, coming out of my ankle bones, and coming out of my kneecaps now. I have fingernails growing through all of my fingers and thumbs, coming out on [the] ball of [my] fingertips where your fingerprints are. I have fingernails coming out of my knuckle joints, my wrist joints, and my elbows."

Up until his death, Harding insisted to be true what now seems so obvious; his job at the federally owned nuclear facility had poisoned him, ravaging his body with mutations. He protested loudly but few listened. Even his list of fifty former colleagues who had died of cancer since he began at the facility didn't move his government bosses.

The US Department of Energy (DOE) insisted that the plant operated within safe guidelines; thus, any radiation exposure that may have occurred wouldn't have caused Harding's health issues and thus weren't related to his employment. Joe's widow, Clara, was livid about the department's ludicrous conclusion and had her husband's body exhumed for an autopsy a year and a half after his death. Her lawyer said that when his bones were tested, they showed a radiation level a thousand times greater than that of the official safe exposure readings shown in plant records. It was shocking but had little effect. Lawsuits went nowhere, and, at every turn, Harding's suffering was ignored or denied by his employers and his government. Richard Miller, who worked as a policy analyst for the Paper, Allied-Industrial, Chemical & Energy Workers International Union said, "The [Department of Energy] took the Joe Harding case very seriously: no dollar was spared in seeking to deny his claims. No effort was spared in their scorched-earth campaign to deny what was overwhelmingly obvious." The DOE knew what Harding's claims meant and what their long-term effect on future cases could be.

Unfortunately, Harding was not the only worker to see these effects. Bill McMurry represented three other employees in a 1999 lawsuit against the private contractors who operated the plant, and his complaint maintains:

"Workers at the PGDP were deceived by their employers; the Plant operators failed to put controls in place which would have protected the workers from transuranic chemicals such as Plutonium and Neptunium. The operators knew that if they instituted controls to protect the workers, it would reveal to the public that the workers were being exposed to the most dangerous chemicals known to man. For forty years, the public and workers were told that the only chemical they were exposed to was uranium, which was a lie."

And it wasn't just workers who felt the effects of exposure. Such little caution was taken when dealing with nuclear waste that an area next to the facility was known as "Drum Mountain." There, thousands of nuclear waste canisters were piled as high as forty feet out in the open, and over time their leakage permeated and polluted the soil and groundwater, creating hazardous plumes that stretched for thousands of feet beyond the perimeter of the plant. The Department of Energy inspector general said later that at least ten billion gallons were contaminated, and some of the polluted water may have reached the Ohio River. For context, in 2010 the oil rig Deepwater Horizon exploded, spilling 210 million gallons of oil into the Gulf of Mexico. It was an environmental disaster. The Paducah Gaseous Diffusion Plant nuclear waste polluted more than forty-seven times that amount of water.

Anecdotal complaints of contamination were everywhere. Residents reported seeing streams running yellow and purple in parts of the county, as well as black radioactive ooze seeping from the ground in 1999 a quarter mile away from the facility. The government was accused of dumping contaminated waste on public property, including a state wildlife area near the plant. Plutonium was found in the wells of at least a hundred local residents, poisoning their water supply. One of them, Ronald Lamb, said government representatives "told us we'd have to drink it for seventy-five years to get any risk. Well, there's no doubt we've had exposures, and if me and my family are the ones at risk from this, that's enough for me." Eventually the federal government changed its mind and agreed to pay for those residents to be hooked up to the city water supply, and it has paid their water bills to this day. Nevertheless, Lamb's family developed digestive problems from the water, and, tragically, his father died of cancer in 1994.

In 1999, after an exposé in the *Washington Post* put the Paducah plant in the national spotlight, the US government finally ended its attempts to hide the contamination. Energy Secretary Bill Richardson admitted the past malfeasance. "In the past, I believe that the government basically said—without any review—that there is no established linkage between the exposure these workers had and their illness." After years, even decades, of pushing aside Harding and other sick workers at the plant, Richardson said the workers in Paducah would now be given the care and restitution they deserved.

The Energy Employees Occupational Illness Compensation Program Act was passed soon thereafter. The bill provided $150,000 and medical expenses for each worker (or his survivors) who developed cancer after working at the plant. No causal link between the cancer and exposure was required to be shown to receive the payments, a barrier that had crippled past recovery attempts. However, as attorney McMurry explains, it was too little too late for most. "Most of those who worked for the PGDP operators were already dead, so the congressional compensation of $150,000 didn't help the vast majority of workers who were exposed. The money went to nearest relatives, and I believe the amount of compensation was inadequate to compensate for the workers' suffering." To date, the plan has cost taxpayers more than $17 billion, even though the bill did not cover residents in the area who were not employed at the plant. Those individuals received no benefits at all.

Not surprisingly, Mitch McConnell has a protracted, tortured history with the Paducah facility and its victims. McCracken County has long been a key component of Mitch's "west of I-65" reelection strategy. In 1988, just as McConnell was gearing up for his first reelection bid, the radioactive contamination was found in the county's drinking wells. Mitch received only 42 percent of the vote in McCracken County in his first campaign and he knew getting a new nuclear facility built in Paducah could be a central part of his platform. The senator claimed that due to his strong influence with the George H. W. Bush administration, he had the sway to get a new plant built if he were reelected. During his 1990 campaign, he even brought Dan Quayle, the vice president,* to the city to see the PGDP facility and make his case, a move that received much attention in the weeks leading up to the election.

The maneuver worked. McConnell turned around McCracken County in 1990, getting 54 percent of the vote on his way to reelection. Unfortunately for the citizens of Paducah, it was the last they heard about the new plant. McConnell never moved legislation to replace the plant and after he won, he rarely mentioned the idea again. Over the

---

* Quayle being vice president was a lot funnier before Donald Trump became president.

next decade, the senator helped secure enough federal money to keep the existing plant open, but the health concerns of the workers was completely ignored.

The dam broke in 1999 with the *Washington Post* reports on the radiation exposure and sick workers. The Department of Energy commissioned an investigation into the health and safety issues at the plant. McConnell and Kentucky's other senator, Republican Jim Bunning, asked the US General Accounting Office to assess the general progress on cleaning up the contamination. The GAO report stated that funding was a huge issue: "The funding available for cleanup had been much less than requested. Most of the site's cleanup funding had been devoted to characterizing contamination (that is, identifying its nature and extent); operating and maintaining the site infrastructure; meeting regulatory requirements; and implementing measures in reaction to immediate threats. According to DOE officials, cleanup at the site, including the removal of contaminated scrap metal and low-level waste disposal, was delayed because of funding limitations."

At the time of this report, McConnell had been sitting on the Senate Appropriations Committee for years. It was his committee's job to fund cleanup efforts, yet the report that *he* commissioned made clear the funding was insufficient. According to the GAO, funding would need to at least triple in order to properly begin addressing the nuclear waste. The estimated cost? A minimum of $1.3 billion over the following decade.

After the report, McConnell did the bare minimum to retain support in the area. Along with Energy Secretary Richardson, McConnell helped push through Congress the bill to pay the $150,000 and medical expenses for the workers and survivors. It provided some immediate relief for those with cancer at the time, but little consolation for those with lost loved ones.

Many in the area—including Bill McMurry—believe not only was the compensation insufficient, it had other detrimental effects. "The health bill did a good job at quieting public discussion of the issue of compensation," he contends, "which discouraged workers from filing suit for getting cancer. The amount of compensation, however, was inadequate to the workers' suffering. But I guess it was at least better than a poke in the eye."

It isn't McConnell's fault what happened to the workers in Paducah. The contamination and cover-up are a blight on our nation's history that began long before he arrived in office. But it is also certainly the case he did nothing to make it better for far too long. Mitch McConnell, at best, stood silently by and watched the federal government thwart nuclear workers at every turn, challenging their cancer diagnoses and actively refusing to help with medical care. Untold numbers of his constituents' lives are worse because of his inaction.

Livingston County

"I Hope This Is Not the Moment This Bridge Chooses to Collapse"

Just northeast of Paducah is Livingston County, an oft-overlooked spot on the map that I knew little about before this trip. I'd never been to Livingston County, had never known anyone from Livingston County, and, honestly, couldn't have placed Livingston County on a map. So when I went into Thompson's Grocery in Smithland, I did so as a tabula rasa.

Thompson's is an older quick-stop grocery store in need of a slight remodel. But when you walk past the racks of soup cans, lottery tickets, and candy bars, it becomes much more interesting. In the back room, slightly hidden from view, is one of the most politically active spots in the entire county.

In most of America, the serious political discussions in a city don't take place in a storage room for palettes of Dr Pepper and Big Red.* But in Smithland, packed in small booths next to the stacked-up rations along the walls, sit Livingston County's greatest thinkers and debaters. Most afternoons, the place is filled with older gentlemen casually discussing the issues of the day and making decisions about the future of Smithland. There's the debating man folks around here affectionately

* If you don't know Big Red, it's terrible—a red "cherry" soft drink that tastes like lighter fluid. No one should drink Big Red. If you do, you should be ashamed.

call "Internet," because every time you argue statistics with him, he goes straight to his phone to find a dubious website to make his point. Louie is also usually holding court, although if you want him to like you, then you need to pronounce it "Lou-*eee*," because he thinks it sounds better. (Everyone here indulges him.*) It is here we meet Daniel Hurt, a wavy-haired young Democratic campaign manager wearing a maroon turtleneck (the only turtleneck we saw in Livingston County) who comes to Thompson's because it's where people shoot straight about his rural, expansive home county.

"Livingston County is famous for several things," Daniel tells us, his thoughtful eyes shielded by large, round glasses. "It's famous for being where the movie *How the West Was Won*, with Henry Fonda, was partially shot; it's famous for having about seven rock quarries, since if you stay here after high school, you'll probably work in one; and it's famous for having really bad infrastructure."

The bridges in Livingston County† are the stuff of horror movies, barely functional and terrifying. The Ledbetter Bridge on the outskirts of the county was built in the 1930s and was in a constant state of disrepair for decades until it was finally replaced in 2014 after years of pleading from local citizens. In the months following its closing, a series of storms caused the bridge to at first drop a few feet, and then completely collapse. It's a result that could have led to a substantial loss of life had Livingston County not been lucky enough to beat the clock by a few months with its replacement. After eighty years of constant use and decades of neglect, the county was just a few weeks from an unthinkable calamity.

After such good fortune, you would think that it would have served as a wakeup call to state and federal officials. But history may be dangerously close to repeating itself just down the road. The Lucy Jefferson Lewis Memorial Bridge is even older than the collapsed Ledbetter Bridge and a main thoroughfare through Livingston County. On US-60,

---

* Matt tries to act high and mighty with these names, but his friends in Middlesboro growing up were named BoBob, Scooter, and Burniel. He doesn't think I know, but I do.

† A poorly received Clint Eastwood–Meryl Streep sequel.

it's the only bridge in the county that connects the northern half with the southern, a bridge traveled by likely thousands of travelers each day. As such, if it collapsed or were abandoned, the folks in this area would suddenly have a ninety-minute commute on alternative roads just to get around it and into (or out of) Smithland. It's the unfortunate result of the odd geography of the area that one bridge could have such importance, but with that being the case, you would assume its stability would be of the utmost importance for the government. You would assume wrong.

The Lucy Jefferson Lewis Bridge is cracking on all sides, and fissures in the concrete are visible everywhere. Slabs of concrete dangle from both sides and below its deck pieces that have fallen are left on the banks of the Cumberland River. The more you observe, the worse it looks. It is terrifying, and as we drive across, I can feel a pit in my stomach. A bridge is doing its job if you cross it and give it no thought. When you cross over this one, your number one thought is "I hope this is not the moment this bridge chooses to collapse, because that's clearly going to happen at some point, and probably soon."

When we asked the Livingston County judge-executive (essentially the mayor of a Kentucky county) about the problems, he noted that county officials ask the state for funds in every budget cycle, and they often hear they are close to getting them. But Kentucky state government is in a pension crisis, and in places like this, infrastructure is often the first thing cut during budget negotiations (due to western Kentucky's small population and little political power). So optimism isn't high. Federal funding could easily fix the problem and would be a godsend for the county, if only someone made it a priority in Washington.*

School buses pass over the Lucy Jefferson Lewis Bridge daily, even though it looks to be held together by rebar and orange nylon construction scaffolding. Their overall weight and the structure's deterioration led the school district to stop letting its buses travel on it for a

---

* Mitch has never had a problem using federal funds to build bridges. When attempting to line up support for his bid for majority leader, McConnell sent infrastructure funds to fellow senator Lincoln Chafee's native Rhode Island in order to shore up his vote.

period of time. But state officials deemed it safe and the cost in time and money of alternate routes has prevented the temporary change from becoming permanent. Amazingly, after you've crossed the bridge (and exhaled from holding your breath) from Smithland, heading north, the first building on your right is—wait for it—a Kentucky Department of Transportation bureau. It is close enough that if you sit inside, you could probably see the slabs of concrete falling below. The irony is overwhelming. Actually, the only thing possibly more ironic would be if Kentucky's highest-ranked, longest-sitting senator (who also happened to be majority leader) happened to be married to someone who runs the federal Department of Transportation, could authorize the funds to fix it, and nevertheless has yet to do anything about it. Why, that would be crazy.

Crittenden County

"You Don't Get Any Real Answer"

While Livingston County barely escaped having one operating bridge collapse and currently has another one striking abject terror in those who have to cross it on a daily basis, Crittenden County actually has a perfectly good, unused bridge sitting in the middle of a field off Highway 64. And when I say sitting in a field, I mean *literally sitting in a field* of tall overgrown grass, connecting nothing to nothing. It is an actual "Bridge to Nowhere."

Its history is a perfect lesson in the ineptness of government in updating our infrastructure in this country. Several years ago, Crittenden County was the only county west of Elizabethtown not to have a four-lane road coming into or out of it. Beyond slowing traffic flow, this crushed its county's economic viability because only certain types of roads are permissible for the widest (102 inches) semi-tractor-trailers to traverse safely. Failing to provide these vehicles access makes it impossible for many types of businesses to function; therefore, widening Crittenden County's roads became a crucial economic priority. After many attempts to get the state government's attention, it was eventually announced that Highway 64 would be expanded to four lanes, opening access to Crittenden and neighboring Caldwell County. However, after construction began, funding was abruptly cut, for reasons that aren't clear.

At that moment, all work on the road ceased. However, the full-size steel bridge that was to connect a part of the revamped highway was already finished. With nowhere to put the bridge, contractors simply left it on the side of the road, where it still sits, years after its construction. The Bridge to Nowhere is a surreal site, a perfectly functioning bridge just sitting in the meadow like an old forgotten truck. It looks to be a nice bridge,* but with no road or body of water attached, it is a bizarre sight. Of course, the neighboring county is desperately in need of a bridge just like this one, but still this one sits abandoned, like a sadistically cruel tease to all Livingston Countians. If Mitch McConnell and the secretary of transportation, Elaine Chao (who happens to be his wife), were ever to pass through, they'd probably be shocked at the waste. That's unlikely, though, since no one can remember the last time either of them set foot in the area.

We take what's left of the uncompleted highway past Stuff Brokers Pawn and Tumble Extreme† to the Front Porch, a massively popular local restaurant known for its catfish, mason jar light fixtures, rustic interior, and extremely prominent (and impressive) front porch.

It's there, over an appetizer of fried dill pickles, that we meet Roger Simpson, an eighty-year-old veteran and retired United Airlines pilot who makes his home in Crittenden County. Roger has a soft-spoken, grandfatherly quality to him but also the firm handshake of a man who could still bring you to your knees if you crossed him. He speaks with purpose, but is kind, alternating in tone between a forceful citizen at a town forum and a grandfather bragging lovingly about his grandkids. Roger is resolute, as seen by the fact that ever since Mitch McConnell became senator of Kentucky, Roger has regularly written him letters,

* We are not, however, bridge experts.

† Located conveniently close to each other so you can take your knee brace to be pawned after your extreme tumbling ACL surgery.

one a year or so, with his thoughts on the major political issues. The letters are polite but forceful, expressing his points in the most direct but considerate manner possible. Roger says he feels that McConnell, as a public servant, should hear from his constituents.

"You know, you don't get any real answer," he says resignedly. "You just get back a generic type of response saying they saw what you wrote and that they'll take it into consideration."

Still, Roger writes. Which is really something; writing letters to one's local congressman is the most bare-bones political activism—a throwback to a bygone era. When was the last time you wrote a letter? I think for me it was 1986, when, as a child, I wrote the Atlanta Braves' Bob Horner asking for an autograph. (A slugging infielder, he once hit four homers in a game, and I was very excited.)* But speaking with McConnell in person is nearly impossible; he doesn't do town halls, rarely travels around the state, and has no real constituent outreach on a personal level. And so Roger writes, and even though I have to think that Mitch McConnell doesn't receive more than a few actual, honest-to-God, handwritten, non-form letters ever, the senator has never bothered to reply, and likely never will.

I can honestly think of no human being on the planet who would be a less exciting pen pal than Mitch McConnell. So why does he do it?

"Sometimes you just get frustrated when you see what's going on," Roger says, crossing his arms defiantly. "It's all just so irritating. These things, they're not simple. It's serious stuff that has an influence on our country. There's just so much hypocrisy.

"I don't know what else to do."

---

* He didn't write Matt back. That's why Matt is now a Cincinnati Reds fan.

Lyon County

"Nobody Thinks, When They Bump Their Knee, 'Oh, It Might Be Cancer'"

"Do you really want to spend that much time of your life thinking about Mitch McConnell?"

That was the reaction of my friend Hubby when I told him about this book project and how it would take me across the state. It was a valid question. There are few individuals less exciting to think about than McConnell. His face and personality are natural prophylactics and because I am considering running against him, I've had to care about him way more than any man ever should. I have read every biography written, searched online archives, downloaded podcasts, and watched so many boring, monotonous, hypocritical speeches of his that I feel as if he is an unwanted part of my family.* McConnell represents the worst of politics, and the more one studies him, the more depressing his power and soulless nature become to contemplate. It does make me wonder if he is worth these six months (or more) of my life.

Then you come to Lyon County, and it actually makes sense.

Eddyville is its largest town, best known as the home of the foreboding Kentucky State Penitentiary and "Jumping" Joe Fulks, allegedly the inventor of the basketball jump shot. I came here to do my morning radio show at the Mineral Mound Golf Course and when it was over, I once again see my Tracker. He is everywhere now and his presence is becoming a regular part of the trip. I don't find having him around as unnerving as I once did, but I am still staying on guard. He is actively trying to make small talk with us and even though I am slightly wary, I ask him how the job is going. He shakes his head and says, "I don't like it very much. I feel weird following you everywhere, and it seems like a waste."

---

* Except even my cousin Steve would have given Merrick Garland a confirmation vote.

He's right. It is. The whole experience is mutually embarrassing. I look at him and he looks away. He films me at times, but it always seems half-hearted and when I look into the lens, he turns red. It is like we are on an awkward first date, only with one of us being paid to ruin the other person's life.

After the show we shake him and head to the uniquely humanitarian restaurant, bakery, and coffee shop Our Daily Bread. Now in its fourth year of operation, Our Daily Bread is run by Rose Fraliex, who prides herself on the faith-based eatery's ability to give back to the community from which it spawned. It is a religious establishment in the best possible way, creating a sense of community in everything it does. It's the type of place that names one of its coffees "the Peacemaker" in honor of the police, "the Three Alarm" for the firefighters, and "Fish Bait" to honor the local fishermen. It's a Norman Rockwell painting come to life, only in a slightly run-down strip mall just off the interstate. Inside is a "Pay It Forward" board, which allows patrons to write down the name of a person or group on a slip of paper and post it on the board for another patron to take down and perform a good deed. The board is full and while we sit in the store, we see two people come and take a slip. It's not just a trite, cutesy thing—it's a real, proactive, and benevolent force in the community.

As I am about to leave, a local says, "Have you met Cullan yet? You have to meet Cullan."

A couple of minutes later I hear, "You know Cullan Brown, right?" A middle-aged woman in a boutique says, "Cullan's very special around here." Another man jokingly refers to him as the mayor.

They are speaking of Cullan Brown, a native son of Eddyville with an amazing story. Cullan is a sophomore at the University of Kentucky and a member of its golf team. Two months before we met, Cullan was diagnosed with a rare form of bone cancer called osteosarcoma, often found in patients under the age of twenty-five. The diagnosis would bench the sophomore National Collegiate Athletic Association (NCAA) golfer during a crucial year of his college career and send him home to Eddyville.

Because he was a UK athlete, I was aware of his condition and had been told that Cullan was one of the kindest young men in the state.

But not until I met him did I realize that was an understatement. Cullan has a broad smile and an easy drawl. He has the countenance of a man twice his age, and is the kind of person so nice it seems impossible, gregariously shaking hands with all comers. He also walks very gingerly, with a cane, and behind the smile, you know he is in pain.

"One night in July I got up in the middle of the night to go to the bathroom and bumped my knee on the foot bench at the end of my bed," Cullan recounts about the events leading up to his diagnosis, "and it just never stopped hurting. In three days, I was still limping, so you begin to wonder what it is. And nobody thinks, when they bump their knee, 'Oh, it might be cancer.'"

After several doctors were unable to pinpoint the problem, Cullan and his family texted the director of sports medicine at the University of Kentucky, who suggested he come in for a magnetic resonance imaging (MRI) scan. The Browns arrived for an MRI on Friday morning, and a few hours later a doctor was sitting down with them to explain that when Cullan had bumped his leg in the middle of the night, he'd aggravated a large tumor growing there.

"It was unbelievable," jokes Cullan. "I walked in that morning with a hurt knee, and now I was leaving on crutches with cancer. I told the nurses that's a heck of a system."

The prognosis for someone like Cullan is positive, as the malignancy was caught early, but it's still nothing to take casually. The disease is serious, and Lyon County has rallied behind its native son. Cullan has joked that it seems the entire county has been through his house since having heard about his diagnosis.

"The thing about this community is that it's been great to me since my diagnosis, but it hasn't changed any," Cullen tells me as we sit down at The Joint, a barbeque restaurant where other diners stop by regularly to shake the young man's hand and sincerely wish him the best. "You have to understand that this community is great twenty-four hours a day," Cullen says intently. "Since my diagnosis, it's been unbelievable, but it hasn't been any different from any other Tuesday at the gas station with some guys. It's amazing how this community has always supported me and been there for me."

As our lunch comes, Cullan asks that we all bow our heads to bless the food. In that warm, friendly drawl, he prays over the meal we're about to share together, the hands that prepared it, and the farmers who helped to provided it. He never mentions himself or the storm clouds over his head. And Cullan Brown, who has days where this rare form of cancer is so tough that it prevents him from even answering the phone, asks us all in prayer to give thanks for the good things in our lives.

I look around the table and notice multiple wristbands that say "Pray for Cullan." I ask for one of my own and have worn it ever since. As we eat, Cullan looks at me and says, "You just have to enjoy the moments you have, like today, and cherish those, and on the bad days, you just have to make it through." I ask him what's next for him, and he says, "Whatever God has for me and giving back to others for all they have done for me."

As we stand to leave, Cullan labors to his feet and takes me to the side. He looks me in the eyes and says, "Thank you for coming. I know you have a tough decision ahead. I will be praying for you too."

Why would I want to spend six months of my life thinking about Mitch McConnell? Because he isn't Kentucky. People like Cullan Brown are.

Trigg County

Fish Are Flying By My Head

"Matt, what would you think about going bowhunting tonight for Asian carp?"

That was the question Lyon County judge-executive Wade White put to me as we pulled up to meet him for the first time. Always up for an adventure, I said, "Why not?" So, at nine thirty that night, Chris and I were trolling slowly in a fishing boat across western Kentucky's Lake Barkley. Now let me be clear. I don't fish. I don't hunt. And I certainly don't "bowhunt." So as we made our way into Trigg County, home of the gorgeous Land Between the Lakes National Recreation Area, I had no idea what was in store. To catch Asian carp, you have to go at night, in the pitch dark. When the lights on Wade's boat are turned off (which is necessary for catching carp), it feels as if we are the only life-forms for miles.

But we aren't. In fact, we are surrounded by the most hated creature in all of this part of Kentucky. Asian carp probably don't mean to be evil, but in this environment, they are. They have overtaken the state and much of the Midwest, and their history in the area illustrates the old adage that no good deed goes unpunished.

Rachel Carson's landmark 1962 book *Silent Spring* condemned the use of synthetic pesticides and exposed the chemicals' harmful effects on the natural world. It persuaded farmers and ecologists to look into alternative methods of controlling vegetation and unwanted bacteria. It was thought that if natural methods could supplement in environments where pesticides were disrupting the ecosystem, things would be better for everyone.

This thinking, noble and considerate as it is may be, led federal government biologists in the 1970s to recommend that farmers stock their catfish ponds with Asian carp, a species that would eat algae out of the ponds and keep everything tidy without chemical treatments. At first it worked like a charm. But then a series of floods hit, the catfish ponds rose and overflowed, and the carp escaped their cozy environs, splashing into larger bodies of water such as nearby Lake Barkley and Kentucky Lake. The unique environment of the waters of western Kentucky was especially conducive for Asian carp reproduction, making the fish more fertile than their brethren left behind in Asia. The Asian carp population began multiplying rapidly.* The fish dominated the environment, wreaking absolute havoc on the vegetative sustenance of the lakes—which indigenous fish eat for survival as well. The Asian carp's aggression made it extremely difficult for other species to survive. Forty years later, this combination of factors has produced lakes throughout the region where Asian carp firmly rule the roost. They're the only game in town. And they've become very, very bad news. Though select world cultures enjoy Asian carp as a culinary dish, locals

* A wholly unromantic situation, I can assure you.

tell us the fish aren't traditionally edible.* Thus, Trigg County—and, honestly, most parts of Middle America that surround lakes—are left with a difficult problem. Fishing, which is so important to these areas as both food and a tourism attraction, is being destroyed by these flying Asian carp.

Wait a minute. Did I mention they fly? Okay, I know this sounds crazy, but Asian carp don't just live in the water, they literally "fly" out of it as if fired from a cannon. Take a second and go on YouTube and search "Asian carp," so you can see what I mean. See that? It's real. Because Asian carp feed at the surface of the water, they get freaked out by our warmer water as well as by the vibrations of boats and bright light. So, when it is dark, and a moving object and/or bright lights suddenly disturb their crib, they will jump into the air in every direction imaginable, sometimes as high as fifteen feet above the water. It is a sight to behold.

For all these reasons, Asian carp are public enemy number one in these parts. And that's why Wade White, along with some other elected officials in areas around Lake Barkley, have spearheaded the War on Carp, a movement that seeks congressional funding to eradicate this scourge from the region's lakes. And it's why we're here, on a Monday night with the judge-executive, on a twenty-foot-long, camouflaged SeaArk 2072 boat, standing on this deck in complete darkness, ready to do our part to pare down those numbers.

Wade and his son, Brandon, have brought us out to bowhunt, which for those of you not of the hunting lifestyle essentially means doing archery on fish as they fly through the air. I would describe bowfishing these sloppy behemoths as a pastime combining recreational hunting, extreme environmental activism, and Nintendo's *Duck Hunt*. As I stated at the outset, I am not a hunter or an outdoorsman. It's not that I oppose the practice, it's just that what it takes—getting up early in the morning, patience, being dirty, and so forth—isn't really my bag. Still, I am a patriot, and if I am needed to enlist in the War on Carp, I will gladly

* The locals describe the taste as "bitter and disgusting," which actually made me want to try it, just to see how bad it was. I am a child in that way. But even though the fish are everywhere here, no restaurant serves them.

volunteer. After a quick lesson in how to fire the arrow, which has a thin fishing line attached to it so one can reel the arrow back in after every shot, we headed out to attack the phenomenon firsthand.

From moment one, it was clear that bowhunting for Asian carp is absolute mayhem. Imagine a war zone where instead of dangerous, deadly mortars whizzing past your head, it's huge, slimy, gray fish attacking from every which way. As Wade flashes the bright lights in every direction, the monster fish become agitated and just start *leaping* from all around us. Sometimes they sail over the boat, other times they land inside with a dull thud, smacking Chris in the leg, me in the stomach. Every body part not covered is vulnerable, and this frenzy is so quick and furious that I begin to freak out slightly. Because I rarely cause fish harm, I have never had them attack me, and the phenomenon is truly disconcerting. The fish strike in packs every thirty seconds, and at six foot four and 230 pounds, I present a big target. While I am ostensibly hunting them, it feels as if *I* am the prey, especially when one smacks me across the nose, nearly knocking me out of the boat. It's sheer madness. Everyone aboard is shouting, fish are rocketing by my head, and about thirty of 'em are thrashing about on the floor of the boat, whacking my knees and ankles. Pure insanity.

But I loved it, especially when I actually shot one out of the sky.* I admit that it was lucky: no one else in the boat hit one, and I have the aim of a drunken Mitch Trubisky.† But somehow, by the grace of God, I hit a fish, and at that moment, I had never been prouder. I let someone else deal with the after-effects (Asian carp are really gross), but I have my picture and memories for posterity. I never really understood the appeal of fishing. It seemed boring, lazy, and a waste of time. But this type of fishing, where the fish fight back—well, that's a different story!

Wade says that Mitch McConnell has actually been helpful in securing funding and is an advocate for the fish's extermination. But like the fish in the darkness of this lake, the effect of Mitch's efforts are hard

---

* No footage of this exists, natch.

† The Chicago Bears quarterback who is, as you are reading this, throwing another interception.

to see. The problem is only getting worse. On this September night, we were proud to have played a part in saving Trigg County. If you are so inclined, I am sure Wade and his fellow warriors would welcome you fighting alongside them. But know that it's a messy fight; there's excitement, danger, and you end up slimy. In the end, you may have to follow our lead and throw away your clothes, because they will smell really, *really* nasty, like decrepit old fish. So be it. Every war has its casualties.

Ballard County

Calling Chuck Schumer

In Kentucky there are four counties no one knows anything about. The four so-called river counties of Ballard, Hickman, Carlisle, and Fulton are rural, sparsely populated areas with a different existence from most of the rest of the state. They are four of the ten least-populated counties in Kentucky, with three of them among the bottom five. They sit on the Mississippi River, but live in a sense of isolation, divided from larger cities in other states by the river and disconnected from their fellow Kentuckians by lifestyle.* Ask most people about the river counties and chances are high they will say you made them up.

But that's not fair. These places matter too. Ballard County has the most people (eight thousand) and sits on the border of Kentucky, Missouri, and Illinois. At first glance, it looks very flat and devoid of all human life, a conclusion only verified on future glances as well. Fields of crops come right up to within feet of the roads, and in the distance, silos and combines swim through them like jagged rocks or shark fins in the ocean. In fact, Hinkleville Road as a whole looks like it just unspools and disappears into a cornfield. We stop at the one happening place, Peedee's Food Mart, where the county starts its day. Old men are sitting in the booth complaining about the St. Louis Cardinals (not enough pitching) and television (never anything good on). I ask one

* Like Shepard Smith on Fox News.

man what there is to do here and he says, "Eat and farm," both of which luckily seem to go hand in hand.

The county's history is mostly wrapped around two sites in Wickliffe: (1) the Wickliffe Mounds, a Native American historical site and burial ground that traces its ancestry to around 1100 AD;* and (2) Fort Jefferson, a military fort established by George Rogers Clark in 1780 at the confluence of the Mississippi and Ohio Rivers. It was commissioned by the brand-new US government and was intended to be one of the key military installations of the newly settled parts of America. Instead, two years later, threats of potential Native American attacks, illness, and starvation led to the fort's abandonment.† This quick retreat is now memorialized by a ninety-foot-tall cross that was built in the 1980s in order to create a monument that could be seen in all three states. Because I am not sure that anything else in the county is higher than around twenty-five feet, you could say the large, imposing ivory cross stands out.

We are here to meet Angie Yu, a Ballard County resident who lives by the old saying "When life gives you lemons, create an international carp processing and exporting enterprise." Knowing that the area had an unwanted surplus of Asian carp and that people in Asia actually like Asian carp but don't have enough to satisfy demand, she had a revelation. Why not just process the Asian carp here and *send them back to Asia*? And the Middle East! And Eastern Europe! And anywhere else that might not have enough of the menacing fish!

While not very popular in western Kentucky, there is still a demand globally for Asian carp. In many Asian cultures, they are a popular food item and, in some cases, considered a delicacy. So, in 2012 Yu established Two Rivers Fisheries with a simple premise: send the carp back where they came from. The facility is remarkably small and intimate given its output, processing yellow, bighead, silver, and grass varieties of Asian carp and exporting them to eleven countries while contracting with local fisherman to catch and provide the fish. Two

---

* We can't really say *how* fascinating because the mounds are closed on Monday and Tuesday, inasmuch as you can close mounds.

† Even the pillow forts I built as a child lasted longer.

Rivers processes upward of thirty to thirty-five thousand pounds of carp per day and expects to export a whopping seventy-eight million pounds over the next six years. A new seventy-two-acre facility is currently being built outside Wickliffe and Angie tells us that getting rid of the disgusting fish is the new Ballard County boom economy.

As Chris continued to learn about Two Rivers's growth, I had to step outside to take a call from a friend in Washington, DC, with some bad news: Chuck Schumer's people had called back, and the Senate minority leader was not interested in meeting with me.

Now, you may be thinking (understandably), "Well, Matt, *I* have never gotten a meeting with Chuck Schumer either, so what's the big deal?" And that would be a fair question, so a little explanation is required.

If you're like me, you probably have a vision of American democracy something akin to this one: citizens across the country all have the right to run for public office. There are, unfortunately, only two major political parties (as opposed to most of the rest of the Western world, where there are more parties and more choices), but candidates pick one, run for office, enter a primary, and, if they are the top choice, become the nominee for the general election. It's a simple process and fits our democratic ideals. However, when it comes to races for the US Senate, it's also completely false.

The real decisions as to who will be both parties' nominees for US Senate races aren't made by voters on Election Day but by a handful of senators and donors in Washington. Each election cycle, Democrats and Republicans recruit potential candidates to run for office via their official campaign committees. If you are chosen, you have a virtual golden ticket to the nomination. The committees introduce you to the biggest donors, coordinate media appearances, and put the force of the party's infrastructure behind you. Since I have never been recruited to run as a Republican, I have no special inside knowledge of what they do, but I am told it's similar to my Democratic experience.* In 2018, after the website Politico ran an extensive profile on my interest in potentially challenging Mitch McConnell, I began to hear from political

* Only with 100 percent more Orrin Hatch.

types interested in my possible candidacy. They all shared the same advice: "You have to get with Schumer; he will ultimately decide who the nominee will be."*

Chuck Schumer takes this role very seriously. The New York senator meets with candidates for every race and conducts the "Schumer interview": a one-on-one conversation in which he grills the individual about their life, why they are running, and their political views. He selects from the potential main contenders whom he believes to be the best candidate and offers his institutional support. Schumer is the judge and jury. He makes the final selection and his decision selects virtually all of the major Democratic Senate nominees in America.

Schumer and the Democratic Senatorial Campaign Committee (DSCC) then go about clearing the path for their anointed choice. They tell the best campaign managers and political staffers that if they work with candidates challenging their choice in a primary, they will then be "frozen" out of working for their choices in future races. That often scares away all the top-tier advisors, making it difficult to find the high-quality staff needed to build a successful campaign. The only candidates with the ability to buck the system are the extremely wealthy ones who can fund their own campaigns. For everyone else, it becomes a massive hurdle. Running for office is hard; running for your own party's nomination against the party itself (without being a multimillionaire) is nearly impossible.

Hearing this, I tried my best to make my case to Schumer directly. Over the better part of a year, I consistently called the DSCC and tried to set up a meeting. My calls were never returned. When a couple of people I knew with ties to the DSCC tried to intervene on my behalf, they were thwarted. I was persistent, but consistently ignored. When I finally got to speak to a DSCC staffer on the phone, I was told politely that no interview would ever take place. The reason why? They had their candidate.

Their choice was Amy McGrath. She checked all the boxes on paper. She had an exemplary military record, killer TV commercials,

* "Get with Schumer" is more professional than it sounds, I promise.

and could raise millions of dollars without even trying. The latter was true thanks to her 2018 congressional run in which her "Fighter Pilot" ad took the nation by storm, making her a celebrity in national political circles. Democrat donors loved her story, glamorized her military service, and gladly gave millions to a random House candidate in Kentucky. She was a money machine.

There was only one problem: she lost. After her Republican opponent, three-term incumbent Andy Barr, released an audiotape of McGrath telling a group of donors in Massachusetts that she was "more liberal than anyone in Kentucky," her campaign plummeted. Her consistent double-digit lead in the polls disappeared almost immediately. Her rural supporters in the district abandoned her and she ended up losing by nearly five points on Election Day. Even though Democrats in eleven of twelve congressional districts nationally with similar makeups to hers all won their races, McGrath was the lone loser, one of the few real disappointments for the Democratic party in 2018.

Despite the poor performance, Schumer still loved McGrath. He thought her ability to raise millions with an unmatched donor list would (a) keep Mitch McConnell busy with a tough 2020 campaign and (b) look great on his national Democratic Senate candidate slate. Even if she couldn't win Kentucky, and, honestly Schumer likely thought, "Who could?," she would help nationally and raise enough money on her own that it would make for one less race he would have to worry about.

Unfortunately for Kentucky Democrats who actually want to beat Mitch, McGrath's Senate campaign launch was an abject disaster. She did raise millions of dollars, but everything else fell flat. Her initial interviews were painful. Her positions were unclear and her starting platform, that she would help Trump "drain the swamp" more than McConnell could, was seen as outlandish pandering by both the Left and the Right. She compounded these problems in an interview on her second day of the campaign in which she said she would have voted to confirm Judge Brett Kavanagh for the US Supreme Court in 2018, despite the past allegations of sexual assault that came up during his confirmation hearing. Democratic outrage on Twitter was swift, especially after it was discovered that she had written an editorial during the Kavanagh hearings saying that he should be voted down. McGrath then compounded the error just hours later by tweeting that after "reviewing his record," she now believes she would have voted against him. It was overconsulted political wishy-washiness at its worst, and a doomed aura settled upon her campaign.

McGrath's troubles made Kentucky Democrats very worried and made it clear to me I needed to reconsider the race. When I had initially heard that McGrath was entering and would have the support of the DSCC, I assumed my potential candidacy was dead in the water. I like a good fight against the establishment, but I am not a masochist. Taking on Mitch was hard, but taking on him and the Democratic establishment seemed nearly impossible. However, after watching McGrath's launch and realizing she may have already squandered whatever chance she had at a general election victory, I had to reconsider.

Calls again came in from people around Washington saying I had to try speaking with Schumer. One of Chuck's fellow Democratic senators, whom I had never met, called me out of the blue and gave me advice on how to approach his New York colleague. "Just be very deferential and tell him what he wants to hear. He really likes people who are intelligent, but also feed his ego." I reached out one last time. Surely after McGrath's bungling start, he would reconsider and look at other candidates. I was told to give it a few days, and they would get back to me shortly.

That response came in Ballard County. I was told by a staffer that Schumer had thought about it, and, despite everything, he was sticking with Amy. He wished me good luck, but said nothing would be changing. The message had come from on high. Kentucky Democrats would have to live with it.

Carlisle County

"They Think He Helps Trump Get Stuff Done"

On this particular day in the back half of September, the temperature as we roll into Carlisle County is a stifling ninety-seven degrees. I am sweating profusely, thanks largely to my poor decision to walk the streets of downtown Bardwell in the middle of the afternoon.* It's barren here. Industry took off from this area long ago. The tiny city of Bardwell isn't close to any major interstate, and even though the Mississippi River borders Carlisle County, Bardwell's seven hundred or so residents have to be content watching barges full of material pass right by without stopping.

Barges *do* stop to unload along the Kentucky banks of the Mississippi, they just don't stop anywhere near Bardwell because there's no physical place for them to dock. The residents of the western county have been hoping for years that a port will be built, seeing this as something of a magic bullet that would help them bounce back from a persistent, tough economic slump. With tobacco gone, farms consolidating, and tariffs imposed by President Trump (even though traditionally tariffs are to Republicans what garlic is to vampires), the economic growth in America is not being felt in Carlisle. The county has become an industrial economic desert, completely on its own.

We pull into the parking lot of the biggest building in sight, Flegles, right off the highway. The air is thick and roasting as we walk inside to meet Andy Flegle and his father, Mark, the proprietors of a once-bustling lumber supply store. The showroom is massive, the type of place you would expect to see in a much larger city. However, it sits completely empty today, and while Andy and Mark are hoping for an

---

* Matt only wears hoodies, regardless of the weather. He has an Adam Sandler-esque fashion sense. I think he would even wear a Minnesota hockey hoodie to the beach.

upturn, the quietness of their showroom on this Monday afternoon doesn't seem to bode well.

Andy and Mark are both slow-to-rile, agreeable types, the kind of people you think of when you close your eyes and picture "Midwestern self-made businessmen." Both are leaning back in their chairs inside the front door waiting for something to happen. They have had an up-and-down go of it here for decades, including closing and reopening again in 1999. The financial crisis of George W. Bush's second term and beyond hit them particularly hard, and the national chain Ace Hardware, once a partner of Flegles, pulled out when the company went bankrupt. Andy has bought the business on his own and is hoping to see it flourish again.

"It's been tough around here," Andy tells me. Even with the intense heat, the doors to the store are open; multiple fans hum gently, circulating air in lieu of an air-conditioning bill. "The factories closed down, and politically—around here at least—everyone blamed the Clintons and Obamas because it happened on their watch." These days the Flegles describe the county's political makeup as zealously Republican, with a lot of love for Donald Trump. Cultural issues are the primary motivator, especially guns and abortion, in this socially conservative area. Andy tells me he tries to stay away from political arguments because most, in his experience, don't seem to end with any change of opinion.* People in the area support Mitch McConnell—not because of affinity for him but for the service he provides to Trump. "They think he helps Trump get stuff done," Andy says.

Mark recounts how in the late 1980s his company used to post $15 or $16 million in profits annually. Now, looking around the county, there seems to be a palpable sense of hard times.

"If we could get a port it would change everything," Mark says.

Andy nods in agreement and chimes in, "A port would be huge for this area."

A port would be a gateway to the economic vitality of the Mississippi River, Carlisle County's best natural resource, but one utterly wasted

---

* Has *any* person's opinion ever changed in the history of mankind due to a comment on Facebook? Just saying . . .

with no access to it. The Flegles say there were rumblings, though no one's sure just how serious they were, of building a port in 2007 and again in 2010, but it never happened.

A port could be built easily, presumably especially so if it attracted the attention of the Senate majority leader and his Department of Transportation secretary wife. An investigation in 2019 showed that McConnell's and Chao's offices coordinated on infrastructure projects in a manner not done with any other senator. Chao assigned a special staffer just to Kentucky, a privilege no other state received.* On several occasions, people McConnell's office identified as "allies" or "special friends" got preferential treatment and other significant funding. Yet the result of all this supposed marital favoritism has produced no results for people in places like Carlisle County. Mitch McConnell hasn't ever paid attention to people here and there is no sign he ever will.

One simple line added to an Appropriations Bill and Carlisle County's entire economic outlook could be transformed. But there are few votes out here and the percentage margins in the river counties are some of the highest for McConnell in the entire state. The good senator probably thinks that if these folks are going to vote for him anyway, why waste his power helping Carlisle County?

Hickman County

"Senator McConnell Looks Out for the People of Kentucky"

Hickman County is empty. And no, I'm not being snarky here. I'm not, like, "Oh, there's nothing *cool* going on in Hickman County!" Or: "It's so *boring* in Hickman County!" No, I mean—seriously, like for real—Hickman County is quantifiably empty. It has the third-fewest people in the state, and it *is* statistically the least densely populated.

In fact, there are so few people walking around Hickman County,

* To be fair, Chao does have to kiss Mitch McConnell on the mouth, so we should give her some leeway.

I can tell you exactly how long it was between sightings of human beings as we drove through it. Twenty-six minutes. Yes, *twenty-six*. At one point, we even tried to stop someplace where we thought others might be: an establishment called Jen's Place. But it was closed. At two o'clock in the afternoon. I won't ever get to know what Jen's Place is. A store? A restaurant? Her house? Who knows? But Jen was not at her place,* and neither was anyone else.

I finally ran into an older lady wearing green pants and singing gospel hymns in Columbus, a town that was once considered as the potential location for our nation's capital. (I know you think I am making this up, but it's true. Look it up.) I ask her where everyone is and she says, "Probably out farming," which is likely true.

Hickman County is a heavy farming community, and the practice is lucrative for the area with a ton of available land and hardly any people. But with America facing a trade war with China, farmers have been caught in the crossfire, an unfair casualty of an overly impulsive president making policy on the fly. Trump's tariffs have hurt farmers across the nation—Kentucky is no exception—but even though no one can remember the last time their senior senator was here, farmers in Hickman County are convinced they have a secret weapon in Mitch McConnell. No one can remember the last time Mitch has done anything to specifically help Hickman County, but many here trust him and say their senator won't let anything terrible happen to Kentucky farmers.

"He's done all that he can do to support the president," says local farmer Matt Latham, who, like many in Hickman County, believes the subsidies being offered to farmers hurt by the tariffs are due to McConnell's involvement. He thinks Mitch has persuaded Trump to help the farmers in his home state he knows are hurting.

"I'm not one to want these subsidies," Latham says. "I'm just like any other capitalist in this country; I want to make my living in the free trade world. But the only way to create a free trade world is if it's free going and it's free coming. I think McConnell has done his part to the best of his abilities. At the end of the day, when it comes

---

* Jen's Place does have great reviews on Facebook so I am sure, when open, it's delightful.

down to the tariffs that have been put on by our president, when our president is making that call, I'm sure he gets input from his Cabinet, and Senator McConnell, being the majority leader, is in his ear, I'm certain of that."

Latham doesn't say why he trusts that these two multimillionaires have his best interests at heart, but he isn't alone. Davie Stephens, a Hickman County soybean farmer who is currently head of the National Soybean Association, has met with Donald Trump personally about the tariffs and considers claims that they are bad for the American farmer slightly overblown. He sees them as a short-term problem that will yield long-term solutions and believes McConnell is doing what he can for farmers from his perch. "You always look at people in Congress in terms of how they affect you personally. There's been a lot of things that I disagree with him on, but there's been a whole lot that I agree with him on."

I admit this viewpoint is baffling to me. The Trump/McConnell tariffs are clearly hurting these farmers' livelihoods, yet their support is unwavering. How do these folks trust Mitch McConnell of all people, a man whom no one can remember ever seeing in Hickman County, when all evidence suggests they aren't on his radar? US agriculture is in a dire position: soybean exports to China are at their lowest level since 2002, pork exports are at a nine-year low, and sorghum exports are down 95 percent. Total agricultural exports to China were around $9.1 billion last year; nearly $15 billion less than their $24 billion peak five years ago. Bankruptcies on agricultural loans are rising rapidly. President Trump insists big agricultural purchases are on the way but all evidence suggests that buyers such as China are finding cheaper long-term sources of supply elsewhere. It all adds up to a very difficult future for anyone in American agriculture.

It is also worth remembering that the actual number of farmers in this area is less than you would imagine. Family farms have been bought up, and the overall consolidation of American agriculture is evident here. Still, the economic impact of farming in these parts is massive, and the success of these few owners crucial. In this staunchly Republican county these farmers still believe, at least for now, McConnell and Trump won't let them down.

"Senator McConnell looks out for the people of Kentucky," says Stephens. "President Trump looks out for the people of the United States. I'm certain that Senator McConnell is expressing to our president the viewpoints of the Kentucky farmers. I believe that. We want free trade, I want free trade, Senator McConnell wants free trade, but he wants it to be fair trade."

Listening to these folks, I can't help but have mixed feelings. I root for them. This part of the state will wither away and die if agriculture doesn't succeed. But the $28 billion in government bulk checks to the farmers (larger than that given to the auto companies in the much-criticized Obama-era bailout . . . and they had to pay them back) are the exact type of anti–free market intervention and government "handouts" that most conservatives rail against when they're given to others. Yet when handed to them, one rarely hears a note of dissent.* They do help explain, however, why, whether by earnest conviction or simply desperate hope, this may be the one place in America where you can find one of the rarest of all political beliefs. Trust in the honesty, good nature, and benevolent heart of Mitch McConnell. I genuinely hope he doesn't let them down. Maybe he will even visit one day.

Fulton County

The Banana Fashion Show

After two full days in the river counties learning about ports and tariffs, it was time to have a little fun. Life isn't all about infrastructure and imposing self-sabotaging taxes on imports to create a global trade war! So it was time to head to beautiful Fulton County—the southernmost county of the commonwealth of Kentucky. Before we go (I am going to

---

* It's worth noting that the Federal Reserve estimates the tariffs will cost a full percentage point of GDP, a huge amount at a time when 3 percent growth is considered high. That works out to $259.2 billion, costing the American taxpayer an average of just over $2,000 per household.

act as if you are currently in the back seat of our car—please ignore the mess, and no eating back there!), you need to know two things:

One, the county seat of Fulton (which, if a county were a flannel shirt, would be best described as "lived in") is split down the middle by the Kentucky-Tennessee state line. Fulton, as it were, is in Kentucky, but its bottom half, South Fulton, belongs to Tennessee. If this were a marriage, Fulton would be the better spouse, and South Fulton would need to start pulling its weight.

Second, you should know that if you are in or near Fulton County anytime in mid-September, you absolutely have to spend a week at Fulton's Banana Festival, a weeklong slate of events designed to celebrate the county's rich banana history. I mean, after all, Fulton was once known as the banana capital of the world.

Yes, you read that correctly: *the world*.

Now, I know what you're thinking: *no way* was the world's banana capital in southwest Kentucky! But while it may be a slight exaggeration, there is some basis for the claim. In the late 1800s our nation's railway system saw the advent and subsequent rise of the first refrigerated boxcars. This was a real game changer, in that suddenly trains were able to transport perishable goods such as bananas farther distances.

If you lived in Detroit in the mid-1880s, there was little chance you'd get to enjoy a banana because (a) the non-tropical climate in Detroit is terrible for growing bananas, and (b) there was no way to transport a banana *to* you in Detroit without it spoiling by the time it reached you from some far-flung tropical region. But then came the refrigerated boxcar.* These cars required ice to keep the goods cold as the trains traveled into America's heartland. But the ice would inevitably melt, as ice tends to do, even in a refrigerated car, and thus it needed to be reloaded.

Fulton stepped in to fill the void.

With one of the only large operating icehouses in the Midwest; consequently, most icy banana cars coming from a tropical climate had to top off in Fulton. At one point, more than 75 percent of the bananas

---

* Part of the great banana technology push of the late 1880s.

consumed in the United States passed through this small Kentucky town. And so Fulton, looking for an identity, became the Banana Capital of the World.

Banana tech has improved these days, so the "a peel"* of Fulton isn't as strong. But the annual Fulton Banana Festival honors the history by presenting over a week of hijinks and the biggest party of the year for the river counties. The events for this year's edition include:

- Miss Banana Pageant;
- Banana Golf Scramble (presumably, regular golf and not "banana golf");
- Banana Bake-off;
- Senior Citizens Rook Tournament;
- Fulton's Got Talent (talent does not have to be banana related);
- Banana Brawl (a wrestling event featuring, this past year, Jerry "the King" Lawler);
- Banana Eating Contest; and
- Closing concert by the group Exile (of the 1978 number one single "Kiss You All Over" and from Lexington, Kentucky).

The festival culminates in an official parade followed by a whopping *one ton* banana pudding served up to the town in Pontotoc Park, a spectacle that screams America.

It's a corker of a festival, one of the longest in the state by my count, and could not be missed. So, when we rolled into Fulton on a Tuesday night in the event's second week, we were bound and determined to take in whatever banana-based fun we could. As luck would have it, the day's only event was to be the Banana Fashion Show. While I wasn't certain what banana fashion might look like, I was excited nevertheless. After all, I like bananas, and I like fashion. Combine them, and it has to be a party.

The event was to be held at Buck's Celebration Center, which is difficult to find in town until someone helpfully points out to you that it is

---

* I didn't want to allow Matt to include that pun, but he insisted. I apologize *for* him.

across the street from the more popular (because it has booze) Buck's *Party Mart.* Once you have that valuable information, it's a lot easier to locate. Tickets were $25 each, which strikes me as high for a Banana Fashion Show, but it was sold out, meaning the banana fashion market is strong. We arrived at Buck's at five thirty (an hour before the fashion show was to start) and began chatting up an organizer who agreed to let us come inside without tickets. It was very kind, considering that we were two adult men, dressed in jeans and flannels, trying to finagle our way into a small-town fashion show for free by saying we were writing a book about Mitch McConnell. I would have been skeptical. Luckily, she was not.

As we walked in, we picked up our courtesy copy of the Official Banana Festival Program, which had this description of the event:

"A full-course meal will be provided and halftime entertainment will be performed by the Broadway Dance Company of Fulton. Fashions for men, women, and children from area stores will be modeled."

It was then I learned that the Banana Fashion Show had nothing at all to do with banana fashion and everything to do simply with fashion. In fact, as we watched the walk-through for the event, it became clear that most of the models were actually area teenagers, and most everyone in attendance was either (a) a local woman who loved fashion or (b) related to the models. That made the sight of us, two grown men, sweaty from ninety-five-degree September heat and smelling like the nearby La Cabana Mexican Restaurant, posted up in the back of the room, quite odd. Scratch that. Let's be real: we probably looked like a couple of creeps—a characterization they couldn't be faulted for assuming, especially once the fashion show started, and high school students began to walk the runway in autumn-themed outfits put together by nearby boutiques. We assumed there would be more banana-themed clothing, and that would have been entertaining and hilarious. Banana hats! Banana pants! Banana bandanas! Instead, it was just two creeps watching high schoolers in prom dresses walk the runway. It was time to exit.

On my way out, a woman ran across the room, grabbed me, and shrieked, "Matt Jones!!! I *love KSR*!!!! Will you be talking about the Banana Fashion Show tomorrow on your show?"

I answered yes to be kind and left hoping that I wouldn't forever be known as "that guy thinking of running for Senate who came to town and hung out at the back of the Banana Fashion Show." With that start, I don't think Mitch's domination of Fulton County will be in jeopardy anytime soon.

Calloway County

"I'm as Republican as Fuck"

Heading back east, we made our way to the only major college in this part of Kentucky, the campus of Murray State University. The moment you arrive in the city of Murray, it is clear you're in a college town. Around ten thousand students attend Murray State, meaning that when school is in session, the population of the town nearly doubles. Unlike most state universities, Murray State sits directly in the center of the city and has attracted businesses that make it the most eclectic downtown in all of Kentucky. Within a mile of city hall and the courthouse, you'll find a glow-in-the-dark miniature golf course, two upscale day spas, multiple coffee shops, a used-bike store, and more craft beer than any person could ever hope to consume. Even the churches have the feel of a college town: the Memorial Baptist Church on Main Street has a reader board out front screaming "Jesus Scored an Eternal Touchdown!"*

With all these young people around, we decided to hit the pavement and find out what the young people of Kentucky think of Mitch McConnell. With access to all the world's information at their fingertips, surely, they all have strong opinions on how this country should be run, and their optimistic energy will one day save us all, right? After all, the children are our future!

We arrived on campus on a brisk Saturday morning ready to talk. Students were everywhere, preparing for a home Racers football game, and the energy on campus meant it was the perfect time to ask about the human sleep aid himself, Mitch McConnell.

---

* But did he then go for two?

Our plan was simple: hand a photo of Mitch McConnell to students and then ask them if they know who it is and what they think of him. No leading questions, no trolling, just pure straight talk. We start with a cheerleader on her way to the game, who holds it, stares for a few beats, then looks back at me. "That's the president," she says.

Rough start.

A couple more passing students stop by to talk to us and offer more constructive takes.

"I feel like he's been in office too long," a girl unloading beanbags from a cornhole board says, "but I'm a wildlife student. I don't really like the current administration too much."

"That's Mitch McConnell," another student asserts confidently. Does he know what office McConnell holds? "No," he says just as confidently. One girl says she doesn't know who he is, and she's been raised not to say anything bad about people you don't know (or, presumably, write books about them).

A trend forms. While some students are able to identify McConnell and know that he's a US senator, the vast majority are completely in the dark. A muscular kid in a tight gray Marine Corps T-shirt can't name Mitch but announces to me, "I'm as Republican as fuck," and asks if the person in the photo is a Republican. When I tell him who McConnell is, he responds, "If you know somebody's party, you can assume things about him; he's Republican, so he's obviously smart." The irony makes me smile.

Another female student, dressed in an oversize Murray State sweatshirt, nods confidently. "That's Mitch McConnell," she says. What does she think of him: "Not a fan; I don't like what he stands for." When I ask what that is, she says, "It's game day and I would rather have fun." Fair enough. Mitch McConnell isn't fun.

Over the next hour, we get a smattering of other responses from those who recognize Cocaine Mitch:*

---

* Bizarrely, this is a nickname Mitch embraces and sells on T-shirts. It derives from some cocaine being found on a boat owned by McConnell's father-in-law. In the past, this rumor would have been one politicians sought to refute. Now they sell it on merchandise.

"Isn't he the governor of Kentucky?"

"I don't like him, probably; I'm just a Democrat."

"That's Bernie Sanders."

"His new nickname is pretty funny—Moscow Mitch."

"I feel like term limits should be a thing, because he's been there forever."

"I've heard his name but don't know anything about him."

It's a depressing set of answers but a part of me regrets interrupting everyone's weekend fun. I feel like a bit of a narc. And I must look like one, too, because an administrator stops me to ask what I'm doing. I explain the project to her and let her know that many of these students don't know who McConnell is. "They're all failing, I'm sure," she says, surprised.

As game time approaches, we send our intrepid research assistant, Eli, into the student section (he is actually college aged) to ask students how they feel about the senator, and, once again, it is alarming how many don't know who he is, even when prompted with the photo and his name. As the Murray State Racers proceed to get thumped by the Austin Peay Governors 42–7,* I can sympathize with the Racers. I'm feeling the defeat as well.

At the end of the day, out of 140 young people we asked about Mitch McConnell, only 27 knew who he was. Twenty-seven! That's both insane and troubling to comprehend. On one hand, here's a man who has been their state's senator for their entire lives, who, in theory, they would have studied in the most rudimentary of civics classes, and yet they have zero knowledge of him. On the other hand, it speaks to why he can dominate in this part of the state. Even though his policies go against most of these young people's values, and the system he has created will saddle them with potentially crippling amounts of student debt, they don't even know his name and likely have no interest in voting for or against him. For a sheer political pragmatist like McConnell, if young people don't follow what he does, why would he care about their thoughts?

---

* As a side note, the giant foam-headed Austin Peay Governor mascot is the only politician creepier than Mitch McConnell.

As we walk away, a young man in a green bandana passes by, and we flag him down, presenting the photo to him. He knows McConnell by sight.

"It stems from what my parents say, but he's stuck in time," he tells me thoughtfully. "He's not progressive. It would be better for the economy and the political environment if he weren't in office."

I thank green-bandana guy! Even though he admits his view is based on what his parents say, it's a satisfying finish to the day. With my unscientific poll showing that less than 20 percent of eighteen-to-twenty-two-year-olds *attending college* are even able to name the second most powerful person in America who is *from their state*, I will take whatever good news I can get.

Caldwell County

"He's Been There Too Long"

Every time we come into a town on this trip, I look for something unique that doesn't exist anywhere else in Kentucky. In Princeton, it's the Cat's Tale, a used-book shop owned by Maggie Gammons. The décor is decidedly cat themed: there are bookends that look like cats, feline-centric artwork, a Monopoly-esque board game called, fittingly, "Cat-Opoly," where instead of Boardwalk, Marvin Gardens, and Baltic Avenue, you can purchase cat breeds such as the Egyptian Mau, the Abyssinian, and the American Shorthair. It might not surprise you to know there are even two cats wandering around the shelves: Gammons's own felines, Pyewacket and Jenny Linkski, who follow us around as we browse. I am not sure where the Cat's Tale ranks on the list of Best Cat-Themed Used-Book Stores in America, but I am certain that very few look and smell more lived in by cats than this one.*

Maggie looks at us with suspicion when we walk in, but I have

* As you might imagine of someone who opens a cat-themed bookstore, Maggie has thirty-five more cats at home.

learned that the best way to break the ice at a small business is to buy something. I walk in the back, take a copy of a biography of Supreme Court justice William Brennan (a steal at $2), and strike up a conversation with her. When I ask Maggie about politics, she says her political philosophy can be summed up this way: "I believe in helping people, of course, but I don't want my freedoms eroded."

It's actually a good summary of the political philosophy of Kentucky, especially in this western part. We can help others, just leave me alone. Maggie and her cats' freedom seem to be sufficiently protected at the Cat's Tale, a place she'd always wanted to open after spending a career working at the nearby cracker and cookie factory on the outskirts of town. A member of the local United Daughters of the Confederacy chapter, Maggie is also of the mind-set that politics is a game of growing wealth in lieu of public progress.

"I get so tired of the incumbents saying the same thing year after year," she tells us, exasperated. "That they'll fix this problem or that problem, and the only thing that changes is that they get richer."

This is certainly true of Mitch McConnell, whose net worth has soared since becoming a senator. It may be the reason Maggie is a proud Trump supporter, but doesn't feel the same about Mitch.

"He's been there too long," she says without missing a beat.

That's an understatement. Mitch McConnell is the living argument for term limits, having been in office for thirty-six years, a quantifiably insane amount of time for one man to hold any elected position. Compare McConnell's stranglehold to Princeton's twenty-five-year-old mayor, Dakota "Kota" Young. Kota* was elected in 2018 and is one of the youngest mayors in the country. He is friendly and seems much older than he actually is—he talks to us like our elder, who has come to educate the youth of the city, yet he has the hip sensibilities and highlighted hair of someone years younger than us. He's friendly in conversation, yet calculating in his choice of words, which keeps us continually off balance. He reminds me of a teenager playing the role of "mayor" in the school play, but doing it so well he wins an award.

---

* This is what his friends call him, and I believe he is my friend, whether he knows it or not.

Young ran for office on a platform of economic development for his hometown, creating his "Plan for Princeton," a ten-point proposal to revive the sleepy city. The bold plan was based on giving Princeton an identity, a reason for people to believe in its future, and was the culmination of a goal he'd had since childhood.

"During my college interview, the last question they asked me was 'What do you want to do after college?' and I said, 'Well, I want to be mayor of Princeton.' They laughed and said, 'Surely you want to be more than that,' but I said, 'No, that's fine for me.'"*

It's one thing to have the goal of becoming mayor and another to go and achieve it at such an early age. It's like the premise of a bad NBC sitcom, but with Young's youthful energy I can see why people want to follow his lead. Whereas most small towns suffer from a lack of motivation or engagement by young people in the community, Young projects an exuberant air of positivity for the future. When I ask a local business leader about the new mayor, he says, "I don't know a lot about him, but I know he works hard and cares about this place, and that is better than most."

Young knows that towns like Princeton get forgotten in America, but he is not deterred. "I don't think there's probably a lot of connection from Washington to little old Princeton," he tells me, "but we still matter. We may be small, and no one may have ever heard of us, but we care about our community, and we're doing our best."

Princeton decided to put its faith in a young elected official with fresh ideas and new views. Young's method seems to be working. He is focusing on creating a cultural presence in the town, holding events for families and attracting outside visitors through artistic projects. It worked on me. I ended up shopping in the new downtown and bought a viola lamp (that is a lamp made from, yes, a viola) for my girlfriend while I was there,† a purchase I did not plan on making upon arrival. Walking down the street, we see a number of young people working in local businesses, and it feels like this is one of the first places on our trip

---

* Kota was born the same year that the R&B group TLC put out "Waterfalls," which is probably why he sticks to the rivers and the lakes that he's used to.

† It was a bummer when he found out she already had three viola lamps.

where we've seen some semblance of youth working toward bettering their local community. The energy is just different here.

It is intriguing to see a young person trying to revitalize an area and a town trying to reform via fresh blood in office. When things weren't working in Princeton, the town decided to try something new, forfeiting experience for energy and a new perspective. After thirty-six years, one wonders if the state of Kentucky will ever be willing to try the same thing.

Marshall County

"We're Not Democrats, We're Not Republicans. We're Marshall Countians"

The morning of January 23, 2018, was a Tuesday like any other. The doldrums of returning after the long Christmas break were starting to wear off, the temperature cool in the high thirties, not terrible for January in Kentucky. Marshall County Schools superintendent Trent Lovett had just dropped off his daughter, a freshman at Marshall County High School, in front of the building around seven forty-five and headed to his office on campus about a quarter mile away. He'd barely parked and come inside, rounding the corner of his desk, when the phone rang moments before eight o'clock. It was MCHS principal Patricia Greer.

"I've got one down," she told him.

Lovett's first thought was that a teacher had perhaps suffered a medical emergency, a situation that might require a last-minute substitute or before-school scramble.

"And maybe more," Greer said next.

Lovett knew then it was something much darker. He sprinted out to his car and tore off for the high school, jumping past a closed gate and dashing across the parking lot. Students were fleeing madly from the building as he ran against the current inside through the gym doors and down the hall toward the eerie quiet of the commons area, where he saw the victims.

Two students were killed and fourteen injured that day inside Marshall County High School at the hands of a fellow student. It is something no administrator wants to imagine until in one moment, their own teachers are running triage inside the school and ushering children to safety. The Marshall County school shooting was one of the most shocking events to ever happen to this area; the type of occurrence usually seen on television in other cities, in other states. Not in Kentucky. Not in Marshall County.

The fifteen-year-old shooter was taken into custody. His trial is ongoing at the time of this writing. But as we walked the halls, it was clear that the community and school administrators weren't interested in reliving the worst day in the school's history. This shouldn't be surprising. We all are aware of the coverage of school shootings and the way they grip the nation for a forty-eight-hour news cycle—although, sadly, their frequency has caused us to become more immune to them every year. But what receives far less coverage is what happens after the reporters and cameramen have left: how communities shaken by such a meteoric tragedy must then rebuild, outside the public spotlight.

The tiny community of Benton in Marshall County made a decision in the hours after the tragedy to reflect inward and turn away the cameras. They worried less about the national media seeking to blast out every detail of the crime, and, instead, wrapped themselves up together to heal. Churches ministered to the students, parents volunteered at every turn, orange-and-blue #MarshallStrong bracelets were on every wrist in the county. The members of the community took it upon themselves to heal one another. They didn't need Dr. Phil. All they needed was Marshall County.

"Every news station in six states was here, plus CNN, ABC, NBC, Fox—all of them were here," Lovett says of the media's flocking to the scene. "I basically said, 'Look, whenever I do talk, it's going to be to WPSD channel 6 out of Paducah, Kentucky.' Because that's our local station, those are the people I'm concerned about." Lovett and Greer talked to administrators from Connecticut's Sandy Hook Elementary School, where in 2012 a shooter killed twenty children and six adults, and Columbine High School in Colorado, site of one of the first school massacres in 1999, for advice, well aware that, as educators, they had suddenly become members of a very grim social club. Greer has since become part of the Principal Recovery Network, a group of current and former school leaders who have experienced school-related gun violence tragedies and seek to impart their experiences to those unfortunate enough to join the group.

"Whenever there's a tragedy, a community has two options," Greer reflects. "It can choose to divide, or it can choose to become strong as one. In Marshall County, it was like one strong person. Our kids did that, our faculty did that, and our community followed."

Greer is careful not to politicize the incident, even though such violent incidents often spark intense political discussions. "Do I have kids that are very well spoken and went to Frankfort and said some very powerful things? Yes. But I think our priority was each other. This wasn't political. It's a school."

Administrators and faculty at other schools that had experienced similar tragedies advised the administration against waiting too long to return to normal, so Lovett and the board of education decided to reopen later that same week. On the Thursday following the shooting, they allowed the teachers back inside—in many cases, having to lead them by the hand.

With a plan in place to renovate the commons area, Lovett mulled blocking it off from the students until a new look could be established, one that wouldn't remind them of the incident of January 23. But Patricia Greer had another idea. According to Lovett, she told him, "That's a great idea, but I want the kids to see it first. I don't want them to think we're hiding anything behind those walls."

That Friday, three days after an unthinkable event had befallen Marshall County High School and the surrounding community, Lovett, Greer, and the administration held a ceremony in the gym before school. Then, nervously, they began to dismiss the classes back to the commons area. First seniors, then juniors, sophomores, and freshmen.

Slowly, on that Friday morning, the students of Marshall County High reclaimed their commons area. That space, which only three days earlier had seen their classmates injured or killed, was not going to keep them in fear.

"To see them head right back to the spots where they were standing or sitting," Lovett says, "and to see them laughing, talking, getting back to things just a little bit . . . it was almost like they were saying, 'This is our house, and nobody is going to take this from us.' That resiliency was unbelievable. I looked at Mrs. Greer, and she looked back at the same time, and we both thought, 'We're not going to block off this commons area.'"

The terror that the students, administrators, and parents of Marshall County High School were put through that January morning was unthinkable, but the strength of a small county to overcome it is mind-blowing. The strength the community demonstrated in the face of such tragedy is a testament to community, small- or large-town, Kentucky or any other state. It brought together the people of that county in a way they'd never been before.

"We were not Democrats, we were not Republicans," says Lovett. "We were Marshall Countians."

After we left Marshall County, a few days later I watched a national town hall on gun violence on one of the major television news networks. Depending on which political philosophy a network adheres to, these "debates" on gun violence always follow the same script. Those seeking major gun control legislation speak of the tragedy of shootings and how restrictions should be placed on these powerful weapons capable of inflicting mass casualties in a matter of seconds. Those against any form of gun control focus on their Second Amendment freedoms, protecting themselves and their families, and the "slippery slope" of any type of regulation. It's all predictable, and for many, school violence becomes simply another weapon to be utilized in our never-ending political warfare. In the end, these debates solve very little, mostly working up anger on both sides and expanding our political division.

Why is our federal government so stagnant? Well, to begin with, no one can agree what the actual problem is. Is it the guns? The media? Our culture? Mental health issues? School security? Or some combination of all these elements wrapped into one? In 1996 Congress passed the Dickey Amendment, a rider on that year's spending bill that prohibited the federal government from conducting any research whatsoever on the causes of gun violence. The provision was added by Republican representative Jay Dickey of Arkansas and was authored by the National Rifle Association (NRA). The goal was clear: to keep the government from looking into the causes of gun violence. While not stated explicitly, the amendment's purpose was to prevent any study that might find that guns are the cause of violence, thus leaving science out of any gun debate.*

Fast-forward to today, and the prohibition is still in place, with extremely detrimental results. The federal government is the only resource in the nation that has access to all the information on school shootings. Due to privacy laws, much of it can't be released to the public, and individual states have no way to obtain the information from other states. Thus, the only entity that could truly and completely understand and study school violence is prohibited *by federal law* from doing so if the study could be used to advocate for any gun control. Our national tragedies continue, with no attempts beyond hypothetical rhetoric utilized to combat them.

This would be an easy fix. Republicans and Democrats should be able to unite and state, "We each have opinions about why our schools have become so unsafe, but before we enact sweeping legislation, let's come together and study the problem as one." But because so many leaders, including Kentucky senator Mitch McConnell, are beholden to the lobbying power of the NRA, this minuscule step is still beyond our reach.

I had been to Marshall County a number of times before this trip. Its annual high school basketball showcase, the Marshall County Hoopfest, is one of the best prep basketball events in the United States. I

---

* Dickey himself, who hasn't been in government since 2001, regrets the legislation and insists that putting a lid on government-funded studies was never the intent of the provision.

was familiar with the school's gymnasium and commons area, but after hearing the stories this day, it has taken on a different meaning. This place is special. As I looked at this community that rallied together as one, turned away from the influences of outsiders whose interests weren't theirs, and focused solely on bettering their community, my thoughts were simple:

What if our national leaders cared less about divisions and more about solutions? What if they were as committed to uniting around our common well-being and as collectively strong as Marshall County? Maybe then our tired political debates would cease, and real change could occur.

CHAPTER 3

Suburbia

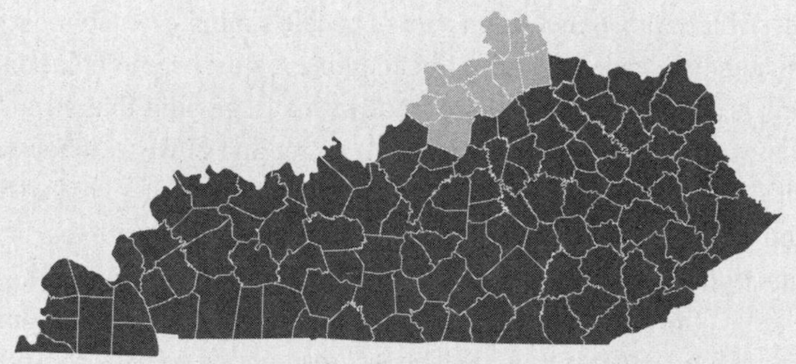

Upon returning from western Kentucky, I took a brief respite from the "Mitch 120" Tour to prepare for the massive Kentucky-Florida football weekend. In Kentucky, the annual battle with the University of Florida Gators in September means three days of excitement, huge live *KSR* shows, and (usually) a heartbreaking loss.

Our show the day before the game was at Country Boy Brewing in Georgetown, Kentucky. Country Boy was founded by a couple of local guys who look like the sons of ZZ Top (but let's be honest: all craft brewers do), and their craft beers have become the hit of the Bluegrass State and a point of pride for those who love to see local boys make good. On this beautiful afternoon, they pack their brewery with five hundred people to listen to the show and celebrate a distinctly Kentucky day. The crowd was filled with college kids, middle-aged drinking buddies, dads with their children, and grandmas in their UK-embroidered vests; it's a cross-demographic party that only sports can bring. It's also part of why leaving *KSR* to run for Senate is such a tough decision for me. It sounds silly to say "leaving sports radio for the Senate is hard," but our show brings people together in a way politics no longer can. Politics divide, and the moment I enter that world, I will never be looked at by many in this crowd in the same way. Abandoning the forum that it took me fifteen years to build only to then be hated by half the state is very difficult.

Due to some local publicity, the discussion of whether I will run against Mitch McConnell is on a lot of people's minds. While most fans in the audience care only about beating the Gators, some talk politics, including one man sitting in the front with a large sign that says, "I'm voting for Matt Jones." After we finish, a long line of well-wishers walk up with messages as varied as "Matt, I love the Cats, but you have to do it!" and "Matt, don't leave 'Camelot' for politics" (a reference to a locally famous quote where Rick Pitino publicly regretted having left his job as coach of the University of Kentucky basketball team for the Boston Celtics of the NBA). Everyone who weighs in does so with conviction. It's clear that my indecision, regardless of their desired outcome for my choice, is strange to them.

Mitch McConnell is a polarizing figure. That I knew. But it wasn't until I really started analyzing this race two years ago that I realized what his impact has truly been. The passion of those who want to see him removed is stronger than I realized. For many, the anti-Mitch sentiment rivals the passion that most people who show up at my live shows feel for the Wildcats. Conversely, for these folks, the idea of leaving a life most sports fans would covet, talking about and following the Cats, to go and likely lose a nasty election to the Senate majority leader seems insane to most in this crowd. But the idea of giving up a chance to change America and rid it of its most negative political influence and instead stay and cheer on eighteen-to-twenty-two-year-olds in college athletics seems equally bizarre to many outside this room. It's a stark realization that no matter which selection I make, many who follow me will be disappointed and find the decision baffling.

Later in the weekend, Kentucky loses to Florida (again) and we head up the road to the suburbs of Cincinnati in northern Kentucky.

Boone County

"How Much Money Do You Think These Billionaires Need?"

When you fly into the Cincinnati area, chances are high your flight attendant will come on the overhead speaker as you approach landing and say something like "We're not actually *in* Cincinnati, we're in Kentucky," as if that little bon mot is going to blow your mind. The attendant will smirk at his or her "Here's a little thing you might not actually realize but *get ready to be shocked!"*-type factoid. Looking around the plane, you will discern quickly who is from northern Kentucky simply by their reaction (or lack thereof). Because the "Hey, the Cincinnati Airport is actually in northern Kentucky" factoid is the oldest and least appreciated schtick in these parts. Yeah, the Cincinnati Airport is in Kentucky. Why wouldn't it be? We are *better.**

Boone County is one of the few areas of the state where the old way of rural Kentucky life runs headlong into the new suburban reality. One moment you're driving past small family farms and open spaces; the next, you're sitting in a Chick-fil-A parking lot, mere feet from a Dave & Buster's and a Costco. So many people who work in Cincinnati now live in the apartment complexes and neighborhoods of Boone County that it just feels like one big Cincinnati suburb extension, expanding every day.

Some locals complain about the suburban sprawl around the county and the continued expansion of the airport, but they don't complain about the jobs it represents. Boone County has its traditional rural

* My favorite such story is about Andre Agassi, the tennis star of the eighties, nineties, and early aughts. Every year, the Association of Tennis Professionals (ATP) holds one of its most important tennis events in Cincinnati. Early in his career, Agassi flew in for the tournament and, when he got off the plane, refused to leave the airport until security came to meet him. A local police officer heard Agassi's complaint and said to him, "Son, you are in Kentucky. Unless you was on *Hee Haw* last night, ain't nobody gonna bother you." Agassi walked away sheepishly.

stalwarts. For instance, the town of Rabbit Hash (and this is true) is on its fourth elected *dog* mayor, the current one being a pit bull named Brynneth Pawltro. There are still plenty of folks holding it down in Big Bone Lick, a state park known for its roving bison. And before you get to Cincinnati, you will see the bright red-and-white-striped water tower proclaiming "Florence Y'all" in big block letters. We ain't too uppity yet.

The reality, though, is that the future of Boone County is its airport and Cincinnati sprawl. It's the fastest-growing economy in the state and an attractive spot for developing industries. Case in point: Amazon. The e-commerce giant is in the process of a massive expansion of the airport, and northern Kentucky will soon become a major center of its delivery operation.

Amazon molding Boone County into one of its primary hubs makes it worth taking a second to think about the obscene wealth of its founder. Jeff Bezos is now one of America's wealthiest citizens, with a net worth estimated at $110 billion. He is part of a growing class of billionaires whose fortunes keep increasing exponentially. Nine years ago, *Forbes* magazine listed the number of billionaires in the world at 793. That tally has now jumped to more than 2,700 in less than a decade. The top .01 percent richest Americans now account for a greater percentage of our nation's wealth than at any time since 1929.

This explosion of wealth for the richest Americans has had no bigger advocate than Mitch McConnell. In fact, if there were a Rich Guy Hall of Fame, McConnell would be a first-ballot inductee. Under his watch, tax rates for the richest Americans have been slashed on all forms of wealth, including income, capital gains, inheritances, and the alternative minimum tax, saving these individuals billions upon billions in taxes in just a few short years. The cuts have been so extreme that people like Bezos now pay, by some estimates, a lower share of their income in taxes than the average member of the working class. The country's tax system has been flipped upside down and, in many states, the result of McConnell's tax cut crusade is that the richest Americans pay some of the lowest overall rates.

The senator always makes the argument that cutting taxes for the wealthy helps the economy grow overall. The problem, of course, is that it's complete nonsense. Tax cuts can provide some immediate, short-term growth, but it never trickles down to ordinary people. The Republicans' pride and joy, the so-called Tax Cut and Jobs Act of 2017, is illustrative. More than $1 trillion in taxes were eliminated immediately for the wealthy and for corporations, with the stated goal being to benefit the economy and trigger new investment and job growth. But we now know that the vast majority of the cuts were used for stock buybacks and investor dividends, with almost no meaningful investment in domestic growth. Sadly, that shouldn't be a surprise. Every decade or so, advocates for the wealthy get a tax cut for the top 1 percent passed, claiming it will trickle down to the rest of Americans. It never happens. Yet they are never taken to task for their lies, and a decade later, they do it all over again.

McConnell's tax bill did include a handful of tax cuts for workers in order to gain popular support. But intentionally, those cuts were meager and temporary. In fact, the working-class tax cut starts expiring in just a few years, while the cuts that Moneybags McConnell* placed for his billionaire buddies are permanent. The net result is a massive increase of the debt that will have to be repaid, either by the middle class, or by cutting government entitlement benefits in the future. McConnell prefers the latter option. Throughout his career, he has repeatedly called for cuts to programs Kentuckians rely on, from Social Security, Medicare, and Medicaid, to spending on education, health care, and infrastructure. In fact, if there is a part of government that the average Kentuckian relies on in his or her daily life, chances are Mitch has tried to prune it.

Most of Boone County is glad to see Amazon expanding its presence in town, and rightfully so. But while Jeff Bezos's company adds to the airport, it's worth remembering that he recently cut benefits for his Whole Foods workers, even as the company received billions in tax cuts. Amazon is now valued at $1 trillion. The average wage against inflation in America hasn't risen in a decade. Some trickle down that was.

---

* Trump shouldn't be the only one who gets to coin alliterative, nasty nicknames for people.

Because of Mitch, the rich are getting richer much faster than they ever have before, while the rest of Americans' share of wealth is dwindling. It is now easier than ever for the Jeff Bezoses of the world to pad their pockets, and harder than ever for his workers or the citizens of Rabbit Hash and their dog mayor to make ends meet. If they were truly being honest, that's the not-so-fun fact the flight attendants should be telling you the next time you fly into northern Kentucky.*

Kenton County

The Intersection of Disaster

Here's what you need to know about Kenton County: it is ground zero in the fight to beat Mitch McConnell.

Why? Kenton County is the third most populated county in Kentucky, and its major city, Covington, ranks fifth. It is growing like a weed, in part because the top quarter of the county is almost functionally a neighborhood of Cincinnati. Cincinnati's sprawl has reached here and created a unique mishmash of urban, suburban, and rural life, all mixed together within the same few square miles. As such, it has more of a city sensibility than most of Kentucky, and an offbeat style all its own.

Case in point: Chris, who once lived in Kenton County, once walked into a Subway sandwich shop, only to be told by the counterperson that they were out of bread. When he asked why they were out of bread, the employee explained, "Someone came in an hour ago and offered to buy all the bread, so we just sold it to him." Now, I'm no sandwich artist, but I don't think that's Subway policy.†

It's also a place where one issue drives much of the local debate.

---

* Matt would make a grim flight attendant.

† Thanks for being there in my moment of need, Quiznos.

Kenton County is the site of the old, degrading, and functionally obsolete* Brent Spence Bridge. Though it is not rated as "structurally deficient," the fifty-seven-year-old bridge connecting Cincinnati to northern Kentucky is still extremely dangerous and hated by all locals. It's a double-decker bridge—the top level goes north, the exhaust-filled second level beneath it runs south—and it has the look and feel of a bridge *at least* a hundred years old. The Brent Spence is a steel monstrosity built to accommodate eighty thousand vehicles a day, but given the growth of northern Kentucky over the past two decades, now *two hundred thousand* rumble along it daily. Goods representing an estimated 3 percent of the US gross domestic product (GDP) value cross it each year. Stop reading for a moment and look around you. Is there any wood within arm's length? If so, I must insist you knock on it. I'll wait. Because the bridge is already starting to show hazardous signs of age.

For instance, take the peculiar case of Jeff Brothers. In 2014 the twenty-four-year-old and his friends decided to tailgate the Cincinnati Bengals home opener against the Atlanta Falcons. Quarterback Andy Dalton threw for 300 yards, and All Pro wide receiver A. J. Green exploded for 130 of those in a 24–10 victory. It was a rare positive Bengals day.†

However, when Brothers returned to his car just a few blocks away from Paul Brown Stadium, the excitement of the day, much like his windshield, was completely shattered. Like many Bengals fans, Brothers had parked underneath the Brent Spence Bridge. During the game, chunks of concrete, some a foot or more thick, had fallen off a support beam for the exit ramp and crashed through the windshield of his 2008 Ford Fusion. A railroad runs underneath the support beam, and Cincinnati police suspected the vibrations from passing trains, combined with the daily traffic of double what engineers designed the bridge to

* I want to joke that this is also how I describe Mitch McConnell, but Matt says that would be mean.

† Some scholars believe this day marked the last time that any Cincinnati Bengals fan ever smiled again.

handle, led to the beam's failure. Police officer Ken Hall told the *Cincinnati Enquirer* the bridge was now an "intersection of disaster." The traffic is horrendous, the accidents are dangerous, and the structure is failing. Something must be done.

For all of these reasons, replacing or repairing the Brent Spence Bridge has been a major priority of national leaders of both parties. President Barack Obama visited the bridge as part of his tour to sell his stimulus package, calling on Mitch McConnell to "help us rebuild this bridge. Help us rebuild America." Obama focused on the Brent Spence Bridge throughout his presidency, but McConnell refused to support its improvement. Then Republican presidential nominee Donald Trump promised support for a new bridge in his 2016 campaign and during his transition; in fact, according to a leaked document, it was second on his list of emergency and national security projects. Even with Trump's backing and a GOP-controlled Congress, Mitch again did nothing. Presidents from both parties remain outspoken on the need for repair, not just for Kenton County but also for the nation. The complaints continue to fall on McConnell's deaf ears.*

McConnell's only use for the Brent Spence Bridge is as fodder for election year campaigns. In his 2014 race, he proposed replacing it, if the money for the bridge could come from reducing wages of construction workers, a classic McConnell effort to distract from his inability to help his constituents by actively pitting them against one another. And in 2018, when asked about its future, he punted in his standard fuzzy language: "Candidly, there is a reluctance both in the administration and in Congress to talk about how to pay for it." Of course, since he (almost unilaterally) runs half of the US Congress himself, that reluctance is ultimately his.

Northern Kentuckians who desperately need the bridge repaired are uniquely screwed. Even though presidents from *both* parties consider it a priority to repair or replace the Brent Spence Bridge, the

* McConnell seems to only care about bridges if he can hide underneath them and scare children.

officials representing northern Kentucky on the national level actively refuse to help.*

Mitch's reluctance to help is particularly odd as he has averaged nearly two-thirds of the vote in the three most populous northern Kentucky cities over the course of his six elections. For nearly a century, this has been the one area of Kentucky that has unwaveringly remained Republican and Mitch has benefited from their support his entire career.

But that might be slowly changing. All across America, the former fertile GOP territory of the suburbs are now flipping Democratic at a record rate due to demographic shifts and the rise of Trump. Nationally, in 2018 all of the top eighty suburban cities and counties saw Democratic gains, including northern Kentucky. In the three most populous suburbs of Kenton, Boone, and Campbell Counties, McConnell had his poorest showing ever in the area in 2014. In 2016 Trump performed even worse. The decline culminated in the 2019 Kentucky governor's race, when Kenton and Campbell Counties voted for Andy Beshear (the state's attorney general and son of former governor Steve Beshear), the first time these counties went Democrat in more than fifty years. Their collective vote provided the winning margin for his election.

All of this means that if there is any momentum in 2020 to "Ditch Mitch," northern Kentucky will play a central role. Will this mean McConnell will finally support rebuilding the Spence Bridge? No. But he will act like it. His modus operandi is to ignore an issue for five years and then, during the next election campaign, make a promise to correct the problem if he wins. It is a promise he never intends to keep.

Maybe inaction will lead to more voter movement in Kenton County. If not, then Mitch McConnell will continue to be a giant chunk of concrete, and northern Kentuckians will remain the windshield of Jeff Brothers's Ford Fusion.

---

* It's worth noting that northern Kentucky is doubly screwed because its House member is Thomas Massie, the most conservative representative on spending in America. He literally votes against nearly every spending bill, even hurricane relief. He ain't worried about helping a bridge.

Campbell County

The Original Sin City

Campbell County is one of the fastest-growing areas of the state. It's the home of that magnificent culinary sensation, Cincinnati Chili (for the record, concocted at Dixie Chili & Deli in downtown Newport, the county's largest city, and if you hate this delicious cinnamon-chili creation, keep it to yourself because we love it). The south end of town remains very blue collar, packed with nondescript storefront dive bars with names like Coach's Corner, Butch's Sports Bar, and Jerry's Jug House, joints the likes of which have been Newport staples for years. Closer to the river, however, things get a little brighter and more family friendly with millennial-wooing new apartment complexes and upscale restaurants on the banks of the Ohio River. There is a place for everyone here.

But beneath this varied exterior lies the reality of old Newport, an Ohio River gangster's paradise. In the 1920s and early 1930s, during Prohibition, the demand for alcohol presented a lucrative racket for the Mob—especially in a state like Kentucky, renowned for its homemade bourbon and moonshine. The typically laissez-faire Kentucky attitude that government should keep its nose out of our business (which still exists in spades around most of the state, actually) led to an atmosphere that was generally tolerant, if not openly accepting, of Mob activities. The unspoken mantra was always "Just don't make too many waves, and we'll look the other way." With Cincinnati across the river and Indiana just a few miles away, Newport quickly became the perfect location for Mob operations.

By the time Prohibition ended in 1933, the Mob was a staple of the town. With illegal alcohol now no longer as profitable, gangsters quickly moved to gambling and sex to bring in the big bucks. Before long, Newport, full of casinos, brothels, fine dining and entertainment, and gangsters who operated like businessmen, became the original "Sin City"—a model for what Vegas would eventually perfect. Newport served as an early playground for celebrities such as Frank Sinatra, Dean Martin, and Shirley MacLaine. There were the high-class "carpet joints" like the Flamingo, the Tropicana Club, and the Beverly Hills Club, where Martin was once a blackjack dealer, and the rougher (and less regulated) "bust-outs," where fair play and hospitality were hard to come by. Newport had something for every sinner, regardless of economic status.

Newport's success led to racketeering, which quickly proved to be too lucrative to resist. In 1937 a Mafia group known as the Cleveland Four decided to muscle its way into town and make its presence felt. They were notorious for using violence elsewhere, including in New Jersey, where they murdered a racetrack owner outside a restaurant just to take over his operations. That same year, the Cleveland Four staked its claim to Newport by burning down the Beverly Hills Club to force out the owner. No sooner did the man rebuild his gambling palace than he sold it to the crime syndicate for cheap, just as planned. For the next several decades, Newport continued to expand, and the Mob was the most powerful game in town.

The town's actual population, which sat at thirty thousand in 1950, would swell to more than a hundred thousand after the sun went down. Newport was the place to party, and at night, venues on Monmouth Street hosted singers such as Marilyn Monroe and Sammy Davis Jr. The town became the hub of all forbidden entertainment in the Midwest. The center of sin east of the Mississippi River was in a little town in Kentucky, where some didn't approve, but no one dared stop this rolling money train.

That all changed one night in 1961, when the Mafia made a decision that crossed every line and ruined the fun for everyone. George Ratterman was a Cincinnati-born NFL quarterback who'd earned letters in four sports at the University of Notre Dame. Playing for the Buffalo Bills, he set an NFL rookie record in 1947 with twenty-two touchdown passes—a record that, it should be noted, stood until Peyton Manning's rookie year in 1998. After his football career, Ratterman practiced law in Ohio and Kentucky, where he became disgusted with the Mob's tactics. As such, he was part of a groundswell of public sentiment against its presence and he decided to run for sheriff of Campbell County, promising to clean up local law enforcement and reform Newport. But as per usual, the Mob had other ideas. On May 9, 1961, Ratterman was arrested after he was found on drugs, lying in a hotel bed with a stripper. The incident was caught by a cameraman who just happened to be outside the room at 2:40 a.m. to document the incident.

During Ratterman's subsequent trial, it became clear almost immediately that the arrest was a setup by the Mob. A doctor was able to prove Ratterman had been drugged with chloral hydrate, and several police officers testified that Detective Pat Ciafardini had orchestrated the bust and asked them to help cover up his attempt to frame the defendant. Ciafardini was indicted* on conspiracy charges for his role, and the whole spectacle turned public opinion. It was one thing to have gambling and prostitution, but framing the local hometown hero quarterback running for sheriff? Well, that was too much. The Mob had become too powerful, too heavy handed; it was no longer welcome in Newport.

Ratterman still won the election and began to clean up the city. He worked to reform the Sheriff's Department, and the governor of Kentucky took the unprecedented step of declaring a state of emergency in Campbell County. State officials began a series of raids of several high-profile casinos, bringing all their malfeasances to light to a shocked public. Robert F. Kennedy, then US attorney general and a fan of Ratterman's from his NFL days, used his story to persuade Congress to target organized crime across several states. Kennedy then used the subsequent publicity as a launching pad for his own political ambitions, and Newport's national racket became public enemy number one.

Eventually, unable to continue raking in huge stacks of cash and tired of dealing with a hostile public, the Mob decided to find greener pastures. The commercialization and corresponding declining cost of air travel presented a golden opportunity to draw visitors from these small-town crusaders to create the new "Havana in the Desert." The prototype worked in Kentucky before those pesky townspeople got in the way—and it was time to go bigger. With far more room to expand

---

* Amazingly, Ciafardini was acquitted and, in classic Newport style, went on to become the city's chief of detectives.

and less oversight, the Mob packed up its operations and flew out west to Las Vegas, and the endeavor proved to be a veritable jackpot.

Newport was never the same. With the glitz and glamour gone, the city hit an economic slump from which it has only recently begun to recover. Over fifty years later, Newport is now attempting to create a new history. Walking the streets on this late-September day, one can see signs of optimism as the suburban boom of northern Kentucky is slowly paying dividends in Campbell County as well. But the renegade spirit of the past still lives on.* Newport remains the gritty uncle of the northern Kentucky family, and they like it that way.

Grant County

Render unto Caesar That Which Is Caesar's

One of the reasons I chose to write this book is that, unlike any other place I know of, Kentucky's people and culture can differ drastically based on nothing more trivial than a few miles and a county line. Every county in this state is different, and the randomness of what side of a county line you happen to be from can help define your personality for a lifetime. Nowhere can this be seen more clearly than here in Grant County, where, just a few miles from Newport, the former Mafia capital of the Midwest, sits the world's only life-size replica of Noah's Ark.

On July 7, 2016, the Ark Encounter—a 510-foot-long, 85-foot-wide, and 51-foot-high re-creation of the Old Testament's most famous boat—opened in Grant County just outside Williamstown off of Interstate I-75. No matter what side of politics you're on, you've probably at the very least heard of the Ark Encounter. If you're a fundamental Christian conservative, you may have already paid the $48 ticket to bask in this faithful, beautiful, and elaborate re-creation of God's glory; if you're an atheist liberal, you've probably smarmily laughed about its

* One of the last bastions of Newport's seedy history still remaining is the Brass Ass strip club; I mean, at least that's what people tell me.

science-scoffing madness at your SoHo wine parties. Either way, it's probably been on your radar.

The Ark Encounter is the brainchild of Ken Ham, an evangelical Australian businessman who began the group Answers in Genesis, a creationist political organization that believes in inerrancy, the idea that all of the Bible is literally true, with the universe six thousand years old and created exactly as explained in the book of Genesis. In 2010 Ham announced the creation of a theme park in Grant County based on the story of Noah's Ark. The idea was to build a life-size replica of the ark, designed precisely to the measurements in the Bible, for people to be able to board and visit. Lifelike models of all of God's creatures saved by Noah during the great flood are on display, including pairs of bears, rabbits, and giraffes, along with pterodactyls and T-Rexes.

Riding the shuttle to the Ark Encounter site, I am struck by the sheer size of this impressive behemoth. This thing is impossibly massive and its craftsmanship is of the highest level. Inside, vertical columns are made from giant spruce trunks, and wide-eyed families and children move through its massive halls as television screens loop the biblical story it is based on. Outside the facility is practically a Christian theme park with zip lines, a petting zoo, a ropes course, and a 1,500-seat two-story buffet. There is also a gift shop where you can purchase coloring books, wooden replicas, and basically any Noah's Ark–themed novelty you can think of.*

Ken Ham's motives, however, are not all solely religious. He is also a capitalist and a heck of a marketer. He intentionally opened the facility on July 7—7/7, or Genesis 7:7, which reads: "And Noah went in, and his sons, and his wife, and his sons' wives with him, into the ark, because of the waters of the flood." Christians instantly understood the subtle biblical reference, but the media, which often mocked the project, did not. Ham knew a fact that most of the world didn't. The most untapped market for entertainment dollars in America is the Christian one. Virtually all entertainment, whether film, television, music, or tourism, is controlled by

---

* Not all of it is *that* friendly. A T-shirt sold online references the end of the flood story with the barbed line noting the ark is "taking back the rainbow." It's sold out at this time, which is depressing.

secular institutions. Genuine religious attractions are much scarcer than the strong market that exists for them, likely because of the unfamiliarity of content producers with the (especially more fundamental) Christian lifestyle. Ham stepped in to try to exploit that balance.

But because something is based in religion doesn't mean it should be excused from following the rules. Many in Grant County feel misled by Ken Ham and wonder if hosting the Ark Encounter is not all they thought it was cracked up to be and that the promises made were overblown at best and outright lies at worst. When Ham promoted building the attraction, he received multiple tax breaks from the state to do so. In return, he said he would invest in the local community, and work to lift up a struggling area. That hasn't happened.

"It's like a church that came in, which is great," says Grant Countian Jenn Williams, "but it's brought no benefit to the county. The county went wet solely because of the Ark, thinking maybe hotels or restaurants might come in, but they haven't."

The bigger Ark issue, though, one that has made national headlines and upset not only Grant Countians but also many elsewhere in the state, was when Ham's Ark Encounter attempted to transfer its property status from a for-profit to a nonprofit organization. By doing so, Ham could avoid paying local taxes as a religious nonprofit. Such a move would have severely harmed the people in Grant County by removing a key part of the tax base promised by Ham initially. They changed their mind though when Kentucky's Tourism, Arts and Heritage Cabinet declared that they were no longer eligible for the $18 million in tax incentives they had been granted. The declaration by the state effectively smacked down the transfer, and Ham quickly sold the Ark Encounter back to his for-profit entity.

In addition, two years later, the Ark Encounter was sued by the Grant County School Board claiming the Ark property was undervalued for purposes of property taxes by about $82 million. The Ark Encounter had been paying property taxes based on a figure derived from the Ark's initial property valuation assessment, a figure that should have risen as the attraction added more accoutrements to its portfolio in the form of a new convention building, restaurants, a petting zoo, and other extras. Even though these additions cost $72 million alone, the

Ark Encounter still claimed the entire property is worth only $48 million. It was an absurd argument. Rendering unto Caesar that which is Caesar's has not been the Ark's mode of operation thus far.

The Ark Encounter has, it appears, sought to avoid taxes, exploit legal loopholes, and avoid promises made to the public, all for the almighty dollar. It acts too often like a Fortune 500 company and less like a religious monument. It has appeared to many that the Ark Ham built was designed less as a religious attraction and more as a way to handle a flood of cash via multiple tax breaks. Because of this, the Ark has soured a lot of goodwill in Grant County, including from some in its Christian base. I am a Christian, and I respect how moving the Ark is to believers even though its lack of scientific basis makes it for others a mocking joke. But I also believe in the Bible verse Philippians 2:4, which says, "Let each of you look not to his own interests, but to the interests of others." It's a message Ken Ham, those behind the Ark Encounter, and many of Kentucky's leaders should seek to take to heart.

Pendleton County

The Town McConnell Forgot

Northern Kentucky is a varied place where each county is defined by its proximity to Cincinnati. Thanks to the business, entertainment, and educational options there, the counties around the Ohio border have flourished, becoming some of the best places to live in the state.

But just a few miles to the south, that prosperity is not shared. The three oft-forgotten northern Kentucky counties of Pendleton, Owen, and Trimble are struggling to find an identity. They are just far enough away from the city not to enjoy all of its benefits and just rural enough that they're routinely overlooked by those whose eyes are drawn to a more lucrative portion of northern Kentucky. It is a difficult situation.

For example, just down the highway from some of the greatest growth areas in Kentucky is the city of Falmouth, in Pendleton County.

Falmouth is home to the state's most empty, dilapidated downtown area. An abandoned old movie theater in the center of town has a marquee that, for some reason, says in crooked letters, "Got Pork"—probably a reference to a restaurant that's also long gone. Most of the storefronts, in fact, are mere shells. One of the very few small business owners I see is a man sitting in a lawn chair at the side of the road, staring into space. A hand-painted sign reads "Bikes for Sale," and next to it stand several clearly used, dull-colored bicycles, their best days long behind them.

Looking through the window of the Assembly Café, for instance, all there is to see is a decrepit dining room filled with broken chairs and a dusty, forgotten old organ shoved up against one of the windows. One empty storefront simply has two giant prop gumball machines inside, gumball-less and left there presumably from some party or event. It's probably very telling that the Pendleton County Community Development Center is locked, and inside sit some ladders and an old salad bar.

Something destroyed this part of town. But what?

I slip into one of the only shops I see with signs of life. It's called Country Patchwork, and it's a quilting and scrapbooking store that at least has a couple of people inside. Inside I meet Sarah Hart, who works in the shop, and we figure we might as well ask her point-blank, *What happened to downtown Falmouth?*

The answer is, simply, "the Flood," one of the largest, and quickest, floods in recent Kentucky history. On March 1, 1997, a heavy rain began as most of the town was in the Pendleton County High School gym watching the district finals basketball game. It turned into a downpour around nine o'clock, and by the time the rains ended the next morning, the Licking River would crest at twenty-six feet above average flood levels, breaching the floodwalls around Falmouth and filling the city with eight feet of river water. The flood lifted houses from their foundations and picked up cars in its path, smashing them into one another like a demolition derby. The nursing home scrambled to move patients to higher ground; the *Falmouth Outlook* newspaper was completely covered, the library destroyed. In all, 95 percent of Falmouth ended up underwater, and there were five deaths.

When the waters receded, parts of the city were buried in at least three feet of mud, and much of downtown was destroyed. A complete, uninhabitable mess. The Federal Emergency Management Agency (FEMA) came to town and set up a makeshift command center at the high school. No one in Country Patchwork, when pressed, can recall any elected state or federal officials visiting.

Eventually FEMA would designate Falmouth for disaster relief, which means affected residents would be eligible for a buyout, paid 75 percent by FEMA, 12 percent by the state, and 13 percent by the local government. The local government would then accept ownership of the land where the properties were sold, and land would remain open space in perpetuity in order to mitigate future flood losses. Although 213 residents applied for a buyout, FEMA only had enough funding for 97. The places that were purchased were never rebuilt, and most of the other flooded buildings were left uninhabitable. Much of Falmouth simply ended up deserted.*

Since the flood, many of the businesses have left and nothing has replaced them; outsiders began to come in and buy up damaged homes to turn a quick dollar on new tenants. "So many greedy people came in from out of town and bought up lots of buildings for pennies, and they don't care about making them look nice," says Lisa Arnold, chatting with friends at Randy's Clothing and Footwear. "They get the rent checks even if they don't fix them up."

It's important to remember—and this is something I keep thinking about—that this isn't some old-time story of a flood that affected a Kentucky river town in, say, 1936. This happened in 1997. You don't think about a town simply going away in modern society. But Falmouth has, and outside of those who live here, no one seems to notice.

It's possible that Mitch McConnell or the other Kentucky statewide politicians at the time visited the area, met the people, and helped the cleanup in the aftermath. Mitch McConnell is the second most powerful man in America, and here in his home state, a town was completely wiped away. The fact that no one can recall if he was around to help is a damning indictment.

---

* It's worth noting that in the past few years, hundreds of millions of dollars have been cut from FEMA's budget. Our next serious disaster could get a much less effective federal response.

For now, Pendleton County moves forward. Most of the business and infrastructure takes place outside of downtown Falmouth because, as you might suspect, people are a little gun-shy to risk rebuilding in the flood zones. Local kid Dontaie Allen is playing basketball at the University of Kentucky, making him the only native Kentuckian on scholarship for John Calipari during the 2019-20 season, a fact that has the county beaming with pride. But the county has been irrevocably changed. Forgotten by its leaders, it has tried to navigate an uncertain future and re-create anew the days before the flood changed everything.

Owen County

Playing Strip Pool

The first time I went to Owen County, it left a strong impression. I stopped at a local gas station/grocery and walked to the back to discover two young men shooting pool clad only in their boxers. I asked what they were doing, and, without a trace of a smile, they said, "Playing strip pool." At four o'clock in the afternoon. On a Wednesday. And they acted as if I was the one who was ridiculous for asking. It still puzzles me to this day.

Owen County is the undisputed champion of local Kentucky signage. From the Sweet Buy & Buy, a quaint house and accompanying barn filled with antiques you can meet on that beautiful shore, to the United Methodist Church's seasonally themed reader board bearing the message "Now Serving Pumpkin Spice Communion," every Owen County sign brings joy. But the most creative sign in all of Kentucky may be standing in front of a local auto mechanic's shop: it simply (and somewhat inexplicably) reads, "Home Is Where You Poop in Comfort."*

* And if you're trying to get home to poop, and your shoddily serviced automobile can't make the trip, you're in big trouble. Any expert will tell you that great marketing addresses a specific need.

I am not sure what that has to do with getting your car repaired, but, honestly, can any of us truly disagree?

The town of Owenton feels like a Pacific Northwest paradise, with tall pines all around us, green and lush. Small businesses dot the downtown area. Bird Dogs coffee is teeming with morning java drinkers. Minch Hardware and Appliance Company looks straight out of a set design calling for "small-town hardware store." Inside Larry Tackett's Men's Wear, which has been in operation in some iteration since the early 1900s, several men are just hanging out and shooting the breeze in the back of the store. Talk to the folks there, and you'll quickly learn several of the county's draws, including the state's largest winery and nearby Eagle Creek, which they say is ninety-nine miles long—only one more mile, and they would be required technically to call it a river. They prefer the word *creek*. Sounds more inviting.

Owenton is isolated. None of the nearby interstates runs through the county, and with no river transit, railroad, or other form of transportation, getting here is difficult. Owenton is surrounded on all sides by major transportation arteries. The county is smack dab in the center of what's known as the Golden Triangle, which has legs made up of I-71, from northern Kentucky to Louisville; I-64, from Lexington to Louisville; and I-75, from Lexington to northern Kentucky.* Yet Owenton does not have direct access to any of them. Even though trucks and business traffic come and go in all directions nearby, Owen County sits in the middle, isolated, watching commerce and economic prosperity drive past every day.

When we think about the inaccessibility of rural locations such as Owen County, we think immediately of the lack of business opportunities. But for Jenny Urie, a world history, arts, and humanities teacher at Owen County High School, such isolation leads to a different consequence. Without the infrastructure of most of the counties that surround it, the day-to-day operations of the Owen County school system have been crippled. The effect is felt across the board, from teachers and students to resources and bus routes.

---

* It's like the Research Triangle in North Carolina, only with a bunch more Arby's.

For instance, with no major road through the county, school buses in Owen County have to travel substantially more miles than those in other counties. "One of the big things we're dealing with as a district, and many districts across the state, are our transportation costs," Jenny explains. "The state has reduced the funding for transportation costs and put it on school districts, and here in Owen County, our buses run almost four hundred fifty thousand miles a year. I mean, this is a big county with a lot of country roads; if the federal government could come pitch in some money for what the state hasn't done, that would be so helpful for our district."

One of the hidden costs of public education is transportation. In the nation's largest cities, transportation to and from school can be difficult, but with the living areas mostly condensed and close to the schools, and public transportation available to fill in the gaps, options exist. But in rural areas, students frequently live great distances from the (often) only school in the county. Arranging transportation across these two-lane, winding roads can be a great burden for local school boards. Throw in the Kentucky state budget crisis, which has crippled all public spending, and small counties are left with a rising cost that they must offset.

The issues frustrated Urie so much that she once ran for the Kentucky State Legislature to try and work to fix them. "We have to get the kids back and forth from school," Urie says. "That's our number one priority, right? And because we spend so much money on transportation, we can't spend that money on professional development or textbooks or even computers."

This is how tight the budget can be: according to Urie, for many of the classes in her school, she doesn't even have textbooks for the students; the ones she has are old copies of books duct-taped together, which Urie has to have photocopied because she can't afford a whole set for the class.

"I have three file cabinets that get me through the year," she says. "I save those copies year after year so I don't cost the school too much in paper, but making copies is cheaper than buying textbooks. But I'll get online and print off a summary of the French Revolution and make thirty-five copies of it, and we'll use it and take notes, and then I'll take them back and put them in my filing cabinet for next year."

Plus, with shoddy Internet service throughout the county, Urie can't assign homework that might require online research. Many kids simply don't have Internet access. "It's very hard to give kids homework; you have to assign homework that you know they don't need to do research for. If they're doing a project, the research time has to be built into my class time, because I know good and well that there are too many students that will not be able to do it."

The same situation applies to extracurricular activities. Fund-raisers help sponsor many of the class trips (even short trips to nearby counties) because it's too much to ask some students to contribute their own money. "If I want to take my kids on a field trip, I have to do a fund-raiser," Urie says. "There's no money for any type of enrichment. If I ask all the kids to bring in ten dollars, a lot of them are going to be left at the school."

It's easy to think that infrastructure problems mainly attack business development and economic growth, but the effects go far beyond those. They cripple public services, causing places like Owen County to survive on a shoestring combination of inventiveness and ingenuity. What is especially frustrating to Urie and others in Owen County is that they know there is federal grant money available; if they could only get Mitch McConnell to pay attention to a county that seems to be consistently off his radar.

"They could give us some grant money," says Urie. "We have parts of our budget that are federally funded by grants. There's all kinds of things the federal government could do for us. If they could just help us out with transportation cost, staffing, or even just textbooks."

As of now, however, Owen County gets nothing. Urie isn't sure if it is because McConnell isn't aware or because he doesn't care. "I don't know that Mitch McConnell would be in touch at all with a place like this," she tells me. "There's no pharmaceutical company, there's no big business, there's no one here who can give him money."

But what they do have is duct-taped textbooks and teachers spending out of their own pockets to educate. Because the truth of the matter is that until Owen County can make itself shiny enough (or give enough money) to catch the eye of Mitch, they'll just have to do the best they can. It's like a game of strip pool: the rules are dubious, it makes little sense, but someone is losing their shirt.

Trimble County

Waiting on Their McConnell Prize

My attention is wavering while waiting on a hamburger as I sit in a booth in Bedford at the Little Town & Country Restaurant. Being on the road for a long time is exhausting, and I am drifting out of focus while watching the ceiling fans turn lazily above me. A giant poster-size action photo of basketball player Bill "Big Eye" Hughes is on the back wall, but his eyes honestly don't look that big to me. This local restaurant could be a scene in about 75 percent of the counties we have visited except that here an older couple, both smoking, size me up from a booth in the corner. The woman staring at me holds an extralong Virginia Slim 120 in her spindly fingers; her husband sits with folded arms while his cigarette smolders in the ashtray in front of him. Neither appears to be eating; their sustenance for the day is nicotine and staring down tourists, and they're clearly filling up on both.

It is a little jarring to see this much smoking in a public restaurant in 2019. I have always hated cigarette smoke. The smell and aftereffects of smoking are disgusting. I tried a cigarette once in my life in college and after two drags I became dizzy and threw up in the basement of my dorm. As a kid in Middlesboro, smoking surrounded nearly every locale I entered except my home. Virtually every public place in town was filled with a perpetual cloud of cigarette haze. A select few restaurants were considerate enough to create a nonsmoking section, but most deemed it unnecessary. Even when I was in high school, one set of doors at the school was deemed the "Smokers' Entrance," and of-age students (and teachers) could use it to take a quick drag between classes. Smoking used to be part of the tapestry of Kentucky life. But it's always been gross and now, even in what was one of the two former centers of tobacco production in America, we have thankfully seen a drastic change in the public acceptance of the nasty habit.

Well, except at the Little Town & Country Restaurant. The sign outside reads "Drive-In" and features an illustration of two children, each with a hand on a shared hamburger between them. One is shoeless, wearing overalls and a straw hat, while the other is an androgynous fair-haired child with a striped shirt and seemingly wearing shorts. I suppose this is the literal, visual depiction of "little town and country," with a hamburger being the common ground on which they can find joy. If not for being overwhelmed by my wheezing on the cigarette smoke, I would find this to be quite sweet, actually. If only sharing a hamburger brought that kind of peace and understanding, I wouldn't have had to write this book and could have just taken Mitch McConnell to Rally's.

Trimble County itself is very rural and sparse. When I ask a local what is good in Trimble County, he says, "Peaches and white-tailed deer," which is a solid combo. But even though prosperous Louisville isn't far away, the county seat of Bedford has clearly seen better days. The local courthouse is nice, but everyone is already out for the day, which isn't a Trimble County thing as much as it is an every-county thing.* The storefronts are all older and most seem forgotten. I can't find anyone around town to speak with except for a shop owner who swears to me that all local politics and politicians are corrupt. Sensing a story, I ask him to elaborate, but when I show interest, he can't give me any specifics and makes me promise not to mention his name (which he never told me). "I'm not going to tell you anything. You can google it. You'll see," he says before wandering off. I googled it. I didn't see.

For Trimble County, this lack of industry or any big-ticket draws means not as much federal attention, which state representative Rick Rand battles constantly.

---

* If I were an investigative reporter in Kentucky and wanted a story, I would take a look at how little time many county officials spend in their offices. Having been to 120 counties, I can attest that you have a better chance of finding a beached whale in most county courthouses during working hours than of bumping into an elected official.

"I think any rural community, not just this rural community, has a hard time attracting federal dollars," he tells me. "So many federal dollars tend to flow where there's significant economic development, and we're really an agricultural and bedroom community. That makes it very difficult in particular to attract federal money. Of course, I'm the state representative up here, so I try to help my community with state dollars—but even those are getting scarce."

As in neighboring Owen, Trimble County struggles because it lost the interstate lottery that decided winners and losers a generation ago. Before the I-71 corridor was built, the county prospered because of local Highway US-42, the best route from Louisville to Cincinnati. With it, roadside markets and businesses were able to succeed, and the local economy flourished. Then, I-71 was built and Trimble County was the only county on the corridor without an exit off the interstate. Out-of-towners stopped passing through, and many business owners have been unable to adapt with the new, much-less-trafficked landscape.

Walking down the streets of Bedford, it's clear this town was once something much greater than it is today. What Rand tells me seems to track with what I've noticed: there just doesn't seem to be a lot going on here right now. The reality is that the modern economy needs infrastructure, and Trimble County struggles with that. Its Internet is slower than molasses, which hurts the prospects of opening a new business in the area, and that causes farmers to fall behind as technology takes hold in the agricultural industry. With no major highways and development, or federal dollars to kick-start them, things just feel very . . . *forgotten* here.

The story of Trimble County echoes the stories of as many as twenty other rural counties in Kentucky. Due to a combination of a lack of infrastructure access, economic downturns (due to manufacturing, coal, and/or tobacco losses), and dwindling populations, many rural areas are being completely abandoned, which is truly sad to see. For Trimble County, it exists now primarily as a bedroom community for the Louisville area. But for those towns even farther from a city, no such lifeline exists.

When Mitch McConnell runs for reelection, he will often make some form of the argument "You can't lose me as a senator, because you will lose all the benefits of my position as majority leader." Of course, it's nonsense. Most counties have received absolutely no benefit at all from having Mitch in a position of power. It reminds me of a famous Chris Rock bit* about O. J. Simpson. Rock notes that the day O. J. was acquitted of murder in 1995, he saw images on TV of his African American supporters screaming and shouting *"We won! We won!"* Rock snaps incredulously, "What the f*** did we win? Every day I go to the mailbox to look for my O.J. prize . . . Nothing!"

Gallatin County

Rubbin's Racin'

Driving back up I-71 toward Cincinnati, I made the executive decision to get off at exit 55 and check out one of my favorite locations in the state: the Kentucky Motor Speedway. If you have never been to a major NASCAR track (and I am guessing many of you reading this, especially north of the Mason-Dixon Line, have not)† then it's hard to truly re-create just what a spectacle it is. The Kentucky Speedway is a one-and-a-half-mile tri-oval that takes up the better part of a milelong stretch of land, with a seating capacity of eighty thousand. It sits visible off the interstate in Sparta, a sleepy agricultural community whose official population is 231; but one Saturday night every year, it becomes the epicenter of auto racing in America.

I love NASCAR. Or at least I *used* to love NASCAR. In the nineties, I fell for the sport thanks to the epic personalities of the day, such as Dale Earnhardt Sr., Rusty Wallace, brothers Terry and Bobby Labonte, and the evil Jeff Gordon. I watched all the races (and not just for the wrecks) and followed the expansion of the series, which, for a short

---

* Likely the first time Chris Rock and Mitch McConnell have been compared to each other.

† And if you haven't, how on earth do you find ways to have your eardrums blown out?

time, was the fastest-growing sport in America. The idea of regular Joes from the country all of a sudden becoming national celebrities while participating in a sport that began as a way to run moonshine in the South was brilliant. Corporate homogenization has made it not quite the same now,* but I always try to make time for an annual appearance in Sparta to watch the Cup Series come to town.

In July 2019 I was invited to a suite with various dignitaries in attendance, including Transportation Secretary Elaine Chao, wife of America's biggest hunk, Mitch McConnell. When I walked in, a fellow radio host and friend, Terry Meiners, came over to me and hissed, "Elaine Chao is here—*don't do anything stupid!!!*" I'm not sure what he thought I would do (I was saving my Dick Trickle jokes for when I met Bill Barr), but I simply introduced myself with a polite greeting and a smile. Secretary Chao was kind. With a sly, knowing smile, she said that she had heard a lot about me recently. I awkwardly laughed and kept moving. It was clear she has five hundred times the charisma of her husband.

As we creep in traffic toward the raceway today, I am reminiscing about the time last year when driver Noah Gragson took me around the track in a NASCAR Xfinity car for my TV show (it was both exhilarating and terrifying), but my good vibes are halted by a text that makes my heart skip a beat. It is from Amy McGrath, whom I hadn't spoken with in quite some time, and for good reason.

When McGrath began her 2018 campaign for Congress, I was hosting my television show, *Hey Kentucky!*, in Lexington. It was a daily debate show about sports and politics that I developed in 2016 from scratch as something of a social experiment. Can an avowed progressive sports guy host a political show aired in a red state and make it work? The answer at first was no, as the combination of my early lack of television acumen and the rising "Stick to sports" mantra in culture combined to keep my initial ratings small. But my staff and I worked hard at improving the program, and over time we slowly built it into an actual hit, rated number one in our time slot, surpassing *Jeopardy!* in

* Fewer accents and fights; more ads for investment banks.

the key ratings demographics.* I even won a regional Emmy for Best TV Host, one of the proudest achievements of my career.

As the show began to hit its stride, Amy McGrath began to hit hers as well. She was running for the House and her candidacy was very intriguing. In addition to her stellar military background and résumé, I was impressed by the idea of a woman attempting to take on the system and pursue public service against a multiterm sitting congressman. Over the course of the campaign she made regular appearances, even once as a cohost, using the show to get her message out to voters. I put together a Democratic primary debate that she participated in (and did well) and, after she won the nomination, hosted a town hall forum with her that aired throughout the district. I wouldn't say we were friends, but I respected her candidacy, and she seemed to appreciate our working relationship.

After she lost the general election to Andy Barr by a surprisingly substantial margin in 2018, our relationship changed. Already McGrath clearly had her eye on the Senate race and as such, she kept her distance from me, presumably because I was rumored to be a potential candidate. I called her in March 2019 and spoke about the possibility of the race. We both talked about our particular potential candidacies and agreed that a primary between the two of us would only harm us both. We agreed to stay in contact and she would call me as soon as her intentions were known (a phone call that never came). Before we got off the phone, she said, "We need to work together for our common goal of ending Mitch's time in Washington."

I still had to do my television show, however, and that included commenting on her newsworthy decision to take on Mitch and her subsequent rough launch. This wasn't just my opinion; it was the consensus of anyone with a political pulse. Even Congressman John Yarmuth, the only federally elected Democrat in the state, was concerned enough about McGrath's electability that he let it be known that he felt she needed a primary opponent.

On my show, I made my opinion known. Because I was contemplat-

---

* Which was not old people—old people *love Jeopardy!* No truer words have ever been spoken.

ing entering the race myself, I always made it clear at the beginning of the segment that people should consider that bias when judging my opinions. I thought doing it that way would allow me to do my job but also be completely aboveboard. The McGrath camp disagreed.

McGrath's advisors contacted my television station, pressuring it to remove me from the show until I decided whether to run. They argued that with my internal thoughts of running, I was unable to treat her fairly and shouldn't be allowed to give my viewpoints on her candidacy. My station manager told me of the pressure and ultimately caved to it, telling me that he couldn't risk a public controversy. I was angry and disappointed. I had made clear for two years that I was considering the race and the only thing that had changed was McGrath's own bungled entry. Her mistakes shouldn't affect my job status. But worry about the loss of potentially millions in general election ad revenue led to a different decision.

I knew McGrath's team was to blame for my departure, but at this point, the public did not. After my removal, her campaign manager, Mark Nicholas, made sure to take credit by bragging in political circles around Kentucky that "I got Matt Jones pulled from *Hey Kentucky!*" His boasts ended up in a story on the national political news website the Intercept and created the narrative that Matt Jones was off the air, and the McGrath campaign was responsible.

I was angry. I had always been kind and respectful to McGrath, and she'd used my show's popularity to her advantage. Now, because she couldn't handle even mild criticism, she sneakily had cost me my job. If she couldn't take a local TV show calling her launch "shaky," how could she handle the barrage that Mitch brings?

My fans were angry, my coworkers worried (their jobs were in jeopardy), and my platform was suddenly taken away. Still, there was little I could do. McGrath's campaign had played dirty, and now my show was gone.*

The tension between the two of us only increased over the next

---

* The station told Matt he could return to the show if he didn't run. But when this book was announced, they took away that option as well and Matt lost his job permanently.

couple of months as our show's fans feuded with her national followers on social media. (She seemed to have little local Kentucky support.) Alienating a sizable chunk of Kentucky voters was a poor decision, especially since at this point I hadn't even decided whether to run. But the two of us never spoke, and she never reached out to clear the air. They assumed I was in the race, and the battle was on.

McGrath's text this afternoon was the first since the day of her announcement. Her text began, "Matt, I just heard about the loss of your father." From there, her sentiments were kind. She said that she had heard my mother recently passed away a few weeks before as well. She mentioned that she had dealt with loss in her life, and she hoped I would take solace in my relationship with my parents and how blessed I was to have had them.

There was just one problem. My father had not died—and neither had my mother. Well, at least I assumed not. We had been on the road for a few weeks, and I hadn't checked in with my parents in a couple of days. I quickly called my mother, who heard the panic in my voice and assured me that my stepfather, Larry Blondell, was fine. She broke my slight panic by making me laugh, saying, "If anything ever happens to him, you won't find out from Amy McGrath." I was relieved.

But what to do next? Chris was sitting with me, and he too was dumbfounded. We debated how I should respond.* Ultimately, I sent a short text saying there must be some mistake, and my father was well. She responded with two words: "My apologies." We haven't spoken since.

Afterward, Chris and I were able to laugh about it. Still, it was really strange. I mean, in a similar situation, wouldn't you say more than "My apologies"? I feel like I would. Not even a phone call or a red-faced "oops!" emoji. The whole incident was completely bizarre. Little did I know, it was just the beginning of the most surreal few weeks of my life.

---

* I alternated between "New phone, who dis?" and a pithy "Condolences on the loss of your campaign." I was overruled on both.

Henry County

Mitch the Environmental Killer

> *Whether we and our politicians know it or not, Nature is party to all our deals and decisions, and she has more votes, a longer memory, and a sterner sense of justice than we do.*
>
> —Wendell Berry

There are few Kentuckians with more accolades and universal respect than Wendell Berry. The poet, novelist, essayist, and environmental critic, who lives a simple life on his farm in Port Royal, Kentucky, in rural Henry County, is one of the most accomplished writers in the state's history. His fiction has produced some of the best depictions of rural southern life since William Faulkner and led to his becoming the first living individual ever inducted into the Kentucky Writers Hall of Fame. But Berry, who comes from a lineage of Kentucky farmers, has also written tirelessly over the years in support of protecting the environment and of small, local farms and communities; precisely the sorts of small farms that are found everywhere in Henry County. Though somewhat reclusive (the only way to reach him, I'm told, is by handwritten letter to a post office box; we wrote him, but to no avail), he is said to still work his farmland with horses instead of tractors, writes in longhand with ink, and maintains the farming practices of eras past in lieu of modern-day agricultural techniques. In short, he is a one-of-a-kind Kentucky treasure.

His lauded polemic *The Unsettling of America: Culture and Agriculture* is one of the best critiques ever written of the economic consolidation of American agriculture. Berry posits that modern agribusiness drives a wedge between the local farmer and the land, creating a distance where there once was an intimate connection. This has a detrimental effect on everything from the farmer to the community to the final food product. Berry's writings imply the disconnect of American agriculture coincides with the loss of greater American ideals in general as well.

Berry, at eighty-five, is still fighting the good fight and has never been afraid to take on partisan politics. In recent years, he has correctly focused his ire on members of his own Democratic Party who have taken to belittling those like Berry's fellow Kentuckians. As he told journalist Amanda Petrusich in a 2019 *New Yorker* interview:

> Since the election, liberal commentators have made "rural America" a term of denigration, the same as "boondocks" and "nowhere." It is noticed now, by people who never noticed it before, only because of its support for Donald Trump. Rural America could have supported Trump, these people conclude, only because it is full of bigoted "non-college" white people who hate everybody but themselves. These liberals apparently don't know that, with their consent, urban America has been freely plundering rural America of agricultural products since about the middle of the last century—and of coal for a half century longer.

The argument Berry makes is critical and 100 percent accurate. My frustration with the national portrayal of Kentuckians in the Trump era angers me nearly as much as the president himself. For decades, rural Americans, but specifically Kentuckians and Appalachians, have been made a mockery of by urban intellectuals and national media. Whereas it was once acceptable to make fun of "hillbillies" and "rednecks," now the comments are more subtle and backhanded. Descriptions of Trump supporters in states like Kentucky are always based on the most negative ideals he condones and not the understandable resentment they have to outside forces that have long taken advantage of them. With elite, wealthy Republicans always working against their interest and the Democratic Party abandoning its working-class roots more each year, rural Kentuckians (and Pennsylvanians, West Virginians, Ohioans, and so on) have been subjected to the double whammy of cultural derision and no counteracting political representation. Standing up for hillbillies is neither popular nor accepted. The fact that Trump was able to come along and exploit this abandonment for his own political gain is less an indictment of rural America than it is of the political climate and two-party system that created him.

But I digress.* There really are few greater minds (and pens) more visible and outspoken about the treatment of Kentucky than Wendell Berry. And he continues to pay it forward to generations via the Berry Center, in New Castle, in Henry County. Founded by Wendell's daughter, Mary, in 2011 to preserve his writings on agriculture as well as those of his father and brother, both accomplished farmers, the Berry Center draws farmers, researchers, professors, and students from around the world to its comprehensive library of farming archives, intimate writings on rural economics. It contains everything from macro-economic agribusiness critiques to practical techniques the Berry clan has used to farm the land for generations.

Berry's commitment to the people and environment of Kentucky is inspiring, and unfortunately, not shared by its leaders. Berry has derisively called Mitch McConnell "our pride and joy," but Mitch's only interest in the environment is to ignore it. During my interview with him in 2014, I pressed McConnell repeatedly on whether he believes in global warming. He refused to answer, only saying, "I am not a scientist."† No matter how many ways I rephrased the questions, McConnell forcefully repeated his proud ignorance of scientific data. McConnell is smart enough to know climate change is crippling the environment but he plays dumb, choosing feigned ignorance for political gain over leadership. He also isn't an accountant, economist, or doctor, but that doesn't stop him from playing the role of expert on taxes, trade, or health care.

It is safe to say that virtually no current US senator has a worse voting record when it comes to protecting the environment:

- NO on including oil and gas smokestacks in mercury emission regulations;
- NO on banning oil drilling in the Arctic National Wildlife Refuge;
- NO on expanding Clean Water Act provisions for rural creeks and streams in coal areas;

---

* On this trip, when Matt begins to get worked up about the treatment of rural Kentuckians in popular and political culture, I always suggest we pull over and get some Skittles. It calms him down.

† For the record, no one ever thought Mitch McConnell was a scientist.

- NO on coal mine safety regulations (even hand-picking a coal lobbyist to be head of the EPA);
- NO on reducing funds for building roads in national forests (satisfying the timber industry); and
- NO on factoring global warming concerns into federal project planning.

When it comes to Mitch's environmental record, no one has said "no" this much since Nancy Reagan sat down with Arnold and Willis Jackson. McConnell votes against environmental issues even when you could make the argument that a yes vote would help Kentucky's economy. He has supported the expansion of oil pipelines and fracking throughout America, both of which have decimated the Kentucky coal industry by allowing them to skip the environmental protections to which coal companies must currently adhere. Even when protecting the environment could help Kentucky, McConnell maintains an out-of-touch and selfish political philosophy for personal gain. He has no regard for how his affirmative negligence will cripple our future.

A website run by the League of Conservation Voters details the voting records of both Senate and House members in terms of their supporting key environmental legislation, ranking them by percentage points on votes for pro-environmental legislation. As of 2020, Mitch McConnell's lifetime rating is 7 percent, among the worst in all the Senate.

The fact that Mitch McConnell and Wendell Berry reside in the same state is both ironic and depressing. Both are coming to the ends of their careers, one trying to build for the next generation, the other clinging desperately to personal power. As Berry once said, "If you don't know where you're from, you'll have a hard time saying where you're going." McConnell was never from Kentucky, and with his continued detrimental policies for the state—he ain't coming back.

Carroll County

Get Shorty

Let's say you are in downtown Carrollton, and you suddenly find yourself in need of (a) a King James Bible, (b) Post-it Notes, and (c) a laser printer all at the same time. You might think, "There is no way I could get all of these at the same place, is there?" Well you can if you are close to Carrollton Office Supply. Beneath the store's name, on a 70s-era sign in large block letters, are the words "Bibles and Religious Materials" on one side and "Computer Supplies" on the other. It's a combo retailer providing two of life's blessings under one roof, similar to the pizza place/tanning salon we ran into in Corbin.*

We are in Carrollton to speak with Harold "Shorty" Tomlinson,† the five-term judge-executive of the county. Tomlinson is a Democrat in a (per usual) increasingly Republican area. He is a friendly older fella with a gray buzz cut, wire-framed glasses, and a short-sleeve button-down with a tie, like if a grandfatherly Howie Long were cast as a substitute teacher. He looks like a favorite great-uncle who surprises you with a crisp five-dollar bill at every family reunion. He's not nicknamed Shorty because of his height, but simply because when he was two years old, a neighbor started calling him that, and it just stuck.

"If 'Shorty' is the worst thing you're being called," he rightfully points out, "I figure you're doing okay."

Shorty is part of a group trying to fix one of the biggest problems for counties along the I-71 corridor. The road is one of only two main arteries north to south in this part of the state, which means that any major

---

* Do *not* get these two mixed up!

† Shorty is a great nickname for a Kentucky public official, but considering I know of a Frog Welch, Duck Moore, Pickle Mills (who defeated Booger Jude to become Martin County constable), Booty Hall, Mutt Varney, Milkweed Wotier, Crawdad Sizemore, and a Mamaw Gulley (who was a man), it won't make the Kentucky top ten list.

accident that occurs clogs up the eighty-three-mile road for miles. And it happens all the time. Wrecks cripple I-71 with traffic multiple times a month, and when vehicles need to be diverted from the interstate, by necessity, they have to come through the small towns along I-71. Unfortunately, because of a lack of investment in the state's road system, the secondary roads are in terrible shape. So when traffic backs up on the interstate, Carroll County suffers.

Shorty helped form a bipartisan collaboration of Democrat and Republican local officeholders to push for a road expansion that would solve this problem for all counties along the route. There is nothing partisan about roads, so, for Shorty, it's a no-brainer. "You really have to stay away from party politics sometimes to get anything done," he tells me. "I've always thought if I could help somebody, I don't care if they're a Democrat or a Republican."*

Matt Lipe, president of the Carroll County Community Center, is a Republican who echoes Shorty's aims and says these cooperative efforts will only help all the counties around the corridor. "These judges have really put a focus on the regional effort and it's not all about 'what is in it for me'—it's about what is for the greater good of *us*."

This mind-set is not just in Carroll County; we have encountered it throughout this trip. The reflection of the country we see on television simply isn't the reality of how people are living in real life. I have yet to have anyone on this trip treat us rudely or unkindly. Many people have had strong opinions, but even with the understanding that they are giving them to a well-known Democrat in the state, they are unflinchingly hospitable. Except for the Republican politicians scared to speak to us on the record because they are worried about McConnell retaliation (it's clear he has the Grand Old Party in this state terrified of him), no one has refused to meet with us. Most people, you may be surprised to know, are normal and . . . nice!

The Washington Mitch McConnell has helped create is a different world. Mitch once bragged about being the "guardian of gridlock" and expressed early in Obama's presidency that his most important goal was to make Obama a one-term president. That political world, where

* Go, Shorty, it's your birthday!

each day's goal is to win a never-ending political bloodbath, and victory is achieved only by destroying the other party, is the preferred living place for McConnell and it is being mirrored online by the greater citizenry. One trip to Facebook and you are sure to see someone ranting about the "liberals ruining America." But when this same person actually encounters one of those liberals, the angry online rhetoric usually disappears, and the regular hospitality shines through.

Our political lives in America are increasingly acted out on social media, where the most rabid of partisans channel their inner Mitch McConnell and root for members of their party to be as vicious as possible to those on the other side. But I think in real life, most Americans want leaders like Shorty Tomlinson: focused on getting the interstate expanded and helping end traffic woes in their communities. Compromise and cohesion over vicious partisanship. I still think America will take a Shorty over a Mitch any day.

Shelby County

"It's Like I'm Just in Somebody Else's House"

The next time you are roaming around a city and see a statue or monument, take a second to really look at it in detail. Kentucky has its regal ones, such as the majestic statue of the most famous racehorse of all time, Man O' War, at the Kentucky Horse Park, just outside Lexington. There are important ones like the bronze statue in Hodgenville of native son Abraham Lincoln seated in the center of the town's confusingly named Lincoln Square Circle. And there are quirky ones like the impressive statue of William Goebel in Frankfort, the unlucky governor of Kentucky who, in 1900, was gunned down by an assassin on the way to the general assembly to find out whether he won the election. He died a few days later, and, as a memorial, the state built what is likely the only monument in America to a governor who served less than a week. (Okay, that statue is kind of sad, but you get my point.)

But sometimes, such as in the city of Shelbyville, in Shelby County, you find insane statues or monuments that defy understanding. It's a twenty-five-foot-tall cast-iron fountain purchased by the city and county from J. L. Mott Iron Works in New York to celebrate the completion of Shelbyville's first waterworks, providing free-flowing water for its citizens—water that is quite functional and lovely.

What makes Shelbyville's city fountain stick out is that instead of a town forefather, or some sort of symbolic figure, or even a historical character local to the area, the Shelbyville fountain honors something more memorable, but one that I am not sure grew up in Shelby County: a woman intertwined with a half-reptilian, half-lion creature with bat wings.

It's as odd as it sounds. On top of the fountain in this tiny Kentucky town is a woman reclined and wrapped around the body of a bizarre creature. They are enraptured together in some sort of throes of human-and-monster ecstasy; think M. Night Shyamalan meets *The Little Mermaid*. Just below the sculpture, water flows from a series of voyeuristic surrounding goat heads into the pool below. It's the kind of thing a town might place in its center if everyone in the town were on acid, which I don't really think Shelbyville is, at least currently.

Aside from its drug-addled monuments, Shelby County is also distinctive in that 9.1 percent of its population is Latino, the largest percentage of all 120 counties in the state. I was told by a shopkeeper in Trimble County that Shelby is known throughout the region as a safe place for Latino workers and families. Latinos often pass through his store asking for directions to Shelby County, where they have heard they can find work and stability. In our journeys across the state, we have come into contact with a handful of Hispanic members of many communities, but Shelby County has a much deeper pocket of Latinos than in other areas, and for those it serves as a home base. It isn't 100 percent clear how this began, but in Shelby County, you'll find many Mexican restaurants, ranging from quick in-and-out to longer-stay sit-down dining, family-owned supermarkets such as Michoacana Mexican Grocery, and nonprofits like Centro Latino, which helps connect Latino people with community services. Shelby County may be the center of Latino life in rural Kentucky.

It is also where we meet a Latino man we'll call Hector, a Honduran immigrant worker who traveled to the United States to reconnect with his family.* He says he came here with the hope of making a better life for himself, and he has found economic opportunity greater than he imagined.

But Hector's main problem is how difficult the process of attaining citizenship can be for those who want to do so legally. The process is so complex and intricate that it is nearly impossible to navigate without professional help. One minor error and you can be shut out forever.

"I have four years trying to get my citizenship, like, the papers," Hector tells me. "It's always something. You know what's the hardest thing? One little mistake can change everything. Even though your papers, your processes, might be going good, but what if you want to go to a job, and you've got to drive somewhere? People like us, sometimes we cannot drive because maybe we don't have a license. It is hard. Then just getting pulled over; for people in the United States, it's just a ticket. But for us, it's a *big* ticket; it's a big something that's going to go on your files, and those files for immigration are dirty now, so, 'We don't want you.'"

Hector's point is important. The US immigration system is arcane, needlessly complex, and hopelessly backed up. Because so many people seek citizenship, the system intentionally punishes any minor mistake, in part so as to alleviate the backlog. During my legal days, I tried to help a friend of mine navigate the process. He had all his papers in gear and followed all the rules. Nevertheless, it was more difficult and complicated than I could have ever imagined. Each step required such expertise that I had to hand him off to an expensive specialist. If an attorney trained in the law struggles with the system, how is a non-native-English-speaking immigrant supposed to jump through all the hoops perfectly?

Hector first came over on a work permit legally but has since let that lapse, making him technically here illegally. "Yeah, it scares me because I'm waiting for my citizen stuff, and I'm on the waiting list," says Hector. "But somebody could say, 'Hey, there's no more people getting approved for this, because it's over.' They can make any rules like that

* For obvious reasons, we are using a different name and nationality. He also asked that we not give details about his family.

in any year. What I always think is, 'This is not my country.' That's the first thing that comes to my head. And then, 'It's their country, the people that have their papers and stuff.' It's like I'm just in somebody else's house. They can decide for anything in their house. Oh, maybe they don't want me here? Gotta go out. You know?"

As for home, returning is a difficult option. He has been gone so long, he has no real family or community left there. "Sometimes I'm sleeping, and I have dreams that I'm back in my country, and I need *something* to live, like a house or something like that. If I go back to Honduras right now, I might have something, but it's not enough for my country. I'm going to be poor again. In my country, you can work a lot, but it doesn't amount to much."

Over the course of Mitch McConnell's career, illegal immigration is one of the issues he has spoken about the least. Like many business-driven Republicans, he is likely happy for the work illegal immigrants provide, and he knows that their presence in the country allows many industries, from food production to agriculture to the horse industry, to keep labor costs down. Thus, McConnell rarely, if ever, spoke of the need for deportation until Donald Trump became president. Now he remains silent even as images of poor treatment at the border and kids in cages under American control show up on our nation's airwaves. Once Trump made illegal immigrants and building a wall on the Mexican border his obsession, the senator abandoned his principles again and marched in lockstep with the White House, calling for strict border security and the wall regularly for the first time in his career.* Everything Mitch believes is malleable, so when the political calculus changes, he changes.

Hector says he doesn't experience racism on a daily basis, and he feels very much at home in Shelby County. But he does feel that the Trump administration has helped fuel negative stereotypes of Hispanic people that is making life here more difficult for him. Even though he isn't Mexican, the routine nasty rhetoric about Mexicans affects him.

---

* The man who criticized the wall when Trump talked about it while running for the Republican nomination used it as an applause line in his 2019 Fancy Farm speech. No stance is too hypocritical for Malleable Mitch.

"I don't get mad or sad or anything when people call me Mexican, but I know you're going to get mad if I call you Canadian. Or maybe not mad, but you might be like, 'Why didn't you ask me first?' It's hard when people are talking bad about Mexicans, because when people are talking bad about Mexicans, that's for us too, because they think we are Mexicans. I don't want people to call me Mexican, but when Donald Trump talks on the news about how they are, we get involved too."

All Hector wants is a chance to be treated as an individual, following the rules and pursuing the American dream, and not be seen as a horrific stereotype from a xenophobic president. He says, "I like it here and get along with everyone. I work hard and don't get in trouble. It's not *all* of us, but he makes it seem like it's all of us."

If America isn't for Hector, a man working two jobs for low wages in order to escape extreme poverty and care for his family, well, then, who is it really for?

Oldham County

"If He's Not Going to Do Anything, He's Got to Go"

Oldham County has a median family income of more than $92,000. It's far and away the richest county in the commonwealth, where the median family income is only $48,000. Another thing about Oldham County—maybe this explains the statistic—is the location of many exquisite communities that are home to a lot of CEO types who work in bordering Louisville. Thanks in part to the desegregation of the Jefferson County schools and the accompanying busing program, many of the wealthiest families retreated outside the area and Oldham County became a popular landing spot for the most well-to-do. Money attracts money, and now a generation later it's home to some of the most elite neighborhoods in the state.

But I tend to feel uncomfortable around rich people. They dress better than I do, and because they get none of my professional wrestling references, we have little to say to each other. They just live a completely different life from mine, and our existences seem to be in two completely different worlds. I am not saying Oldham Countians are out of touch, but when you tell them it's time to change the oil, they say, "Extra virgin or white truffle?"*

My favorite part of Oldham County is the train that runs right down the middle of Main Street in its largest city, La Grange.† I think this bears clarification, as a lot of towns have trains running through them. But when I say this train runs through the center of La Grange, I mean this train *runs right through the center of La Grange*. As in mere feet from the parked cars on either side of Main Street upward of thirty times a day. You could literally be standing in front of Old Oak Frame House having a conversation, step off the curb, and potentially be hit by a train. It all seems very dangerous, to be honest. You're warned by the pleasant dinging of a bell, and moments later, here comes a giant blue-and-yellow CSX locomotive hauling fifty boxcars.‡ It's cool, sure, but it strikes the plaintiff's lawyer in me as a tort waiting to happen.

With all the excess coin floating around, La Grange looks like a picturesque town in Cape Cod. Every shop here is just a little bit nicer than similar shops on most Kentucky towns' Main Streets, from the upscale flea market called the Copper Awning (way nicer than most Kentucky flea markets . . . I didn't see one Hank Williams Jr. "Bocephus" flag), to the emblazoned brass-on-aged-wood shingle hanging over the door of the Ink Well tattoo parlor. In Oldham County, whatever the business, they make it classy.

La Grange is so aristocratic and quaint, in fact, that it looks like the setting for a Hallmark movie. And, in fact, it was. The movie *The Ultimate Legacy* aired on the Hallmark Channel in 2016. It centered around a narcissistic young man whose grandmother (Golden Globe winner Raquel Welch) will permit him to inherit the family fortune

---

* Matt has a joke for every county, but I don't tell Matt I know most of his come from *Parks and Recreation*. It's better that way.

† Matt also had a guy go to his truck and threaten to pull a gun on him in front of the courthouse in La Grange while he was filming a legal commercial for his old firm. He doesn't talk about it a lot. It might come out in the sequel.

‡ It's the most absurd train layout since *Silver Spoons*.

only if he adheres to a strict and loving moral code for a year. (Spoiler alert: he does.) It is as terrible as you would presume, but still a point of local pride.

Everyone in town tells us we have to meet Elsie Carter, a former mayor of La Grange for eight years and owner of the Metal Matrix, a futuristic industrial art shop, filled with cut metal pieces made into signs and sculptures. When we walk into her store, there's a Kathy Bates–esque woman behind the counter where Elsie might be.

"Well, I don't know," she responds. "She might be around here somewhere. Or she might have just left to go someplace. Can't really say."

Then she cracks a grin. "Just kidding. I'm it."

Immediately, you know the type. Elsie, as it turns out, is just as colorful as everyone says. Her aunt Pearl Carter Pace, the first female sheriff in the state of Kentucky, served as Republican chairwoman for Kentucky from 1948 to 1957 and was appointed by President Dwight Eisenhower to the War Claims Commission in 1953. Elsie comes from a long lineage of tough, successful women, and she wants me to know she's as Republican as it gets.

"I don't consider myself a Republican," she says, "I *am* a Republican."

Elsie is a die-hard Donald Trump supporter and a straight-ticket voter, to the point that if she suspects one of her customers is a Democrat, she'll troll them by going to the back and producing a giant "Trump 2020" flag. But she insists she isn't one of *those* Trump supporters who seek deliberately to antagonize. She's just joyous about life, about her town, and, yes, about her president. If it's GOP, it's for her, with one exception. Mitch McConnell. She's not a fan. Not anymore, at least.

"I had a restaurant here twenty years ago and threw a party for him in the back garden when he was running, and that was cool," Elsie explains. "But he's changed. I don't hate him, I just want him to do the right thing. I don't think he always does the right thing."

Elsie believes McConnell has completely forgotten about his constituents. "There are traitors everywhere," she says. "And I don't think he's a traitor, I just think he's evolved over time to where he's only taking care of himself. It's not about Kentucky. That's the atmosphere in Washington, though. It changes people."

Even though she is a politically active citizen in a wealthy county who once *threw a party* for the man—I mean, she's Mitch's key demographic, but still he doesn't care. Regular Republicans in Kentucky are no longer his constituency. Millionaires and billionaires are. She tells us a story about a grant for La Grange's historic district, written during her time as mayor, that needed sponsors. It was, as Elsie describes it, an impeccably written grant and was taken to McConnell for sponsorship consideration.

"We tried to call Mitch, but he didn't even respond. He didn't want to hear anything from us, and if you don't take care of the people, you don't deserve to be there," she says firmly.

Elsie's political rationale for disliking Mitch is probably different from mine (he doesn't help Trump enough, in her opinion), but her complaints about his lack of help for the community are familiar and bipartisan. It's a recurrent refrain we hear across the state, even from Republicans. Complacency, apathy, the flagrant dismissal of Kentuckians who reach out to him. They don't like him, they feel let down, yet they still vote for him—simply because they want someone who they think is capable of helping them. It doesn't matter that he doesn't; the potential is enough. They like the idea of having someone in that catbird seat, even though time after time he ignores requests for action, pawns constituents off on his army of aides, and refuses to even respond.

"Do you know why they vote for him?" Elsie asks rhetorically. "It's because he's the man who should be able to get things done—*if he will.* But if he's not going to do anything, he's got to go. I don't care who you are."

CHAPTER 4

Coal Country

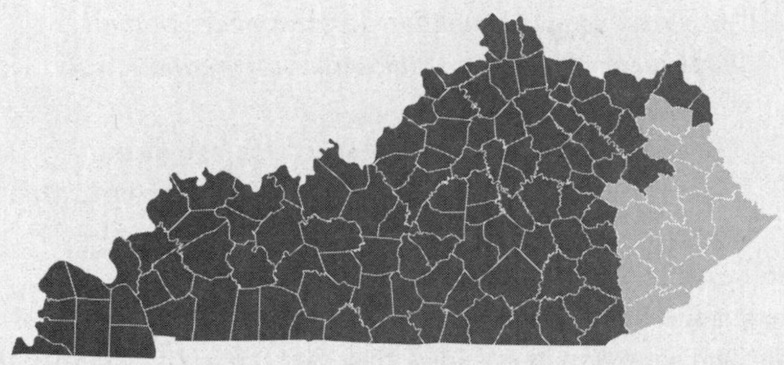

To understand Kentucky, you have to understand coal. Its impact on the state goes far beyond economics. Even at its peak, coal was not the main driver of the Kentucky economy. But its cultural and social relevance to the region extends far beyond the revenue it generates. The culture of Kentucky is tied to the eastern Kentucky mountains and the culture of the mountains is tied to coal.

I grew up in the mountains. I know firsthand that Mitch McConnell has been the most destructive political figure for eastern Kentucky in its modern history. While claiming to be a "Friend of Coal" (a political organization created on behalf of mine owners that, with strong marketing, became a rallying cry for the region), McConnell has single-handedly fought to end mine safety protections, eliminate miners' rights, and perpetuate the lie that coal will return to its past glory. In his time as the second most powerful person in America, the coal industry has collapsed. Not only has he done nothing to prevent its downfall, he has sold false hopes of its return to obscure his inability to help replace it. When the final history of coal mining in eastern Kentucky is written, McConnell will be one of its chief villains.

Leslie County

They took us to the scene of that disaster
I was so surprised to not find any sign of death at all
Just another country hillside with some mudholes and some junk
The mines were deadly silent like a rathole in the wall

—"Trip to Hyden" by Tom T. Hall

To get to Hyden, you have to *want* to get to Hyden.

It's not the kind of place where you're headed from one town to another, and all of a sudden realize "Oh, hey, I'm in Hyden. How about that?" To get to Hyden, you have to make a concerted effort to arrive, navigating a county with town names such as Thousandsticks and Hell for Certain. After you head down Highway 80 past the Begley Lumber Company, This-N-That Indoor Flea Market, and a road called Tim Couch Pass (named for the favorite son who grew up playing in these mountain hills and went on to start five seasons as quarterback for the Cleveland Browns, who made him the top pick in the 1999 NFL draft),* you will arrive in the small Leslie County community. The county courthouse sets the county's mood with two large embossed signs warning "No Spitting in the Water Fountain" and "No Cigarette Butts in the Urinals."†

October is the best time to come to Hyden. There aren't many places in the United States more enamored with Halloween than Hyden. Even

---

* If you are an NFL fan, you are probably going to make a snide remark about Tim Couch. Well, don't. We love him, and he is still the most successful Browns QB since the second franchise was granted in 1999.

† Conversely, you are allowed to spit in the urinals, but still no cigarette butts in the water fountain.

though the holiday is still a couple weeks away, Main Street is decorated with pumpkins, painted windows, and banners. A gaggle of chatty nurses are turning their storefront into the Ghostbusters' headquarters (complete with a mural of the character Slimer) and tell us that Halloween gives the community a sense of pride, especially now that it is overseen by Mayor Carol Joseph.

We visit Mayor Joseph in her office, which is decked to the nines in skeletons, monsters, and ghosts, one of which triggers loud, hysterical, screeching laughter as I activate its sensor by sitting down on a chair. Joseph is a former teacher, which explains a lot of this commitment to décor, as well as her leadership style. In a town that has experienced more than its fair share of hardship over the years, Carol is the type of person who keeps the spirits up and the excitement flowing. Everyone in town tells us she's a great mayor, and when I ask her why, she laughs. "Well, I should be, because I work really hard. I've worked harder at this job than at any job I've ever had. My daughter moved here and I saw her three times in three months. I guess I'm married to the city of Hyden." Her phone rings and rings. It's another person calling asking the plan for this year's trick-or-treat. Because in Hyden, when you want to know when trick-or-treating begins, you can call the mayor directly and she tells you.*

Hyden's obsession with Halloween is fitting for a place that has always done things its own way. During the height of the coal boom, in the decades following World War II, most of eastern Kentucky coal mining was carried out in union mines, leading all the counties to be staunchly Democratic. Not in Leslie County. It remained nonunion and Republican, traits that left it unique in the mountains and an object of suspicion by many in other counties. The love of the GOP was so strong here that Richard Nixon chose Hyden for his first public appearance after he'd resigned the presidency in disgrace in 1974 rather than face impeachment for his role in the Watergate scandal. A local Republican donor was such a fan he persuaded the county to build the Richard M. Nixon Recreation Center and Gym to honor the defrocked president. On June 2, 1978, Nixon came to tiny Hyden, followed by the world's

---

* Someone please try this in New York City with Bill de Blasio.

press corps, eager to witness the reception for the return of "Tricky Dick" to public life. Natives still remember it as the most exciting day in Hyden history, and the Rec Center still bears his name.*

Nixon's visit came eight years after the most traumatic event in Leslie County history: the Hurricane Creek (pronounced "hurr-uh-cun") Mine Disaster. In December 1970 a coal dust explosion rocked the Finley Mine, causing the death of thirty-eight of the thirty-nine miners inside at the time. The thirty-ninth, blown sixty feet from the mountain and into a road, was the only one who lived to tell the tale. The Finley Mine was nonunion and, prior to the explosion, had racked up thirty-four safety violations within three months of its opening. It was even labeled an "imminent danger" by the US Bureau of Mines just one month before the accident. Even after giving the designation, the bureau neglected to close the mine, only scheduling a follow-up inspection that never occurred due to a lack of inspectors.

As one of the deadliest coal mining accidents in America's history, it shocked the entire nation. The country's focus on the tragedy, described in the Tom T. Hall song "Trip to Hyden," and the passage of the Federal Coal Mine Health and Safety Act (following an even deadlier explosion that killed seventy-eight miners in West Virginia) just a year prior made the event a national focus. Mayor Joseph takes us through winding roads to the Hurricane Creek Mine Memorial, a sobering, solitary remembrance. Deep in these Leslie County mountains, the memorial showcases thirty-eight bronzed mining helmets, hanging on wooden posts, each bearing the name of one of the dead miners. A cursory view hammers home not only the scale of the tragedy but also its enormous effect on such a small community. Many families lost multiple relatives. The victims included four Collinses, three Couches, three Hensons, and three Wagerses. Among the killed were twin brothers, a man and two brothers-in-law, and many other individual tragedies, each commemorated beneath a polished statue of a coal miner. At its center, a plaque honors the miners "who gave so much so that future generations may benefit with a better life." It's beautiful and heartbreaking.

* Leslie County schoolchildren still play the popular recess game "Find the Tapes."

If you aren't from Appalachia, it would be very easy to look at this tragedy and think, "Who on earth would *want* to work in a coal mine?" I can understand the question. Even though I grew up in the area, it's one I've asked myself at times as well. But for people in the mountains this isn't a reflective calculation. Mining isn't good or bad, it just is. It is (or at least was) an available, well-paying job that at some point became a profession. It allowed you to support your family and better their lives while staying in the hills you loved, where your family roots were strong. Coal mining in this area was a profession celebrated by the community. Honest, hard work that provided not only income but also energy for this isolated area. The memorial at Hurricane Creek, and the words emblazoned on it, are an example of the truth that politicians outside the mountains have never understood. Coal mining isn't just a job, it's a way of life. The safety of the mine at Hurricane Creek was ignored in the quest for the almighty dollar, and thirty-eight men, their families, and a community were left with suffering that still lingers nearly fifty years later. But even here, in this spot of such destruction, the memorial to the terror of the mines celebrates the practice of coal mining. The fabric of eastern Kentucky culture includes coal, and even with its inherent dangers, it's a part of who we are.

Letcher County

"Last I Checked, He Was Sleeping with Your Boss"

There aren't many places in America like Whitesburg, in Letcher County, and that's a shame. In a state full of isolated rural enclaves, Whitesburg is maybe the most unique. The sign outside of town (which has a large sponsored RC Cola logo on it) says "Welcome to Whitesburg, Kentucky: Population 1,534 Friendly People Plus 2 Grouches."*

* It used to say "1 Grouch," and then a woman called and complained the sign gave the town a bad image. So, the man who put it up climbed up to it and changed it from a *1* to a *2*.

It's a haul to the nearest interstate (probably I-26 in Tennessee), but the best way to enter is up Highway 119, where at the top of Pine Mountain you'll find the prettiest, most panoramic view of the Appalachian Mountains anywhere in their existence.

I love Whitesburg because it represents the best of America. The people here have very diverse backgrounds and viewpoints yet they work together peacefully and happily for the greater good of the community. Letcher County is most certainly Trump Country; driving into Whitesburg, I counted four houses with Trump flags hanging on them on the major highway alone (one house had three, one on each visible door). It is a place that loves Jesus, guns, the Kentucky Wildcats, and Trump, in that order, and all four are to be respected.

However, it's also the location of one of the most progressive pockets of Kentuckians outside of a major city in the entire state. Parts of downtown Whitesburg look like they could be a small liberal arts college town in Vermont. On first pass, I notice a rainbow-banded flag flying unabashedly on a Main Street business and the sound of loud European pop music emanating from the Roundabout Music Company on the corner. Summit City, a local restaurant, flashes a neon sign in the window: "Coffee & Art," and inside both seem to be in abundance. It is unlike any other Main Street in Kentucky, and illustrates that Whitesburg is just different.

For further proof, you need look no further than Appalshop, a media, arts, and education center located right here in the heart of the Appalachian Mountains. Appalshop occupies a large, avant-garde wooden building that houses a theater and a radio station. It has existed for fifty years as an under-the-radar headquarters for some of Appalachia's most progressive filmmakers, artists, and musicians. Think Andy Warhol's New York City studio the Factory, only with bluegrass music and a mountain accent.*

Herby Smith, one of the founding members of Appalshop, is showing us around on this drizzly early-fall evening. With his wry sense of humor, long, white hair, and white handlebar moustache, he has a bit of a Jerry Garcia vibe to him; he looks like at any given moment, he might

* Less coke, more 'shine.

break out a banjo, whittle on his front porch—or hand you an edible. His excitement about Appalshop is infectious. Walking us past photos of bluegrass icons Ralph Stanley and Alison Krauss, Herby fills us in on Appalshop's unique history. It began in 1969, when New York City's Community Film Council, in conjunction with Los Angeles's American Film Institute, set out to establish local film workshops around the country in order to help procure funding from the National Endowment for the Arts.

"They realized if they were going to continue to get federal money, they would have to get a diversity of people," explains Herby, "that the people behind the cameras couldn't just be white men from urban areas, they had to have a more diverse group of people making the media. We realized there was all of the media—*The Beverly Hillbillies, Hee Haw, The Dukes of Hazzard*—one after another, promoting all these images of who people thought hillbillies were. So, we set out to make something different. We felt like our job was to show, for mountain people, their world as they see it."

A community of hippie types in the late 1960s setting up shop in rural Whitesburg—it's a premise that seemingly could have been a sitcom in its own right. But the town realized quickly that the eclectic filmmakers wouldn't be a problem. "A lot of them realized, 'Yeah, they have these strange ideas, but don't worry about it; they're good people who pay their bills,'" Herby says with a grin. They also came to discover that Appalshop was there to help tell their story. Since those early days, it has become the place to learn about mountain life from actual mountain voices.* Its documentaries, with topics ranging from coal miners' strikes to the lifestyles of the most isolated in the mountains, each paint a picture of eastern Kentucky that's both unique and refreshing. In a world where being a "hillbilly" is seen as a pejorative, Appalshop showcases mountain life at its fullest and is a truly special resource.

Herby walks me through the town, the sun dipping behind the nearby mountains, to see Wes Addington. An attorney who hails from a family of local coal miners, Addington is executive director of the

* A better source than the TV series *Justified*, which was great, but isn't totally realistic. We don't drink that much moonshine for breakfast.

Appalachian Citizens' Law Center, a small nonprofit law firm that represents miners and their families regarding black lung disease and mine safety issues. He works tirelessly to draw attention to the health issues faced by miners and former miners, whom he feels have gone unprotected over the years by their employers.

The worst of these issues is black lung, the severe inflammation of the lungs due to long-term exposure to coal dust. Because the body cannot break down the toxic particles, they build up in the lungs, incapacitating respiration over time. "Severe black lung is worse than it's ever been in the United States," Addington says, shaking his head. "That's a nineteenth-century disease. We know how to prevent it—you just have to limit exposure to dust—but the miners never get that help. It's simple as that. So now even though the government is supposed to be watching this, we've got guys that are dying. I mean, we're getting some guys in their late thirties with terminal lung disease because of this job."

At one point, black lung was said to affect more than 30 percent of all coal workers in the United States. In the central Appalachian region, cases are currently at a twenty-five-year high, and with more sophisticated early diagnosis available, the number is expected to keep rising.

"You have deep-sea fishing that we see on TV, and that has really high fatality rates," Addington points out. "But in coal mining, there have been over a hundred thousand coal miners die on the job in this country." He believes employers have either ignored or affirmatively caused black lung, even accusing some of monkeying with coal dust samplings before regulators would test them for exposure. "There are things that are done underground," he adds, "that would have people prosecuted for manslaughter if they were done in the sun."

Addington, like many who work to help coal miners stricken with black lung, has little positive to say about Mitch McConnell. The senator's record on mine safety has been well documented: he has virtually always sided with mine owners over workers. Bob Murray, CEO of Murray Energy, until recently one of the nation's largest coal companies; his company; and his company's political action committee (also called Murray Energy) have together donated more than $7 million to candidates, almost exclusively Republicans ($330,000 to McConnell himself). In the notes of one meeting we had with mine safety officials, Murray was quoted as insinuating that they should be careful because of his warm relationship with McConnell: "Mitch McConnell calls me one of the five finest men in America, and the last I checked, he was sleeping with your boss." That boss, of course, being Elaine Chao, then the secretary of labor.

The brazenness of the comment is infuriating. One of coal's biggest barons felt empowered to say that because of his relationship with Mitch, regulators were beholden to him, not the safety of miners. He likely felt emboldened because for decades the coal industry has flooded McConnell with campaign donations. They expect return on their investment in the form of lax safety standards across the mining industry. That expectation has been met again, again, and again.

McConnell's attitude toward coal miner safety may be best summarized by Bill Banig, the director of governmental affairs for the United Mine Workers of America. He notes that the group counts a number of Republican and Democratic senators as champions of miners, willing to tour mines and promote safety legislation. But not McConnell. "He's not done anything to help us with mine safety. It does seem odd, given the state that he represents."

Pike County

"He Feels Like Nobody Can Bring Him Down. I Am Sure Gonna Try."

Pike County is beautiful, nestled deep in the Appalachian Mountains. The largest county in Kentucky by area, Pike's 786 square miles include some of the most remote sections of the entire state. The mountains are steep, the hollers are deep, and the hardworking people there are among the kindest folks in the entire state. They have spent their lives toiling too hard, often with not near enough in return. Even though this is the place that gave the world half of the violent Hatfield and McCoy families' feud in the late nineteenth century, if I had to choose anywhere in Kentucky to be stranded because my car broke down, it would be Pike County. I know I'd be sure to get a helping hand.*

Few counties in America have been hit harder by the decline of coal than Pike County. It was Kentucky's leading coal producer for nearly fifty years, but now production has decreased by nearly 75 percent since 2000. Accordingly, the population has cratered from eighty-two thousand at its peak in 1980 to just fifty-eight thousand now. It's an effect that has been noticed all over Pike County and it makes life here a struggle for many. Diana, a middle-aged woman in a UK basketball hoodie standing outside the post office, explains, "In its heyday, coal was a wonderful thing. Kids would grow up and see their daddy carry a lunch pail to the mines, and then they grew up and that's what they knew, so that's what they did. You could have a good life. Now people just live day to day. It's just really hard."

Losing coal has also been a tremendous hit to the local tax base, limiting the amount of money available for local services such as roads and education. The exodus of the mining industry has dramatically decreased the "coal severance" money: a tax created by the Kentucky State Legislature to force coal mining companies to pay a tribute on the land they mine due to the fact that the mineral resources they extract can never be replenished. These taxes formed the backbone of local public spending, and their dramatic decrease has left many counties struggling to provide even basic governmental needs.

It's another example of how this region continually faces systemic problems that make their progress difficult. It has become common in recent years for books such as J. D. Vance's *Hillbilly Elegy* to place the blame on the Appalachian people and their culture for the region's struggles. But such arguments are insulting and overlook the region's historical difficulties. Few groups have worked harder for less reward and been forgotten more quickly than the people of Appalachia.

---

* As opposed to some other places on this trip where, if our car had broken down, I would have told Matt to abandon the car, run, and buy a new one when the sun came up.

That is why there was such anger here when a group of miners recently traveled from eastern Kentucky to Washington, DC, to speak with federal legislators about the Black Lung Disability Trust Fund and the Coal Miner's Pension Fund. Both funds, which are intended to help ensure black lung benefits and pensions for miners if the companies they work for go out of business, have had a rough few years. Multiple bankruptcies have depleted the funds, causing Senator Joe Manchin of West Virginia, a Democrat, to propose the American Mines Act, which would have replenished the funds with money from other mining tax sources. The bill should have been uncontroversial, as it has bipartisan support and takes care of the miners who helped bring energy to America. But due to his allegiance to the big coal companies, Mitch McConnell refused to call a vote on the bill and held it up for nearly a year.

Think about that for a second: McConnell represents the state with more coal miners in need of the funds than any other but was the one senator who refused to allow it *to come to a vote*. Manchin was particularly furious, saying McConnell was "the sole person that is blocking a vote on my amendment to the NDAA [NDAA is the acronym for the National Defense Authorization Act] that would secure coal miner's health care and pensions. Our coal miners," he continued, "are running out of time, and I refuse to play Mitch McConnell's political games with their lives."*

McConnell's obstruction led the miners to go to Washington in August 2019 to help stir action. Jimmy Moore, the president of the Black Lung Association of Southeastern Kentucky, was present for that trip, which the Appalachian Citizens' Law Center helped to fund through regional donations and sponsors. A Greyhound Bus was loaded up, and the group of displaced and slighted miners was on their way to make their voices heard.

They spoke with a number of legislators on the trip, and most, according to Moore, listened to their plans. But there was one notable exception. As about thirty-five miners gathered in a large room waiting

---

* It's worth noting that just prior to the publication of this book and after a year of delay, McConnell eventually signed on to allow a similar bill to proceed. The fact that he did so to kick off his election year campaign I am sure is only coincidental.

for the powerful senator from their state, Mitch found a way to fail to meet their already low expectations.

Moore sets the scene:

"McConnell came into the room, he walked down and introduced himself, and we asked him about black lung and miners' pensions. He said, 'We've got a plan—we don't know exactly what it is yet—but we've got a plan.' Well, we asked, 'What is your plan?' and he repeated, 'We don't know what it is yet, but we've got a plan.'"

And with that, Senator Mitch McConnell, our man in Washington and friend of the coal miners, left. Just . . . left. After sixty seconds.

"That's what we was left with," says Moore sadly. "I came out of it feeling like an idiot, coming all the way up there and spending my time trying to talk to him. It's like it just goes into the wind, it just evaporates, and goes on out. It doesn't go anywhere."

Moore, in addition to suffering from black lung himself, was there also to represent his adult son, who has such a complicated case of the disease that he couldn't even make the trip. For Jimmy Moore, going to Washington, DC, could not have been more personal.

And he got *one minute*.

"What I would have loved for him to have done is to have come in there and recognize us," says Moore. "That we were from eastern Kentucky, and that he understood what black lung is, and that he understood we had a promise with our miners' pension, and that, most of all, he understands each one of our stories. He could've stayed in there thirty minutes and had a little bit of compassion for us after we'd traveled ten hours on a bus and stayed all night to meet him. All he needed to say was, 'Jimmy, I understand your son's got a mass on his lungs that's gonna grow and grow until it smothers him down to where he can't breathe, and he dies. I have compassion for you for that.'"

Some have defended McConnell's actions by pointing to how busy the senator is in his role as majority leader. But that explanation doesn't work for Moore. "I don't think there was an emergency that came up," Moore tells me. "He just didn't want to be with us; he didn't want to be connected with eastern Kentucky. I could ask anybody in that room, 'What has Mitch McConnell done for eastern Kentucky?' Nothing I know of."

However, the retired miner and advocate left with resolve. "He feels like nobody can bring him down," Moore says. "I'm sure gonna try."

Floyd County

"Well, That's What Christianity Is Supposed to Be About, Isn't It?"

I didn't expect to have a moment of enlightenment while walking around on an October Tuesday night in downtown Prestonsburg in Floyd County. We came to the town late, hoping to find somewhere interesting to have dinner and learn about an area that has seen a severe decline in recent years.

Shops are beginning to close up for the night, and as the sun drops behind the mountains, the view is gorgeous. The now near-empty streets show little movement absent lights from a lone old-school barbershop, complete with the candy cane pole and window full of older gentlemen shooting the breeze. If there is one thing I have learned from being in small towns, it's that barbershops are where you find out what is truly happening. So we make our way inside.*

Walking inside Wright's Barber Shop is like entering a time machine and being transported to Floyd's Barber Shop in Mayberry, from *The Andy Griffith Show*. Aged wallpaper covers the area behind posters, signs, and mirrors unchanged since what looks like the late sixties. The floors are linoleum and four big steel swiveling barber chairs sit on each side. There are old magazines, read and reread, and a giant bucket of bubble gum for kids able to sit still long enough for their fathers to get them haircuts. The scene is familiar for any male who grew up in the rural heartland, and if you did, you totally know the décor by heart. Here, at least, it hasn't changed since you left it.

We're ten minutes from the opening prayer of the Wright's Barber

---

* It was either this barbershop or Sassy N' Peaches Clothing and Décor (which is a real place).

Shop Men's Bible Club, which meets weekly to discuss a new chapter of the Bible. The men welcome us in, gesture for us to sit in two empty barber chairs, and then continue to chat as they wait for their leader to arrive. The barbers have long since gone home for the day, leaving these men to lock up. The men are funny, as old men sitting around barbershops tend to be, and—as old men sitting around barbershops tend to do—they talk about the good old days of Prestonsburg.

"I remember as a kid coming into Prestonsburg, and if you ever wanted to see anyone who lived in this town, you'd come sit on that wall out there, and eventually they'd walk by," says Richard Price, a substance abuse counselor and the baby of the group at sixty-three years old. "It was a vibrant town, a prosperous town, but then small towns started dying around here."

"It sure makes me sad," sighs seventy-six-year-old Mike Craft.

"Prestonsburg's on life support," Price says. "It's on a ventilator, and the power is running out. We're not getting any industry; when Lyndon Johnson declared the War on Poverty, we got a shot in the arm we thought would revitalize everything—but it was just euthanasia."

The study group, which I learn was founded twenty-three years ago by the barbershop's owner, Gary Wright (who passed away just months earlier but is commemorated by a large, pomaded portrait on the wall), was meant to bring people together, and politics too often divides. The six men are of varying political ideologies but find cohesion in their Bible meetings. "We try to keep politics out of this, because it's a Bible study," says Craft, "but this is eastern Kentucky, so anything you see or do, politics is involved a little."

Politics is a hot topic here today because even though Prestonsburg is very small, one of its native sons is running for state attorney general. Democrat Greg Stumbo is controversial here (for reasons ranging from his supposed liberalism to the amount of time he spends in Lexington instead of Prestonburg), but at one point he was Kentucky's Speaker of the House. I assume he would have some fans in the room. I ask how many people plan to vote for him in a few weeks in the AG race, and no hands rise. I am a little surprised, and when I ask why, one man blurts out, "'Cuz we *know him*!" The room echoes with cackling laughter, as if he'd said aloud what everyone else was thinking.

I ask the group how Mitch McConnell has treated the area.

Seventy-four-year-old Gary Brown, sitting up in one of the barber chairs, exclaims, "He's a rat!," which sets everyone laughing again.

"Why, he won't do anything for this part of the state," says Gary. "He'll come to coal miner rallies in Pikeville and stay two minutes. Two minutes! That's not giving them people justice. Nothing."

Before I get a chance to ask more, the suspendered Brother Paul Burke, tonight's study leader, arrives, hobbling in with his cane. He greets everyone and takes a seat at the front of the shop. Political talk is suddenly and reverentially over. I understand, but it's a bit of a shame, because I think it was just about to get good!

Gary Brown gets up and strolls over to a stack of Bibles in the corner, then hands one to me and one to Chris. Not fresh, brand-new Bibles. Not hardcover, the church-just-bought-a-bunch-of-new-Bibles Bibles, but worn and tattered Bibles. These are studied Bibles. Mine uses as a bookmark a baby announcement postcard from thirteen years ago. We're invited to stay and participate—tonight's verse is the book of Mark, chapter 4, about the sower and the seeds—and we do, reading aloud when it's our turn.

I don't remember much about the specifics of what the men said, but I was struck by the camaraderie and the fellowship. Here was a group of six men, none younger than sixty, who see two random guys walking the streets (and, honestly, looking haggard after weeks on the road*) and they invite them to sit and be a part of their group Bible study, no questions asked. They don't know us, but they treat us as equals and as people whose lives and opinions have worth. As we leave, I thank them for their hospitality and for letting strangers be a part of their night.

Mike Craft looks at me with a smile and says, "Well, that's what Christianity's supposed to be about, isn't it?"

---

* We didn't smell great, either. *I* certainly wouldn't have invited us in.

Martin County

"He Could Have at Least Lied to Me"

In one unscripted moment in January 2018, Martin County went viral and entered the national spotlight.

At an emergency meeting of the county's Fiscal Court, the gallery was packed with more than 1,400 citizens who were unhappy, to put it mildly, over nightly shutdowns of the local water supply. Homes had little to no water at all, sometimes for hours at a time. Judge-executive Kelly Callaham declared a countywide state of emergency and said he wasn't sure when full water service would be restored. That's when Gary Michael Hunt, an imposing man seated at a bench in a navy blue T-shirt, black suspenders, and ball cap, decided he couldn't sit there and listen to any more.

Hunt rose from his seat, shook his finger at the county water board executives, and told them what he thought. His family needed water. He was tired of being screwed around by the county and not receiving even the most basic of public utilities. His voice rose as he threw in some curse words and began advancing toward the bench at the front of the room. He didn't stop until a Kentucky State Trooper powerfully grabbed him by the throat and ejected him from the courtroom. The video of the confrontation made the rounds across the state. What happened in Martin County that led to a moment like this?

To understand how this evening came to be, we have to go back to the terrible environmental accident in Martin County on October 11, 2000. A nearby seventy-two-acre impoundment (a collection of coal waste) owned by Massey Energy broke through the ground and sent some 306 million pounds of coal slurry—liquidized coal waste from mining operations—gushing into the Tug Fork River. This impoundment failure and spill, thirty times greater than that of 1989's well-documented *Exxon Valdez* oil spill, but with a fraction of the national media coverage, contained arsenic and mercury. The toxic combination not only killed all life in the river but also contaminated the drinking water of twenty-seven thousand residents. Because the Tug Fork River supplies much of the county its water, the tainted sludge infiltrated the pipes used by the nearby Martin County Water Treatment Plant, compromising it immediately. The county seat of Inez and the tinier ones surrounding it were left without clean, drinkable water.

The Mine Safety and Health Administration (MSHA) began an investigation, but, following the declaration of George W. Bush as president by the US Supreme Court, it was abruptly closed. In the new Bush administration, the person put in charge of overseeing the investigation was Mitch McConnell's wife and newly appointed labor secretary, Elaine Chao. From there, things moved quickly. Prior to Chao's appointment, investigators had anticipated hundreds of thousands of dollars in fines and were considering pushing for charges of willful and criminal negligence. The accident, which poisoned nearly an entire county's water supply, was determined by investigators—better sit down for this—to warrant federal fines totaling only *$5,600*. A slap on the wrist, *barely*. Not surprisingly, Jack Spadaro, one of the investigators on the job prior to Chao's appointment, has expressed the view that McConnell was the driving force behind crippling the investigation. The fact that coal industry donations to Republicans tripled in 2000 from the previous presidential election suggests he is probably correct.

Fast-forward to nearly twenty years later. Though an alleged "cleanup" was performed according to EPA standards, the pipes supplying water to parts of the county were still permanently damaged. The aged facility became inoperable in many places, and the local water board was forced to intravenously shut off service to various parts of the county. A number of citizens, many of them poverty stricken, ended up without water for days or weeks at a time. The impoverished county, already struggling due to the lack of coal severance money, was left without funds to begin the massive work needed to repair the treatment facility. The citizens of Martin County faced a full-fledged water crisis. If water was available at all, it often emerged from their taps brown or yellow with sediment; many children couldn't even bathe in it, and there were serious concerns that the water could be dangerously toxic. It was an all-systems failure, caused by the neglect of a coal company that wasn't even around anymore to help fix it.

So that's why Gary Michael Hunt had finally had enough.

At the time, on *Hey Kentucky!* (the McGrath camp had not yet ridded me of my television program), we aired the viral video of Hunt's ousting from the Fiscal Court meeting. Our viewers were shocked. Most people equated the idea of not having access to water as a problem that only occurred in the world's most undeveloped countries. It couldn't be happening here in Kentucky. After all, Inez here in Martin County was where Lyndon Johnson first declared the War on Poverty in 1964; it was unimaginable that fifty years later, the very land he stood on would now see its water supply so contaminated that it was unusable. Even the nearby federal prison refused water from the poisoned supply and procured it elsewhere; the federal government knew its level of contamination and made sure the outside prisoners at least had healthier water than the citizens of Martin County.

To call attention to the problem, our show conducted an investigation of the crisis. We met Asher Maynard, an elderly man living in a tiny trailer deep in the county. When we entered his tight quarters, the water was so filthy that he couldn't even wash his hair. Maynard turned on the spigot as we spoke, and little more than a pithy stream of water no wider than a pencil leaked from the faucet. Sometimes, he explained, it would come on a little more than that; sometimes not at all. When he could get it, he'd tirelessly fill empty gallon milk jugs with the dirty water just to clean himself or try to cook some food. He said he didn't understand why the county couldn't afford to provide its citizens water. But he had no other options so he had to try to get by.

Our reports on *Hey Kentucky!* were able to shine a small spotlight on this plight, which attracted the attention of the state and some help to the county. Donations of clean water poured in from around Kentucky. Environmental activist Erin Brockovich (known for the eponymously titled film dramatizing her battle against a California electric company, which won actress Julia Roberts an Oscar for her portrayal) saw our report and sent the environmental group she works with to intervene and do what they could to help. Movement began in the state capital of Frankfort to try to find solutions.

Jimmy Don Kerr was one of those tapped to serve on the county's new water board and try to fix the mess. "It was one of those situations where I was reluctant to come on, because I knew it wasn't good," he says. "One of those situations where you realized the bed was on fire when you jumped in, you just didn't realize how high the flames were.

"Our first meeting was a room full of people, and we had to have the sheriff's office there because the temperatures were so high," he recalls. "I literally couldn't go to a ballgame. I couldn't go to the post office. I couldn't go to the supermarket. I couldn't go anywhere without getting jumped on, and I had literally been on the board for a month. I had nothing to do with any of the past stuff, but I was the face of it. They needed a villain, so it became me."

Kerr knew that the crisis simply could not be fixed locally. It was too big. So he began looking to the state and federal government for help. State and federal officials from both parties reached out to offer sympathy or help with finding solutions, save one.

Guess who?

"During this water situation, I heard from Governor Bevin; I heard from Congressman Hal Rogers; I heard from our state representative, Chris Harris; I heard from Rand Paul's office. I heard from everybody at some point. I don't recall ever hearing from Mitch McConnell. He could have at least *lied* to me and said, 'We'll get you some federal help.'"

"He could have at least lied to me." Expectations for Mitch McConnell are so low that not only is help not expected but it's assumed it won't occur at all. But the desperation just to be heard makes flat-out lies better than blatant disregard.

When people ask me why I am considering running for Senate, I often talk about Martin County. After generations gave their labor and their lives for the mining of coal, a company's negligent (at best) behavior drains them of their most basic needs, and the federal government does nothing but look the other way. The company causing the disaster doesn't care and the political bribery of Mitch McConnell gives him no moral compulsion to act. Elaine Chao helped sweep under the rug an environmental disaster to protect a company and industry that has helped fuel her husband's political success. Some two decades later, the same community loses its drinkable water. The state is full of examples of McConnell regularly ignoring its needs, but this one is particularly egregious. In their toughest moments, the people of Martin County deserve someone who cares about their well-being and will fight for their basic dignity. Mitch McConnell has never been that person.

Perry County

Friend of Coal

If you are traveling down Highway 80 in Perry County, I highly recommend you stop at Clark's First & Last Chance Liquor. Either you are headed to Perry County and you are dying for a sip of bourbon. Or you are headed to Leslie County, and, knowing you are entering a dry county, need to stock up on bourbon before you arrive. And no matter which direction you're headed, sometimes—like this day—there are two chickens fighting a dog in the parking lot, which is quite a sight to see.*

Let me make something clear from the top: Hazard, the largest town in Perry County, is not—and I repeat, *not*—the Hazard from the TV show *The Dukes of Hazzard*. Everyone in Hazard would like you to know that in advance, so you won't make some stupid joke about it when you meet them. That Hazzard, spelled with *two* *z*s, for starters, was fictional and in Georgia. This Hazard is real and beautifully surrounded by the mountains of eastern Kentucky. There is no 1969 Dodge Charger nicknamed the General Lee, nor is there a Boss Hogg; but there is a Mother Goose House, which, bizarrely, features a roof in the shape of a gigantic goose. Completed in 1940, the home was built to scale using an actual goose skeleton, with the goose's neck and beak protruding over the front. I drive by it on every trip to Hazard, and it's as weird as it sounds.

The reason for its existence is, not surprisingly, also strange. In 1935 George Stacy was eating goose with his family for dinner, when he saw the carcass left on the table after they finished. He looked at his

* The chickens seemed to have the early advantage.

wife and said, "Honey, I'm going to build you a goose house to match that." And he did. She would have probably preferred jewelry.

Culturally, Hazard is uniquely mountain. Take the Hampton Inn, for example. In early 2019 an employee of the Hazard hotel brought a lawsuit against his employer alleging he was being punished for disobeying his supervisor's orders. You are probably thinking, How can someone sue for that? You don't do what your boss says, you suffer the consequences. Except in this case, the man's superior insisted he undergo an *exorcism* to expel the dark forces causing him to consider a divorce from his wife. According to the claimant, when he refused, his supervisor changed his shift and even had members of her church assemble in the hotel lobby and pray for him while customers were checking in—which, as you might imagine, could be a little awkward. I am fairly certain exorcisms are not specifically approved of in the Hampton Inn employees manual.*

Hazard is the home of WYMT television, the only major network-affiliated television station in the mountains. It is one of the most popular local stations in America, and the most utilized news source in all of eastern Kentucky. Its placement here has caused Hazard to be a centralized hub for the regional politics of coal. For instance, take the 1997 visit by a liberal Democrat from Minnesota, Senator Paul Wellstone. It's a story told to me by Tony Oppegard, who at the time was the directing attorney of the Mine Safety Project, a public interest law office that represented miners in legal actions related to mine safety. Wellstone visited Hazard to make the plight of coal miners a national issue and in so doing, he highlighted the difference in priorities between he and McConnell.

"Wellstone was considering running for the Democratic presidential nomination, and he was retracing the steps of Bobby Kennedy's poverty tour," Oppegard tells me. "I got a call from Wellstone's staff telling me the senator was coming to eastern Kentucky. They'd been given my name, and they were wondering if I could arrange for him to meet with coal miners. So I organized it. There were maybe a dozen

* I do always stay at Hampton Inn because of the terrific complimentary continental exorcisms from 7:00–9:30 a.m.

of us. We had one widow of a man who had been electrocuted in Pike County, and the rest of them were coal miners.

"We had the meeting at city hall," Tony recalls, "and the same day Wellstone met with the miners in Hazard, Mitch McConnell was meeting with coal operators an hour away in Pikeville. It was very emblematic: here we have a senator from Minnesota who cared more about mine safety than the senator from Kentucky did. McConnell never did anything for mine safety and health, and was not the kind of man who meets with coal miners."

McConnell's focus has always been on mine owners, his one true coal constituency. He gave them all the time they needed, the support they desired, and the friendship they utilized to avoid regulation. While the Kentucky senator proclaims often and loudly that he is a "Friend of Coal,"* that friendship has never extended to the miners injured in work-related accidents, those crippled with black lung, or those seeking to have their health and pension benefits restored. For those men, McConnell's time is too valuable. He has bigger fish to fry, and those fish have large checkbooks.†

At the Wellstone meeting, miners told the Minnesota politician about their difficult jobs, safety issues, and health struggles. The Midwestern senator from a state almost a thousand miles away showed more compassion that day than their senator down the road ever had. Aides said he would later recount that it was one of his most powerful meetings ever as a US senator. Wellstone was killed in a small plane crash in 2002, along with his wife and one of his three children, but that day changed how the local mining community would forever remember him.

"Wellstone told the miners there, 'I'm not going to forget about you, and I will be an advocate for you in the US Senate,'" Oppegard says. "And after that day, he was."

---

* Definitely "friends with benefits."

† And keep their money in river banks.

Harlan County

"He's Not Pro-Coal. I Don't Even Think He's Pro-Kentucky."

July 1, 2019, began as a typical Monday at the Blackjewel coal mine in Cumberland, Kentucky. The first shift worked its regular eight hours below ground; the second shift followed. However, after two hours, the second-shift employees were told abruptly to go home for the day. For miner Colin Cornette, who had worked at the mine for eleven years, the work disruption was odd, but he wasn't too concerned. "We were used to that company kind of being late on their bills and checks. I wasn't too worried, because I knew that was just how they were."

Things changed two days later. That Wednesday, the 320 Harlan County miners began to hear from their local banks that the paychecks they had received the previous Friday for the last two weeks of work had been pulled back by the mine, and the money would no longer be available in their accounts. For miners who had child support or arrears taken out of their paychecks, those would not be forwarded, and they would be in automatic violation of the provisions. Concern spread among the mining families, as it quickly became clear this was a different scenario from before. The miners suspected that Blackjewel mine CEO Jeff Hoops was to blame.

Cornette noted, "Men go down in that mine every day and put their life on the line for that man to make money, and we knew he was trying to scam us."

Two weeks later, with the men still not back to work and the wages still not paid, rumors began to spread that Blackjewel was sending trains to the mine to pick up the last of the coal for takeaway. The miners were furious. They'd mined that coal and hadn't been paid for their labor. Five men decided to take action. They went to the train tracks and stood there, using their bodies to block the coal train from passing.

Their resistance ignited an organized fight for workers' rights that Harlan County hadn't seen in nearly a generation. This county was the site of a violent coal miner's strike in 1973–74 against Eastover Coal Company, which was the subject of the Oscar-winning documentary *Harlan County, USA.* So when I first visited the protest site a few weeks after it began, I wasn't surprised to see a community standing together with a singular purpose. Harlan County has always been a place where people fight, both literally and metaphorically, for their rights. Just off the highway in Cumberland, a couple of tents were erected, signs were placed saying, NO PAY, WE STAY, and a rotating group of men occupied the area next to the tracks. An agreement with the state police kept them off the actual tracks, but their presence was strong, as was the support from the community. Local businesses brought food and supplies, while residents went and sat with them all hours of the day and night. The county was unified against the villainous coal mine defrauding the workers out of their hard-earned wages and retirement-plan contributions.

Local officials, along with lawyers for the miners, began to explore remedies to force Blackjewel to pay the miners. Harlan County judge-executive Dan Mosley was at the forefront of the fight. Dan is Harlan County to the bone, with a buzz cut and a deep mountain accent that, if you aren't from the area, you might not understand at first. He's the most dedicated of elected officials, deeply committed to the area and very active in his care for Harlan County. "I was a child in the fourth grade who saw my dad get laid off from the coal mine, and I know what it feels like. I wasn't going to not fight for these men," Mosley said.

They went to work, keeping in regular contact with state officials, including the governor and the attorney general, both of whom came to visit, as well as the US Labor Department and advocates in the Trump administration. Mosley says it was "a classic example of bipartisan leaders working on a daily basis to make these miners whole." Many miners spoke of their pride in knowing that local, state, and federal officials were prioritizing their concerns and trying to make it right.

One person they didn't hear from, however, was Mitch McConnell. Not only didn't he visit Cumberland (come see constituents in a time of need? Yeah, right!) but also he never responded to miners' attempts to reach out to him. "Several miners told me they were upset they called the DC office and didn't get any response," Mosley says. Colin

Cornette, asked about McConnell's lack of intervention, expressed outrage, saying, "He's not pro-coal. I don't even think he's pro-Kentucky."

Then Republican governor Matt Bevin and Democratic attorney general Andy Beshear—two men historically at each other's throats personally and running against each other for governor—put aside their differences for the cause. Their offices came up with a legal strategy to help the miners recover their paychecks, and it worked. After meetings with the Department of Labor and negotiations via their attorneys, the men ended the protest on September 26, receiving their full pay.

Mosley says the key now is to help the miners find new options. Through workplace training grants, many are now going to school to learn new trades, and a number have started new professions. Among those is Cornette, who tells me the experience has led him to get trained in machine tooling, a process he hopes will help him grow a career in the future.

But the anger about what happened still rages within Cornette, and much of it is centered around the senator. "Mitch McConnell does not care for the people of eastern Kentucky. He is so disrespectful to miners, to the people around here. He just doesn't care."

I ask Mosley about McConnell's response, and he tries not to be overly critical. He says that Mitch is probably busy in Washington with national politics, and that can have a negative effect on Kentucky. But he does note that actions reflect a senator's priorities. "It's all a matter of what kind of senator you want to be. Do you want to be like Joe Manchin," of West Virginia, "and be locally focused and help your people? I'd like to see Mitch focus on bringing economic development to the area. I just don't know if that is his top priority. The confirmation of judges seems to matter more."

Cornette is more blunt: "Mitch McConnell does not care for us. He is one of the most powerful people in the United States, and we are one of the poorest states. Nothing else needs to be said."

Johnson County

"There's Just No Opportunity Here for Our Kids"

If you're a country music fan, you may have heard of the Country Music Highway in eastern Kentucky. Highway 23, stretching 144 miles, from Greenup County up north down to Letcher County, is the official Country Music Highway because of the bumper crop of country music superstars who either were born or lived around it, including the Judds, Billy Ray Cyrus, Keith Whitley, Tom T. Hall, Patty Loveless, Dwight Yoakam, Ricky Skaggs, and Sturgill Simpson, among many others. Johnson County alone, located roughly in the middle, can claim country-crooning residents Loretta Lynn, Chris Stapleton, Tyler Childers, and Crystal Gayle. That's a lot of musical talent for such a small area, and it is the central base for what I call "real" country music.*

In Paintsville, the county seat of Johnson County, the Country Music Highway Museum draws its fair share of visitors, but the rest of the city is having a more difficult time forging an economic future. Though once a vibrant eastern Kentucky hub, where coal money made Paintsville's downtown bustle, the town is now sleepier and less stable. Though it still maintains a certain bygone charm, Paintsville's tight streets are emptier now, and the vacant buildings seem to multiply by the year.

This reality is concerning to a trio of women in a boutique clothing store. All three have strong opinions about the state of Johnson County, but when told the book is about Mitch McConnell, they ask to be left anonymous.† Like many in Kentucky's rural towns, these mothers say

---

* Don't even get Matt started on this point, or soon he will be going on and on about how current country music such as Luke Bryan and Florida Georgia Line is neither country, nor even really music. He then will make you listen to ten George Jones songs in a row. Just let him go. It's not worth it. Trust me.

† It is interesting to me how many folks we have found in rural Kentucky like these three. Mitch legitimately scares these people and they almost see him as

it's growing harder to keep young people interested in staying and living here. An unfortunate side effect of the downturning local economy in the area is that places like Johnson County don't pique their kids' interest or offer them a bright future. Keeping high school and college graduates around is difficult, and their exodus away from these rural counties is tough for older generations to watch.

"There's just no opportunity for our kids to make real money here," says one mother wistfully while browsing the store. "People here are defeated," says another, "You can just see it in their eyes." The third adds, "We'd love to someday have our grandkids nearby, but it's just not going to happen."

They explain that drugs have infiltrated the community to the point that they don't even want their kids downtown after dark due to people they refer to as "walkers"—drifters who roam the streets late at night in search of drugs. One admits she won't even jog after dusk without carrying mace. It's startling to hear. Paintsville doesn't strike me as dangerous, and I certainly feel safe. But for these women, they feel a different reality.

All three grew up in Johnson County, yet all three actively hope their children will leave for better opportunities elsewhere. "When I was growing up here, everything was so different than it is now," says one mother. "There were businesses up and down the street, there were things for children to do—now most of these buildings are empty."

During the 2016 election, Hillary Clinton proclaimed proudly that if she were elected president "a lot of coal miners and coal companies would be put out of business." This area will never forget that statement, and it almost single-handedly changed the political landscape of the region. You cannot overestimate how important that statement is to understanding eastern Kentucky politics. It is still brought up virtually any time national politics is discussed in the region. Clinton claimed it was taken out of context, and maybe it was. But the sentiments behind it were careless at best, and it set in motion the rise of Donald Trump and the distrust and demonization of the Democratic Party. Hillary's

---

a dark force of doom. As one said to us in another county, "I worry he will send his people after me if I do talk to you." It really is bizarre.

seeming dismissal of the coal economy, and more broadly eastern Kentucky's way of life, was striking. There were actual, real people behind her flippant statement, and their communities have been shattered, with almost no regard or sympathy for their futures.

It's easy to criticize Mitch McConnell for his lies on behalf of the coal industry and lack of concern for coal miners in the state. He deserves every bit of that scorn. But in the last decade a Democratic Party that once fought alongside coal miners' unions on behalf of workers' rights and safety has now seemingly abandoned this section of its loyal base as collateral damage to their environmental agenda. Democrats have celebrated the demise of the coal industry but have proposed far too few of the dramatic solutions needed to help spark a new economy for those it has left behind. The result is an area that now sees Democrats as enemies, fighting against their very way of life.

Eastern Kentuckians already know Mitch McConnell doesn't care about them. But now they don't feel the Democrats do either. And that's why many of the mothers like these three in Johnson County are ready to encourage their kids to go elsewhere to find the future that no longer seems possible here.

Breathitt County

Bloody Breathitt

"Bloody Breathitt" County has an outlaw history of mountain feuds, vengeance, and justice that would rival any script that Hollywood could produce. (The one it did, the 1997 action flick *Fire Down Below*, starring Steven Seagal, was uniformly terrible.) The nickname derives from the overwhelming bloodshed over power that erupted in the tiny streets of Jackson more than a century ago. While the Hatfields and McCoys get more publicity, the tales of their feuding were tame compared with the all-out warfare that was a normal, everyday occurrence in Breathitt County. This was politics at its most hardcore.

The area was best described by the *New York Times*, which came to town in 1903 and reported, "It is evident that a republican form of government does not exist in Breathitt County, Kentucky. Civil authority, represented in the person of the sheriff, has broken down. Martial law was proclaimed, and a company of militia went into camp at Jackson." In Breathitt County, political rivals literally gunned each other down in the streets. In fact, the Kentucky government sent state militia to occupy the county courthouse three times during this period and still couldn't put a stop to all the brawls and assassinations.

Thankfully, today Breathitt County is quieter and much more tame. Yet the Bloody Breathitt spirit is still alive and well in state representative Cluster Howard. He is the kind of eastern Kentucky politician I love: a man with new, controversial ideas he is willing to fight for regardless of the political cost.* Cluster is a relaxed, affable guy with gray hair and a matching goatee. He reclines casually on a sofa here at the local college where he teaches health, and tells us in his slow, confident drawl why he is a unique sort. He is one of the singular high-profile Democrats in an area that includes staunchly Republican voters. He has held on because people like him, and he tells the truth.

Cluster Howard's positions aren't easy to compartmentalize. He says he bases his choices on what he believes will benefit Breathitt County, regardless of his personal opinion. For instance, Howard isn't particularly pro-gun but realizes his district is, so he votes against gun regulation. He also fights adamantly against the attempts to get rid of the Affordable Care Act expansion, because he knows how important the insurance has been to his people.

It's his focus on his constituents that has led Cluster to file a bill legalizing marijuana in Kentucky. Howard believes that with the coal and tobacco industries fading in the state, legalizing cannabis, and not just for medicinal purposes, could provide a sorely needed economic shot in the arm. It's a rather bold move to be the legislator who puts his name on it, but Howard believes it's both a smart move and getting

* Plus his name is Cluster. I have a bet with Matt that there are no other Clusters in the world. If you know a Cluster, call Simon & Schuster and I'm sure they will patch you through to us.

ahead of the future. "It's the right thing to do because in ten to fifteen years, it's going to be legal everywhere," Howard says.

At its core, Cluster sees marijuana legalization as a way to ease many of the problems in the region by reducing prison overcrowding, making a dent in the opioid crisis, and slowing budget cuts by bringing in new revenue. "All we ever hear in this state is 'Cut, cut, cut, cut health care, cut education, cut everything,'" Howard says wearily. "This is a way to raise some revenue. Legalization of cannabis is not going to save us, but it's still a step forward."

When I note that Mitch McConnell will almost certainly not be in favor of his bill and will use all of his political power in the state to oppose it, Cluster responds forcefully, "Mitch McConnell doesn't care about these people here. We can't wait on him to help us, because he never has."

Cluster, though, isn't just a weed advocate. He suggests we go visit the Southfork Elk View Station, a wildlife preserve that has been opened as a tourist attraction and reclamation project for the mine that used to occupy the land. Strip mining is the most controversial of all types of coal mining.* It occurs when companies chop off the tops of mountains in order to reach the pure surface coal that is much easier to mine than the coal secreted deeper in the mountains. Its practice is highly controversial because after the area is plundered of all its coal, the remnants are unsightly (as is any mountain without its peak) and unusable (as all the resources of the land have been taken away). Figuring out what to do with old strip mines is a consistent issue in these areas, and Breathitt County has tried to solve it by creating a nature preserve.

The drive to Elk View is long, winding, and isolated. Once there, we saw a stunning landscape, with miles upon miles of wild horses ranging in the wilderness. The high open setting provides a panoramic view of the Appalachian Mountains virtually unmatched anywhere and a sense of peace and serenity. It is truly beautiful. Elk View is Breathitt County's attempt to reclaim old coal lands and repurpose them for future benefit. Toward the end of his presidency, Barack Obama, realizing the

---

* And not, as its name would imply, the sexiest.

importance of such projects for the future of Appalachia, along with Republican congressman Hal Rogers, put together a proposal called the RECLAIM Act (an acronym for Revitalizing the Economy of Coal Communities by Leveraging Local Activities and Investing More),* which would disburse $1 billion over five years to communities struggling with the decline of the coal industry. The money would be used to reclaim the old strip mine sites in an environmentally conscious way and create economic development in the depressed areas. Even though Rogers was a strong critic of Obama's coal regulations, he signed on to cosponsor the bill, saying that he owed it to the area to "partner with anyone who wants to create opportunities in southern and eastern Kentucky." With Obama and a conservative GOP representative from the area on board, the bill should have passed easily.

Which is exactly what Mitch McConnell did not want. Kentucky's senior senator refused to support the legislation for two years, and single-handedly held it up. He made clear he didn't want to give Democrats a "bipartisan win" in coal country prior to the 2016 election. Mitch made sure the bill stalled, delaying help for Kentucky for his own political gain. But then, after Trump was elected, McConnell had the audacity to not only support Obama's bill but to refile it, this time as a *sponsor.* For Mitch, it was never about the policy or even his state. It was all about scoring a political win and defeating his enemies.

Egregious, right? But also *very* McConnell. Fast-forward to the present day, and the bill still hasn't passed. Even though both the newly Democratic-controlled House passed it in 2019, the bill hasn't even gone to a vote in the Senate. Five years after its introduction, even as he publicly sponsors it, McConnell refuses to bring it to a vote, letting it languish for no discernible reason.

My prediction? He waits until right before his 2020 reelection, passes the bill, and takes credit for "saving" Appalachian land. Nothing would be more par for the course for such a cynical partisan hack like Mitch McConnell.

---

* A round of applause for the brainstorming team that stretched this acronym to its furthest limit to make it work.

Wolfe County

Fighting the Opioid Epidemic

I attended college at Transylvania University, in Lexington. (Yes, those of you outside of Kentucky, it's a real college; no, we did not major in "sucking blood," and that's only the five thousandth time we've heard the joke.) Transy, as we called it, is a small liberal arts school with only a little more than a thousand students, where Chris and I became friends. It was a great place to go to college, the first university west of the Allegheny Mountains,* and counts John Marshall Harlan (the "Great Dissenter" in *Plessy v. Ferguson*), Stephen F. Austin (the father of Texas), Jefferson Davis (president of the Confederacy), and Ned Beatty (*Deliverance* pig squealer) among its famous graduates.

The reason I bring up Transy now is because I think of it whenever I hear mention of Red River Gorge in Wolfe County. The Gorge, as it is known, isn't a state park but rather a geologic area with steep cliffs, dense forests, and absolutely stunning rock formations. It's like our own little Appalachian Grand Canyon. When I was in college, the Gorge was where students headed for the weekend to camp. Well, actually, what this really meant was they were going to the Gorge to smoke weed, because the Gorge, just an hour away, was the secret marijuana escape for college students all over Kentucky.† I never visited Red River Gorge to take drugs or do anything else (I was lame, and I don't like sleeping outside because the ground is hard), but have enjoyed its beauty a lot in recent years.

In 2020, however, Wolfe County faces a problem far worse than the skunk weed of yesteryear. Like most of eastern Kentucky—honestly,

---

* Transy claims to be the first everything "west of the Allegheny Mountains," a point of reference that no one else in America uses.

† It was a different time. People thought you would go to prison for decades if you got caught with pot on campus. Nowadays, I believe colleges issue it as part of the welcome packet.

like most of rural America—Wolfe County has been absolutely devastated by opioid abuse. In nearly every town we visit, when I ask local officials or even random citizens on the street the biggest problem in the county, they all say "drugs," "pills," or "dope." Wolfe County and its county seat, Campton, are no different.

Wolfe County was never home to many coal mines, but the residents here serviced the mines elsewhere by driving trucks, fixing equipment, and providing support to them. Many also commuted the short distances to work in the businesses around the mines. When the coal economy declined, the secondary jobs held by many in Wolfe County dried up with them.

The environment was thus ripe for the opioid epidemic. It started with a perfect storm of predatory corporate greed and medical aloofness. Pharmaceutical companies pushed shoddy research about new "miracle drugs" that could help treat all types of chronic pain without being addictive. They marketed them aggressively to doctors via high-pressure sales reps incentivized handsomely to make sales. Doctors, even well-meaning ones, took the research at face value and began overprescribing painkillers such as hydrocodone and oxycodone at astounding rates. Eventually, because patients develop a tolerance to opioids, they gradually lose their potency. The "solution"? Increase the dosage, which led to addiction and overdoses. The crisis snowballed, and after a crackdown on overprescribing "pill mills" across America made the prescription versions more difficult to obtain, desperation led many users to turn to stronger (and cheaper) narcotic painkillers such as heroin and fentanyl, drugs that can cause instantaneous death.

Gay Campbell, former mayor of Campton, has watched the problem get worse over the years. "It's bad. It's real bad," he says. "Drugs are a huge problem, it's unreal. And it's not just Campton, it's all these little communities around here."

Campbell describes watching as the jobs moved out, and the pain clinics moved in. "It seems like there is a new pain clinic opening up here every month. I don't know why we need so many pain clinics," he tells me. "You'll see them line up at the pain clinic just outside of town, they'll come out high as a Georgia pine." There are now more prescriptions for opioids in Wolfe County than there are people.

The city has tried to fight it. Campbell worked to help Campton secure a grant a few years back to make improvements to its downtown area. The city of Campton modernized walkways, fixed roads, built a new park, upgraded the library, and in general made the community seem, at least visually, like a town out of *Southern Living* magazine. Shortly after the park was completed, though, residents started finding drug needles there, making them apprehensive about taking their kids to play. "What we need here are more jobs," Campbell says firmly. "If we had some jobs, where people could get out of bed in the morning and go to work, they might not need to have so many pain pills."

Mitch McConnell's record on the opioid epidemic is mixed. It wouldn't be fair to say he hasn't helped at all, but his contributions are hugely overshadowed by what he *hasn't* done to combat the epidemic. If there is one thing we have learned about the senator, you can always trace his choices back to the money. McConnell has received more campaign donations from Big Pharma in the 2020 election cycle than any other senator. Thus he has had no interest in overhauling the marketing regulations taken advantage of by the opioid manufacturers. The United States is one of only two developed countries that allows drug companies to market directly to consumers. They spend billions each year marketing their drugs to doctors and misleading them about their effects. Taking orders from Big Pharma, Mitch has no interest in that changing.

In 2018 McConnell held up a near-unanimous bipartisan bill that aimed to help with the opioid epidemic. Insiders assume it was because he believed passing it before the midterm elections would help Democrats in Republican-leaning states, especially West Virginia, where Senator Joe Manchin was vulnerable and up for reelection. Thankfully this was seen as a bully tactic and after a public outcry and accusations from industry experts that he was once again putting politics over people (which were true), McConnell backed down and allowed the bill to move forward. It passed almost unanimously—one month before the midterms.

Lawrence County

The City of Hope

As we drive south on US-23 from Ashland to Lawrence County on this crisp autumn morning, the fog dissipates into the October air. The effect is like being in a postcard, and it's a terrific welcome to Louisa, a wisp of a town on the northeastern edge of the county, next to, but thankfully not in, West Virginia. Lawrence County itself has a population of nearly sixteen thousand people, and Louisa's tiny main drag includes the prerequisite post office, county courthouse, diner, and Marcum Custom Graphics, which has nothing in the window but a cardboard cutout of *Halloween*'s Michael Myers standing ominously. I do my radio show inside and the Tracker shows up, standing by himself in the corner during the festivities. After hearing me say the Tracker is in attendance (we have spoken about him so often on the air that he has become a mini-celebrity; fans even take selfies with him at my shows), a local restaurateur includes the Tracker in the lunch he brings us after the show. The Tracker seems genuinely surprised to be included in this kindness. Louisa welcomes all visitors in diverse ways.

It is here in downtown Louisa where we find the home of one of the state's best allies in the fight against opioid abuse. Addiction Recovery Care, known as ARC, has quietly turned a waning downtown into the model of how to change the stigma of the disease of addiction.

Matt Brown, chief of staff at ARC and himself a former addict, sits across the table from us here at lunchtime in the Masterpiece Café & Painted Cow Art Gallery. He tells us that just a few short years ago, downtown Louisa was in shambles and beginning to see businesses pull out. ARC decided to set up a rehabilitation facility that utilized a number of the newly vacant downtown buildings. ARC wanted to not only treat addicts but also change the landscape of the town as well. "We believed it was important to be in the middle of town and not hide the problems we face. Everyone could then see the impact addiction was having on the community and how it could be transformed," Brown observes.

ARC created a faith-based recovery program, designed with a holistic approach to overcoming addiction. ARC tailors the treatment to the addict, using not only religion and the church but whatever method is best suited for the individual.

"There are a lot of groups that are counseling only," says Brown. "There are a lot of groups that are faith based only, and there are a lot of groups that'll just give you a job, and they think you'll be okay. We've never lived in just one of those; we've combined the best of all of those and treat the entire person, so you've got the mind, body, soul, and purpose."

All addicts at ARC are placed in a facility away from their hometown, where they are almost certainly surrounded by other users and simply too much temptation. "When you first come into treatment and you're actively addicted, you're not making great decisions. The cravings for your drug of choice are so intense that the farther away you are from that, the better," Brown explains.

"So, for me, I lived here, but when I went to treatment, the treatment center was in Fleming County, near Morehead. I was about an hour and a half away from home, even farther if you're walking, and so that first week or two, it's good to not be able to just walk outside and call your dope dealer."

ARC has had a great deal of success and currently has thirty-six facilities, both outpatient and residential, around the region. In order to help graduates maintain sobriety, they are given internships and job training. But ARC itself has also become a major employer for its graduates. Fully half of its six hundred employees have graduated from the program, including the company's CEO, Tim Robinson, both a former attorney and alcoholic. The idea is that those who come from ARC are more invested in its success and eager to give back with their employment, a process that makes them more likely to stay on the correct path.

What makes ARC fascinating to me is the degree to which it has celebrated the humanity of its clients while they are undergoing therapy. Most rehab facilities are usually situated on the edges of town, far away from its central activity. In contrast, ARC has placed all their facilities on Main Street, next to the courthouse and most of the town's businesses. They are making the community part of the process and demonstrating to people that their once-addicted friends and neighbors can be helped and are worth saving. Rather than hide the problem, the town of Louisa is now part of the recovery process, allowing huge numbers of recovering citizens to find ways to deal with their addiction without the accompanying stigma.

In return, the patients have helped revitalize the city. Everywhere you look, you see the impact of work done by recovering addicts, in the form of repainted buildings, newly opened businesses, and renovated homes. Over on Watermelon Hill Road, you'll find Second Chance Auto, staffed by recovering members of the ARC program, with the slogan "Changing tires and changing lives."

This is what true community means and is why some have started calling Louisa the "City of Hope." Brown says that a key reason for the program's success is the money made available by the Affordable Care Act.

"Kentucky is leading the way of all of Appalachia when it comes to the drug epidemic," says Matt Brown. "And the reason that I can say that with confidence is because Kentucky was the first state in all of Appalachia to expand Medicaid. It created a comprehensive benefit for all levels of care of substance use disorder treatment."

ARC is transforming lives all around eastern Kentucky and is the type of care that would be lost by repealing the Affordable Care Act, a fact that many Kentucky leaders must know but choose to ignore. The change here is inspirational and the effect transformational, not only in individual lives but also in communities as a whole. A few of Kentucky's leaders would be well served to visit and learn.

Carter County

"It's Like Being Dr. Jekyll and Mr. Hyde at the Same Time"

Carter County feels a lot like summer camp. It's densely wooded, nestled into the hills, and small, cozy cabin homes dot the banks surrounding you on all sides of I-64. The largest town of Grayson is still very small and appropriately quirky: barbeque joint The Hogs Trough is only open Thursday through Sunday (fiscally smart), The Man Cave Discount Store sells both tools *and* live bait, and Divas and Dudes is currently making a bid for more market share ("We used to just be Divas but we wanted to branch out," a blue-haired stylist tells me).

We have come to Carter County to talk to Eric Bush, a former addict who now works at ARC helping others get treatment. We often hear of the stories of the lives lost due to the power of opioid addiction, and it can be difficult to comprehend. So we asked Eric if he would share his experience with addiction in his own words:

> On January 11, 2016, I remember lying facedown on the concrete of a local parking lot. I was being arrested that day for a number of drug-related crimes, and it was definitely the worst day of my life to this point. I'd been arrested several times before, but somehow this time felt different, like there was no escape and no hope. I finally realized that something would have to change. The following weeks, as I sat in jail, I began praying several times a day. It's not uncommon; many people find jailhouse religion, but during this time, I began to feel a little bit of hope. In a short time, I got out of jail on a surety bond, with an ankle monitor around my leg, and a month later, ended up in rehab as a patient for the last time.
>
> For years, I let my addiction control me like a puppet on a string, as I put my next fix in front of everything I claimed to love. My life had four steps: one, find a way to get dope; two,

get dope; three, get high; four, repeat. I repeated this every day for years, minus the times I was forced to get sober for a while. I was an IV user and could not break the cycle of addiction.

It's certainly not easy to understand why an addict does what they do, and it's not easy to understand what it's like for a person living in addiction. Addiction causes an incredible, ultimate temptation that is constant and never ending. It's like being Dr. Jekyll and Mr. Hyde at the same time, except an addiction doesn't change back and forth from one to the other. As an addict you are both at the same time. As an example, like I mentioned before, it's like being a puppet with all the normal human feelings of shame and guilt, but while being forced and controlled to do things the "good" side of us doesn't want to do. Addicts and alcoholics see the negative effects of their actions, but the craving for the drug is so much more powerful than the thought of those consequences. Therefore, we continue to hurt others and make poor choices while we watch our lives crumble.

Long term, the mental addiction is the hardest part to defeat. However, the short-term sickness caused by opiate withdrawal is like having every symptom of the flu. It's truly a horrible feeling that lasts for nearly a week. Combining the mental addiction and the physical dependence is why we continue to see the relation between crime and addiction. Mentally, an addict's mind continues to have intense, nonstop cravings and desires the only thing that can end their physical sickness. This is why the cycle repeats.

For a normal person, lying facedown on the pavement with guns drawn on them would probably be enough to make them stop using. However, normally, I usually got out of jail and got high on the same day. Over the course of the next month, I still used occasionally and strategically so I wouldn't get caught by the drug screens I was taking. The last time I used any form of mind-altering substance was on February 26, 2016. A few days later, I left for drug and alcohol treatment because my arrest had violated probation on a misdemeanor shoplifting charge. I'd lost count of how many times I'd sought treatment, but here I was, sent to rehab to satisfy the courts again.

On March 7, 2016, while talking to the pastoral counselor at Lake Hills Oasis (LHO), I felt the calling and made a decision to turn my life over to the care of God and accepted Jesus Christ as my savior. I was inspired by the LHO staff, many of whom were sober and in recovery and truly made a life of sobriety seem attractive. I was patient with my sobriety and allowed life to come as it may. I didn't feel the need for anyone to be proud of the change taking place in my life. I had begun to understand a valuable lesson that I live by to this day: if I am faithfully putting my trust in God, then I am right where I need to be.

After thirteen months of being sober, I was offered a job with Addiction Recovery Care (ARC) at a residential treatment center called Belle Grove Springs. Here, I did my best to inspire the same hope that was inspired in me a year earlier. I shared my experiences with others to give them the best advice I could in order to help them discover a new way of life.

At the end of 2018, I completed Carter County Drug Court without any sanctions or warnings. This was a choice I made by putting God, drug court, and my recovery above everything else in my life. I used to see people complete drug court and then throw a party for themselves, which would only take them back to the same mistakes of the past. In order to find success after completion of a drug court, outpatient, or any other sort of drug-related program, the participant must continue doing the things that have helped them find their success. It isn't over that day.

At one point I considered January 11, 2016, the worst day of my life. Now I see it differently. Good and bad are often about perception. At that time, things only seemed dark and hopeless because I didn't know what the future could hold. But now I see that what seemed bad was the major turning point in my life. Because of the events of that day, I was sent to rehab. Because of the events of that day, I was enrolled in drug court.* Through drug court, I found Belle Grove Springs. At Belle Grove Springs, I found my home church. Through all of these things, I found a new way of life.

The only reason I ever share any of my own story is to inspire hope for others. Change can happen, and it's never too late for something new to take place. A life that seems hopeless can change, but we have to either consciously attempt that change, or find ourselves facedown on the pavement with guns drawn. Either way, we must do the work to change, or we will die in our addiction. I have done it, and I know others can too.

Knott County

"It Usually Began for Them with a Prescription"

I got a good sense of Knott County life when, ten minutes past the county line, I saw a concrete building with a sign on the side advertising, in giant lettering (and in this order):

ELECTRONIC CIGARETTES
HOME VIDEO
CHILD CARE

All my needs taken care of in one stop.† Top that, Walmart. Lest you think, however, that Knott County is not cultural, I'd like to point you

---

* Drug courts are used as alternative punishments to incarceration for low-level drug offenders in Kentucky. Most small drug crimes within the state are now processed this way.

† The place is great. I dropped my six-year-old off there for the day and she brought home a VHS copy of *Judge Dredd*. Still trying to wean her off the e-cigs, though.

to the fact that it also has the small college town Pippa Passes, named after an 1841 verse drama by English poet Robert Browning. It's a wildcard, this county, so keep your mind open.

Case in point: we are in downtown Hindman on a rainy afternoon, touring Knott County's Appalachian Artisan Center, a partially federally funded institution designed to help support not only art in the mountains but also Appalachian artists themselves. The center functions as a bit of an art showcase house, allowing mountain artists to refine their craft and found businesses without the up-front cost of an individual office. It's a bright, cheerful place and as director of fund-raising and development Christy Boyd shows us around, her pride in the facility is infectious. Christy is talkative and funny, introducing us to each artist in their studio and telling us a bit about each ("Her jewelry is amazing," "This pottery is unlike anything you have seen"). It's a celebration of the area's culture, and she's the perfect host.*

Christy explains that the Artisan Center was born in an effort to create jobs for Appalachian artists, but over time it has seen its role expand to help the Knott County community at large as well. In 2017 a $475,000 grant from New York's ArtPlace America, a group made up of foundations, agencies, and financial institutions created to help fund art projects, allowed the center to launch a program called Culture of Recovery, a cultural response to the opioid epidemic ravaging eastern Kentucky. "We wanted to do something nontraditional in getting these people toward recovery," explains Boyd. "We realize that idle hands lead to bad things, and we wanted to do something to help a growing problem in this area."

The program allows recovering addicts to learn a craft during treatment, hopefully to use it upon release. She takes us to the Troublesome Creek Stringed Instrument Company, in the old Hindman High School, which manufactures high-end guitars and mandolins, and, with only *six* employees, is proudly the first factory in Knott County history.†

---

* Matt asks if he can have an area to showcase his whittled spoons, but he's told politely that they're "good on spoons right now."

† I found this difficult to imagine, but it's true. No fact better crystallizes the way this region's economy was dominated and controlled by the coal industry and how hard it is now to rebuild.

Troublesome Creek works with the center to hire workers from the Culture of Recovery program—men such as Nathan Smith and Jeremy Haney, both recovering opiate addicts who've taken to the structure and challenge of manufacturing stringed instruments.

Nathan is a big, friendly-looking giant of a man, with a long black-gray beard; he looks like the beloved Hagrid from *Harry Potter*. Jeremy is shorter and walks with ginger steps, having been diagnosed at birth with spina bifida, a congenital malformation of the spinal cord; the condition has kept him on disability much of his life. After years of struggling with addiction, they both ended up at Troublesome Creek Stringed Instrument Company by force: Nathan through the drug court, Jeremy through the nearby Hickory Hill Recovery Center.

Each tells a familiar story: their addictions were cemented by first becoming hooked by legal means. "I'm thirty-nine now," Nathan says. "I was addicted for twenty-five years, and probably ninety percent of the people I associated with during the time I was using, if it were pills, they were hooked, and it usually began for them with a prescription." The nation's opioid crisis didn't start due to illegal pill pushers crossing the southern border and selling product. It started from Big Pharma using young sales reps to charm doctors into overprescribing massive amounts of highly addictive medication, hooking regions of the country on narcotics they simply couldn't handle.

Nathan has now been clean for more than two years, and at Troublesome Creek, he spends his days perfecting his craft of guitar making, or luthiering. "It's been amazing," he says. "It's kept me busy; it's helped me stay focused. I took to it quickly, having worked in woodshops, but in a month or two, I knew it was really what I wanted to do. And when I saw that first instrument I made, that done it for me. That's an amazing feeling."

Troublesome Creek and the Appalachian Artisan Center are examples of the resiliency and ingenuity of a region's people to find ways to not only celebrate the arts and music of the area but also help those tormented by the pain of drug addiction.* The program relies on an

---

* To paraphrase Jefferson Starship, they built this city on acoustic guitar and dulcimer music.

annual arts grant distributed via the National Endowment for the Arts. Without the NEA grant trickling down to Knott County, the project would likely disappear entirely.

And, not surprisingly, it's the type of grant Mitch McConnell consistently opposes. In 1993 ultraconservative senator Jesse Helms of North Carolina went on a crusade to end all NEA grants after he was made aware of art funding used to create work he deemed obscene. He repeatedly tried to take NEA funding out of the annual budget and had a dependable friend in Mitch McConnell, who always voted to end all grants to the NEA. Not surprisingly, then, since the Appalachian Artisan Center opened, McConnell has yet to visit the facility. If NEA funding ever comes up as an issue in the future, it's almost certain McConnell will again try to strike them from the budget. If successful, it would be dire for the center and Knott County. Not only will the arts be diminished, but folks such as Nathan Smith and Jeremy Haney will suffer as well. Here in Hindman, the arts are more than just a reflection of local culture; they also save lives.

Elliott County

"Hey, Rocky! Go Get 'Em!"

Only 614 people live in Sandy Hook, Elliott County's largest town. It sits in the middle of an enclave in the Appalachian Mountains, isolated to such a great degree that when you arrive via what may be the state's windiest highway, you feel like you have left the real world peacefully behind. (In part because you likely don't have cell phone service.) When we arrive, it's getting close to dinner so we stop at the world's most Keith Whitley–loving Frosty Freeze.

If you're not familiar with Keith Whitley, here's a short primer: Whitley's melancholic baritone may be the best male mountain voice in country music history. I will fight anyone who disagrees. He grew up in tiny Sandy Hook and played in country legend Ralph Stanley's band, before moving off to Nashville in 1983 to make his fame and fortune as a country music star. He had hits such as "I'm No Stranger to the Rain," "I'm Over You," and "When You Say Nothing at All." The local boy made good. In 1986 he married fellow country star Lorrie Morgan, making them the biggest country couple since George Jones and Tammy Wynette. Whitley, however, struggled with alcoholism and eventually drank himself to death on the morning of May 9, 1989, at the age of just thirty-three; the cause of his death: acute alcohol poisoning. The singer-songwriter left behind his final song, a rudimentary recording of "Tell Lorrie I Love Her" as a final gift to Lorrie and the world. Stop what you are doing right now and find it and listen. I'll wait.

Now tell me that song isn't the saddest thing you've ever heard. True love has never sounded so powerful and its ending so tragic.

The Frosty Freeze adorns its walls with Whitley headshots, sheet music, handmade drawings, and album covers. As a matter of fact, you'd be hard pressed to find anything hanging in the Frosty Freeze that doesn't focus on Keith Whitley except a TV airing Fox News and a sign by the entrance for a missing black-and-tan German shepherd who answers to Henry. (If Henry's owners are reading this, I hope you found him. He's a beautiful dog.)

You'll also notice in the center of Sandy Hook's tiny downtown the Rocky J. Adkins Public Library—named for the county's former state representative and the House majority leader for thirteen years. Adkins is a tall, lean former local basketball star who took his talents to Morehead State University, located just down the road, where as a senior he helped its 1982 team reach its first NCAA Tournament in school history. He is also a former coal miner and teacher, with an endearing drawl and an ability to pick the banjo, a combination that makes him as pure Kentucky as any public official could be. If you meet Rocky, you will notice two things: he is both a consummate politician and extremely likable.

Adkins's reputation as a Democratic voice for the working man in Kentucky has made him known in rural counties at every end of the state. He ran for governor in 2019 as that rarest of birds: a pro-life Democrat seeking to bring back the blue-collar tradition of the Kentucky Democratic Party. Even though he had far less funding than his two opponents and received less than 10 percent of the votes in Louisville due to his antiabortion stance, Rocky came ever so close to pulling off one of the biggest upsets in modern Kentucky political history. His defeat only enhanced his folk hero status in eastern Kentucky, as he remains the one Democrat in this Trump-loving region that citizens believe "actually has some sense."*

"It's easy for me to talk to coal miners," Adkins says, "because I worked in the coal industry for thirty years of my life. While coal will remain a part of our region, I think everybody understands we've got to diversify the economy of the region, and we've spent the last thirty years building infrastructure to give ourselves that opportunity."

Rocky is correct. But his opinion still takes courage. Mitch McConnell and most Republican politicians in Kentucky still insist to voters that coal is coming back. But the reality is that cheaper forms of energy now exist, and eastern Kentucky coal is some of the hardest and dirtiest to mine in America. The proof is in the numbers. Coal employment is now less than 10 percent of what it was in 1979, and most estimates put the number of coal jobs in the entire state at less than six thousand. No serious discussion about the future of eastern Kentucky's economy can only center on the magic of coal.

Rocky knows these statistics, and that is why he fights for the region in Frankfort and Washington. But he doesn't believe he has a strong enough ally in Mitch McConnell, whose status in DC has done little to boost the region's economy. For all the supposed power of the Senate majority leader from Kentucky, the region's deterioration has all occurred on his watch, with virtually no movement in action to fix it.

"I've not seen the personal attachment or engagement in our region that's needed from Mitch McConnell at the federal level," Rocky says of the senator. "I mean, he serves as the majority leader in the United States Senate, and the focus of somebody with that authority and that kind of influence needs to be there in order to diversify, to assist our region, help lift up our economy, lift up our people."

Rocky might even be underselling the point. In our entire travels in coal country, we did not meet one—I am serious, not *one*—person who said he or she was a fan of the senator. Many claimed to have voted for

---

* This is a massive compliment around these parts.

him because they considered the other option worse, but none claimed to be a supporter.

Contrast that with Rocky—and this is no hyperbole—whose name is on the tongues of people all over this state. He's present and engaged. When walking with him through Hillbilly Days, an annual festival in the streets of Pikeville in the state's far eastern tip, it was nearly impossible to get through a sentence with him without someone screaming, "Hey, Rocky! How are ya! Go Get 'Em!!!"

Rocky's problem politically? His stance on abortion, which makes him persona non grata with a great deal of the Democratic establishment (but only more popular with GOP voters). It's unfortunate because a strong case could be made that Rocky would have the best chance of anyone (including me) of beating Mitch McConnell. He is Mitch's diametrical opposite, on-the-ground and fighting for those who feel disenfranchised, while Mitch is distant and aloof. Both are career politicians, but only one seems to actually represent Kentucky.

As I leave Elliott County, I stop at a gas station, and a man behind the counter tells me he listens to the show. He then says with a sly smile, "So . . . you down here to decide who is running, you or Rocky?" I laugh and say no, I am just visiting. He gives me a wink and responds, "Well, you two figure it out. One of you better step up. We gotta get ol' Mitch out and that's the only way."

Magoffin County

Magoffin County Cadillac

I have a strong affinity for Magoffin County, and it all originates with one catchy song. Bluegrass guitarist Laid Back Country Picker is an eastern Kentucky legend, and his tunes about the area are local cult classics. The high school social studies teacher who doubles as a hell of a picker is formidable at first glance: 6'4", mutton-chopped sideburns, long gray hair, a fiftysomething musician who is missing a tooth in the front of his mouth. He's also, behind that rowdy visage, a thoughtful and conversational intellect known around these parts by day as his alter ego, David Prince. David wrote the definitive song on Magoffin County and says he did so because the county is its own unique beast.

"It's hard to put your finger on, man," Prince tells me in a deep bass drawl. "Magoffin County is surrounded by much larger cities, but it's kind of off on an island of its own."

Prince cut his teeth in a country band playing the music of George Jones, Merle Haggard, and Waylon Jennings (his moniker is an ode to a Jennings song of the same name), and the highlight of Prince's set list is his signature "Magoffin County Cadillac," an ode to the auction-purchased Ford Crown Victorias—usually ex–police cruisers—that dot the county. The song is dedicated to the area's unique love for the vehicle and notes how locals drive them proudly as if they have a prized piece of machinery. I always assumed the reference was a playful, loving jab at a neighboring county, but then we arrived in Salyersville, in fact, and immediately saw several. One was parked in front of the old gas station on Church Street, while another was commandeered by an elderly lady over by Betty's Pizza who could barely see over the wheel. Everywhere we turned, another showed up. Magoffin County Cadillac is not just a clever song title, either; it's an honest-to-God ode to the offbeat brand loyalty folks have to the cars here in this area.

"They're a real thing; they're here." Prince notes that the concentration of Crown Vics in Magoffin County began when a local car dealer began purchasing the durable automobiles at local police auctions and bringing them back to the area to sell.

"I bought my first one for about $1,500 and I have 350,000 miles on it," Prince tells me, "and all I've really done is change the oil." He says that back in the day union workers would have jobs sometimes a hundred miles away offsite—the durable, tanklike Crown Vics were easy to pile a bunch of guys into to get back and forth to jobs. They caught on from there, and people in Magoffin County love them. "Usually people who own one have two more in the yard," Prince says with a laugh.

We're standing at the four-way stop where all roads meet in downtown Salyersville when we see a maroon Crown Vic idling in front of the news offices of the *Salyersville Independent*. We wave, because now everyone in town seems like a friend. Head east from this intersection and you'll hit the Mt. Sinai church just a block down; north takes you up toward Crace's, where taco salad is the special of the day. Having eaten already, instead we head south and walk a little more than a block when we discover Magoffin County Pioneer Village, a collection of rebuilt, rustic log cabins sitting right there along the downtown street, next to the historical society. It's an odd sight, not one we've encountered in any county's downtown yet, but seems oddly in step with the unconventional Magoffin County.

It's here at Pioneer Village we meet Todd Preston, a past president of the Magoffin County Muzzle Loaders Club, an organization over a hundred years old in the county and a stalwart for men of the area spanning generations. The muzzle-loaders have long prided themselves on protecting a past way of eastern Kentucky life, from firing traditional muzzle-loaded rifles to preserving the very log cabins we see here in Pioneer Village. Preston, grizzled with blue eyes and a denim shirt, shows us around the collection of log cabins, relocated log by log by the club's members downtown over the last few decades in an effort to save the forgotten cabins of Magoffin County. Preston has an affinity for them himself; his father grew up in a one-room cabin that housed his parents and ten brothers and sisters. And he may be the last person still keeping the tradition alive. "All the men who helped me build these cabins one-by-one are dead and gone, but we are trying to preserve that tradition," he says.

Preston's love of Magoffin County history is obvious, and we follow him to his house, where he shows us more artifacts. His trophy room walls are lined with an ode to the Magoffin County outdoors. There are mounted deer heads, antlers, a belt buckle made from a snapping turtle foot, a necklace made of sharpened turkey talons, and several skunk-hide hats hanging from hooks. Preston is clearly an old-school eastern Kentucky "mountain man," and the spirit of the past lives in him. "Those times were simpler then, for sure—but they were a lot harder, too."

Preston participates in shooting competitions in Kentucky and neighboring states wherein he wears traditional buckskin garb and tests himself in time trials and accuracy challenges against other muzzle-loading shooters. He takes Chris and me out back to illustrate, stuffing a three-and-a-half-foot rifle full of gunpowder and a lead ball to allow Chris to fire a muzzle-loader into a nearby bank of trees. It's the type of rifle once used by mountain scouts—dangerous Civil War snipers in their own right—who knew these woods like the back of their hand and could hide in the trees and spot you long before you spotted them. As the rifle explodes with a pull of the trigger and a sharp and sparky pop, Chris fires the lead ball into a paper plate target from thirty yards away; as Todd grabs the target and shows him the perfectly round hole in the plate he made, I don't mind telling you that I was proud. My coauthor having his mountain man moment.

The county's most prominent car is a former Crown Vic police cruiser; downtown is filled with re-created log cabins; citizens participate in muzzle-loaded rifle shootouts on weekends. Magoffin County is eastern Kentucky's eccentric cousin that marches to the beat of its own drum. It's old-school but lots of fun, and maybe the quirkiest county in the state. It's also very different from Washington, DC, where I have been summoned to prove my mettle.

Washington, DC

Begging for Dollars

When I initially considered the prospects of running for office, the part I dreaded most was raising money. I hate asking people for anything. I have always taken the view that if I never ask people for something, I won't risk ruining a positive relationship. It is a great mantra for life, and it has served me well.*

This, however, doesn't work in politics. Unless you are super wealthy enough to fund your own campaign, raising money is one of the most important skills for being a successful politician. Our current political system has two methods of winning elections: either be filthy rich or

* Unless you have ordered fried pickles at dinner. He will totally ask for, and take, your fried pickles.

become beholden to donors and special interests via their donations. There is no way around it. If you want to win in said system, especially against the money behemoth that is Mitch McConnell, soliciting donations is simply a required part of the game.

Over the course of my Senate decision process, I have been advised by a handful of people whose opinions I've grown to trust and whose advice was important for a political neophyte such as myself.* All believed I had a legitimate chance against McConnell—or at least said they did. All believed that if I were the Democratic Party nominee, raising the necessary money wouldn't be an issue due to the intense hatred for Mitch across the country. But all saw Amy McGrath and her $11 million campaign war chest as a huge obstacle for me to take her on in the primary and one that would be very difficult to overcome.

So, I was advised that I needed to set the table for a potential candidacy by meeting with some high-level donors and see whether they would be amenable to my potential run. I hated this idea intensely. As I stated earlier, extremely rich people freak me out. I have almost nothing in common with them, and the sense of entitlement that often comes with their wealth just might be my least favorite quality in humanity. I try to avoid the ultra-rich, and the few friends I have with money usually hide it well. But if I wanted to do this, my populist anger at the entire system would have to be put aside. With the national party winds at McGrath's back, I was going to have to suck it up and play the game.

It was decided that I should go crash a meeting of wealthy Democratic donors in Washington, DC, to make my case. I was told the name of the group was something pretentious and aristocratic, like the Captains Club, and that it was an annual gathering of major Democratic political donors with connections to the Obama administration. They meet in Washington over two days at a DC, hotel, and most of the major national Senate and House candidates approved by the party come to

---

* A reminder: Matt can't tell you who any of these people are because they don't want their names shared. They are scared that by simply talking to Matt, they won't be allowed to work on any future major Democratic campaigns. Welcome to politics in America, everyone!

make the case for their candidacies. Basically, the donors sit regally in a room, and the candidates come one by one and grovel for money.* Simply by being wealthy, these individuals get access to all the major candidates and get to have their voices heard. It went against my inherent populism and all my ideals, but I was told it's the world we live in, and I needed to do it.

There was just one little problem: the group only meets with candidates approved by the national Democratic Party and I was not such a candidate. In fact, quite the opposite: I was considering *challenging* the party's handpicked contender. Thus, I wasn't invited to the DC political beauty pageant and was not permitted to strut my political stuff for the judges. At least not officially. My trusted advisors were sneaky, however: they set me up with an illicit conference room in the same hotel, one floor above the event, where I could meet a select group of the donor elite class at an unsanctioned lunch. I was told to dress the part and look like a future senator. I wore jeans, a blazer, and Jordan 6s—which I don't think was what they had in mind. I say that because, upon my arrival, one of my advisors sidled up to me and asked, "What time will you be changing?"

As the twenty or so donors walked in, I saw quickly that my worst fears were being realized. The room was nearly all men, every one of them wearing either a suit or the "rich guy business casual" of Burberry jackets, argyle sweaters, and a handful of scarves. The room combined the fashion taste of a Princeton University faculty lounge with the jewelry accoutrements of an investment bank board meeting. I was out of place, but I also had nothing to lose.

I began my spiel. Here is the simple version:

- Mitch McConnell is the greatest threat to American democracy today.
- Mitch McConnell has done nothing for the people of Kentucky.
- Mitch McConnell needs to be defeated, but to do so requires accepting some hard truths.

---

* It's like *American Idol* for Democratic fund-raising, but with no Paulas, just Simons.

  - The national Democratic Party as currently constituted doesn't understand rural America and has no idea how to communicate with them.
  - Because of this, we can't win in Kentucky, and we are losing in formerly Democratic bastions such as Pennsylvania, Wisconsin, and Michigan.
  - If we want to change this, we have to get back to our blue-collar roots and become a party that stands up for working-class America.*
- In my career, I spend every day talking to Trump voters. I understand them and can speak to some of their causes. I am one of the rare Democrats who can win them over in Kentucky and thus beat Mitch McConnell.

I spoke with authority and conviction, hiding the awkwardness I felt about being in the room. When I finished, I thought my monologue had gone well so I asked for questions. The first was from an older gentleman and was direct: "Chuck Schumer says Amy McGrath is the better choice. Are you saying he is wrong?"

This one was easy. "Chuck Schumer knows nothing about Kentucky, he knows very little about rural America, and his strategy of picking candidates has led to Mitch McConnell as the majority leader, so I am not sure why you would start listening to his supposed good judgment now."

The room appeared shocked. But then, gradually, a few of them began to smile, and one man chuckled loudly. It was clear they weren't used to a potential candidate speaking so frankly, and my candor amused them. They asked me a couple policy questions, before the meeting came to a close when one man spoke for the group.

"You were a delight to listen to. I need to say, though, Schumer found out we were meeting with you, and he asked us to come up here and talk you out of running. But now I think I can speak for the rest of

* Left unsaid was that this means turning away from the policy choices preferred by many of the people in the room. Donor-business Democrats are all very progressive, until you get to workers' rights. Then the room gets silent.

us and say we are going to go back and tell him he needs to meet with you as soon as possible."

I laughed. I said I had been trying for more than a year to talk to the New York senator, so I wasn't sure that would work, but I thanked him for his support and for their attendance. As the group headed toward the door, nearly all stopped and encouraged me to run, with one offering to write a check right then and there. I told him I couldn't accept any money yet, but I thanked him for his consideration. As the room cleared, my two advisors (both from DC) started clapping. "I can't believe I am saying this," one of them said, "but your whole hillbilly thing really works. It's magic."

Sliding into the cab to head to the airport, I got on my phone to check my email and see what I had missed in the world. At the very top of my in-box was a message from Chuck Schumer's office asking if I could meet with him within the next two weeks. After a year of ignoring my every attempt to talk to him about the election, one conversation with a group of powerful donors and ten minutes later, he wanted me in DC. I guess it's all in who you know.

CHAPTER 5

Mitch's Base

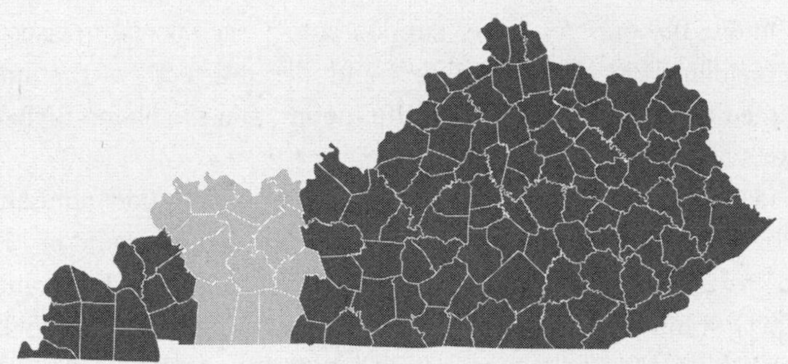

The area west of Interstate 64 is where Mitch McConnell finds his most consistent voting bloc. The region surrounding Hopkinsville, Owensboro, Henderson, and Madisonville used to be a Democratic stronghold, producing a century of Democratic Party representatives that guided western Kentucky and the state.

McConnell, however, realized before nearly anyone else that at the heart of this area was a strong religious core he could exploit to win elections. By turning his back on his pro-choice, pro–civil rights, pro-union, secular background in Louisville, McConnell knew he could place a huge dent in the traditionally Democratic support by using religious, cultural, and social values to his advantage. The transformation of this region may be the biggest factor in Mitch's electoral success—so I went west to check it out for myself.

Christian County

"People Want to Be Heard"

We began in a town that for one day, in 2017, was the center of the world. On August 21 of that year the world witnessed a solar eclipse (you know, the one you were supposed to wear special glasses for, but President Donald Trump didn't and stared directly at the sun as it seemed to emerge from behind the moon), and the nation turned to Hopkinsville for its view.

The National Aeronautics and Space Administration announced that the best place on the planet for viewing the eclipse would be "Hoptown," as the locals call it. The city would be treated to two minutes and forty seconds of complete solar blackout*—longer than anywhere else—making it the prime destination for amateur astronomers around the globe.

After the announcement, local businesses were flooded with calls and projections began building that at least two hundred thousand visitors would descend upon the area. A wide range of people inquired—from fringe-religion practitioners to top-level NASA scientists—ensuring the town's six hotels were full immediately. Hopkinsville dubbed itself Eclipseville USA, with a festival the night before and events designed to take advantage of the opportunity. This was Hopkinsville's two minutes and forty seconds in the world spotlight, and it wasn't going to let it go to waste.

I brought my show, *Hey Kentucky!*, to a local farm that claimed to have the "best viewing spot in America" for the celestial event. Admittedly, I was skeptical about the whole thing, probably because, as a child, I'd once gotten a day off from school after a preacher had prophesied that an earthquake would cause the entire state of Kentucky to

* One minute and forty-five seconds longer than the average Mitch McConnell constituent meeting.

sink into the ground. (Spoiler alert: it didn't.) But when the moon began passing in front of the sun, I have to admit, I was impressed.* Suddenly day became night, a phenomenon that defies description if you have never experienced it. The mass of people around me stared awestruck at the spectacle in the sky, as the sun and moon condensed sundown to sunrise in the span of just under three minutes. Great job, universe!

While I was impressed, I hate traffic with a passion and was born with a sixth sense to avoid it. I knew that once the eclipse ended, returning the world to normal, bedlam would erupt, as hundreds of thousands of out-of-towners who had flooded into tiny Hopkinsville hopped in their cars and made for the exits. I was wrong: it wasn't bedlam, it was *apocalyptic*. To beat the mother of all traffic jams, no sooner had the sun reappeared than I maniacally dashed to my car and, following my Waze navigation app's winding route through the back roads, high-tailed it home to Louisville. It took me three and a half hours, an hour longer than usual, but all in all, not too bad.

Others, however, didn't have the same luck. As folks pleasantly meandered to their cars for what they expected to be a leisurely ride home, they encountered traffic levels never seen before, with highways and interstates quickly clogged and not moving for hours at a time. The local roads were overwhelmed. Speaking of which . . .

If you were to bring up the eclipse to Chris today, he would spit directly in your face. My friend and traveling companion left Hopkinsville a mere fifteen minutes after I did, but by that time it was too late. His journey home took more than thirteen hours. It's a sore subject, and I try not to remind him (read: gloat) that if he'd hit the road just five minutes earlier, he could have saved ten hours. It is also why at night on our current expedition around Kentucky, I often find him cursing at the moon.

This time our trip to Hopkinsville was much more pleasant. As part of my political exploratory committee, I'd scheduled a few meetings with local Democrats throughout the state to gauge their interest in my potential run against Mitch McConnell. This one was on a Monday night in downtown Hoptown at a place called Jazzy Souls. Few locales

* Matt had a total eclipse of the heart.

can claim to be a rare combo of rural Kentucky jazz bar/Democratic Party headquarters,* but Jazzy Souls pulls it off and was filled to capacity. I spoke to the group, listened to the people's real frustration at having McConnell as their longtime senator, and came away with a sense that there was a palpable desire for change in the area.

I wasn't, however, the main attraction at Jazzy Souls. If two or more are gathered in Christian County, you will always be playing second fiddle to County Judge-Executive Steve Tribble. He is the guy everyone knows, who, when you go in for a handshake, grabs your hand with a hearty bear paw, pulls you toward him with a smile, and just begins laughing at a joke he hasn't even told yet. Seventy-two years old, tall, with graying hair and a thick moustache, he's funny, loud, and instantly endearing; the kind of man who's never met a stranger. It's Politics 101 to watch Tribble work the room, shaking hands, gently needling people, and checking in on how everyone is doing. He makes everyone around him feel special, a valuable trait for any politician.

As I wait to speak, Tribble greets every single person in attendance (if we are honest, many likely came at his behest), finding some unique anecdote to tell all of them. I consider myself a decent small-talker. But after I say hello, ask the person where he or she is from (which isn't helpful here, since everyone is from Hopkinsville, including Steve), make a pithy comment about John Calipari ("Love the guy, but he should play zone more"), and thank them for coming, I am often tapped out. Tribble, on the other hand, lives for it. If he has four minutes with someone, he will know all her kids, her favorite movie, and her SAT score, while joking it's better than his. He is impressive.

I call Tribble a few days later and ask what is his secret to communicating so well with the people he meets. It's eight o'clock in the evening, and he's still at the office. "I think I've returned every call for the last twenty-six years, as far as I know; unless I lost a note or something, I've always called everybody back," Tribble tells me. "People want to

* In Kentucky, county Democratic headquarters can be anywhere, from old scrapbooking stores, to hat stores, to health food groceries—usually unmarked. Try to find yours!

be heard. They want you to hear what they have to say and see if you can help them."

Tribble tells me most people don't expect to agree with everything you do, but they do remember how you make them feel. "When I leave this world, I want people to think I worked hard for them, and did a good job for them, and cared about them," Tribble says. "That whole thing about treating others the way you want to be treated, it's old, but it's certainly true. It's true in politics, and it's true in everything."

In that respect, Tribble is the anti–Mitch McConnell. To call Mitch a "people person" would be like calling Jared Kushner a "self-made man." He has no real charisma, no discernible people skills, and seems to possess none of the traits that make for a good politician. And few ever are. On this trip, I can count on one hand (maybe less than three fingers) the number of people who claim to have spoken directly to Mitch McConnell.

In fact, at its core, this is probably one of the best explanations for McConnell's unpopularity. In a state as friendly and personable as Kentucky, Mitch McConnell just isn't like the rest of us. In Kentucky, we prefer our politicians (and friends) personable, like Steve Tribble, polite and returning phone calls. Mitch is dour, unpleasant, and standoffish. One wonders if it will ever catch up to him. He is not, most certainly, a jazzy soul.

Daviess County

Kentucky's Official Granddad

Owensboro is the most underappreciated city in Kentucky. Even though it doesn't sit on any of the major Kentucky interstates, it has one of the state's nicest downtowns on the river, a ton of restaurants, and even stores you forgot existed (well hello there, American Eagle!). Also, no place better embodies the change in Kentucky politics and the rise of Mitch McConnell's power than this small city. For more than a century, Owensboro elected Democrats almost exclusively. It was a consistently reliable mass of votes for anyone seeking state elected office with a (D) next to their name. If you couldn't win in Owensboro, you probably weren't a Democrat fit to hold public office in the first place.

One of those Democrats was Senator Wendell Ford, a local boy who rose all the way from the banks of the Ohio River to the governor's mansion, and then to Washington, DC. A lifelong Daviess County resident, Ford was the embodiment of the old Democratic Party in the Bluegrass State. He is universally remembered fondly throughout Kentucky. The annual Democratic Party state dinner and the state party headquarters are both named after him. When politicians speak about the need to reignite the Kentucky Democratic party, the phrase "get back to the party of Wendell Ford" is repeated endlessly.

I came to Owensboro in part to find out who Wendell Ford really was, and to see if the admonition "If you run like Wendell Ford did, you can win" was true. Wendell Ford was certainly a winner. He was elected governor in 1971, serving three years before running for US Senate, a position he held from 1974 until his retirement in 1998. He was known as an advocate for the "little man" in the state, spending virtually all his time in Washington fighting for Kentucky small farmers and working-class issues. While he also had an interest in aviation (the main airline safety bill that governs American air traffic bears his name), the majority of his efforts reflected a senator worried less about national politics and more about the people at home.*

I met Ford's grandson Clay Ford for pizza in downtown Owensboro on a dark and chilly night. Clay is a longtime friend whom I consider one of the brightest young leaders in the state. He hasn't gotten into politics yet (although I urge him to, often) but is a local businessman who personifies the phrase "hope my daughter brings someone home like him."† Clay now works with the Wendell H. Ford Government Education Center, a nonprofit set up to help teach young people about government. Clay speaks of his grandfather with reverence.

---

* It's true. Ford never met a group of Kentuckians he couldn't charm. He was like Kentucky's official granddad.

† A phrase no father has ever said about Lindsey Graham.

"His number one priority was meeting with constituents," Clay tells me. "If someone from Kentucky was in Washington, his staff would let him know, and he would try his best to meet with them. It didn't matter if they were Democrat or Republican."

When traveling the state, Ford sought out interactions with average Kentuckians, especially those of the working class. "Anywhere my family went, if we stopped in a restaurant, or if someone was having an event for him, Granddad would want to go and talk to the people who worked in the kitchen. It was something he did almost everywhere we went."

John Calipari, the University of Kentucky basketball coach, is known to do the same thing. One day when I was praising him on my radio show, noting how that behavior had impacted me, an older gentleman from Owensboro called in to say, "I am glad Cal does that. But that was what Wendell Ford did back before it was normal." Ford's care for the common man may have been his most distinctive trait.

Mitch McConnell and Ford were colleagues, but not close friends. Still, both respected each other and found ways to work together. However, when Ford retired in 1998, Mitch saw an opportunity. He made Owensboro, the fourth most populated city in Kentucky, a priority, sensing that without the beloved local politician, the area could be quickly transformed into Republican territory. The Catholic Church has a strong presence in Daviess County, and the largest Right to Life (Right to Life Owensboro) organization in the state is based there, hosting an annual dinner that draws more than a thousand people. McConnell began an offensive, earmarking a number of major grants to the area and making numerous appearances.* Outside of Louisville and Lexington, there is no area Mitch has visited more, and with his cultivation, he was able to use the area's socially conservative views to flip the region's politics.

Now in 2020 the fruits of his labor are everywhere. All public officials outside of the sheriff and the property valuation administrator

* It was the political equivalent of going after your old college roommate's girlfriend after they break up, only instead of flowers, you give her a partial-birth abortion ban.

(PVA) in Owensboro are Republican.* Daviess County has voted Republican in every federal race in the last twenty years, with Mitch McConnell winning the county in his last three elections. Democrats are still here, but their presence and influence has waned.

It is fascinating to think how different the McConnell legacy will be from the one left by Wendell Ford. No matter who you speak with in Kentucky, regardless of party, if someone was touched by Senator Ford, they remember it and speak about him with a sense of universal respect. Ford knew that when a person meets his or her senator, it's a moment he or she will remember forever. Leadership, in part, is about how you make people feel and whether you can lift up those around you. By that measure and others, Wendell Ford was a great leader.

Contrast that focus on average Kentuckians with the leadership style of Mitch McConnell. The idea of Mitch hanging out with coal miners, fishing on Lake Barkley, walking the streets of West Louisville, or even celebrating a Kentucky basketball victory is not only difficult, it is laughable. McConnell's legacy will be that of a nasty partisan who forsakes his own state for individual power. All earthly gain is temporary, but for both of Kentucky's longtime senators, their legacy will live far beyond.

Henderson County

Mitch Doesn't Like You

When it comes to midsize Kentucky cities, young professionals seem to stick around Henderson,† a rare change from what we've found in

---

* It is a fascinating phenomenon that, in virtually every county in the state, you find a Democrat PVA. It might be the final vestige of the populist, antielitist sentiment that has a deep strain in the state. "Yeah, you might screw us around, but we are going to make sure you pay your full property tax!"

† Unlike Jackson, which isn't in Jackson County; Grayson, which isn't in Grayson County; or Carlisle, which isn't in Carlisle County, Henderson is in Henderson County. Hooray for rationality!

most of our travels. Located along the northwestern ridge of the state, on the banks of the Ohio River, Henderson's revitalized downtown boasts a number of outlets that attract a younger crowd, such as a brewery (the Henderson Brewing Company), a juice bar (the Henderson Juice Co.), and a yoga studio (*not* called the Henderson Yoga Company, in what feels like a real missed opportunity). This growing hipness is rare outside Lexington or Louisville, and it's a good look for Henderson, a town where chicken processing and agriculture are the top employers in the surrounding area.

The improvements to the Henderson Riverfront District are one of the only solid answers any community has given me to the question "What has Mitch McConnell done for your area?" In most places, people can't point to any tangible benefit to their county from Mitch's tenure in office. But here, even the senator's harshest critics agree that the Henderson Riverfront improvement came about because of money earmarked by McConnell. So, three cheers for Mitch, right?

Well, no. Even when McConnell seems to have earned praise, there's still a somewhat icky alleged backstory behind it. While in Henderson, we're told that a prominent hospital administrator in the city is one of McConnell's few close, personal friends. The senator is said to have called him and disclosed that the federal transportation budget had a surplus of several million dollars. Was there anything Henderson wanted? The administrator suggested that the city could use a new waterfront district, and that was that. Mitch's friend had spoken. One sentence, and it was done.*

Look, I get it. I understand why the people of Henderson would like this $8 million project. It's quite nice. Good for them. But is that really how we want our federal government to distribute resources? Rather than systemically assessing the needs of all 120 Kentucky counties, many of them saddled with, for one thing, crumbling roads (as I can attest), the senator telephones his old buddy and lets him decide in a matter of minutes. Hey, I am all for Henderson getting its riverfront area spruced up, but it probably would have been a wiser expenditure to replace the

* I hope if Matt runs and wins, this means I can get a waterslide on my street.

rickety Lucy Jefferson Lewis Memorial Bridge in Livingston County, you know? I guess it pays to be friends with Mitch McConnell.*

We met with Dorsey Ridley, an animated former Democratic state representative and senator who has worked with Mitch over the years on various projects. He appreciates the grant that McConnell helped obtain for this area (and a corresponding grant in Owensboro) but remembers the odd moment when the senator came to town to celebrate.

"He came to the dedication," says Ridley, "but let me tell you what he did. We set up the dedication ceremony down in this beautiful district—a great thing for us—with a big tent on the riverfront. There were seventy-five to eighty people out there, and when Mitch pulled up, instead of getting out and walking through the crowd to come up to the stage, he gets out and makes the hypotenuse of a right triangle, bypassing all the people who are there to see him, goes straight to the podium, and says, 'Let's go.' When he left the stage, he went through the crowd, but with a female aide dragging him by his arm. He hardly spoke to a single person."

Ridley said that while the rest of the politicians were taking time to bask in the achievement for the city and talk to the citizens, arguably the person most responsible spoke to no one. Ridley said he was shocked because he believes moments like that are where it's great to be in politics. "He could've thanked them for coming, he could have *let them thank him* for doing so much for Henderson, and instead, he hurries up, and he is in that car and he is gone. I was a sitting state senator—man, I'd have eaten that up!"

To be honest, it's sometimes hard to understand why McConnell likes being in politics. He isn't an ideologue (his positions fluctuate based on the political winds), he doesn't like attention (he does few interviews for a man of his power), and he hates being around people. I had an admirer and close political supporter of McConnell's† once tell me that, in some ways, he is saddened by Mitch. He respects his keen

* Still a high price for having to hang out with Mitch, though, if you ask me.

† Not an imaginary friend; a real person.

intellect and believes he is a master tactician at accomplishing conservative ideals. But he wondered if Mitch was ever happy personally or if he could enjoy his success. "I honestly am not sure he has many friends," he observed. "Politics is his life. There is nothing else."

McLean County

"Let's Call a Spade a Spade: It's Not Working for Farmers"

The chill of fresh autumn is in the air as we pass into McLean County early this Tuesday morning. McLean County is made up of a patchwork quilt of fields and farmland—in places it looks more like the stretched-out plains of Kansas rather than the soybean fields of western Kentucky. After maneuvering so many hills and mountains on this trip, it's unique and calming to encounter long, open roads for a change. We certainly don't have to worry about any hairpin turns, as every inch of the two miles ahead is visible.

Calhoun, the county seat of McLean, is fairly uneventful on this bright morning, with few people out and about. A sign for Calhoun reads "The Capital of Green River Country." That very river runs alongside the town, wooded on all sides and interrupted only by the occasional boat ramp. Greeting the few people we do see yields kind, countrified responses such as "How do" and "I'm doing all right, thank ya Lord." (One of the biggest distinctions between Kentucky life and most big-city life is the accepted conversation between passing strangers on the street. When I visit Manhattan to see my girlfriend, my country friendliness on the streets is met with near-universal disdain.)

McLean has a lot of towns with *fantastic* names. For instance, there's Cleopatra and, maybe ten miles south, Buttonsberry—a reflection, obviously, of McLean's multicultural Egyptian and rural English heritage.* There's Island, where the Dairy Freeze's Island Burger is

* We are not sure if this is true, but we choose to believe it.

so good, people come from the surrounding counties daily just for a taste.* There's even Poverty, which, according to legend, was founded and named by a sarcastic local physician who didn't like the way his snobby, rich neighbors looked down on the poor, so he named a town to give those less fortunate a place to feel welcome. No one here has ever seen McConnell visit. Not surprisingly, Mitch is very out of touch with those in Poverty.

We end up in Rumsey, Calhoun's neighboring town to the south, at the farm of Tommy Howard and his son, Nathan. The Howards are part of a long tradition of McLean County family farmers, growing soybeans and raising cattle in the small community. Nathan drives up across the field to us on a bright-green 9410 John Deere tractor, a snappy and clean behemoth with huge yellow-hubcapped wheels taller than I am. He is a fan of our show and tells me that today, whether I like it or not, I'm learning to drive the tractor. I am up for it because he seems friendly—and also looks like he might put me in a headlock if I don't.

I climb up the ladder, slide into the driver's seat, and am struck immediately by how high-tech this whole thing is. If your only notion of a tractor is from a Kenny Chesney video,† you don't know modern farming (or good country music). There are computer screens, ground sensors, and automatic alignment steering that make Howard's tractor seem more like an airplane cockpit than the stereotypical John Deere of yore. *Green Acres* this is not. The gregarious and chatty Nathan gives me instructions, letting me know when to let off the clutch, hit the gas, and plow the wide strip of ground before us. It feels a little like mowing the yard—that is, if your lawn mower weighed thirty-eight thousand pounds, and your mowing evenly spelled the difference between success and failure for thousands of dollars' worth of crops.

As we ride across the field, I ask Nathan how the current political climate is affecting Kentucky's family farmers. He says Trump's farming tariffs are hurting his operation every day.

"As a soybean farmer, I've been disappointed over the last few years

---

* I can attest it's a heck of a burger—so good it defines the entire town it resides in.

† "She Thinks My Tractor's Sexy"—yes, a real song.

about the tariffs on our market," he says. "I like free trade; I like to be able to sell to the person who wants it for the price established for it, so putting tariffs on soybeans isn't the answer. I'm not going to lie; I'm a registered Republican, but I can't say that Mitch McConnell has helped farmers much. He's let things slide because he's trying to keep power in Washington. He won't stand up to Trump on the tariffs for farmers because he's afraid Trump will turn on him, and when Trump turns on you, you're done."

Trump's popularity in Kentucky puts McConnell in a bind. Tariffs go against Mitch's free market philosophy, and he knows that, long term, they will not help the American farmer. But Trump is exponentially more popular than he is in every corner of the state. The quickest way for Kentucky to "Ditch Mitch" is if he turns on Trump, a fact of which McConnell is keenly aware. Thus he casts aside his role as the "grown-up in the room" and accepts Trump's worst impulses. For a man obsessed with his own political power, he has no other choice.

"People here think Trump can do no wrong, but let's call a spade a spade: it's not working for farmers," says Nathan, who thinks the subsidies are at least Trump's way of acknowledging he is hurting the farmers. "As far as Mitch is concerned, though, I can't remember the last time he was in McLean County. He's in Louisville, Lexington, and Washington. That's where he's at. He's not holding up his end of the bargain."

Nathan knows subsidies can't last forever, and he believes the American farmer can compete straight up if allowed to do so. He worries that Trump's imposing tariffs will drive China and other consumers of US agriculture to seek other, more permanent sources of food supply. He notes that this is happening already in South American countries such as Brazil, where the Chinese may create stable markets they can better control for the future. If that happens, the American farmer will be shut out. "We need to see the big picture," Nathan says, "and I am not sure that is happening right now by anyone in power."

Hancock County

Buffering . . .

Kentucky's magic lies in its regional delicacies. Depending on where you are in the state, you could go hog wild on burgoo (a spicy stew), benedictine (a cucumber and cream cheese spread), or a hot brown (a turkey and bacon sandwich with Mornay sauce). It's rare to find any of these beyond a forty-mile radius of Kentucky, but all are deliciously unique. In a homogenized food culture, where nearly every food item has been repackaged and refurbished for mass consumption, Kentucky still boasts largely untouched pockets of food heaven. (Speaking of pockets, Hot Pockets are made in Winchester, Kentucky.)

Take sorghum, for instance. Many of you have probably had the pleasure of enjoying a true southern breakfast. The Kentucky version is like a Thanksgiving spread of eggs, country ham, sausages (patty and link, no messing around), cornmeal mush, pancakes, fruit, grits, fried potatoes, and biscuits and gravy. If you're eating one in Hancock County, be careful when you reach for the maple syrup for your plate of hubcap-size pancakes because chances are you might be grabbing a wide-mouthed bottle of sorghum instead. *Don't freak out.* Give it a chance.

Sorghum is, in fact, utterly fantastic—and it's often a staple in some southern farming regions. Sorghum is so loved here that Hancock County is home to one of the state's three annual Sorghum Festivals.* Sorghum plants grow tall like corn, with little wheatish tops, and serve a number of agriculturally important purposes, such as producing ethanol and feeding livestock. The sorghum plant can also be boiled down into a very sweet syrup that goes perfectly on almost anything you'll

* Look, I like sorghum as much as the next quasi-southerner, but I feel like we could have stood to hold only *two* sorghum festivals a year. Either Morgan County or Washington County needs to back off.

eat on a southern breakfast table. And it has the added bonus of being gluten free.*

While sorghum evokes memories of a bygone area, present-day Hancock County perfectly illustrates the potential successes (and challenges) of Kentucky's future. The county is flush with industry, with around 65 percent of its jobs and seventy-two cents per dollar coming from local manufacturing. Those are astounding numbers for Kentucky and the envy of nearly every other county in the state. Due to its prime location next to the Ohio River and with easy access to many transportation centers, Hancock has a scrap metal and aluminum plant, a lumber mill, a paper company, and other stable major employers to keep its economy humming. In an era when the manufacturing economy continues to erode, Hancock County is a booming success story.

"We're not the barefoot, bib-overall-wearing hillbillies here whose lives have been decimated like some think," says Mike Baker, head of the Hancock County Industrial Foundation.

The big dilemma facing Hancock County is that almost everyone who works here resides outside the county, in nearby Owensboro or across the river in Indiana. "We just can't get people to stay here," Mike Boling, the circuit court clerk, tells us. "The issue for us is that sixty-two percent of this county's income is leaving at six o'clock every night."

The reasons are numerous. Many folks prefer other areas, including Owensboro, because they are wet, while Hancock County does not permit the sale of alcohol. Furthermore, Hancock County lags behind in housing, restaurant, and hotel options, issues that are important to the workforce they attract. However, the biggest hindrance to fixing all these issues is the county's terrible Internet service. In Hancock and, unfortunately, many parts of rural Kentucky, Internet and cell service are iffy at best, and in some places, all but nonexistent.

"Down here, where we are right now, we're on flat ground," Boling tells us. "Out elsewhere in the county, I can literally see a service tower from my window, and yet my Internet service bounces all over

* This one's for you, vegans!

the place." With limited cell service and virtually no Internet, it is impossible for Hancock County to keep the type of middle-class families the industries bring to the area.

The problem, as usual, is how the state and federal law are currently set up, which is not pro-consumer. "In Kentucky," Baker explains, "there's a regulation that an electric co-op can provide only electrical business. If these companies in rural areas want to branch out into Internet service, they have to start their own business and lease their own poles, and they can't afford it. At some point, the federal government is going to have to get involved in this, because we don't have the population density to draw an independent Internet provider to come into this community."

Corporations in Hancock County get around the problem by paying for their own access, but individuals don't have the same opportunity. This lack of Internet access is a statewide issue that continues to divide Kentucky counties into haves and have-nots. Osama bin Laden was able to have continuous Internet access as he moved from remote cave to remote cave around the most desolate areas of Afghanistan and Pakistan while on the run from American justice; it feels like Mitch should then be able to help fund a project to make sure the people of Kentucky have online options greater than an America Online CD and a hard-line phone connection.

Hancock County officials have been seeking federal government assistance for such a project for years, but their pleas to their senior senator have repeatedly fallen on deaf ears. Local leaders have done a tremendous job attracting industry, and those businesses love the workforce and the centralized location. But they can't take the next step and create a vibrant community because the federal government won't help provide the infrastructure. The result? Their workers go live elsewhere—say, Owensboro, or even worse, across the border in Indiana, costing the Bluegrass State desperately needed tax dollars.

As we begin the drive to our next stop, we turn on to Highway 60, which runs right through the center of Hancock County. Chris fishes out his phone to get directions to nearby Butler County. But we can't—even with two massive factories employing hundreds within eyesight, there is still no cell service until we pass the county line. So we navigate like the great explorers of old did, using only the sun, and head south.*

Butler County

The Giving Table

It's around three thirty in the afternoon as we enter Butler County. We pass the Southern Elementary School, where the reader board notes, "We Love Our Grandparents!"† Around the corner, an elderly couple sits on a porch swing, the man's arm wrapped sweetly around her shoulders, perhaps happy and content knowing they are loved by Southern Elementary School students. At the end of the road sits the Farm Boy Restaurant, my favorite spot for catfish in the entire commonwealth of Kentucky. It was the place a few years ago where a stranger in a plaid shirt and camo pants came up to me with no context, tapped me on the shoulder, and whispered, "I know what you are up to, but I ain't gonna say nothing." I am glad he didn't. It was a close one.

Morgantown is a nice community that, to be honest, has seen better days. After weeks of travel, I have learned you can judge a county's well-being by looking at the courthouse square. Whereas most county seats have new, shiny courthouses, with people milling about, Morgantown's is quiet, and the area is empty. The courthouse's paint is peeling badly, and the grass needs mowing. Most of the shop fronts on Main Street are empty, shuttered, or sealed up with flattened cardboard boxes behind the glass windows.

One store is open, however: Five Seasons, a brightly lit family-owned flower shop mixed among the neighboring darkened windows. A large banner over the front door reads "The Best People on

---

* There was also a big sign that said "Butler County" with an arrow. That helped too.

† I do, too, but there is no need to shout.

Earth Walk Through These Doors." We take that seriously and go inside. The room is a bit cluttered but friendly, with flower arrangements and miniature gifts placed all around. Next to the front door is a medium-size card table stacked with canned goods, vegetables, toothpaste, and a sign encouraging those without food or groceries to take what they need. From the looks of things, the table seems to be used often.

Roger Moore* is the shop's proprietor. He's more than happy to chat with a couple of strangers who've wandered into the store on what seems to be a slow afternoon. I ask him about the canned goods he's amassed for the needy on the front table.

"My son came up with the idea," Roger tells us. "He said to me, 'You know, there's a lot of people in this community who have stuff to give, and there's a lot of people in this community who need stuff.' Some kids around here don't get enough food, so we tried to help."

Roger estimates that about fifty individuals take advantage of the free table, including a man who lives just outside of downtown in a tent and cooks food over his fire in the tin cans. He says he asks nothing of those who take the items except that they take only as much as they need. The table is restocked up to three times a day, and local churches donate goods to help him keep up his supply. He shows us his supply closet, which is packed full of shaving cream, feminine products, boxes of crackers, and stacked cans of food. His unquestioning support for those less fortunate in Butler County is inspiring.

Five Seasons—he admits that the name was pulled out of a hat and doesn't mean anything specific—opened forty-six years ago, and Roger has been here the entire time, running the shop with his wife. He knows the community is struggling and wonders if it will be able to bounce back, but in order to do his part, he shops only at locally owned establishments. For example, he won't buy something from Walmart that he can get at the new hardware store around the corner, even if it costs a bit more. He cares about Morgantown first and has no interest in politics.

"When anything political comes on TV, I just turn the channel,"

* Not James Bond.

Roger says adamantly, "because I just don't want to deal with it. I feel like, years ago, I tried to keep up with it, but I've realized they're going to say and do whatever they want to do. I'd rather worry about something around here, something that I can help take care of."

As I often do when in these counties, I quickly take a look at how Mitch McConnell performed here in the last election. He carried Butler County handily, with nearly 70 percent of the vote. I talk to four local citizens and none can remember Mitch ever being here or point to anything he has done to help it in any way. Their answers and overall tone in discussing him don't suggest satisfaction with his thirty-six-year reign. Yet all four tell me they've voted for him. It doesn't seem to make sense. When I ask why, three of them shrug and say they aren't sure, one adding, "I never really thought about it."

In areas such as this, it seems McConnell is just the devil they know, and their prevailing skepticism and cynicism toward all politicians makes it easier for Mitch to survive. When you believe all of government doesn't have your best interest at heart, then you become resigned to whatever fate your current senator bestows on you. Put another way, if all politicians are the same, why not Mitch?

Muhlenberg County

"Mister Peabody's Coal Train Has Hauled It Away"

You know Muhlenberg County. Well, perhaps you at least know a song about Muhlenberg County. The one-time hotbed of coal, western Kentucky may be the most famous of all Kentucky counties for no other reason than John Prine's 1971 song "Paradise." I have listened to Prine my entire life, as he is my mother's favorite singer, and this song, his signature creation, details the decimation of his parents' beloved hometown due to strip mining of its beautiful land:

Then the coal company came with the world's largest shovel
And they tortured the timber and stripped all the land

Well, they dug for the coal till the land was forsaken
Then they wrote it all down as the progress of man.

And Daddy, won't you take me back to Muhlenberg County?
Down by the Green River where Paradise lay
Well, I'm sorry, my son, but you're too late in asking
Mister Peabody's coal train has hauled it away.

Behind the refrain that most Kentuckians know by heart is a sentimental and sad song that recognizes the environmental destruction the "world's largest shovel" did to his childhood memories of visiting this small Muhlenberg County town. That shovel is a reference to the Peabody Energy "Big Hog," which is said to have uncovered eighty million tons of coal over its two decades in use, including strip mining large parts of Muhlenberg County. Prine notes in the lyrics that "Mister Peabody's coal train has hauled . . . away" his paradise in Muhlenberg County, which is fitting, as it's how strip mining works, extracting minerals and leaving virtually nothing in its place.

Well, not nothing. Coal mining has left countless miners with debilitating black lung. In Greenville, we find Brent Yonts, an attorney who has spent the past thirty years representing those with the disease, caused by years of inhaling coal dust particles. Yonts's office in Greenville is a virtual museum to the administrations of both Abraham Lincoln and Bill Clinton, with commemorative plates and framed depictions of the men's greatest moments in every free space on the walls and shelves.* Yonts's two greatest loves are politics (he was once a state representative) and working on behalf of coal miners.

Although coal mining in Kentucky used to take place deep in the mountains, that's no longer the reality in 2020. Now most of the coal in America is mined from the Midwestern flatlands, including in Kentucky. It is cleaner, easier to extract, and a more modern source of energy. But its effect on the miner is still the same, ravaging the air passages of the lungs.

"Those with black lung usually die," Yonts says bluntly, sitting

* One was followed by Johnson, one followed his Johnson.

behind his desk in his office. "It's devastation. The person will gradually get worse and worse; they can't bend over to tie their shoes, they can't carry a gallon of milk from the refrigerator to the table, they can't do any yard work or household work. They're basically confined to a chair with little mobility, sometimes needing assistance just to change clothes. It's a deadly disease that only gets progressively worse."

Yonts represents miners tasked, sadly, with having to prove they have the illness in order to receive the care and appropriate federal benefits for their recovery. And if you think this is easy, you clearly don't know how either government or insurance companies work. Yonts has handled more than four hundred federal black lung cases, and the way he talks about them, it's clearly never a simple matter.

"The insurance companies fight all of them no matter what," the attorney explains. The excruciatingly frustrating process begins with a Department of Labor field office examination, at which the patient receives a chest X-ray; a blood gas test, to measure the amounts of oxygen and carbon dioxide in the blood; and a full physical examination. An opinion is rendered based on the X-ray and testing positive on either the blood gas assessment or the physical exam. Oftentimes, the government determines the miner has "failed" both tests, even though he exhibits symptoms of black lung. That's when attorneys such as Yonts have to intervene.

It's a very complicated process,* involving multiple doctors, tests, and hearings. It is one that intentionally requires miners to jump through many hoops, while giving multiple layers of medical professionals the ability to deny claims. On the second floor of Yonts's office is a room full of giant file boxes. He hoists one and places it on the desk, showing me a full binder of color-coded papers, each segment representing a different step in the process. And each miner's case has multiple binders like this. This particular file, he tells me, is for one person and still open. In fact, Yonts says the entire process—from opening the case to a final ruling—can sometimes drag on for *more than three years*. And when you take into account that by the time a person first sits down in Yonts's office, he or she may already be at an advanced

* Obscenely overly complicated.

stage of black lung, the cruel reality is that some don't live to see the final ruling or the first benefits check.

"That happens pretty regularly," says Yonts. "It depends on their age. I had someone sitting in that very chair earlier this morning; I was looking at his reports. His ejection fraction"—the amount of blood pumped by the heart with each contraction—"was thirty to thirty-five; I told him that if you're under fifty in your ejection fraction, you're about to die. And he said, 'I know that.'"

The way we treat those with black lung in this country is shameful and unforgivable. McConnell helped create and refine the broken system for processing the benefits claims of ill miners for whom time is of the essence. It exists solely for the benefit of insurance companies, which rely on needless bureaucratic red tape to delay or deny victims' claims. In Kentucky, about one in five coal miners are currently diagnosed with black lung. Yet the system for obtaining benefits is as maddeningly protracted as ever, leading to even longer waits for all patients.

Mitch McConnell surely didn't cause black lung. But he has done nothing to try preventing it through government safety regulations. While representing a state where miners are literally crippled by the disease, he has stood silently in the wings as afflicted workers continue to contend with unconscionable delays in getting their eligibility approved. He has no shame, and one trip to Yonts's office shows the dramatic effect of his indifference.

Logan County

The Pro-Life Democrat

Barbeque is big in western Kentucky. Even though the area didn't create a BBQ style (except for mutton BBQ, which is delicious), nor do they do it particularly uniquely, what this part of the state lacks in originality it makes up for in sheer quantity. No place in America can claim a greater per capita rate of BBQ restaurants than western Kentucky. In every town—and I mean literally *every* town—barbeque restaurants pop up like Russian donations to a Moscow Mitch SuperPAC, with each claiming to be the "best" barbeque you've ever tasted (a mathematical impossibility). The same dynamic occurs everywhere we go. We arrive in town, and the locals *insist* that we *must* try their local hometown BBQ restaurant, followed by a predictable "Best barbeque you'll ever taste!" We try to be kind to our hosts (even though we have had barbeque for six straight meals) and eat at the local version. It's likely owned by the person's brother's cousin's son, and we tell them afterward how wonderful it truly is. They are all fine but, honestly, at some point they start to taste alike. I mean, it's barbeque.

But sometimes you find one that delivers. Like, *really* delivers. And since 1983, Roy's Bar-B-Q, in Russellville, has held itself to a higher standard, drawing huge crowds daily. If I were to give a Best BBQ award in western Kentucky, I am going with Roy's; I make a point to stop there anytime I'm anywhere near Russellville. It's a small, funky little building right off the highway, its walls decked out with photos of famous University of Kentucky athletes and Kentucky politicians, in addition to a few mounted fish—a perfect encapsulation of the state's culture.

We've done our *Kentucky Sports Radio* show from Roy's on more than one occasion. In fact, not to toot my own horn, but on this trip, I see that a photo of my radio crew at our last appearance here now adorns the wall as well. I'm happy to be among such elite company as Ronnie Milsap, the country singer; NBA pro and onetime UK Wildcats forward Kenny Walker; and the late Kentucky senator and baseball Hall of Famer Jim Bunning.

Unfortunately, my pride is short lived. When I sit down at my table, I see that my smiling visage has been hung near a framed photo of one Addison Mitchell McConnell, complete with the signature "To the great folks at Roy's Pit Bar-B-Q, thank you for the wonderful Bar-B-Q, you're the best." It's a younger version of Mitch, less grizzled, though equally as creepy, and it seems to be staring deep into my soul.

I look across the room and see the Tracker once again—still following me and doing nothing except looking sad; what a terrible job this must be. He sees me see Mitch's picture and writes a note on his pad. I can't imagine what it says, but I wonder if it could be important.

I really can't shake this guy. They say that when McConnell sets his sights on you, he doesn't let up until he wins. And maybe this is true. He has the Tracker following my every move. I am hearing through the grapevine that the McConnell camp is *very* upset that I am writing this book and has been considering ways to try sabotaging it. At first, I sort of assumed this was nonsense, but now I have to wonder. The picture, the Tracker, the continued reluctance of people to speak—maybe Mitch is zeroing in on me. Either way, the picture does show Mitch has at least been to Logan County, a fact that puts it ahead of 80 percent of the counties in this state.

We pay a visit to the office of the Logan County judge-executive, a Democrat named Logan Chick. As we walk in, he remains seated in total relaxation behind a large wooden desk. He's leaned so far back in his chair that it's a wonder he doesn't topple over. His desk is surrounded by large boxes of giant maps and flags—all important judge-exec stuff. Chick has a gruff but friendly drawl and a cheeky grin at all times, as if he's letting you in on an inside joke he shouldn't be telling. He explains to us the contours of the county. There are four cities in Logan County: Adairville, Lewisburg, Auburn, and county seat Russellville. Land ownership is important to the people here, as it is used for farming or for leasing to those who want to farm on it. Logan County is home to the Red River Meeting House, site of the nineteenth-century religious movement known as the Second Great Awakening. It is also where, later in the 1800s, the outlaw Jesse James once shot a bullet into the metal fish weathervane at the top of the courthouse as he rode out of town, spinning it around and around. The townspeople were so honored, they left the weathervane and the bullet hole there to this day.*

As I noted earlier, many Kentuckians put social issues before economic issues when picking which political party they support. They tend to feel very strongly, one way or the other, about abortion, gun laws, and gay marriage, even though these issues probably don't impact

---

* This state loves their Jesse James stories. On this trip we have visited about ten counties that have some memorial to something he shot in their county. He really did a number on this state.

their daily lives. After all, there is only one abortion clinic in the entire state, exactly *no one* is proposing taking away their guns, and gay marriage is a settled precedent that hasn't caused the breakdown of society. Still, to the citizens in these parts, such matters *feel* more substantial and pressing than questions about economic policy. Logan Chick is one of those people but, unlike many, he is a Democrat.

When I ask him to tell me about his political positions, he leads off by saying, "I'm pro-life," pointing at us as he speaks.

This doesn't catch me terribly off-guard; during our travels I've met several people who are Democrats but have traditionally socially conservative beliefs. It's not all that rare here. Logan is a very religious man, and he tells me that despite those personal morals, he doesn't believe that, in his position, he should impose them on others.

"In my position I don't have to vote, but I do," he says, his fingers tented on his stomach, "and the reason I do is because I think the people in my county need to know where I stand. If you get to legislating morality or immorality, you might not have the freedom to go down the stairs and tell people about Jesus. I always say, We can walk down the stairs and tell people about Jesus today, but now you get to legislating morality; one day, someone else might be in charge, and we might lose that opportunity." Logan says he is against gay marriage (he no longer officiates marriages at all so that he won't have to perform a homosexual one), but now that the Supreme Court has ruled, his personal opinion doesn't matter. Just because he believes something, doesn't mean the government should. He offers as an example a recent county debate on an LGBTQ issue (he didn't specify which one), in which he voted against his personal beliefs. "I was against it, but I wasn't going to pass an ordinance saying the county was against it just because I was."

It's an interesting take, and one I haven't heard articulated a great deal on any political level. Logan Chick's socially conservative personal beliefs are as strong as anyone's. But he says he sets them aside in his role as a government official. It's actually a belief in "personal freedom" consistent with what many Republicans say they believe in other areas. For Logan, government isn't just about his beliefs or that of the majority of the masses, but it's for the rights of the minority individuals as well.

Nationally, there used to be many Democratic politicians and voters like Logan Chick, even just a generation ago. But in the hyperpartisan arena of today's politics, a large number of conservative Democrats have switched parties. You'll hear arguments about whether a litmus test on controversial issues such as abortion rights should be required in order to be a "true" Democrat. But if Democrats are going to win in states such as Kentucky, there has to be a place for a Logan Chick. He concurs with the party on the vast majority of issues. He believes that Mitch McConnell doesn't care about the working class, he fights for the poor, and he supports social programs. If his faith influences him to take a different position on a couple of issues such as abortion, should that disqualify his similarities on everything else? The Democratic Party preaches tolerance. But tolerance has to be shown to the Logan Chicks of the world, even if their views are antithetical to ours. If it isn't, then they will end up forced to line up with Mitch McConnell and his GOP brethren, simply because they feel they have been given no other choice. That result isn't good for anyone.

Hopkins County

Skatepark Resistance

Hopkins County has something for any athletic enthusiast. You can play a little sand volleyball over at Festus Claybon Park; on Grapevine Road you can test your skills at the 18,000-foot indoor range of the West Kentucky Archery Complex; or you can take in a Madisonville Miners game at historic Elmer Kelley Stadium. While these options are beloved by one and all, the city of Madisonville wanted to spruce the place up a bit more by recently building a $475,000 miniature golf course in the city. Unfortunately, they made one minor miscalculation. The course is right next to Elmer Kelley Stadium, and the lights from the golf facility wreak havoc on the pitcher's line of sight. Thus, any time the Miners are at home, the course has to be closed. Since that takes out a lot of summer nights, the city's mistake closes the course during the time it's most likely to be used. They do tell me it is something they are working on.

Hey, we all make mistakes. Madisonville does have its share of hits, however. The Skyview Skatepark is the only indoor skating facility in Kentucky, and it is packed on this particular Saturday. It occupies a large warehouse on North Franklin Street, and as we walk in, we get our fair share of side-eye glances. I guess they're stereotypically assuming I can't goofyfoot into a Caballerial,* and so they wonder who these lames are. I wave, trying to ease the tension, but make myself only look older and more out of place in the process. I couldn't have felt older if I had Macarena'd into the park with a *Reader's Digest* handing out Werther's Originals.

At Skyview's front desk we meet Jessica Short. She greets us warmly, a young mother in skater gear and stylish glasses. The park is owned by Jessica and her husband, Luke; she is an ex-newspaper journalist who switched careers, he is a longtime skater himself. The two opened the skate park when the property opened up, creating a safe place for young people to congregate while pursuing their passion for skate culture.

As we chat, the kids in this skate park slowly surround us to eavesdrop, and all seem good-natured and friendly. They listen in on our conversation until they hear me mention the words *politics* and *McConnell*. Then they immediately turn up their noses and head back to the ramps. I guess we aren't exactly a fun Saturday-night hang.†

Jessica tells us that the skaters here follow politics a bit, but it's not much of a hot topic. "I'd say no one in here likes Trump," she tells me, adding, "No one in here likes Mitch McConnell. But this is a place people come to forget about all that stuff."

While that's understandable, Jessica does say she is involved in a group that not only cares about politics but is trying to make a difference locally. "There is a group of younger people in this area that get

---

* He googled these terms.

† "You guys want to get crazy and analyze the voting trends in Todd County? We'll buy the Sunkist!"

together and try to get people like that out of office," she confides. "They'll try to take on roles even as small as city government to push those types of people out. It's a group of people who just got sick and tired of it all."

She is talking about Resist Kentucky, a protest-minded group founded by local people in the community trying to fight the good fight. Jessica explains that they organized via Facebook and began figuring out how they could effect change in places such as Madisonville, rather than simply accepting the status quo. They thought a good first step would be finding people who shared their goals and getting them elected to the city council.

Cody Lander, who is both a member of Resist Kentucky and the head of the Pennyrile Pride Alliance in Madisonville, tells me, "Right after Trump's inauguration, I was invited to an all-private online group chat with like-minded individuals, and we decided we wanted to make an impact. We formed Resist Kentucky. Most of them do not like to be named because of their jobs and what people might say, but I have been acting as a face both for Resist and the Pride Alliance since then."

The group decided that at least in these parts, protest would not be the most effective means to fight the Mitch McConnells of the world. People would just ignore their words. They had to focus on elections. They decided to channel their energy first at a local level and target officials who worked against their beliefs by backing their opponents, whose policies the group could support. It was resistance through the system, and it ended up with Resist Kentucky backing Misty Cavanaugh, an openly gay Madisonville citizen running for city council.

Lander says the group wanted to get more transparency on the city council and have a voice connected to the younger citizens in the community. While talking with Misty one day about local politics, he saw she agreed with the group's ideals and suggested she should run for city council. Soft-spoken but direct, Cavanaugh ran on a platform of refocusing the city toward its youth, diversifying the identity of Madisonville, and building a culture in the town. Resist Kentucky went right to work, and Cavanaugh attended town events and focused on getting her message out to voters via social media. Lander was surprised how little backlash they encountered.

"The parties aren't strong here until you get into the state and national levels, and then people start caring about party name," Cody tells me. "But on the local level, party lines are very blurred. We had no issue when we were knocking on doors; Misty had a card stating she was a military wife, and people would ask, 'What branch does her husband serve in?' We'd tell them her *wife* is at Fort Campbell. Nobody had anything negative to say about that."

Her opponent was an older businessman in the community who represented the city's old guard. He was against adding a restaurant tax and promoting any funds for tourism or development in the county. He campaigned very little, had no social media presence, and was absent from debates held by the city. His absence only made Misty work harder.

On election night Cody, Misty, and others joined a packed throng within the exposed-brick walls of Madisonville's The Crowded House gastropub to watch the results. The group was confident Cavanaugh could win but were shocked by just how much—the team watched in awe as Cavanaugh nearly doubled the votes of her opponent. A scripted phrase painted on the wall at The Crowded House read "*Meeting Place of the Revolution*." It seemed completely fitting on that evening.

"Being both kind and direct can go a long way in a small town," Cody tells me. "You may not be the person who pushes your way to the front of a room, but if you get your two minutes to talk, you can make that difference."

What's next for Resist Kentucky and the movement as a whole in Madisonville is unclear. Cavanaugh has settled into her city council role and preferred not to talk to us for this book because of its political nature (the first time a politician has told us they won't speak to us about politics). After the group's electoral success, they have taken a bit of a step back, focusing more on their regular lives and less on political activism. But the symbolism of the win remains, and the subset of citizens in Madisonville, from the members of Pennyrile Pride Alliance to the skaters in the skate park, now have a voice they believe will listen to them. That's not a political revolution, but it's a start.

Webster County

Smelly Chickens

What if I knocked on your door and told you that if you'd let me build about four houses in your sprawling backyard, and each house would have, let's say, *one thousand chickens* as tenants, then all you would need to do was house them and feed them, you could make a large profit. Would you do it? I'll give you the houses and the chickens; all I need is your backyard. I'll bring the feed to you; all you have to do is just let the chickens live there. Everything else will be easy.*

Well, that's the situation that played out just over twenty years ago when Tyson Foods moved into Webster, Henderson, and McLean Counties. The food industry giant wanted to build a large chicken processing facility, the extent of which would spread out across the three counties. Each county would get a portion of the plant, but farmers in each county were needed to help house the countless chickens Tyson raises in order to mass-produce its various chicken-based goods. Webster County had the most fertile land and the most available acreage as a number of farmers there were struggling financially due to the tobacco decline. Many said yes, and Tyson moved in to begin work.

Here's the thing, though—and I forgot to tell you this when I knocked earlier. These chicken houses produce the most disgusting smell ever known to man. If you have never had the pleasure of driving past a chicken farm, I would describe the odor as a combination of decaying garbage, animal feces, and burnt hair, with a hint of raw eggs thrown in for good measure.† I got a whiff on my initial drive into Webster County and it was no joke. It was hideously unpleasant.

---

* Take as long as you need, but just know this is a rhetorical question, not an offer for a business transaction.

† This will be the only in-depth description of chicken feces for the rest of the book.

It also became an unexpected nuisance for the county's economy. "There were some other people here at the time who were trying to create some economic development, and they could see that we have water as well as a low cost of energy in coal firing plants," Paul Vernon Westerman, a former educator and school principal, tells me. We're sitting at a table in the back corner of Papaw's Poole Mill Restaurant, where the pie is alleged to be the best anywhere around. "But," he continues, "if you're an executive, and you come here, and all you smell are chicken houses, you're probably not going to bring your plant to Webster County."

Tell me about it. I can't imagine living with the daily smell. Paul's wife, Sonya, chimes in. "There were probably a hundred of them within a couple of miles of our house," she says. "We really can't smell them if there's a breeze, only if the air is still. But then it really hits us."

"Chicken guts and burning feathers," says Paul.

Not exactly a great tagline for a brochure from the chamber of commerce. Also sitting with us is Jim Townsend, the former county judge-executive who, in the 1990s, helped make the call to bring Tyson into the area. "It was one of the hardest decisions I ever had to make," he reflects, "because it was going to bring a lot of jobs in. But there were three judge-executives at the time. None of us could build the package just for our county without the other two. So, it worked out that McLean County got the hatchery, Henderson County got the plant, and we got the grain facility."*

Townsend was the Democratic judge-executive in Webster County for many years, but just as in much of the state, these days Republicans rule the proverbial roost, and Sonya says that things have started to get bad for the Democrats left hanging around.

"They won't even let us have a rally in the Dixon Community Center," Sonya tells me. "Even though when Jim was in office, he always let Republicans do what they wanted. Once the Republicans took office, they said no political events could be held there; they stopped us from meeting."

Changing the rules after you take power is, of course, a Mitch

* And the smell.

McConnell signature move that we have seen many times in recent years. Since taking over as Senate majority leader, he has systematically eliminated long-standing Senate rules and policies for his party's political gain. Nowhere can this be seen more clearly than in the confirmation of judges. For decades, the Senate operated under the "blue slip" policy, in which no federal judge from a state could be confirmed unless he or she received the blessings of both senators from that state.* This operated for decades and was observed by both Democratic and Republican leaders to bring some order to the judicial confirmation process. Then, when Trump was elected president, Mitch ended the policy, allowing the GOP Senate to confirm numerous ultra-conservative judges in very liberal states without any hindrance.

That's to say nothing of his handling of the vacancy on the US Supreme Court following the sudden passing of conservative justice Antonin Scalia in February 2016. Despite the fact that Barack Obama still had nearly a quarter of his term left in office, McConnell invoked the made-up "Biden Rule" to prevent the Senate from even considering the president's Supreme Court nominee, an esteemed US Court of Appeals judge named Merrick Garland. McConnell held the empty seat hostage for the remainder of Obama's final year in office, then delivered it to the new Republican president, Donald Trump, as a White House–warming gift.† With a GOP majority in the Senate, Trump's conservative pick, Judge Neil Gorsuch, was quickly confirmed to maintain the conservatives' 5-to-4 edge. You don't have to be from Webster County to know that tactic was chicken shit.

Forcing people to choose sides and then pitting them against each other in all-out political warfare has been McConnell's political strategy for a long time. But now its effects are being seen in everyday life. All three of the Webster Countians at our table agree that it's a tough row

---

* This policy wasn't exactly the most democratic in the world, but Mitch had no problem enforcing it in the Clinton and Obama years.

† A little better than what George W. Bush left Barack Obama: matching Millard Fillmore salt and pepper shakers.

to hoe for Democrats in the new Republican landscape. Sonya pulls out her phone to show us a Facebook page called Bluegrass Under a Red Sky, an invitation-only group where Kentuckians in majority Republican counties can share their ideas for the state out of sight of prying social media neighbors who might take umbrage at their views. She says the group allows them to express their opinions freely among people who will not judge them, something that used to be possible in Webster County, but now? Not so much. I take a look at it and find a mixture of interesting articles, jabbing memes, and liberal discussion—I can see how it could serve as an online oasis for suffering Democrats.

"There's definitely a Democratic underground," Sonya explains. "We can't really go out and in public talk about our political beliefs if we want to remain friends with some people. There are definitely people who, if they knew our feelings, wouldn't be going out to dinner with us anymore. There's a division being made, both in this country and here in this county, and it's not good for anyone." She shrugs before taking a bite of that sweet, sweet bipartisan Papaw's pie.

Union County

"This Is the Business We Have Chosen"

Union County, for all intents and purposes, seems to be doing pretty well at the moment. One-third of all coal in the state comes from here. If you're making your own "Uses of Kentucky Coal" chart at home, you should know that coal mined in the eastern part of the state tends to be used for steel and metallurgic purposes, while coal from western Kentucky generally fuels power plants. The deep, rich soil here also makes it ideal for farming, and as icing on the cake,* Union County even struck oil recently, adding another lucrative industry to the northwestern part of the county. Locals are also proud of the Union County

---

* Do *not* use coal as icing on your cake.

High School Braves wrestling team. The eight-time state champions have won four of the last six titles, procuring a national ranking in the process.*

With an upbeat economy, many prospects for entrepreneurship, and, apparently, no discernible ceiling for its high school wrestling aspirations, Union County is pretty happy. The overall optimism of the area can be seen on the face of Jimmy Baird, the president of Jim David Meats, one of the greatest business success stories in these parts. He is the epitome of a self-made man, starting out as an eighteen-year-old farmer with just a handful of hogs and ending up the owner of the largest independent major ham manufacturer in America. Baird, stout, clean-shaven, and wearing a blue denim shirt and a baseball cap, has a handshake that grabs you and pulls you directly into his body. As he speaks, he gestures with his hands often: the more forceful the point he is making, the more expansive his arm movements. Baird frequently flashes a slight, natural grin of a man who's got the world figured out and knows it.

Jim David Meats is the processing facility that Jimmy Baird built from the ground up and turned into one of the largest employers in the county. When we arrived after lunch, he was excited to give us a tour. Not many meat processing facilities are going to let you drop in and show you around (most are pretty secretive about things), but Baird is clearly a different breed.

The operation is sprawling, with a massive assembly line that turns hogs into processed ham. I will spare you the details; but if I'm being honest, it is gross—which, of course, is no fault of Baird's. As Hyman Roth, the fictional mobster in the film *The Godfather: Part II*, put it, "This is the business we've chosen." But seeing the processing of meat from start to finish is . . . eye opening.

He shows us every step of the process, from the hog meat coming in, being put together as a ham, then bound and packed to ship. Giant vats of crimson by-product pop against the stark white walls as rolling barrels of viscous meat whizz by on the way to their next destination.

---

* I made the mistake of saying this didn't seem like a big deal and a fourteen-year-old immediately put me in a full nelson.

It's like *Charlie and the Chocolate Factory,* but with a lot more blood, guts, and hog parts.* We are sanitized to the nines with hairnets, boots, boot covers, and long overcoats. Baird knows that a single mistake can compromise an entire facility like this, and so nothing is risked. "We can be shut down if we score anything less than a ninety on a safety evaluation," he explains, understandably protective of the investment he's made.

Even with the inevitable mess, what's so impressive about Baird's operation is how meticulously he seems to have thought of everything. This is not Upton Sinclair's muckraking (and yuck making) 1906 novel *The Jungle,* with its grotesque commentary on the meat industry; it is a sterile, clean environment that runs like a well-oiled machine. Baird tells us exact details of how much time is spent on every step of the process, the various standards he requires before each ham can be sent out, and his entire packaging and shipping methods, all of it done in-house. Even though the facility is located in this rural county and is still run by the same individual owner, it is no small-time endeavor. Baird's ham, chicken salad, and other products are shipped as the store brands of supermarkets such as Walmart and Kroger all over the United States. When we reach the shipping room, a massive hangar of palettes of boxed Jim David Meats is being prepared, each labeled with its destination, from North Platte, Nebraska, to Miami, Florida.

We walk around the messier parts of the meat production area, where virtually all of the employees are Hispanic. I ask Baird if there is a lot of immigrant labor in the area, and he says, "Thankfully, yes." According to him, his Hispanic workers are among the hardest working he has ever hired, and he points out that they take on jobs in the packing process that he can't get anyone else to do. As with many employers we have met in rural Kentucky, he remarks that unemployment benefits in Union County have become more attractive for many citizens than a full-time job. Baird grows animated as he says, "We've got to get rid of food stamps, get rid of all that bullshit." He believes an attitude of dodging employment in favor of government assistance is taking over

---

* *Matt and the Ham Factory.*

the county and makes finding good workers in Union County nearly impossible.

Based on those comments, I wasn't shocked when Baird said he is also a big Donald Trump fan. (I ask about McConnell, too, but he just smiles and changes the subject, waving his hand with a dismissive "Naaaah.") He tells me he thinks Trump has been a very good president. But when I ask him about Trump's demeaning comments about Hispanic workers like the ones who work for Jim David Meats, he defers and says he doesn't approve of that. He likes Trump's work on the economy and likes that he is a straight shooter, a tell-it-like-it-is kinda guy. He looks past the rest and doesn't pay it too much attention. It is a common theme I find in a lot of my travels. Many Trump fans don't like his outlandish and sometimes downright disrespectful comments, but they minimize them as being irrelevant, like the sketch they don't care for on an otherwise great episode of *Saturday Night Live*.

Jimmy Baird's success is inspirational. He is a lone active owner, taking on companies that are much larger than his with efficiency and ingenuity, traits that are at the heart of the American dream. Baird loves his workers, including the Hispanic ones that he seems to see himself in, the ones working diligently to make a better life for themselves and their families. But then he also likes Trump, a person who has villainized those that are expressing the exact traits Baird says are so hard to find in the everyday citizen of Union County. When I see Trump on television ranting about Mexican immigrants, I wish I could take the people in the crowd cheering and bring them to Jim David Meats. In order for all of us to eat the hams that will be a part of our holiday meals, Hispanic laborers are working long hours, doing messy, difficult jobs that, according to Baird, others won't do. These workers do the daily grunt work necessary to give us the food supply our nation craves. So why do all of us let our leaders villainize these men and women just for political points? They are just the modern version of Baird—taking chances, working hard, and sacrificing, all while trying to pursue the American dream.

Todd County

The Life of a Migrant Worker

As we head into Todd County, we run into a sign for the town of Tyewhoppety, a "town" that consists only of a handful of homes bunched together, with a wooden sign in front on which the following is carved:

WELCOME
TO
TYEWHOPPETY KY
POPULATION 33
MAY GOD BLESS
AMERICA

I'm not sure what happens to this sign when a person is born or dies in Tyewhoppety. It looks like it's been there for quite some time without anyone carving new numbers into it, so maybe there is a "one-in, one-out" rule to the place. It's like Todd County's most exclusive bar, only the reward is empty farmland.*

We pass the Jefferson Davis Monument, a 350-foot-tall ode to the president of the Confederate States of America, placed in his hometown of Fairview. Even though Kentucky was not part of the Confederacy, the monument was built in 1924 by a group of southern boosters who wanted to create a rallying point for future Davis admirers. It is obscenely tall, the second highest obelisk in the world, and it literally sits alone in a field off the highway. I am not a Jefferson Davis guy (I have a bias for those who didn't secede from the Union and bring about a bloody civil war, but I am weird like that), but it's quite a structure. When we went, the elevator was out of service, so we couldn't get to the top. While some hard-core Jefferson Davis fans have dreams of the South rising again, maybe they should start by getting their elevator to rise first.

---

* You don't have to go home, but you can't plow here.

We head to visit the farm of Jerry Wayne and Shea Simons, tobacco farmers who host a group of Mexican migrant workers each year for six to eight months, depending on demand. That's not a rarity around Todd County. The area is heavy with large farms, and farmers need the extra hands on deck to turn around their harvests each year.

The Simonses' farm is huge: about sixty acres of tobacco, fifty acres of watermelons, and some thirty acres of pumpkins and cantaloupe. They're also trying to grow hemp right now, to see how successful the new crop will be and if it can replace the dying tobacco crops they have farmed for so long. That's a lot of farmwork to be done, and as Shea, a slim blond woman in boots and jeans, walks us around the land, it's clear that it would take a substantial amount of labor to turn around so much yield each year. She and her husband learned long ago that they couldn't find the labor necessary in Todd County, so they joined the federal system that allows the entry of seasonal agriculture workers from Mexico. It works really well for them and they agree to show us more about the workers' lives.

Shea echoes the claim from Jimmy Baird in Union County: not only do the migrant workers provide support, they do so working at levels that simply cannot be matched by workers here. "We absolutely could not function the way we do without them," Shea tells me. "Have you ever been in a tobacco patch? It's the middle of summer, it's a hundred ten degrees, it's sticky, and these guys are working like nobody's business. I think Americans overall couldn't hang with what they do."*

The Simonses host the workers during their stay on the farm. Even though almost none speak English, they've developed a good working relationship, and so they tend to have the same individuals back every spring. Simons takes us through their housing as we chat, and it is eye opening. Depending on the time, twenty-five to thirty men live in one house, spread across a number of rooms, with bunk-bed-style sleeping arrangements. With thirty men under one roof, it looks about as you would imagine: dark, quite messy, and there is a lived-in odor in the air. Food simmers on the stove, laundry is hung to dry, a TV hums with

---

* I agree with Shea. I'd never cut it in a tobacco field. Five minutes of walking in downtown Elkton and I had to stop and eat two scoops of ice cream.

news in front of a big, worn-down sofa. Photos of wives, children, and family adorn the walls; some of the guys have made makeshift curtains around the bedframes to give themselves some privacy. It's crowded, but it works. This house, Simons tells us, is built according to federal code, which requires furnishing enough sinks, refrigerators, and bathroom facilities for the entire crew. Anything above thirty, Simons says, and they'd have to build another housing facility.

"Twenty years ago," she says, "the wage for a migrant worker was $5.50 per hour, but now it's up to $11.63, almost four dollars higher than the minimum wage in Kentucky. The workers do put in more hours, working six full days a week, with a guarantee of one free day each week. We spend time with the guys; we form bonds with them," Simons emphasizes. "We respect them, and in return they respect us. A lot of the farmers, the older men, don't treat their workers well. About eight or ten years ago, seven or eight of the guys had left another farm, where they were being treated very poorly, and we picked them up." It angers Shea when she hears about mistreatment at other farms, because she knows those workers are no different from her employees.

"They all have small children, for the most part, and they miss them," she says empathetically, "but they know they have to be here to make money to send back home. And even though we can't understand each other, we laugh together, we eat together, we do fun things together with them outside of work. They're just people. They're good guys."

The current heated national rhetoric around immigrants bothers Simons.

"They're our family," she says. "So, I guess like with anybody, if somebody says something negative about your family, you're automatically going to be defensive." As Simons explains, the manual labor that these immigrants provide literally keeps the farms in operation, which, in turn, allows the economies of these rural counties to continue to flourish.

Mitch McConnell has always been a supporter of the guest worker program and has repeatedly voted to increase the number of guest workers allowed in the country. But at the same time he stands silently by while the president not only engages in hateful rhetoric against them but also refuses to establish any pathway to citizenship for those whose labor have helped build the country. Here is the reality that very few want to admit: that food you ate tonight? It's relatively inexpensive compared with what much of the developed world pays. You want to know why? Because labor costs are kept low through programs such as the guest worker visa, the special set of farm labor laws, and, yes, illegal immigration. Without all three—yes, including illegal labor—your food would be double the price. Cost is low because immigrant labor is available to do jobs other Americans won't, and they do the work for low wages. Every single government leader knows this. Every one. It's the reason most Republicans cheer on Trump's border wall rhetoric but ultimately don't vote to fund it. They know that without a comprehensive immigration strategy, building a wall would kill the US agricultural economy.

Rather than fight back against the rising tide of hate directed toward immigrants, particularly those from south of the border, McConnell chooses to remain silent. For our nation's migrant workers, the message is painfully clear: "Do the work, but don't stay. And while you are here, we will demonize you." It's ugly enough in theory. But if you take the time to go to places like Todd County and see the hard labor these men and women give to the American economy, far away from home and under difficult conditions, it becomes infuriatingly despicable. Economic realities make it so that immigrant and migrant labor is necessary for US success. The least we can do is treat those who make up the backbone of our country's agricultural infrastructure with dignity and respect.

Ohio County

Bill Monroe and the Best Beef O'Brady's

Beaver Dam is a small town off the Western Kentucky Parkway. We enter from the north, passing combines harvesting beige fields throughout the county. We are headed to the Beaver Dam Amphitheatre, the symbol of growth for a community that is centered around music. This is the birthplace of Bill Monroe, the father of bluegrass music, and in tiny Rosine on Friday nights in the summer, the Rosine Barn Jamboree brings in some of the best gospel, country, and square dance artists from around the country. They play deep into the night, jamming with fellow artists to honor Monroe's legacy. The amphitheater even goes a step further, bringing national touring artists from all sorts of musical genres to the small town, including Jason Isbell, Sheryl Crow, the Temptations, Old Crow Medicine Show, and Poison just in the past year.* Its existence has helped revitalize the town, making Beaver Dam a centerpiece for entertainment in the area.

Economically, we are told, the timber industry is thriving here, with sawmills and hardwood manufacturers doing quite well. Apparently, there are more jobs than people, and the only problem townspeople can seem to think of is that there aren't enough good places to eat. The area's newest restaurant, located in an old town bank building, is a sports bar chain called Beef O'Brady's. We stop in late in the afternoon. All across America, Beef O'Brady's are closing left and right, as consumers move to other sports bar options. But not in Beaver Dam. People here are so happy about life that they are pumped about their Beef O'Brady's and proclaim loudly that they have the best one in the country. (I see no reason to dispute this fact. I don't rank Beef O'Brady's but if I did, it would be #1.)

In fact, the one moment I get excited thinking something crazy may happen, Ohio County's happiness disappoints. As we meet with a group of local Democrats in the Beef O'Brady's, the Republican state representative for this area, Scott Lewis, walks in the front door. Uh-oh. When they tell me who he is, I become concerned that he's here to spy on behalf of McConnell, as this happened to us in another location. Instead, he walks up to our table, exclaims, "Well, *there is Matt Jones*!!!" and gives me a big, friendly slap on the back. Then he pulls up a chair to sit and hang out with his Democratic friends. No controversy, just Democrats and Republicans schmoozing at the thriving Beef O'Brady's. Life is good in Ohio County.

---

* Poison played "Every Rose Has Its Thorn," in case you were wondering. And it's still great.

I am not saying Ohio County has no problems. But they don't seem to be major; I can't find anyone with an ax to grind. A young librarian tells me she wishes they had a new movie theater since the drive-in down the road closed. Yeah, that would be nice. A radio host who has a regular segment called "What's Your Beef?" says a frequent caller complaint is that the city spent too much money on Porta Potties for a festival celebrating Bill Monroe a couple of years ago. Think about that. Have you ever even had two seconds' worth of thought about what your city paid for Porta Potties in your life? Well, in Ohio County, it is the biggest complaint! And it happened two years ago!

After encountering so many frustrating issues in other parts of our journey, Ohio County was a welcome reprieve. I am sure there are problems here, but the overall vibe was positive, and it seemed like a good place to stop our week five travels, as I had a flight to catch. So, after a round of Boom Shrimp at the world's most happening Beef O'Brady's with my bipartisan friends, I headed off to Louisville to get ready for a big day.

Washington, DC

Good Luck Chuck

Early the next morning, I board a seven o'clock flight to Washington, DC, for my meeting with Senator Chuck Schumer. I knew of Schumer only from what I'd seen on television. He strikes me as the consummate Washington politician, glasses perched on the tip of his nose, figuring out the next political move, always ready for partisan warfare. My assumption is he is taking this meeting simply to satisfy the donors, tell them he did it, and then move on and ignore me going forward. But it's still an opportunity. As word began leaking in Democratic political circles that Schumer was willing to talk to me, I was getting calls from people wanting to help. I have no idea how these people find this stuff out.

I didn't return a single call, sticking with the policy that had gotten me this far. Go with my gut, and if it is supposed to work out, it will.

I was met in DC by my small team of trusty advisors. As we grab a quick bite down the street from Schumer's office, they go over the talking points. The expectation is that he will yell at me and try to bully me out of the race. He is already committed to Amy McGrath, but the senator hates contested primaries and does everything possible to avoid them. Their theory is that my performance with the DC donors has him worried about possible momentum, and thus he has brought me here to talk me out of running. And if that doesn't work, he'll try to find a way to push me out of the race. They all tell me to stand my ground, give away as little information as possible, and promise nothing. The advice is good, but tempered a bit by the fact that all want me to not mention their names due to possible retribution against them. Stick your neck out, they seem to say, just don't stick ours out too.

This trip is a heady experience for me. For the first time, this potential run now feels truly real. The Senate minority leader is taking my potential candidacy seriously enough that he wants a one-on-one. Regardless of whether it's to talk me out of it or simply to extend the necessary political courtesy, I am genuinely excited. It's one thing to be a sports radio show host from eastern Kentucky and think you can run against the second most powerful man in America. It's another for others to make the same assumption. I take a deep breath and look around. I want to soak in this surreal moment before it passes.

The meeting is in the Democratic Senatorial Committee building, a drab, depressing rowhouse across the street from the Capitol. Rules prohibit political business in the hallowed halls of Congress, and thus the true nitty-gritty party talks take place in old, cramped buildings such as this. As I wait in the lobby for Schumer to arrive (he is a little late due to the latest impeachment developments against President Trump, occurring just a few hundred yards away), I watch staffers move quickly in and out. They walk with a purpose, but each makes sure to say "Hi, Matt!" as he or she passes by. It's a little startling. I don't know any of them.

A little more than twenty minutes late, the senator rolls in and greets me with a big smile. "So, you are this Matt Jones I have heard so much about," he says. He points me in the direction of his office upstairs, and we walk toward whatever fate awaits me. I look behind me as I move toward the steps, and the young woman working at the front desk makes eye contact and gives a quick smile, as if reminding me to maintain a positive attitude.

When we enter Schumer's office, I notice immediately how barren it is. He uses this only to meet with candidates, and there is virtually nothing in it except a big-screen television, which he immediately turns on to a live feed of the Senate floor. The only other person in the room is a DSCC staffer who sits to the side silently. Schumer gets behind the desk, I take a seat across from him, and we begin with him asking questions about me. I do the usual biographical speech about being from eastern Kentucky, going to law school, and then starting a sports radio career.

"So, sports radio?" he says, perking up. "How did you get into that?"

Sports is the great male icebreaker. Whenever I am talking to a male sports fan,* the moment I say I do sports talk radio, my listener bolts upright in his seat, and gets all googly-eyed. It doesn't matter how famous or powerful they are: for men who like sports, the idea of getting paid to blabber about them incessantly every day seems like a dream.

Schumer confides, "I have always thought about doing that. I am a huge Bills fan . . ." With that, he then drifts off into Buffalo Bills football talk for the next five minutes. I smile, nod, and make references to Bruce Smith and Steve Tasker, two stars from the franchise's early-1990s pinnacle, when Buffalo made it to the Super Bowl four seasons in a row—only to lose each time. In short, I play the role to which I am accustomed: letting the powerful person play out his sportscaster dreams.† It works like a charm every time.

The change in topics loosens Schumer up and he becomes much more casual. He asks about my stances on issues (concrete proof that the process for Senate races is more substantial than my experience with the House), then says he would like to ask me some political questions "if that's okay." I had been warned about this prior to the meeting. Schumer likes to feel out potential candidates by quizzing them on the

---

* Maybe this is true of women, too, but they hide it much better.

† Be prepared for Chuck Schumer's *Buffalo Sports Radio*, coming this fall.

ideology of famous politicians. He uses it to get a sense of your political acumen (at least according to his scale). He gives potential candidates a list of names and says, "If 'one' is Jesse Helms and 'one hundred' is Paul Wellstone, where would you put these people on the ideological scale?" He then reads off a list of names, from Hillary Clinton, to Mitch McConnell, to Elizabeth Warren, to Ted Cruz, and gets your opinion. I give him my percentages (Hillary 70, Mitch 20, Warren 85, Cruz 5, etc.), and they seem to correspond to his. He asks where I am on the scale, and I say, "Sixty," a number that also seems satisfactory. He then comes to what I have been told is the most important question: Where do I rate *him* on the scale?

I was prepared. I knew from talking to a close friend of Schumer's that he sees himself as more moderate than his general public persona, and it is flattering to him if candidates recognize it. So, I said (only partially believing it), "Sixty-five," and he nearly leaped out of his seat. "Exactly! People never realize that about me! I am always seen as this New York progressive, but I can work with people on all issues." He goes on to talk about upstate New York, how he won every county in the state in his last election and how the party needs moderates. He then says with a nod, "I like the way you look at this."

We move on to talking about Kentucky. I tell him about this book and the plan to visit all 120 counties in the state. He is shocked to learn that I am going to visit every one in ten weeks, noting that he hits all the counties in New York once every two years (as opposed to Mitch McConnell, who visits one county every two years). He asks me how I would go about winning if I were a candidate, and I explained my thinking.

To win in Kentucky, any Democrat has to win Louisville and Lexington big, compete well in northern Kentucky, and then cut the margins in rural parts of the state. What I believe I can do differently is actually win in the mountains of eastern Kentucky. I am from there, have a strong connection to the area, and understand the issues important to them. If a Democrat can win the mountains, it changes the whole political calculus of the state. McConnell is particularly vulnerable there because of his poor record when it comes to caring for coal miners.

I can tell Schumer is intrigued. He cuts right to the chase:

"What about Amy McGrath? Can't she do the same thing?"

"No, she can't," I say bluntly. "The launch of her campaign was horrific. No one knows what she stands for, and she is running for office by trying to avoid tough stands and align herself as more favorable to Trump than McConnell is. That is an insanely stupid strategy that no one believes is authentic or real, and if she utilizes it, she will lose by fifteen points or more."

He asks how I would deal with Trump's popularity and I say, "I think Kentuckians respect authenticity and honesty. I will say to Trump voters what I always say. On the issues, we agree more than we disagree. We all want better education, health care, and workers' rights. The only difference is I don't like Trump and you do. That's fine. But we both don't like Mitch."

Schumer pauses and grins at me slowly. "You have thought a lot about this, I can tell." He then goes on to say that while he can't say it publicly, he agrees the McGrath strategy has been poor and that the campaign doesn't listen to anyone and believes it can do it without any help whatsoever. He is frustrated with their actions.

Feeling emboldened, I deliver the message I came here to say.

"Look, if you don't mind me being real, here's the deal: you guys picked Amy McGrath not because you thought she could win but because you knew she could raise a lot of money and would be a big help for your national ticket due to her impressive background. You don't think anyone in Kentucky can win, so why not pick her? I get it. But the reality is, Mitch McConnell is beatable, and you guys are too stubborn to realize it. You need someone who can relate to Kentucky and has a chance of convincing those Republicans who like Trump and hate McConnell to vote Democrat. I can do it. She can't. I need to figure out if this is the right race for me, so I need you to stop blocking me from talking to staff, hiring pollsters, and doing the research needed to figure out if I am going to run. Stop tilting the game and let me figure out if I can compete with her straight up."

Schumer was taken aback. He responded quickly, "We have not endorsed her! And I haven't told anyone they couldn't work for you or not to support you. We don't do that!"

I shook my head and fired back, "Look, I like you. I like your style, and I enjoy talking with you. But I don't believe you. I know you are telling people not to support me, or else they won't have a job working for your candidates again. They have told me that is the message from this building. I don't want your endorsement. It will only hurt me in Kentucky, where people don't really like you. Just stop tilting the game, and we are good."

Schumer paused and smiled. He ignored my accusation and instead said, "You mean people in Kentucky don't like me? Really?"

"Actually, that is probably harsh," I said. "They don't even know who you are."

With a shocked expression, he let out a loud laugh. Another powerful person not used to being talked to with that level of directness. "Ha-ha, well, you call it like you see it, I guess," he said. "Fine, if you want to hire someone, and they are worried, have them call me, and I will tell them they can work for you directly. We won't make an endorsement until we see what you decide and how the campaign goes. Does that work for you?"

"Yes," I said. "All I want is a chance to make a real choice. Beating McConnell will take the most intelligent campaign in Senate history. I need to see if I can put it together and if I am the right candidate to do it."

Schumer then looked at me and said, "Well, honestly, I kind of hope you do it. We need more people like you in the party, and even if you don't run, I hope you will keep active."

He shook my hand, and after more than an hour in the office, I left to fly back to Kentucky. Contrary to my expectations, Schumer wasn't there to blow me off or scold me. He was taking me seriously. And I had to admit, I liked him and his style. He was someone open to me talking to him directly, even if I did think he was slightly full of it. He knew McGrath wasn't working, and by not standing in my way anymore, I could now decide on a run free of the obstacles of the DSCC juggernaut working against me. The meeting was much more successful than I could have ever imagined.

Now it was really real. The choice was clear. Do I fight Darth Vader to try and make history, or continue my normal, happy life away from the political madness? No more excuses. The decision was now all mine.

CHAPTER 6

Returning Home

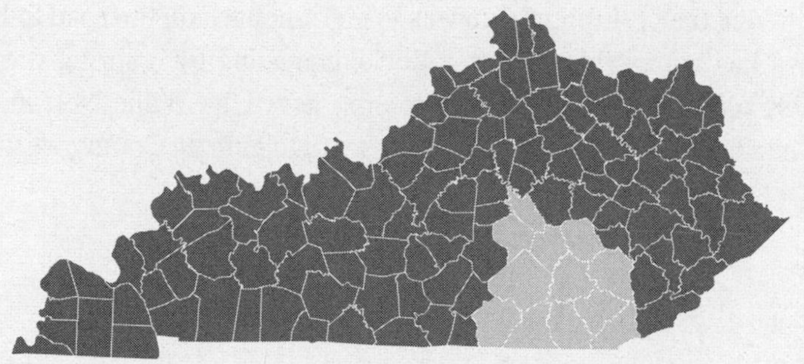

Things changed swiftly after my meeting with Chuck Schumer. I'd promised the senator I wouldn't leak details of our conversation to the press, and I didn't. But even though there were only three people in the room, news of my trip spread quickly. Politico's *Playbook* newsletter didn't help by running the following the very next day:

> Spotted: Kentucky Sports Radio host Matt Jones milling about at Reagan Airport while waiting for a flight to Louisville.

Really? Senator Rand Paul and Kentucky congressman John Yarmuth were both on my flight as well, but somehow *I* was the one worth writing about?

Still, the calls began pouring in. The "vulture" class (as I began to refer to them)—which included campaign managers, consultants, pollsters, and fund-raisers—started reaching out, seeing potential dollar signs that would come from being associated with a big-time campaign against Mitch McConnell. Some top-level staffers began contacting me, including one young progressive campaign manager offering to leave his current role with a presidential campaign and come work for me because it would be "punk rock" to take on McConnell. The Bernie Sanders wing of the Democratic Party loved the idea of me taking on the establishment, even though, from an ideological standpoint, I was one of their unfavored moderates.

It was a lot to take in. To be honest, more than I had bargained for. I determined the best thing to do was to go right back on the road in Kentucky. I had gotten this far in my decision-making by ignoring the DC chatter, and there was no reason to stop now. Like Willie Nelson, the road had become my peaceful retreat, so off to Lincoln County we went.

Lincoln County

"I Hope Other Candidates Will Fairly Soon Either Shit or Get Off the Pot"

When you arrive in Lincoln County, you notice immediately that it's a place where being a patriot matters. Its high school's mascot has the look of a scowling, menacing soldier in an America Revolution–era tri-cornered hat, as imagined by a Marvel Comics cartoonist. Signs supporting these "Patriots" are everywhere. In the county seat of Stanford, multiple businesses have adopted the name as well: you can clean your vehicle at Patriot Car Wash, order flowers at Patriot Petals, and even take care of that W-2 at Patriot Tax Service. Even the local preschool is called Little Patriots Preschool,* preparing young Lincoln Countians to love their country for years to come. Whatever you do in Lincoln County, you might as well love America while you do it.

We headed out to Chicken Bristle Farm, a spacious piece of land outside Stanford, to meet a real American patriot, Mike Broihier, who,

* Like their New England brethren, these Patriots spy on other preschools to win games of kickball.

unlike me, has had no qualms about throwing his hat into the ring to challenge Mitch McConnell. Broihier, tall, muscular, with a buzz cut and a firm handshake, and dressed in a denim shirt and jeans, greets us outside as we arrive.

He shows us around the farm, which is absolutely beautiful. Miles away from the nearest town, it sits atop a small hill with seventy-five acres for his livestock and asparagus. Broihier was a lieutenant colonel in the US Marine Corps, and when he and his wife, Lynn (also a marine), retired from the service in 2005, they systematically searched the entire country for the perfect place to put down roots and farm the land. Using a computer, the two of them inputted every feature they were looking for in a home (farm acreage, weather, population, and so on),* and the search engine told them the perfect place to settle would be Lincoln County, Kentucky. So, they did.

Mike wasted little time in becoming an active member of his new community. He became editor of the local newspaper, the county emergency coordinator, and the health department's preparedness planner, and even worked occasionally as a substitute teacher. But as he watched the political circus enveloping the country after Trump's election, he decided he needed to act, and in July 2018 he became one of the first Democratic challengers to announce his candidacy to take on Mitch McConnell.

Broihier explains all of this while leading us into his home, where Lynn is waiting. They are both cordial, welcoming people, and as we sit down in their warm, pastel-colored kitchen, I notice on one of the walls a giant print of the anonymous British street artist Banksy's *Flower Thrower*, which depicts a young revolutionary preparing to hurl what we assume will be a rock or grenade but instead is a colorful bouquet of flowers. It is a beautiful piece, but one I wouldn't have expected to see in the home of two former marines. The Broihiers, however, live to defy expectations.

When Broihier announced his candidacy, his introduction video included some of the most liberal messaging a serious candidate for

---

* The last time I inputted that much information into the Internet, it was on Buzzfeed and only told me I was a Miranda.

statewide office in Kentucky had ever produced. The first image is of a woman holding a chalkboard with the word *Bitch* on it. She is followed by a number of Kentuckians, each holding up his or her own chalkboard with a stereotypical label, such as *Thug*, *Hillbilly*, and *Baby killer.* Broihier, the narrator, tells us that Mitch McConnell employs these and other derogatory terms to divide Kentuckians. A major goal of his campaign is to unite the state, specifying the need for inclusion and respect for homosexual and transgender Kentuckians specifically. It's a bold launch video, and very compelling.

The message might seem at odds with the stereotypical image of a retired marine officer, but according to Broihier, it was his military service that shaped his viewpoints. "You can't help being changed by traveling around the world and seeing how things are outside of our view," Mike tells me. "We've got this beautiful little bubble here on our farm, but the military helps us see the world in a much different light. The Marine Corps was surely formative without a doubt—you're going to see people literally starving to death, or with dysentery, and that leaves a mark. Everything you thought was right or wrong is subject to review after you see things like that."

Broihier says he is tired of watching Mitch McConnell divide America. He had never considered running for office previously but felt compelled, as someone has to step up to take down Mitch. "It was the only fight worth running," he says. "He *is* the problem. Donald Trump is a symptom, but McConnell and people like him are the problem. It's a complete absence of morality, just being driven by power and money. He is constantly accumulating power and screwing people. He burns people. He's without morality."

Because McConnell is a divider, Broihier's entire message is one of Kentucky unity. "That's the whole gist of the campaign," he says. "I'm not going to run on 'Mitch McConnell's stopping Donald Trump from draining the swamp.'* No one buys that. It's an inclusive campaign because Kentucky is diverse and growing more diverse every day. There are a lot of perceived divides, but you take a look on the west side of

* This is an implicit shot at Amy McGrath, who used that ridiculous messaging as the launching point for her campaign.

Louisville and then Appalachia: they both have drinking water problems. This campaign's purpose is to try to bridge these gaps."

I love Broihier's optimism, and his passion comes through as he speaks, but I can't help but wonder if he has a tougher path than he realizes. Candidates who can't trade on name recognition, whether politically generated or via past media coverage, have a hard time gaining traction for their campaigns. Without that coverage, raising money can be difficult, which in turn makes it even more difficult to get name identification. It's a vicious cycle that is hard to break. At the time that I met him, Broihier had been in the race for a few months but had made little headway; he remained virtually unknown except to political insiders.

This fact is underscored at the county courthouse later in the day, when I speak to a group of thirty Lincoln County Democrats who are encouraging me to run. I ask if they realize that there is a person living in their county already in the race. Only one of the thirty has even heard of Mike Broihier—and he lives down the road.

Broihier and I discuss our similar frustrations with current frontrunner Amy McGrath. He, too, resents some of the behind-the-scenes tactics her campaign has been utilizing. I can tell by his tone that even with these commonalities he is also perturbed by my indecision about whether to run. I get the sense that this very serious man sees me as an unserious interloper who doesn't realize the gravity of the fight that the race will be. I've experienced that reaction before from people who don't really know me or my motives for considering a campaign. Toward the end of our conversation, he says pointedly, "For those of us in the race, it is very important that we know where we stand. I hope other candidates will fairly soon either shit or get off the pot."

Broihier couches the comment as a general one, but it is clearly aimed at me as the audience of one. I understand his frustration. On paper, Mike Broihier has many more qualifications than I do to take on Mitch McConnell. He is a decorated military veteran, has held numerous positions in local government, and doesn't spend his days talking about college students playing sports.* Yet my potential candidacy has gotten exponentially more publicity than his actual one.

* Also, I've had Matt's asparagus, and it's terrible.

If I were him, I would be frustrated as well. I promise him that I will decide very soon.

Driving toward Jackson County, I think a lot about Broihier and the race. He is an impressive man, and even with his very liberal platform, he would likely have a substantially better chance of beating McConnell than Amy McGrath has. Yet he doesn't have the backing of a clueless national party or his own sports radio show to help him attract attention. In a perfect world, a candidate like Broihier wouldn't be an afterthought, he would be an important voice with a legitimate chance to compete. But the sad reality is that is not our world, and unless he can find a way to break through the noise, his message of unity will unfortunately barely be heard.

Jackson County

"If the Lord Himself Came Back as a Democrat"

What's rarer than a Duke Blue Devils fan in Jackson County? A Democrat.

Of the county's thirteen thousand residents, 89 percent voted for Donald Trump in 2016, and that number is expected to be even higher in 2020. (One person here jokes, "He's won some of the others over.") It's a small county, with some of the worst poverty in the United States. In fact, its largest town, McKee, holds the distinction of being the poorest town in the state, with an average income of just $10,418 a year. Yet when you talk to people in this community left behind by the country's economic resurgence of the last decade, you will still find near-unanimous support for Donald Trump—and universal disdain for all things Democrat.*

McKee is quiet on this drizzling, dreary morning. Henry's Billiards & Games, on the corner, is a decent gathering spot, but it doesn't open until later this afternoon (and no one is sure exactly when). We drive

* In McKee, there may be more Whigs than Democrats.

around looking for a bustling business, and the only one we find is the Save a Lot discount grocery on Highway 421. It's kind of a typical Save a Lot, to be honest, but it does have a good special going on right now: five Totino's Party Pizzas for $5.55. At least three people seem to be taking advantage and are quite happy.*

We search the town trying to find a Democrat. It isn't easy. Cell service here is virtually nonexistent, so there is no one we can call.† We go in Sassy Scents & Silver, a charming little business in town, and ask if they know any Democrats around here. Teresa Moore, one of the proprietors of the store, just laughs. This is definitely not AOC country.

Eventually a friendly older lady points us to a couple of unique ones and they admit they're having a tough go of things. "Jackson County, tell you the truth, I don't think it'll ever change unless something big and crazy happens," says J. B. Estridge. He says McConnell is bulletproof here solely because of the (R) next to his name. "They're all Republicans here, and no matter what he does, he's still going to carry it ninety-nine percent here, even though he don't do nothing for Jackson County. He's still going to carry it. That's just the way it is."

Estridge says it's frustrating because while he believes Democrats have tried to do things for the area (Bill Clinton once visited Jackson County during an Appalachian tour to find out what he could do to help), the county remains dark red. In fact, no Democratic presidential candidate has ever carried the county since its inception in 1858, and few have even come close.

"They think Trump is the greatest thing since sliced bread, they do—they think he's a really smart man, old Trump," Estridge tells me. "They think the Democrats are the devil. Republicans don't do nothing here because they know they're going to get seventy, eighty, ninety percent of the vote, so why should they do anything here?"

That is the catch for Jackson County and similar red counties throughout the state. Because their vote is consistently Republican, elected officials don't try to curry their favor. Plus, since there are so few residents

---

* Say what you want, but I think we all can agree that getting a pizza for $1.11 is a savings party.

† We even logged on to PelosiFriendFinder.com. Nothing.

in the county as a whole, there isn't much reason to reward their loyal supporters, either. State Democrats see it as a lost cause and pay the county little attention, leaving the citizens to continue pulling the Republican lever every time.

Randy Vickers, a postal service worker and chairman of the Democratic Party in the county, agrees that it's puzzling that the county remains so conservative when they haven't seen much from the party for which they continually vote. "Mitch doesn't do anything here," he says. "If we get down on our knees and beg a bit, we might get a few things, but nothing major as far as helping us with businesses or anything like that. People here, they've just got their minds set that Democrats are horrible, with abortion and the gun law, and all that."

I actually feel sorry for the many McConnell voters here. (I wouldn't say "supporters," as even here I still can't find anyone who really likes him.) They continually give the man their loyal vote, and in return, they get nothing, not even a courtesy visit.

Yet Mitch will continue to win here. Despite no signs of any reward for their support or even an acknowledgment of their loyalty, Jackson County will still be a Republican stronghold. "Anything that a Democrat does, nobody recognizes," Vickers says, sounding defeated. "I believe if the Lord himself came back as a Democrat and somebody ran against him on a Republican ticket in Jackson County, they'd win. That's just the way it is here."

Rockcastle County

What's the Worst Thing You've Ever Done?

Rockcastle is named for the fifty-four-mile-long river that runs through it. Stunning rock cliffs border the Rockcastle River on each side, a rare sight in this otherwise green state. The county seat was originally named White Rock, for all the rocks and such, but then changed to Mount Vernon, to honor George Washington's home. The father of our country isn't from this area, and there is no record of him having visited, so the decision seems odd. But until I looked this up just now, I always assumed it meant he had, which means whatever shenanigans Rockcastle County is trying to pull, it's working.

Vape shops are alive and well across Kentucky (three constants in nearly every county we've visited are tattoo parlors, CBD oil stores, and vape shops), but it's only here in Rockcastle County where you'll find James 4:14 Vape Sales, named after the New Testament verse reading, "Why, you do not even know what will happen tomorrow. What is your life? You are a mist that appears for a little while and then vanishes." Touching words for certain. WWJV?

Rockcastle County is home to the Renfro Valley Entertainment Center, a country music hoedown venue that dates back to 1939. It's like a smaller version of Nashville's Grand Ole Opry but focused more on bluegrass and Kentucky culture. The forties and fifties saw Renfro Valley become a hot spot for bluegrass musicians, comedians, and gospel singers. Local and national acts all performed here, among them Homer and Jethro, Slim Miller, and the Coon Creek Girls, one of the first all-women string bands to perform on the radio, beginning in the late 1930s.

Renfro Valley isn't what it once was*—most of the hotels and shops that once benefited from the venue's massive crowds have long since fallen into disrepair—but occasionally big names like the Oak Ridge Boys and the Platters will still keep the site on their touring itineraries, restoring the past glory of the once-mighty Renfro Valley, even if just for one night.

We sit with Joe Bullen, an eightysomething local Democrat in a navy-blue sweatshirt and baseball cap, at the Limestone Grille in Mount Vernon. He remembers the thrill of those musical evenings at Renfro Valley and blames its decline in popularity on the fact that the valley now serves alcohol.

"It's not been doing too good," Joe tells me, while focusing on a cup of coffee in his hand. "They started serving drinks down there, and that's okay. But the older people, well, they came all the way to the valley from as far as Michigan, and they didn't like it. You don't see them as much now."

---

* Even though, let me tell you, old people *love* Renfro Valley.

Joe says the recent wet-versus-dry vote continues to divide the county, an issue we've observed quite a bit on this trip. There are still some dry counties in Kentucky, and as they gradually vote one by one to allow alcohol, citizens in the counties inevitably end up at odds. The divide is between older and more conservative groups, who make up a lot of Kentucky's small-town population, and a younger, progressive crowd who see alcohol sales as a path to economic development and just want the freedom to have a beer when they choose.

As Joe expands on Rockcastle's divide to Chris, I walk out to the car to return a phone call. On the other end of the line, a friend tells me that the McGrath campaign is seeking a private detective to do background research on me and has approached his coworker about the job. At the same time, I check my email and find a message from a different friend, who was contacted by a reporter investigating a skit we once did on *Hey Kentucky!* Minutes later, another call comes in from an acquaintance in Louisville, letting me know that a "whisper campaign" concerning my status as a bachelor is beginning against me in political circles in the city.

It's a lot to digest quickly. I have known all along that to run against McConnell would open my life to being investigated and my entire past dissected. Unfortunately, it comes with the territory. None of these issues worries me particularly: hiring an investigator is to be expected, the skit in question was a stupid, nonsensical parody of *The Bachelor,** and stirring up rumors through a whisper campaign can happen to anyone in the public eye. But now it is no longer hypothetical; it's real. I am squarely a target for both the Republican Party *and* the Democratic Party.

I get Chris's attention and tell him I need to go back home to Lexington. He agrees to meet with the group of local Democrats we had

---

* This was literally a scripted comedy sketch that was being investigated as if Matt was actually a contestant on a dating show. It's like investigating Steve Carell to see if Jim and Pam of *The Office* had checked with HR before they started dating.

assembled and I ask him to please convey my apologies.* I just need some time to think.

I drive to Lexington and go to my restaurant, KSBar, to watch a football game and try to get away. As I walk in, I see the Tracker, sitting at a back table by himself. He catches my attention and waves me over. He had no way of knowing I would be here, so his presence surprises me. I sit down and with a serious expression he looks me in the eye and says, "Look, Matt, I like you and just thought you should know, they are going to be following you in New York now when you visit your girlfriend. That person probably won't be as nice as me, so be careful."

Wow. Clearly naive, I hadn't even considered they would have the audacity to follow my girlfriend around New York. It's clear the McConnell people are ruthless and playing for keeps. The Tracker tells me he disagreed with the decision, but thought it was only fair that I be made aware. It's actually very kind of him to warn me, and honestly, after all this time together on the road, I actually trust him. I feel like he realizes this decision is as ridiculous as I do and, seeing what my daily life is actually like, a complete waste of time.

With no political record to speak of, it's clear that a major component of the attacks on me will be about my personal life, past and present. It's hard to step back from your life and judge all your past behavior. I am sure everyone reading this has done something in their life that they regret and wish they could change, especially since, in the age of the cell phone camera and the Internet, a perfectly innocent but perhaps embarrassing moment might get shared online without their knowledge. I didn't grow up in the era of social media, but I have lived within it for a decade and am sure I have done something stupid during that time frame.

Knowing what running in a race against McConnell would mean, I have racked my brain and gone through a thorough examination of my entire life and all that I have done. As one nationally prominent political

---

* When I go to meet with them, they are quite disappointed that it's just me and not Matt. One lady grabs her purse and upon seeing my face, wordlessly stands up and leaves.

commentator told me, "Think of the worst thing you have ever done and assume it will become public. Are you okay with that? Because if you aren't, you shouldn't run."

Having completed this process, I think my answer is yes. Sure, like everyone, I have embarrassing moments I wish I had back, but nothing serious for which I am ashamed. I have a much more mundane personal life than most people would imagine. I rarely drink, don't really go out much, and was way too much of a dork to ever get into trouble in my youth. As I have gotten older, the most "scandalous" thing about me is that I am forty-one years old and single, a rarity in Kentucky. This leads some to assume I am gay and, at the same time, some to assume I am some wild playboy, neither of which is true. The last two years I have dated the same wonderful TV producer in New York and I spend most of my free time with her watching Netflix and reading.

When I was first considering a run for public office, I followed the recommendation of almost every political expert I spoke with and paid to have what they call opposition research done on me. I hired a professional company to create a file of research on me that, presumably, the other campaigns would also collect. It was an expensive and somewhat surreal process to pay someone to dig up dirt on me. But it was also necessary. I ended up with an eighty-page report, most of which was, well, as boring as my past. But because I'm in media professionally, the vast majority of those pages contained references to past writings of mine, as well as social media posts and comments I made on the air. In addition, there was a great deal of information on what people who have worked for me have said publicly, as their comments could be imputed to me as well. None of these were scandalous, mind you, but a lot of them were immature and fratty, and not at all what I would write or say now that I'm in my early forties.* What's more, *I'm on the radio*. It's my *job* to inform and entertain, and sometimes that involves being provocative and off-the-cuff. I have said the occasional thing that looking back, I wish I hadn't. But that is what doing multiple hours a day on live radio entails. Having heard from friends and even the Tracker that

* I told Matt at the time: fewer posts on how great the band Fall Out Boy and basketball star Latrell Sprewell are. He didn't listen.

the campaign to savage me is underway, I can't help but dread knowing that they'll have fifteen years' worth of daily material to sift through and then manipulate to make me look bad.

As far as Mitch McConnell and Amy McGrath are concerned, the race is on and this is war to them. No matter how pure my intentions are for considering this race, they will be out for blood. The question is, Am I? And will I be ready to take the hits and fight back?

Pulaski County

A Day of Pride in Somerset

Remember how I said all of western Kentucky is obsessed with barbeque? Well, it is the same in the eastern half of Kentucky, but for Mexican food. In every single town, no matter how small, there are multiple Mexican restaurants, most with names along the lines of El Poncho, Rio Brava, Casa Fiesta, and Mi Rancho Grande—all seemingly formulated by pulling two random Spanish words out of a hat. Each establishment serves essentially the same food selections, but in every Kentucky town, folks insist that *their* Mexican restaurant is the best in the world. In Somerset, the largest town in Pulaski County, the choice is Speedy Tacos, and it's a good starting spot for our day.*

Somerset and Pulaski County are what folks around here call "rock-ribbed Republican"† territory, full of generations of rural conservatives, protective of their rights (particularly religion and guns), and not particularly interested in ultraprogressive values.

However, the area is slowly starting to evolve. Thanks to the tremendous local economic success in the region—due in part to the fact that local congressman Hal Rogers excels at lining his hometown with pet projects—the town continues to grow. And with new arrivals

---

* The food was awesome, but the service a little slow, but I guess "Lackadaisical Tacos" didn't test well.

† Probably due to all the tacos.

and opportunity, different viewpoints are being expressed. Earlier this year, few were surprised when the Somerset City Council unfortunately voted 10 to 1 against a proposed local fairness ordinance prohibiting discrimination against the LGBTQ community in employment, housing, or public accommodation. But a few eyebrows were raised as, in response, Somerset became the first town in Kentucky outside of Lexington or Louisville to host a LGBTQ Pride Festival.

After our quick taco feast, we resist the urge to stop off at a bingo hall on Highway 27 (bingo is the fourth major sport in Kentucky), because we need to meet Kat Moses, a gay citizen of Somerset and local librarian, who, following the city council decision, was one of a handful of the town's residents who went to work. "After the fairness ordinance was struck down, there was a growing sense of 'We can't be ourselves in our own home,'" Moses says. "Someone made a flippant comment that 'What we really need is a Pride festival,' and I said 'Okay, if you want to have a Pride, meet me in the library, and we'll talk about it.' A collection of fifteen random individuals came and we met over five months to organize Somerset's first public Pride event."

One of those who joined her was Mona Eldridge, a local language arts teacher who became involved with the issue because she has a gay son. She wanted to become a force for positivity, so she helped create a Facebook call for interest in the event. "All of a sudden, on the Facebook page, people kept marking themselves 'interested' and 'coming,'" says Eldridge, "and it just kept growing daily until we had eight hundred people who'd responded that they were going to the event."

The support from such a conservative area surprised and energized the organizers. It came from all angles: a local brewery signed on as the first public corporate sponsor, a few local churches volunteered to set up booths and tents, and the Somerset police agreed to provide security as well. Moses and Eldridge originally thought the first Pride would be small and controversial, but as the support rolled in, it grew to a size they couldn't have imagined.

On the day of the event, the organizers were thrilled to see hundreds of area citizens come out and celebrate. Not only did people from Somerset attend, but also former residents and visitors from Chicago, Washington, DC, Tennessee, West Virginia, and Ohio all made the trip home to support the weekend. Even drag queens—decidedly not the norm in an area like this—performed for huge crowds in town on Saturday. Moses notes, "It was unafraid and unashamed, and that's what made it beautiful."

Unfortunately, it also drew some small protest from the community. "Sixty protesters, easy," Moses says with specificity, "plus five Nazis."

It didn't matter. As the protestors tried to advance toward the festival, the attendees locked arms to create a wall forbidding them to pass through. A young girl faced down dissenters with a handmade sign reading "Jesus Loves All," while a fourteen-year-old boy stood in front of an outspoken religious group and held up a poster board bearing the words "These People Do Not Represent My Faith." "We found that day that we had more allies in Pulaski County than we ever thought we did," says Mona proudly.

Moses and Eldridge practically glow as they tell us about the weekend; it's clear that they didn't expect this kind of unadulterated success. Now the group is planning to make the Pride Festival an annual occurrence. They believe over time even more people in the community will become accepting of their presence, as they slowly realize that their neighbors aren't as different as they might presume. One similarity is the fact that in this deeply religious area, many in the LGBTQ community have the same Christian faith they do.

"I feel the immense love of people around me who have supported me through the process and accepted me for who I was," Moses says. "But I've also met other LGBT people of faith who shared their feelings and the concept of Christ being all-loving and Christ being with the sinners. I couldn't imagine a God that created me that way only to set me up for failure. Why create something that you would only damn to hell?"

I ask Moses about Mitch McConnell; she says she feels like he isn't an advocate for her lifestyle at all. She is right. While McConnell hasn't made his stance against homosexuality a trademark of his politics, he has voted against virtually every provision ending discrimination against the LGBTQ community. He is against gay marriage, all equal-rights legislation, and expansions on prohibiting workplace discrimination. But Moses also points out that other Kentucky politicians, including many Democrats, have dropped the ball by remaining quiet on the issues.

"Any politician who won't take a firm stand on equality and fairness for all, regardless of whether that's geared toward sexual identity or gender politics, isn't one I'm interested in supporting," she says.

McCreary County

"The Affordable Care Act Saved My Neck"

Earlier, I noted that Jackson County was one of the poorest counties in the state. The reason I said "one of" is because the poorest county in all of Kentucky is McCreary County, located in deep southeastern Kentucky, on the Tennessee line. It is an ultra-religious area and the Christian influence is everywhere, from the Ten Commandments painted broadly on the entire side of a large downtown building, to the Lord's Cafe (all the bread and fish you can eat), to the Lord's Gym (where you can become "John the Buffest"). In Whitley City, the county's largest town, I even saw a man wearing a T-shirt that said simply, "Spiritual Gangster," with an arrow pointing up toward his face. It's not a hard-knock spiritual life in McCreary County.

Two miles south, tiny Pine Knot (population 1,680) is home to Crowley's Country Cafe, where, just inside the door, you'll find this sign:

WARNING
YOU ARE ENTERING
A RED NECK AREA
YOU MAY ENCOUNTER
AMERICAN FLAGS
ARMED CITIZENS
THE LORD'S PRAYER
& COUNTRY MUSIC
ENTER AT YOUR OWN RISK.*

* Oddly, we didn't encounter any of these. But at least we were on notice.

I presume this sign is hung to discourage delicate snowflakes like us from coming in, but it doesn't work. Good food is good food, and Crowley's comes highly recommended, so we indeed entered at our own risk.* A letter from Mitch McConnell hangs behind the cash register, congratulating Crowley's on its ribbon cutting and referring the owner to a field representative if he needs anything. To avoid human contact, Mitch always refers people to his "field representatives," who are like Smash Mouth fans—rumored to exist but rarely seen in the wild.

We are here to discuss the Affordable Care Act (ACA), as McCreary County is one of the areas helped most dramatically by its implementation. In the last decade or so, McCreary County, like most of eastern Kentucky, has seen a sharp increase in the number of citizens who now enjoy health care coverage thanks to the ACA. The Affordable Care Act, enacted in 2010, has many features, but the one most important to rural Kentucky was the provision that allowed states to expand Medicaid coverage. Now states were given the opportunity to offer health care to individuals who made too much to qualify for Medicaid—the federally and state-funded insurance program for the very poor—but couldn't afford to buy insurance on the open market. The ACA set up government-subsidized marketplaces where these individuals could finally receive health care coverage, many for the first time, at an affordable price. Kentucky's then governor, Steve Beshear, became one of the first governors in the United States to implement the expansion. More than a million Kentuckians immediately qualified.

The fact is, no state has benefited from the Affordable Care Act more than Kentucky. People's health care options have increased dramatically, and the regional health of parts of the commonwealth has taken a major step forward. Between 2013 and 2016, the number of uninsured people in Kentucky declined by *63.8* percent, a number that far exceeded even the most optimistic of expectations. In addition, the ban in the ACA on coverage denials due to preexisting medical conditions protected countless more Kentuckians as well. After Beshear left the governorship, he was asked why he'd been so gung-ho about implementation. "Very simple," he replied. "It was the right thing to do."

* Matt's lying. The LibSnowflake restaurants in McCreary were all full.

It has literally been a lifesaver for Kentuckians such as Rhonda Wilson, a sixty-six-year-old former welder and hairdresser in McCreary County. We talk to her outside her home, wind chimes tossing and clanging in the cold breeze.

"I feel very positive about the ACA," she says. "I feel like it really helped people here, because without it, there's no way we could pay for insurance." Her husband, a diabetic, died in 2013, before certain crucial provisions of the Affordable Care Act had been implemented. Virtually all of the couple's savings went to pay for his insurance and treatment, and as a result, Rhonda wasn't able to afford health insurance for herself.

"I went without insurance for twelve years," she says. "I had this problem, I had a bone that was shattered between my neck and my shoulder, and I had it for seven years before I could ever get any insurance to get it fixed." Rhonda was in constant pain and had to prop up her elbow just to use her hand. She said she didn't have enough strength to lift a cup.

According to Rhonda, the ACA Medicaid expansion has "saved my neck." After she qualified for Medicaid, she saw a doctor who noticed a clot in her left leg. He told her that if she had waited much longer, they would have needed to amputate. The ACA not only helped her get the diagnosis but covered the surgery as well. "I would be in really, really poor health without it."

Mitch McConnell was against the passage of the ACA from moment one. During the political debate on the bill, he made certain that it received no Republican votes, and refused to be part of any negotiation on its passage. He told senators that if any broke ranks, they would receive a primary election challenge and the party would do nothing to help them. McConnell believed that if the bill were seen as bipartisan, it would be considered a "win" for President Obama, something worse to him than the health of a million Kentuckians. So he unsuccessfully fought tooth and nail to prevent its passage.

In the ten years since, McConnell has been on a mission to avenge his loss and see the ACA repealed. He has attempted to overturn the bill legislatively, administratively, and legally, failing at every attempt. As a last resort, McConnell has proposed new plans with significantly worse coverage, but none have received sufficient support.

Kentucky has been a model of success for the ACA, and hundreds of thousands of its citizens' lives are better off for its passage. That fact makes McConnell seethe, but as of now, he has been unable to reverse it. For Mitch, politics is always more important than people, and thankfully for Kentuckians, this is one of the few issues where Mitch has taken a political loss.

Wayne County

Saving Rural Hospitals

There is no more beautiful place to spend a lazy summer evening than in a boat on Lake Cumberland, off the Conley Bottom Resort dock in Wayne County. I know this because despite being deathly scared of water (I am not a strong swimmer), I love Lake Cumberland. It's known as the "Hillbilly Riviera" of eastern Kentucky because, to be honest, it gets rowdy. Thousands of visitors come to Lake Cumberland each summer and make Wayne County's lake areas a wild local party destination. Holidays and special events such as the annual summer Raft-Up can bring tens of thousands of tourists to the area at once, creating an economic boom that sustains the region all year. Their visits and the large number of houseboats produced in the area have earned Wayne County's small city of Monticello the unofficial title of "Houseboat Capital of the World." At its peak, nowhere else in the country produced a greater percentage of the houseboats you see on lakes all across America.*

This tourist influx has helped Wayne County to be blessed with an advantage that many rural communities in this region are not: its own hospital and emergency room. However, like other similar small-town hospitals across America, its financial situation is always tenuous.

---

* In Wayne County, being on a houseboat means you love the outdoors and are a person of leisure. In movies and television, being on a houseboat means you live on a houseboat and are a murder suspect.

Because such a large percentage of the residents who utilize the hospital are poor, its financial stability is wholly dependent on patients' insurance status. And that is why before the passage of the ACA, Wayne County Hospital and other similar rural medical facilities around the United States were on the brink of collapse.

The reason is simple. Under federal law, all hospitals receiving federal funds must accept anyone who turns up in the emergency room for care. Before the passage of Obamacare, the vast majority of patients who came to ERs in places like Monticello were either on Medicaid or, more likely, had no insurance coverage at all. The hospitals were still required by law to provide care to the uninsured, knowing that they probably wouldn't receive a dime in reimbursement. Compounding the problem, says Shawn Crabtree, director of public health in the Lake Cumberland region, is that "When people don't have insurance, they have a tendency to go to the emergency room even more"—including for routine health issues that ordinarily would be tended to at a doctor's office. Financially, it was a no-win proposition for hospitals.

But with the passage of the ACA, the calculus changed. As Crabtree explains, "If you have insurance, you can go to a primary care physician instead of to the emergency room, which isn't necessarily the correct location for that care. So it's diverting some unnecessary treatment from the emergency room to an appropriate treatment modality. And it's better for the people who actually need to go to the emergency room."

Now, when those with coverage from the ACA do come in to the emergency room, the hospital can receive partial reimbursement from Medicaid. The money is not reimbursed at the same levels as private insurance, but it's better than zero dollars. So long as the citizens of the area are signed up for ACA coverage, the rural hospitals get reimbursed, giving the medical community an incentive to encourage more patients to sign up for coverage. The result is multiple parties working to have more citizens insured, the hospitals remaining financially solvent, and the health care of the area improving.

But what happens to these rural hospitals if Mitch McConnell gets his wish and repeals the ACA? The simple fact is that most will end up closing. We tried to contact the CEO at Wayne County Hospital, one of the centers that would be most at risk if the ACA is repealed, but he declined to comment for a book that is at its core an indictment of Mitch McConnell. I understand. In the CEO's stead, we talked to a former health care official in Wayne County, who told me that "Rural hospitals, and particularly the one here in Wayne County, rely on Medicaid funding. Restrictions to Medicaid that limit the eligibility of individuals *will* close these rural hospitals."

Another health care administrator told me, "If you run a small hospital in a poor community, to say you would be against the ACA would be like saying you are against breathing. It just isn't working without it."

Insurance providers are some of the biggest donors to Mitch McConnell's campaigns; among active senators who haven't run for president, only one has received more money from insurance providers than the majority leader has. From a legislator's perspective, there's no campign money in fighting for people's lives but a lot of money in siding with insurance providers. In 2009 and 2010, when the Affordable Care Act was being debated, the insurance industry spent $102 million lobbying against it. Making these companies happy is key to McConnell's and Republicans' political success, and explains much of their vociferous opposition to the ACA.

McConnell favors a system where private insurance companies can deny policies based on any criteria they choose. This system, where the poor have no coverage, the working class struggle to find minimal coverage, and the sick are locked out completely, should be called McConnellCare. Under McConnellCare, a half million Kentuckians would lose health care instantly, rural hospitals would close permanently, and insurance companies would get rich. It's Mitch's dream come true.

Now a full decade since the passage of Obamacare, neither McConnell nor the Republican Party has ever proposed a genuine health care alternative to the ACA. They're still peddling McConnellCare, which would return us to the days when a sizable portion of Kentuckians, and Americans, were left out in the cold.

During the health care debate of ten years ago, Democrat Alan Grayson, then a first-term congressman from Florida, put the GOP's position in stark terms: "If you get sick in America," he said, "the Republican health care plan is this: die quickly."

Garrard County

Getting Help from McConnell Is Like Winning a Lottery Where No One Knows the Rules or How to Play

I'm about to give you a top-secret tip about Lancaster, Kentucky, one that also applies to the rest of the state: folks in Kentucky pronounce the names of some of our towns and cities differently than you might assume. For instance, you'd probably assume that Lancaster, the largest town in Garrard County, is pronounced "Lan-*kass*-ter." But you'd be wrong. We use the Old English pronunciation: "*Lank*-uss-ter." Same thing with Athens, Kentucky: Pronounced "*Ath*-ins," correct? (Cue game show buzzer sound.) Gee, sorry, that's not the right answer. We say it "*Ayy*-thens." Likewise, you non-Kentuckians continue to insist on calling Louisville "*Loo*-ee-ville," but we prefer sounding like we are chewing marbles and saying, "*Luhl*-vuhl." Even more bizarrely to outsiders, most of you probably presume Versailles, Kentucky, is pronounced the same way as that *other* Versailles, in France, with its palace and gardens and castles: "Vuhr-*cy*." We, however, prefer the much more unique "Vuhr-*say*-uhls." Go ahead, say it out loud. We Kentuckians do things our own way. Deal with it.

Garrard County is the hometown of country music's singing brothers Eddie (of the duo Montgomery Gentry) and John Michael Montgomery. The two have both become huge country stars, but they still reside in the area, and the county has served as the inspiration for a number of their hit songs. Garrard County is beautiful, friendly, old-fashioned, and just an hour away from Lexington if you need any big-city stuff.*

What we found in Garrard County does have the true makings of a country song, or at least a great short story. The premise goes something like this: a doctor, having grown disillusioned with the hassle of

---

* Like Montgomery Gentry CDs.

his regular medical practice, opens a local clinic that treats the uninsured and underinsured, but for some reason, he can't seem to get the town of Paint Lick out of his head. He and his wife drive there one day and discover a small brick building that is exactly the type the doctor had imagined, complete with a blue Chevy truck door (and nothing else) out front, with the words "Press On Regardless" painted on it.

Entering the building, they find a woman who has been trying to attract a doctor to open a practice in Paint Lick; the doctor, inspired, decides to use her brick building for the clinic, and the rest is history. The nurses even go fishing on their lunch breaks. It's like a real-life version of the 1990s TV comedy-drama *Northern Exposure*, about the life of a solo doctor in a fictional small town in Alaska, only with less moose and more bourbon.

It also has the benefit of being true and explains how Dr. John Belanger started the Paint Lick Family Clinic nearly twenty years ago. Dr. Belanger's concept was very simple: every patient pays $20 a visit to get the care they need. No questions asked. The clinic got through its first decade on a shoestring budget and Belanger's hard work, but ten years ago he was afraid he might have to shutter the organization completely, as nearly his entire base of patients was uninsured. Thankfully, the Affordable Care Act became the clinic's saving grace. By having patients who now could afford insurance, the clinic was able to get enough reimbursements from Medicaid to become financially stable. In 2013 Belanger turned over administrative duties to the White House Clinics network, the clinic was renamed, and the doctor was able to focus just on medicine.

Without the ACA, the clinic closes down, and Paint Lick has no doctor. The act literally saved the only medical lifeline of this small community, enabling it to keep its doors open. Just across the street from the clinic we run into Mark Gumbert, who runs Copperhead Environmental Consulting. He has an office on the second floor and is turning the first floor into a restaurant with raw, epoxied wood—it's going to be gorgeous. I ask him about Dr. Belanger, and he's clearly a fan.

"The number of people that come in and out of that clinic when it's open is unbelievable," he tells me, adding that most of those patients are—in typical southern ailment fashion—unwilling, unable, or sometimes too stubborn to go to a hospital, and without the clinic, the patients would end up suffering.

Clinics such as this one in Paint Lick serve understaffed rural areas all over the state. Few are as lucky to have a benefactor like Dr. Belanger, but all meet vitally important needs. It's bizarre to think that Mitch McConnell wouldn't appreciate these resources and want to protect them. Over the years, the senator has been willing to give temporary health funding for areas selected usually based on what makes the news. He obtained some funding for temporary mobile medical screening clinics in occasional years; a handful of detox programs for addicted mothers; and Kroger bottled-water purchases for areas upended by contaminated water supplies.

But when it comes to permanent help with care, McConnell has no interest. It has been said that getting funding from Mitch McConnell is like winning a random lottery where no one knows the rules or how to play.* It is impossible to know what will trigger the grants, and it isn't clear that those who need assistance the most receive it.

But the ACA is different. We know it helps poor citizens throughout the state and the health of rural areas in general. So why would McConnell be against it? Studying McConnell and his positions on issues like this can be depressing, but thank goodness we have places such as the White House Clinics and people like Dr. Belanger in Paint Lick. Even with their own senator working against them, they fight for health care for Kentucky's most vulnerable citizens out of the goodness of their heart. They are Kentuckians worth celebrating.

---

* It's a scratch-off game where first prize is your diabetes medication.

Whitley County

Hanging at Glen's Restaurant

I am going to tell you folks a secret at this point in the trip: we are currently on county 69 of 120, and Chris and I are starting to get a little tired. Each county in the state is great and all, but there are a lot of them and sometimes they start to run together a bit. Then there are the moments when you see something unique and, suddenly, it is all worthwhile. While driving along Highway 92, a narrow, winding road that is the best route between Williamsburg and Barbourville (which is not to say it's a *good* route), we discovered Glen's Restaurant. It was a ramshackle, bright-blue cottage, crumbling in spots, its door garnished with crushed cans of Dr Pepper and strewn candy wrappers, with a sign that read simply "Glens Restaurant." The place looked abandoned, honestly, but as if a force had overtaken me, I jerked the wheel and pulled over.

Junk was everywhere. We crept up to the front door gingerly, dodging the leftover packaging boxes and red Solo cups on the steps. I hesitantly approached the door, a lone note about a lost dog taped on it, when a voice shouted from the parking lot, "Go on, you can go in!"

Glen's is a combination restaurant and grocery store crammed into two rooms, each the size of a college dorm room. It's a "restaurant" in the sense that Glen has a frier behind the counter on which he can make you grilled cheese, chicken nuggets, or, if you have the time, a hamburger. He cooks with a microwave, a toaster, and a small residential stove in a dark side space, with an old 1980s refrigerator holding the goods. It's a "grocery" in the sense that it sells these items (listed in no particular order): a giant can of yellow cling peaches, two boxes of Wheaties, three jars of tartar sauce, a Saltines box of indeterminate age, a children's bubble set, a homemade Ziploc bag full of gumdrops, two flyswatters, a ceramic figure of a sad clown, ten or so water bottles indented by time, a guitar-shaped clock with Willie Nelson's face on it, a coat hanger draped in colorful scarves, and a family of porcelain manatees swimming among seaweed. That's just a sample of Glen's inventory. Despite the room's tiny size, behind every item is another, different item, slightly more baffling than the one in front of it. I moved three cans of StarKist tuna, which revealed a Pez dispenser and a pack of 1999 Fleer baseball cards. It was magical.

Glen's Restaurant is the last of a nearly extinct breed: the country store that serves as an isolated community's only shopping center.* By necessity, such stores stock one of nearly every kind of item imaginable. However, for Glen, time has made all but the barest of necessities unavailable via suppliers, and thus he is left with whatever random trinkets he can acquire from whatever random salesmen come through the door.

There wasn't anything particularly insightful about Glen's place, except for the fact it gave us the realization that we were in an establishment of a bygone era. The only two people in the store are Glen Peace, a man in his seventies, rail thin, wearing a flannel shirt and old jeans (and who grinningly refers to himself as "Peace of the Valley"), and his sole patron for lunch, Jim Perkins, a soft-spoken, white-haired man, also in his seventies, with a round belly, who is sitting in the back room eating a lunch of breaded fish and a side of peas.

Glen tells us his restaurant has been in this same spot since 1989; his brother owns one up the road as well, called Blue Store. When I ask him why it's called Blue Store, he looks at me with a puzzled expression and says, "Because it's a store and it's blue. Blue Store." Glen says he comes to work every single day, never taking a vacation because he doesn't want one. "I'm a hard hitter, a go-getter," Glen says, "because I always believe a feller should work. If you don't work, you shouldn't eat, I always say."

Glen isn't politically minded because he says he gets enough commentary day-to-day from the store's patrons. "When you work like I do, you sit here and listen to that talk all day long; they'll stay in here with you all day and take you to the parking lot on it," he says

* It's crazy to think of the time before these stores existed, when people had nowhere to go to buy a ceramic clock shaped like a boat's steering wheel with a smiling sea captain leaning against it.

dismissively. "You get tired of it." He's had politicians come into the store but doesn't remember any of their names. "They wasn't too impressive," he said.

Glen says his customers have changed over the years and nowadays he can't treat them the same. "I used to give four hundred people credit, now only three. Can't do it no more, though. Most of 'em won't pay. Old timers'll pay, new generation won't pay," he says. Glen also won't hire young people because they goof off too much. "They play games, stay up all night and sleep all day. They won't work," he tells me.

We go to see Jim in the other room, who has been loudly giving commentary on our conversation from the back. Glen notes that the table Jim is sitting at is known around these parts as "the Liar's Table." I ask Jim why and he replies, "Because you know who sits at this table? Preachers and deacons. They're the biggest liars of 'em all."

Jim is a lifelong bachelor but tells us even with his ability to swing, he doesn't date a lot of women anymore in Whitley County. "I used to date a lot of women in Illinois. They's good women in Illinois. Very few women around here, though. I'm just an old hillbilly so I can tell you hillbilly women are the hardest women to get acquainted with you'll ever find," he tells me. "They's tough; you gotta watch 'em. They don't trust nobody."

Jim is preparing to move to nearby Williamsburg, into a new low-income housing unit, but plans to come back out to the country because he has to feed his "pretty good size" tomcat, because "if I don't, who will?" He tells us he worries about Glen because there is a new Dollar General down the road, and he doesn't know if Glen can compete with their prices. The thought of his favorite store going away makes him sad.

"'Bout all there is to do around here if you can't work no more is sit around and get the blues," Jim says. "You can't do nothing about it if you've got 'em; you can't do a thing about it."

We thank the men and head out the door of the two-room shack. The whole time we were there we didn't see a single customer other than Jim, but Glen never stopped smiling. Two old-timers who have seen the world pass them by but are stubbornly holding on to their old ways and the world they miss. On the way out, I see the Dollar General store Jim had mentioned, its parking lot full of cars. They seemed to have no problem drawing a crowd, and I am sure the selection was much better.* But it's a shame. I wish the world had more places like Glen's Restaurant and Blue Store. This is what America used to be about, the little man and his small business serving the community. Soon Dollar General is almost certainly going to take that from him, and Glen knows it. But if I lived in Whitley County, I would do my shopping at Glen's little shack off Highway 92, just outside Siler. I might not be able to get my essentials, but I can get a serving tray with the cast of the *A-Team* on it. And really, what else do you need?

Knox County

"It's Time to Put Stitches on the Wound"

Feeling renewed after our visit with Glen and Jim, we get in the car and head to Barbourville or, as it's pronounced in these parts, "Barrrvuhl." The town's claim to fame is that it's the site of Union College, a perfect place to go to school if you're the outdoorsy type. Mountains, lakes, and trails are everywhere, so if you want to spend as much time out climbing a tree as you will on your clinical psychology thesis, no one will bat an eye (though, please, take your clinical psychology thesis seriously). It's small and cozy, surrounded by hills, and a great place to go to spend four years if you are okay with being slightly off the grid.

As we park in the center of town, memories of my childhood come flashing back. Union College always hosted the Thirteenth Region High School Tennis Championships, making it the site of some of my most bitter athletic defeats. On these hallowed grounds I lost my chance to advance to the state tournament in boys' doubles, as Chris Thompson and I were taken down at the hands of the evil Nick Cook

* They probably had actual prepackaged bags of gumdrops.

and Jay Fleenor duo from down the road in Corbin.* I have silently held this against Union College every day since, even finding myself rooting against its sports teams.

I know: not healthy. It's probably time to move past the disappointment, so I face my demons and we walk across campus to meet Dr. Joseph Pearson, a history professor at the college.

Pearson has conducted a great deal of research on Henry Clay, Kentucky's most famous senator before Mitch McConnell took the throne. Henry Clay is known as one of this nation's greatest statesmen, given the nickname the Great Compromiser. McConnell, the Great Partisan, has often cited Clay as a role model; at the University of Louisville, he even wrote his senior thesis on Clay. While McConnell has expressed allegiance to few members of history, Clay still holds a special place for him—even though he's rarely if ever emulated his highly principled home state brother during his six terms in the Senate. This seeming contradiction has not gone unnoticed by some of McConnell's foes. In 2011, during a debate to avoid a government shutdown, Nevada senator Harry Reid leered at his Kentucky counterpart as he said, "Remember the words that are so important in what Henry Clay said is 'mutual concession.' And we have done far more than anyone ever thought we would do." The implication was clear: McConnell may like Clay, but unlike him, Mitch never gives an inch.

Professor Pearson finds the idea of McConnell sharing any traits with Clay laughable, saying that at this point in his career, the senator doesn't ever see fit to compromise.

"McConnell's certainly no Clay," he says with a laugh. "Clay spoke to the better parts of people. He was a guy who built coalitions, who voiced unpopular opinions, who compromised, and who was willing to work across the aisle with Jacksonian Democrats—people he might have hated personally—to pass legislation. He worked with *people* and didn't really do a lot of work on the larger scale, and that cost him the presidency on several occasions."

* And their girlfriends are probably not being followed around by Mitch McConnell, so they are still winning.

Mitch McConnell, says Pearson, is almost the polar opposite. His description of McConnell the politician is as accurate as any we have come across: "The cold calculation of McConnell is almost Machiavellian. Clay was really good at crafting broad-based platforms that could draw support from a lot of different kinds of people. That's really, *really* important when you talk about Kentucky history. We're kind of America written small: we've got our rural parts, we've got our urban parts, we've got more faith-minded people and more progressively minded people. I think Mitch appeals to the absolute worst. He's about calculation over compromise. He's about defamation."

I ask Pearson how he believes McConnell will be judged by history. He says McConnell's legacy is pure partisanship, and history tends to look down on such figures.* But he's quick to note, "I don't think Mitch would really care either way what we decided about him."

On that depressing note (we may need to get Pearson a drink), we exit Barbourville and head up Highway 25-E toward the town I used to dread entering, Corbin. When I was growing up in Middlesboro, Corbin High School was our most hated rival and Corbin our least favorite town. Thanks to fifty-plus years of fierce competition between the two sports teams, the Redhounds were eastern Kentucky's hoity-toity neighbors who thought they were better than us and, therefore, had to be defeated at all costs (we usually lost). It spawned my bull-like aversion to any sports team that wears red (I'm looking at you, Louisville).

But now that I'm a grown-up, I can say objectively that Corbin is a beautiful and fascinating place. It is the gateway to the Appalachian Mountains and the birthplace of Kentucky Fried Chicken—yes, the launchpad for (honorary) Colonel Harland Sanders's world-conquering fried chicken enterprise. You can still visit the original location, and guests at the annual Nibroc Festival (*Corbin* spelled backward) celebrate its crispy-poultry legacy.† Plus, Corbin is the only city in Kentucky that occupies three different counties: Knox, Whitley, and Laurel.

* He has zero chance of making *Distinguished Chin* magazine's Top 100 of the Century.

† Each Kentuckian is taught one of the colonel's eleven secret herbs and spices as a young child. Mine was turmeric.

Not only is this illegal—according to state law, a city may spill over into a second county, but that's it; however, I guess they decided not to arrest the entire town*—but it's also odd considering that Corbin's population is only around 7,500.

Corbin has a tortured history, most notably the 1919 labor unrest that led to race riots. The turmoil ended when its white population forced all two hundred black residents onto a train and sent them out of the town permanently. It was a horrific moment, part of the Red Summer of racial violence that swept across America. In the years that followed, while there was no law on the books keeping African Americans out of the town, the practical impact of the riot was that none ever chose to live in Corbin. It is astounding to consider now, but even when I was in high school in the mid-1990s, Corbin had almost no black residents and was known in the mountains as a place you didn't go if you had African American players on your team, like we did. It shows how naive I was at the time, that I didn't question why this was the case. It was just assumed that black people weren't welcome in Corbin, so we'd grab something to eat in nearby London instead.

Thankfully, things have changed dramatically since. In the last twenty years or so, the new generation of Corbin residents has taken steps to overcome their hometown's history of bigotry through affirmative outreach. In 2005 Corbin became one of the first towns in America to reach out to Hurricane Katrina victims, with a local church volunteering to house and feed more than forty people from New Orleans in the months following the disaster. While only a few chose to remain in the town permanently, all found Corbin residents hospitable and welcoming, a signal of Corbin's strides forward. This year, the town went further as the mayor commissioned an exhibit and memorial acknowledging the one hundredth anniversary of the incident. It included a display of firsthand accounts of those African Americans who were displaced a century ago, an important step for a community confronting its past.

I think of this history as we sit in Si Señor Mexican Restaurant in Corbin's downtown. Things have changed to such a degree that many

* Don't go anywhere yet, Laurel County. We have some questions!

younger people in the town aren't even aware of its history. A group of high-school-age boys, four white and two black, sit near us, laughing and cutting up as if they have no cares in the world. It is a scene that could be repeated easily anywhere in America, but it is strikingly refreshing here in Corbin. I have visited the area many times since childhood, and my old sports bias against the Redhounds faded long ago. But I am proud of my southeastern Kentucky neighbors for confronting history and moving forward. Nevertheless, there is still work to be done, but the town seems committed. As resident Nathan Flynn, an organizer of the exhibit, told a TV station on the anniversary: "There is now a Band-Aid on the wounds, but it is not closed. It's time to put stitches on the wound."

Laurel County

Christianity in the Trump Era

Laurel County is a success story, growing as fast as any other rural area in the state. The population has doubled to more than sixty thousand just in the last thirty-five years, and its location as the final industrial center before entering the Appalachian Mountains has led to huge growth. London's downtown is a weird hybrid of old-timey and new, evidenced by modern-day brick-and-glass buildings standing next to aged, classic storefronts. It's as if a business developer came to town to try to buy up the whole city, but only half were selling. The result is hip modern banks, tattoo parlors, and breweries that rub shoulders with old antique stores, barbershops,* and decaying office space. A city in transition.

Laurel County is also home to a very conservative political base, built in part by a population with fairly fundamentalist religious beliefs. London may be the centerpiece of Kentucky's evangelical Christian

* Though to be fair, the barbershop is called the Tonic Room, which is the most hipster name for a barbershop ever.

political scene, as witnessed by the fact that Vice President Mike Pence has come to town three times since taking office. That's a whole lot of Mike Pence for me (or for anyone but Mother), but people around here seem to like it.

I am a Christian and grew up my entire life in the church. Both my parents are accomplished musicians (my dad plays the bass violin and my mom the piano and sings),* and I spent most of my childhood traveling with them on Sundays as they sang at churches around the community.† I went to a Christian-affiliated university and have maintained a strong relationship with God ever since. However, as a progressive, I get asked often, "How can you be a Democrat *and* a Christian?" On the face of things, it's an absurd question. There is no scenario I can imagine where my relationship with the Lord requires me to vote for an immoral narcissist like Donald Trump, but many Kentuckians believe that their faith compels them to do just that. As for Mitch McConnell, the senator rarely, if ever, speaks about religion, and it isn't clear if he is even a churchgoer. Yet if I run, there will be many Christian Kentucky voters who will somehow believe that casting a ballot for him is their religious duty. Combatting that would be a difficult task.

With that in mind, I spoke with Brian House, a London pastor whose family has lived in the area since 1801. House tells me that in a town as conservative as London, he's seen firsthand how politics and religion mash together, even though House himself has self-proclaimed liberal views. He tries to keep things nonpartisan—at least, as nonpartisan as the crossroads of religion and politics can get these days.

"You have to be very careful when you're pastoring a church," he explains. "I always tell my congregations, you'll never hear me preach a particular party from the pulpit because my job is to love you and take care of you. But when it came to trying to live as Christ calls us to live, if those views were deemed progressive and liberal by other people who

---

* Daddy plays bass, Mama sings tenor.

† I'll see and raise Matt on this one. I literally share a name with Grammy-winning Christian music artist Chris Tomlin, whose fan mail I sometimes receive. Some of you may still think I am him now. If you haven't figured it out yet, I am not, but I can do a mean rendition of "How Great Thou Art."

went to other churches, I didn't care. It was not politics per se if certain political parties adopted positions that we felt were consistent with the New Testament. That's the prerogative of the party. We were simply trying to live as we interpreted the gospel."

House admits it has become hard in recent years to know how to handle the political landscape in which we find ourselves, especially as it relates to President Trump, a leader who is supported by the vast majority of rural Christians.

"I struggle with that all the time," the pastor says. "Christians cannot hand over the governance of their country to people like Donald Trump; just because you're Christian doesn't mean you're passive. What you have to do, if you're going to engage in social activism, you have to do it in a way that's consistent with Christ, and that means we can't be violent, we can't be profane. We can be vigorous, and we can be very energetically involved in voting and contesting issues—all of those things we should be doing. So much of what Trump does is absolutely antithetical to what Christ was about."

When I was growing up, the idea that Christians would rally around a man like Donald Trump would have been unimaginable to me. A man with multiple divorces, repeated instances of infidelity, a constantly cursing tongue, arrogance that knows no bounds, and hateful disdain toward those who disagree with him would have been against every principle that Christianity is said to stand for. And that doesn't even get into his treatment of immigrant families, his disdain for helping foreign allies, and his attempts to take away benefits from the most vulnerable Americans. In January 2016, on the eve of presidential primary season, candidate Trump spoke at Jerry Falwell Jr.'s Liberty University in Lynchburg, Virginia, quoting a Bible verse like this:

"Two Corinthians 3:17, that's the whole ballgame. Is that the one you like? 'Now the Lord is that Spirit, and where the Spirit of the Lord is, there is liberty.'"

Of course, any Christian who has even the most basic familiarity with the Bible would know that it is "Second Corinthians," not "Two Corinthians." But, of course, the gaffe isn't surprising, as there is exactly zero evidence that Trump has spent any time with the Bible or religion as a whole, either in action or in deeds. (Also calling his piety into question, he cursed twice during his speech.) And yet in 2020 there is a Christian voting base who will vote for Trump and those who support him, such as McConnell, regardless. Many believe his leadership is destined by God, with some going so far as to argue that Trump is the "imperfect being" sent by God to do his work on Earth. It is an unbelievable whitewash of essentially Trump's entire life. When an editorial in the publication *Christianity Today* dared to suggest that defending Trump wasn't defending Christian behavior (with examples as to why), many readers chose Trump.

How is Trump, with his myriad personal flaws, seen as God's warrior, but Barack Obama, a lifelong churchgoing Christian, is regarded with such disdain? The main reason is social policy. Trump's personal transgressions are ignored because of his stated positions (all of which he flipped just before running for president) on abortion, gay marriage, and other social issues. However, Pastor House believes that due to these oft-discussed issues, other facets of Christianity are being ignored. What about some of the basic tenets of Christ's teachings, such as caring for the poor, respecting your fellow man, and loving one another as God has loved you? These tenets are rarely invoked and completely forgotten by Trump and most modern-day GOP leaders, including Mitch McConnell. If we are supposed to care for the least of our brothers and sisters as we would for Jesus himself, how do the actions of so many politicians get a pass?

"I don't think Mitch McConnell has a great deal of compassion for the poor," says House. "He's not demonstrated it in all of these years, and he's certainly not used his power as Senate majority leader to do anything for the poor. He has been a lot about Mitch, he's been a lot about the wealthy, and making the people who are entitled likely to be more entitled. I think his legacy will be one that will be very disappointing to Kentuckians thirty years from now."

Clay County

Mitch McConnell Was Wantin' to Know If There Really Was Someone Praying for Matthew Jones

"For I know the plans I have for you," declares the Lord, "plans for welfare and not for evil, to give you a future and a hope."

—Jeremiah 29:11

I would doubt that any potential candidates considering a run against Mitch McConnell read this verse out loud just before kneeling on a floor to pray in a small house in Clay County. But then again, most potential candidates aren't as blessed as I have been to get to know Jason Root.

I first met Jason a few months prior, when my mother called and told me that a stranger in Clay County had contacted her to say God had told him to pray for me, as he knew I would be making a big decision soon.

Jason Root is a very unique individual. He is a mountain preacher, forty-three years old, with short hair and a large frame, kind and gently spoken. He loves to smile, and when he speaks, he does so with a deep mountain accent and a rhythmic cadence. He takes few pauses as he speaks, often in one long run-on sentence, rocking rhythmically back and forth as his voice rises and falls in ways the best rural preachers know will bring you along with them. His cadence is that of a soft impassioned plea of delicate information he is imparting only to you—punctuated every now and then with "'n' so on."

We came to see Jason after taking a long drive through Clay County, passing the largest town of Manchester. Jason lives beyond the federal corrections facility, the largest employer in the county, where prisoners in jumpsuits shoot hoops behind tall chain-link fences. These winding roads in the mountains can make you dizzy, and we are relieved when we reach the top of a slight hill and arrive at Jason's house.

He lives in a small one-room building next to his mother's house.

Jason is fully blind and stays in this small room because it's easy to navigate. Inside his home is a veritable museum of University of Kentucky sports memorabilia. A quilted Wildcats blanket hangs on the wall, along with posters commemorating the biggest victories and best teams of the past eras of UK basketball. An autographed photo of 2012 Wildcats phenom Anthony Davis is clearly a prized possession. The place is warm and friendly, and Jason sits right in the middle of it all, rising from a recliner to meet us. His eyes closed, grinning, he clutches Chris's and my hands like we're old, familiar friends.

Jason often calls us by our names as he talks in his personable, caring, genuine manner. He turns to Chris and leans back in the recliner.

"When I was five years old, Chris"—he settles in to tell his story—"I was diagnosed with retinitis pigmentosa. I was born two-eighteen-seventy-six. My dad was in the Vietnam War. I have a brother; he has retinitis pigmentosa too. They call it 'RP' 'n' so on. It eats the rods out of the eyes 'n' so on. And I didn't know what that meant when I was five years old. Your life's going great, you've got no problems. But God knowed what it meant in the future. I went all through grade school, didn't have problems with my vision. First year in high school, my vision went to 20/2100. I was fifteen years old. Us Christians, sometimes, Chris, we think nothing bad is ever supposed to happen to us 'n' so on. But that ain't the way it is. And I got mad at God. I said, 'God, why are you making this happen?' He told me, 'You don't know the big picture for your life,' so God gave me peace with it."

Jason's life changed dramatically. Soon after, he lost his eyesight, a victim of the chemical Agent Orange his father had been exposed to in Vietnam. His brother, who lives next door in their mother's house, has the disease also. Both are legally blind.

"Got out of high school that summer," Jason continues. "I had a headache for thirty days. I laid in bed. Couldn't get out of bed except to eat 'n' so on. Was in so much pain. And God gave me peace again. Then in 2001, September twelfth, I woke up with another severe headache, and I was blind. Got mad at God, I was depressed. Didn't even really want to go on. And God gave me peace again. So I went really to praying for people, focusing on other people besides me 'n' so on. His best gift is to keep our minds on other things when we have problems. That summer, God called me into preaching. I told him, 'I ain't preaching. I don't want to be a preacher, God.' And then I went to a revival, and God spoke to my heart and said, 'You can do this the easy way or the hard way, but you're gonna be a minister either way.'"

And that was that. Jason decided to spend his life seeking out people with problems or difficulties and trying to make their lives better. As I watch Jason tell Chris his story, I think of my first meeting with him. In the summer, my parents drove to Clay County to bring Jason to a live radio show I was doing in my hometown. When it was over, I met him at my parents' house, and he asked if he could pray for me. For five minutes, he held my hand, and we closed our eyes, and he asked the Lord to bless me and help give me strength as I decided whether to run for office. In words that still touch me to this day, he said, "Lord, I know you have something for Matthew, a gift he is going to share with the world. I don't know what it is, Lord, but he cares about us, and he cares about mountain people, and I pray you help him see your will." It was powerful stuff, causing me to cry in the middle of my parents' living room. In part it was the message, but it also was the messenger: a special man who had been touched with so much personal tragedy but still wanted to heal others in pain.

Jason's manner of speaking naturally draws you to him and makes you lean in, hanging on his every word. He tells me God calls him to pray for people—people who are sick, people having difficult times—and that God called Jason to pray for me. Well, more accurately, Jason explains, God told him to call *my mother* first, which he did, although it was a little awkward even for him.

"So, I called her," he says, chuckling, self-aware of the uniqueness of the moment. "And I prayed with her. I don't even know why I called her. And next week God let me know that I was supposed to start praying for Matthew, and that he had a big decision coming. So, I started praying for him, and that Bible verse that you read, Jeremiah 29:11, that's the Bible verse that God speaks to me every time I pray for Matthew."

And pray he does. He calls my mother weekly, asking which counties I will be visiting that week so that he can pray for our blessings. He asks for guidance for me, my girlfriend Rachel, Chris and his wife, and even my radio show cohosts, Ryan, Drew, and Shannon, who, as he puts it, "don't know what the future holds neither." Jason never tells me what he thinks I should do, he just says, "God will let you know." He believes whatever decision I make will be the right one.

Whatever I end up doing, Jason's opinion of my possible opponent isn't a positive one, even though he considers himself a strong Republican. "That's what Mitch McConnell don't do neither, Matt, is what you do, unite people," he says. "As a senator, governor, Congress, whatever, you have to unite the people instead of divide them 'n' so on. And I don't think Mitch McConnell unites the people in this state. He don't get no new jobs for Clay County, and he don't get no new jobs for nowhere. They talk about how he's the most powerful person in the country besides the president. And this whole state ain't got nothing, and I think we got sixteen pharmacies and drug stores here in Clay County. Why you think we have so many drug problems? There's no supercenter here, there's no Kroger here, there ain't no big-time grocery store here. I think Mitch McConnell should be helping more businesses come into the communities 'n' so on, but I'm forty-three years old, and he ain't done it since I been here."

A few weeks prior to our meeting with Jason, I did a podcast with veteran radio host Tony Vanetti on which I told him about Jason and his prayers for me. I spoke about how his belief in me touched my heart and gave me confidence that I was on the right path. Little did I know, someone else was listening as well.

"It was one Sunday," says Jason. "I got up and listened to my Bible, then I prayed, 'n' so on. I had a buddy call me—he's the richest man in Clay County, and he's friends with Mitch McConnell. He said, 'I called you because Mitch McConnell was wantin' to know if there really was somebody in Clay County with the Binghamtown Baptist Church that was praying for Matthew Jones.' And I said, 'Yes sir, I'm praying for Matthew, because I feel like God has great work for him to do.' And I told him, I said, 'I don't know what that work is, but God knows what it is.' And I prayed with that man too."

I am floored. Mitch McConnell took the time *personally*, not via a surrogate, to call a supporter in Clay County to question if my story about Jason was real. He clearly presumed I had made Jason up for political gain and thought he could catch me in a public lie. Such dripping cynicism says a lot about how McConnell looks at the world. To him, people like Jason Root don't exist, and it is completely foreign to his experience to imagine such self-sacrifice. In Mitch's mind, a relationship like the one we have must either be about political motivation or simply be untrue.

"I believe I'm just supposed to help connect you with the church people 'n' so on," Jason says, nodding. "And I'm just telling you, and I don't even know what you're going to do—God knows. But if you decide to do that, we'll do our best, with the help of God, to help."

I give Jason a hug and tell him thanks, meeting his family on the way out. Chris and I walk out the door in silence, and I look at him, and we both have tears in our eyes. Mitch McConnell may have all the political power in the world, and Amy McGrath may have all the money the establishment can generate, but I am not sure either has the support of Kentuckians like Jason Root. If McConnell wants to confirm his existence, he should call Jason. Maybe he would learn something.

Bell County

"Dig Up Any Dirt You Have on These People!"

After leaving Jason's house, I headed to Middlesboro in Bell County to visit my parents and spend a night in my hometown. Middlesboro is situated in a bowl in the heart of the Appalachian Mountains, created by a giant meteor hitting the area two hundred to three hundred million years ago. The crater that was left behind allows Middlesboro to be placed below everything around it, like a candle that has burned unevenly only in the center, creating a sinking depression below the hardened wax above. Driving into the area, I passed the relatively new welcome sign that on top informs visitors the city is home to "Lee Majors," and on the bottom, "Kentucky Media Personality: Matt Jones." When you are the Six Million Dollar Man, you need no descriptor.

I moved to Middlesboro at the age of four with my mom, who was returning to her hometown to start a law practice. I loved growing up in this small community, and the mountains of eastern Kentucky shaped who I am as a person. Only around ten thousand people lived here, and, during my childhood, Middlesboro saw the peaks and valleys of the greater economy of the region. Coal was a big deal during my youth, with many of my classmates having parents who worked in the area mines. But during those years, the secondary economy was solid too. A local leather tannery, meat processing plant, and Coke bottling company were among the many businesses that kept Middlesboro's economy afloat. It was a poor area, but not destitute by any means, and, as a child, it seemed like a perfect place to grow up.

Now things have slowed down. Industry has left and most of the mines are closed. I drive into town and pass the Middlesboro Country Club, the oldest continually played golf course in the United States, a title few would believe could come from this area. It is a semipublic golf course where I spent a lot of time playing golf as a kid and as I go past, I see the effect of the economic downturn on the area in its slightly worn appearance. I head to my parents' house for the night and walk in as Larry, my stepfather, is finishing his work in the yard. Larry is a dead ringer for actor Patrick Stewart of *Star Trek* fame and looks like he could take over command of the starship *Enterprise* at a moment's notice. My parents divorced soon after moving to Middlesboro, and my mom married Larry a few years later. Because I have no relationship with my biological father, I consider Larry my dad, and he has happily taken on that role in my life. We are very different. He is quiet, introverted, and a handyman, all traits I do not possess. A retired middle school guidance counselor (a profession you must be a saint to undertake), he is likely the kindest man I have ever met.

My mom and I sit in our den, adorned with framed pictures of me at various ages and begin chatting about how the tour is going and my thoughts on the race. It is a somewhat delicate subject to discuss, because I know it makes her nervous to think about her son having to take on Mitch McConnell on the national political stage. Whether she realizes it or not, my mother, Karen, is my hero. She moved to Middlesboro as a single mother in her late twenties and started a solo law practice in rural Kentucky, something that just wasn't done at the time. She ran for the position of Bell County commonwealth's attorney twice, losing the first time by just fifty-seven votes but winning the second by a two-thousand-vote margin. In that year's election, she and two other women became the first female state prosecutors elected in the history of Kentucky. She was a trailblazer and took risks that now, thirty-plus years later, are hard to comprehend.

Now my mom is one of the most renowned prosecutors in the state, winning the annual Kentucky Prosecutor of the Year Award twice in her career. As a kid, I loved going to watch her in jury trials. She was known for her exceptional skill at closing arguments, and she has a unique ability to bring together facts and tell a compelling, conclusory story in a way that is both relatable and powerful to jurors. Even more impressive to me than her talent is her confidence: when making those closing arguments, she was doing what she felt was morally right, protecting the community from crime, and it drove her to excel at the highest level. When I speak to groups now, I feel like, at my best moments, I am trying to channel that same skill and confidence I saw in her in that courtroom many years ago.

But my mom is also a mother, and I can tell she is nervous about my decision. We agree that my running against Mitch McConnell will be difficult but is a fight that is noble. We also firmly believe that I am one of only a couple of people who could actually beat Mitch in 2020, but that the battle will be a nasty one that will have a long-term impact on my life, for better or for worse.

I can see she is worried about me, knowing that he will attack me personally and in vicious ways. As a mother, she is terrified I will get hurt. We talk about the primary and all the money Amy McGrath will have at her disposal to try to crush me. I confide for the first time that most of the personal attacks on me that I am hearing about are not from the McConnell camp but rather from inside McGrath's campaign. Getting bludgeoned from the left and the right would be the reality of this race—one neither of us relishes. My mom is very strong, but I know if I choose to do this, watching me get attacked constantly for twelve months will be awful for her.

The next morning I wake up, do my radio show, and tell my parents goodbye. Before I go, I take a driving tour around town to reminisce. I go past my old elementary school; my grandparents' house, where

I spent nearly every afternoon after school; my friend D. J. Sharpe's childhood home, where I gained my love for professional wrestling—you know, all the important locations. I drive out farther, past my high school, and continue until I reach an area they call Noetown; it's a poorer part of the community, with a number of churches and run-down houses. I look around, reminded of the fact that these are the people who have inspired me to consider this race in the first place. They are invisible to most politicians. Democrats act like they don't exist and Republicans do nothing to help their futures, leaving them with little hope of changing their paths in life. Folks like this desperately need someone to fight for them and to have a seat at the table. If nothing else, I know I would do exactly that.

But as I drive out of town, I also think about the cost of entering this race on a personal level. I have epilepsy, and the occasional seizure while I am sleeping is part of my existence. The biggest factor in their occurrence is stress and I know if I run, it will have a detrimental effect on my health. I also would be under constant scrutiny, and it would make it very difficult for my mother in her role as a state prosecutor. Any negativity about me could be used against her, which is unfair but an unfortunate likelihood. Then there's my girlfriend, a very private person living in Manhattan to pursue her lifelong dream of becoming a TV news producer on a national network. If I run, she will be taken off the network's political coverage during the campaign and will have her entire life dissected in an unfair manner she never asked for. The Tracker told me that people are now following me around when I visit her in New York City, and the idea of her having to go through an ordeal like that for a whole year? Well, it breaks my heart. She says she can handle it, but I hate to put that on her.

Then there are my lifelong friends. I haven't even declared yet, and already seven of their names turned up on a sheet of paper that had been handed to a private investigator I happen to know, along with the instructions "Dig up any dirt you have on these people!" None asked for this scrutiny, and their lives will be invaded all for the "sin" of having chosen me as a friend decades ago.

For me, Bell County represents this dichotomy: people who need someone advocating for them daily in Washington as much as anyplace in the country but currently have no one. I know I would work harder for them than any other candidate would. Yet it's also the place that will be ground zero for the campaign of personal destruction that will come my way if I enter the fray, taking out those I love the most as collateral damage. Putting my name on the ballot will be signing them up for a hellacious experience they didn't ask for. Everyone who gets into modern politics knows the risk he or she is incurring. But to do it to others who didn't ask for it? That just seems cruel.

At a Kentucky Chamber of Commerce meeting in July 2019, I did a panel with Scott Jennings, a McConnell campaign advisor. I was speaking about the potential race and I pointed to Jennings and said, "If I run, these guys will try and personally destroy me." Without missing a beat, Jennings responded, "We won't try and destroy you, we will destroy you!" The crowd let out a gasp and Jennings laughed at his comment. It didn't go over well in the room (or with my mother in the audience) but I tried not to get offended. Jennings and I are friendly, yet I do believe there was truth behind what he said.* McConnell's campaign style is personal destruction. Am I, a political neophyte, ready for that battle against Darth Vader and his Death Star of personal attacks? It's an agonizing decision, one I've wrestled with for months. I can make a rational case for either path—a realization that only makes the final choice more difficult. But I still have four weeks left to decide and miles to go before I sleep.

* For the record, I have advised against this friendship. I don't trust him.

CHAPTER 7

"We Never Existed"

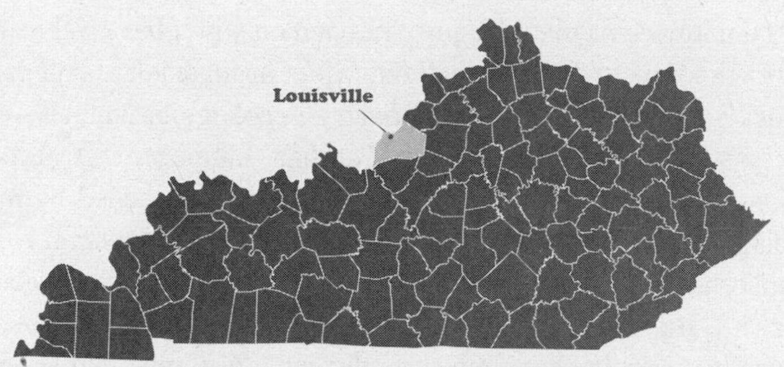

Jefferson County

I Can't Say Mitch Let Us Down, Because to Him, We Never Existed

Louisville is the largest city in Kentucky, and by far its most progressive. In a state that continues to trend more and more red, Louisville is an outlier, becoming a more solid Democratic stronghold each year. It's the strongest economic engine for the state as a whole, and its growth in recent years has made it one of the most desirable midsize cities in America. However, Louisville often feels apart from the rest of Kentucky, both politically and culturally.

Mitch McConnell's political life began in Louisville, but he's become more detached to the area by the year. Whereas he once won Jefferson County by taking nearly 60 percent of the vote in 2002, his total in 2014 was only 42 percent of the vote there, and it is assumed he will struggle to crack 40 percent in the 2020 race. Even though the senator is the most important benefactor to the University of Louisville, has played a part in area politics for nearly fifty years, and even lives in the same moderate-sized house in the middle of the city's most progressive neighborhood, the Highlands, the city is over Mitch McConnell. Louisville will be the most important location for any serious attempt to throw Mitch out of office.

It also is likely the area in which I am the least popular. In Louisville, I am known as the "UK guy": the person who goes on the air to support the Cats and knock the Louisville Cardinals on a daily basis. Kentucky-Louisville is the biggest rivalry in college basketball—even more passionate than Duke-North Carolina, although that is a discussion for a different book.* The UL-UK rivalry is fueled by many components: city versus country, urban versus rural, Democrat versus Republican. Steeped in the state's history, it is based as much on culture as it is on sports. Even though it may seem insane to an outsider, the two fan bases see themselves as distinctly different, and crossing that barrier will be difficult for me.

When the University of Louisville found itself in a series of basketball scandals involving illegal payments, FBI probes, and strippers in the dormitory,† I was on the radio taking glee in the situation. It was exactly the role you would expect the biggest UK fan to take. I was happy to play the heel, assuming that listeners realized sports isn't a life-or-death endeavor. But for many, trash-talking rivals is not behavior they normally associate with a US senator. As a broad stereotype, the UL fan base is predominantly Democratic; the UK fan base, predominantly Republican. Thus, the idea of the main UK voice becoming a Democratic candidate for senator is tough for many Cardinals fans to accept. That, too, will present a genuine hurdle for my potential campaign, especially in a Democratic primary.

This concern led me to an event in Louisville on a fall Sunday afternoon at the house of Christy Brown, a local philanthropist and

* Our next book, "Thanks a lot, Rickhead!"

† It was quite the scandal. We tried to write about it in this book, and our editor said it was too dirty.

Democratic political donor. Brown is arguably the most important Democratic donor in the state and has been an early supporter of my potential candidacy. She loves the state and has been a wonderful help in navigating the unfamiliar landscape of Louisville Democrats. She has introduced me to many in the city and has set up this meeting at my request to have me speak to the most active progressive Democratic figures in the area, the biggest activists, thought leaders, and donors in the city, all of which are important to success. This group is likely skeptical of me as a candidate, not so much because of sports but because of policy. I am seen as a moderate, and Louisville is the one place in Kentucky where that may be a bad word.

Driving to Brown's house, I go through a part of the city I have never seen before. The neighborhood is a bastion of old Louisville money with beautiful and grand homes. In a city that always seems congested to me, this community on the eastern edge is isolated, surrounded by nature and beauty, a few miles and an entire lifestyle away from the rest of Louisville. The path to Brown's house is convoluted, with a number of turns on roads with no signs, causing me to get lost and turn around twice. It's the kind of place that isn't easy to navigate in part because, if you don't know how to get here, folks who live in these neighborhoods may not want you visiting.

Brown welcomes me to the gathering warmly, saying she hopes this meeting will encourage me to jump into the race. She has been a constant presence in my ear, pleading for me to run and promising that she will be an advocate for me if I make the leap. I believe her and do appreciate her advice, but I am most definitely conflicted. I am often uneasy around her and the other wealthy liberals in Kentucky. Even though I feel completely at ease in nearly every corner of the commonwealth, for some reason, at these get-togethers I am at my most uncomfortable. They are refined and dignified, while my own deficiencies in those areas make me feel like a hillbilly interloper who just happened to drift into the wrong room.

Brown's estate is gorgeous, and the view from her house overlooking the city is one of the best I have seen anywhere. It is packed with guests, and I chuckle thinking about the last time I was in a house with this many people in Louisville. It was a World Wrestling Entertainment

(WWE) Royal Rumble party, and my excitement cheering Shinsuke Nakumara on to victory was likely much more fun than this will be.

Brown introduces me to the room as we begin and notes that Democratic congressman John Yarmuth will be listening in over speakerphone as well. She sets the phone right next to where I am standing, further rattling my nerves. Approximately fifty people are in attendance: doctors, lawyers, artists, professors—a good cross section of the Louisville cultural elite. I introduce myself and give the same general Mitch speech that I have on other occasions, focused on health care, workers' rights, education, and equality. It seems generally well received. I finish and ask for questions.

One by one, I am peppered with questions on a litany of progressive issues: the Green New Deal, immigration, abortion, impeachment, and so on. I note that I am pro-choice, not in favor of the Green New Deal until I see actual legislation behind the label, against the wall, for raising taxes on the wealthy, to support universal healthcare, and so on. My answers are met with general positivity, and I feel like the event goes well. Some of the progressives seem unconvinced, but I don't think I hurt myself in the process.

The final question comes from an older African American man who introduces himself as a doctor in the community. He has watched me the entire time with a serious face and has rarely showed any emotion. His question is simple and direct: "If you were elected, what would you do to help the black community?"

I completely bungle the answer. I had focused so much of my speech and questions on particular responses to individual policies that when a more general question about priorities came, I wasn't ready. I mumbled something about criminal justice reform and equal opportunity, but admittedly, it wasn't well thought out. I tried to fix the mess by saying I needed to listen and rely on the wisdom of others, but the damage was done. Sitting in the crowd, if you had noticed the ease with which I dealt with other issues and then the awkwardness with which I spoke on race, you'd rightly think I didn't have the plans needed to address the issue.

I looked for the man after the event to apologize. I felt embarrassed by my answer, but, more importantly, by my lack of preparation on a crucial topic. He said, "Matt, no need to apologize. I can tell you are sincere. But you need to take some time to focus on the policies that you will encourage for the black community. We don't need a savior, but we do need someone who will listen and who cares."

I took his words to heart and made my way to the West End of Louisville. When you say, "the West End of Louisville," everyone in Jefferson County knows what you are talking about. Louisville is as racially segregated as any city in America. Three-fourths of its black populace live on just 5 percent of the land: the area west of Ninth Street, referred to as the "West End." Long after official segregation has been outlawed, it remains an economic dividing line between whites and blacks, the haves and the have-nots.

By the time you get to Ninth Street, the major businesses cease, and what follows are ten to fifteen blocks of liquor stores, fast-food joints, and dollar stores. Beginning on around Twenty-Fifth Street, vacant lots overtake the premises, cleared-out property paved over with concrete. The homeless walk the streets, and you begin to see low-level housing. With each passing block, the view becomes less promising. The most progressive city in the state, divided by one street that everyone knows serves as its permanent racial and economic barrier.

I used to do a radio show in this area but the last time I was here was in 2016, when Muhammad Ali, Louisville's most famous native son, passed away. Born in the Parkland neighborhood in Louisville's West End in 1942, the magnetic three-time heavyweight boxing champion became an international icon who transcended the world of sports. Driving into Louisville on I-64, you can see a magnificent building-size banner of him looking thoughtful and smiling next to the words "Louisville's Ali," in giant print. In 2005 Louisville spent $80 million to open the Muhammad Ali Center, a huge museum and cultural center that fleshes out the city's skyline with images of shadow boxers dotting the outside walls. Upon his death, Ali requested to be buried in Louisville's Cave Hill Cemetery, but not before his hearse drove him one last time through his old neighborhood in the West End. The procession was one for the ages, with the entire city lining the streets and an international audience watching on television. Ali received the royal treatment from a nation, and a city, that hadn't always treated him with the respect he deserved.

In his autobiography, Ali tells of returning home from winning the light-heavyweight gold medal at the 1960 Summer Olympics in Rome and finding he had less respect in his hometown than in a foreign country:

"I sat down and asked for a meal. The Olympic champion wearing his gold medal. They said, 'We don't serve n***ers here.' I said, 'That's okay, I don't eat 'em.' But they put me out in the street. So I went down to the river, the Ohio River, and threw my gold medal in it."

Ali's struggle for acceptance in Louisville mirrors the experiences of most African Americans in the city as a whole. Louisville remains one of the most residentially segregated cities in the United States. The racial segregation began during the Jim Crow era, when, in 1914, the city passed an ordinance prohibiting racial mixing in real estate. A black person was forbidden from buying, or even dwelling in, property that was located on a white-majority block. A challenge to the ordinance made it all the way to the Supreme Court. In 1917 the court ruled against the city of Louisville, contending that even under the "separate but equal" doctrine of the time, the ordinance was in violation, as it didn't allow African Americans to buy the same houses as their white neighbors. Official government segregation in private housing was ruled unconstitutional.

The city of Louisville didn't stop there. No longer allowed to officially ban the races from living in the same neighborhoods, city officials utilized the tools of zoning to enforce de facto segregation. In the late 1930s, the Home Owners' Loan Corporation (HOLC) implemented a strategy of "redlining," the effect of which is still being felt in Louisville to this day. As part of the New Deal legislation, which was intended to encourage home financing, cities were allowed to create maps that labeled neighborhoods on a desirability scale based on traits such as owner occupation, social status, and economic sustainability. Thanks to the work of Harland Bartholomew, an urban planner who believed in segregationist housing, cities such as Louisville devised maps that abused these scales to systematically rank the minority neighborhoods as "undesirable," thus denying them access to credit, mortgages, and any outside investment. Businesses refused to move into these now official "undesirable" areas, and systematic unofficial housing segregation in Louisville was set in place. White property owners fled the city, and black neighborhoods became permanent second-class areas, unable to flourish with the rest of Louisville.

In 1968, following the assassination of Dr. Martin Luther King Jr., the racial tension in the West End boiled over. On May 27, 1968, on the corner of Twenty-Eighth Street and Greenwood Avenue, in Ali's Parkland neighborhood, a group of black protestors congregated after having learned that a white police officer who had been suspended for excessively beating a young black man was going to be reinstated. Raoul Cunningham, then the twenty-five-year-old director of the Kentucky Christian Leadership Conference, was there.

"It was a little bit scary," he admits. "Louisville had not experienced anything of that nature at that time. I witnessed the protests and the rally that had been scheduled for Twenty-Eighth and Greenwood. One of the speakers tried to incite some discord by saying the police would not allow Stokely Carmichael to land his plane." Carmichael was, at the time, a member of the Black Panther party and a civil rights leader coming to town to be a part of the protests. The rumors of his supposed banishment from the city were spreading. But Cunningham notes, "That was just a blatant lie, but after that, the police gang busted in."

Before long, what started as a peaceful protest turned into a riot spanning at least ten city blocks. Rioters were seen vandalizing, looting, burning cars, and breaking windows. The governor of Kentucky called in nearly seven hundred National Guardsmen, and a curfew was set for the city. Violence ensued for days, with four hundred people arrested and two teenagers killed before tempers and emotions finally cooled.

Chris and I visited the corner of Twenty-Eighth and Greenwood to see where it all started. The 28th Street Barber Shop, surrounded by empty lots and vacant buildings, shows the only sign of life. We walk in to ask about the protest and subsequent violence, and see it memorialized in photos mounted on the shop's walls: speakers standing on cars, addressing the crowd; burning vehicles that had been turned upside down; young men throwing bottles; the National Guard marching through the street, rifles at the ready.

The smell of burning incense fills the air, and we look around at the five fish tanks on display, as well as small slap stickers tagged with images of barbershop poles smoking weed.* It's a unique atmosphere, alive with history. One barber tells us that back in the day, every city had a "Black Main Street" where minority life was centered, and in Louisville, in 1968, that was Twenty-Eighth Street. It was vibrant then, teeming with people and full of stores and other local businesses. Now it's deserted, and Simon Wallace, who opened the barbershop in 2013, explains, "In most cities, after a race riot, the city eventually reinvested and helped to develop that part of town. Here, the city hasn't done a thing; they have left us on our own."

In 1975 a federal judge ordered the city to institute a busing policy in order to alleviate the effects of discrimination lingering from the residential segregation of the Jim Crow era. It was an extremely controversial policy, leading to widespread protests and even acts of violence. School buses bringing black students to white neighborhoods were pelted with rocks, and the busing issue became the defining question for local politics for a decade.

It was in this very tumultuous environment that Mitch McConnell began his political career. In those early days, while working for Republican representative Gene Snyder, he claims to have snuck out onto the Capitol steps to observe Martin Luther King Jr.'s landmark "I Have a Dream" speech on the National Mall on August 28, 1963. Many who worked with McConnell at the time considered him progressive on civil rights, something he played up heavily when he began his political career in Jefferson County.

But McConnell also knew that busing was causing tremendous angst among much of the county's white population. Many abandoned the downtown area or the county altogether, in what was called white flight, and Mitch knew that making the wrong decision could end his political career before it started. In his classic calculating way, he took no position, stating only that the incumbent county judge-executive was wrong to support busing. McConnell never came out against it, mind you, but his criticism of his opponent implied otherwise. As with abortion, unions, and other hot-button issues, Mitch took whatever stand

* Which I need in my house.

would benefit him most at the time, sacrificing his previous pro-civil-rights viewpoints for political expediency.

Democratic state senator Gerald Neal, a representative of West Louisville since 1988 and a key figure in the civil rights movement, says that initially McConnell was somewhat supportive of Louisville's black community. But, according to Neal, he turned quickly.

> I met Mitch McConnell when he was county judge, and I worked with him. In fact, we worked well together. I had high regard for Mitch McConnell at that time. But you know they've got a saying, "Power corrupts, and absolute power corrupts absolutely." I don't know if that necessarily fits McConnell, but I will say it this way: I do not recognize him today from what I knew then. In fact, when he ascended to his Senate position, it became quite apparent that this was someone I did not know that I thought I knew. I thought he was the kind of person that I could go to, and we could sit down and work out problems, and work out a resolution. But then I began to realize that he's corrupted the system by the way he's conducted his business. I'm embarrassed for him. He is not the human being that I thought I knew in his early career and my early career. I don't know him.

It's a sentiment you hear quite often from people in Louisville who worked with Mitch McConnell in his early days. They describe someone who had conservative beliefs but who was also willing to try to help those in need or even those who disagreed, if it was for the greater good. That Mitch has disappeared and left us with the destructive figure we have today. Now the West End of Louisville and the black community are afterthoughts to Mitch McConnell.

I call Charles Booker, a thirty-five-year-old Kentucky state legislator who represents the West End, and ask him about Mitch's impact on his home area. "Truthfully, Mitch McConnell doesn't have a record with African Americans in Louisville," he contends. "We aren't even on his agenda or his political radar. I can't say he has let us down, because to us he is a nonfactor. To him, we never existed."

That feeling of invisibility is what has led Booker to try to end the McConnell legacy. Charles is running for the Democratic nomination against the senator, and even though he and I could end up challenging each other in the primary, we remain friends. I met Booker while attempting to help organize a West End group a few years back to try to give a political voice to young African Americans in Louisville. Booker worked with me in helping form the initial group, and I have always been impressed by his love for and dedication to Louisville and his commitment to public service. Booker was born and has lived his whole life in the West End. He still calls it home today, and, unlike a lot of people running for public office, Booker is still very much a part of his community.

He says the divide between white and black Louisville is frustrating and real. "It's between the haves and the have-nots," he comments. "You can feel it when you drive across Ninth Street and go west. You can feel the resources aren't here, and the farther you go toward Sewanee Drive, the less there is."

He also is furious with McConnell and his GOP colleagues who use race to frame the issues that lead to disparate treatment between the communities. "Take opioids," Booker says. "Now people are saying that opioids are a public health issue, which they are. They are killing our state. But when it was just my community and affecting my family, it was a criminal justice issue. McConnell's a big part of that."

Booker is a product of the Louisville busing system that sent him across town, an hour each way, for schooling. The experience helped inform the political views he holds today. "Making that trip," he reflects, "that is how I knew a lot of things weren't right. On the school bus, when they would take me home through the West End, a lot of people would make jokes. I didn't invite my friends over because we didn't have air-conditioning. I decided then that it was my responsibility to fight for change and not turn my back on where I was from."

Booker takes me on a tour of the West End today, showing me where he grew up and the surrounding neighborhoods. It is a world completely removed from any other part of Louisville. The buildings are deteriorated, the houses crumbling, and long stretches of the streets vacant. Ironically, it resembles some of the impoverished areas of eastern Kentucky, where I grew up. Booker notes, "Pick a list, and we don't have it. We have only two sit-down restaurants in the entire place. Just a couple of small grocery stores. Nowhere to buy stuff for your home but a dollar store. You could take a picture of a home in the Russell neighborhood, and you would swear it's in some of those counties in the mountains."

It is that commonality between the problems of black Louisville and rural Kentucky that Booker is relying on to make an insurgent challenge for McConnell's job. He knows it's a long shot, but is determined no matter what. "Mitch is such an institution and so woven into the fabric of Kentucky that it will take something dramatically different to shock the conscience and flip it on its ear. Part of this is divine for me. On one hand, someone may try to hurt me or try to hurt my family. But I know what I am doing is morally right, and thus I know I am protected."

Witnessing Booker's passion for what he's doing is inspiring to me. He is in it for the right reasons. Like me, he loves his home and his state, and believes he can help effect change. It's part of why I have ignored the advice of many of my advisors who have said I should try to talk him out of running. They have made the political calculus that if Booker isn't in the race, the national progressive donors who are dissatisfied with Amy McGrath won't be split and will give me the money I need to run. They also worry about the visual of me, a white man, running against a woman and an African American in a Democratic primary.

That's all fine and dandy, but who am I to tell a man as committed as Charles not to run? He is in it for the right reasons and is exactly the type of person who should be in politics. "Look," he tells me, "I'm still a young guy trying to keep the lights on at his house and help his mother. I live the challenges these other politicians just talk about. Now I just have to go and try to fix them."

CHAPTER 8

Moscow Mitch

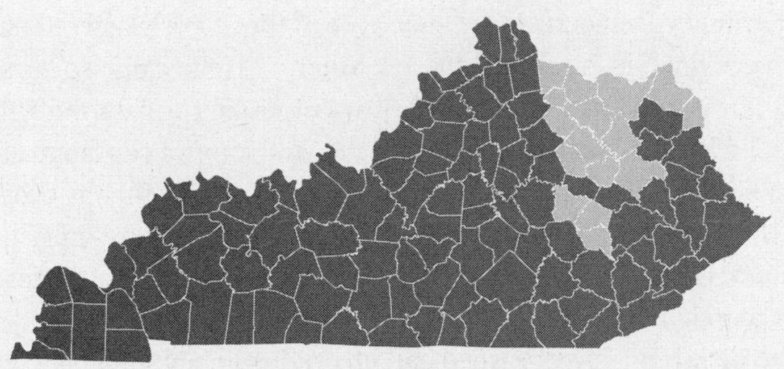

Winning as a moderate Democrat in Kentucky requires doing well in the three traditional Democratic areas: Louisville, Lexington, and eastern Kentucky. I always felt good about Lexington and, after having met with the donors last week, much better about Louisville. The mountains, though, would be the most difficult nut to crack. On one hand, our radio show is more popular in the mountains than in any other part of the state, and since I am from the region, I have some natural advantages. Nevertheless, the national Democratic Party is becoming a four-letter word here, thanks in large part to Donald Trump. His popularity in these parts is high and those who support him see him as a culture warrior fighting on their behalf. With him on the ballot along with Mitch, it will be an uphill battle to be given a chance.

The final leg of our trip through these mountains will give me some insight to see if, outside of the most progressive circles of the state, the appetite is out there to "Ditch Mitch."

Boyd County

Moscow Mitch

Mitch McConnell is not an easy dude to get riled up. He is notorious for his ability to maintain his composure, rarely showing emotion. Which is why Kentucky Democrats take such glee in the anger plastered on his face every time he is called "Moscow Mitch."* He became so enraged at the phrase that as #MoscowMitch was trending across the United States, he said, "It's an effort to smear me. You know, I can laugh about things like the Grim Reaper, but calling me Moscow Mitch is over the top." Naturally, his statement only made people say it more. In fact, the Kentucky Democratic Party even raised $500,000 in sales of Moscow Mitch merchandise in just a couple of days.

The nickname is well earned and its origins lie not in his big, furry *ushanka* hat, but in his dealings with the aluminum company Braidy Industries in Boyd County. Ashland, the county's largest city, was once the site of one of the largest industrial economies in the state. The Ashland Works location of the American Rolling Mill Company, better known as ARMCO, was a massive steel mill that employed thousands from the early 1920s through the early 1990s. Along with Ashland Oil, which maintained its corporate headquarters here until the early 2000s, it made Boyd County a viable and vibrant place to live. The city had a very distinctive smell (kind of a mix of gasoline, rotting eggs, and both natural and passed gas) that welcomed visitors across the state line from West Virginia, but it was the smell of economic prosperity to the locals provided by a company supplying good-paying jobs for generations.

Now, a little more than twenty years later, the area has changed dramatically. ARMCO has left, and an area that once was flush with money—I can remember as a child being amazed that a place in the mountains of Kentucky had a Mercedes-Benz dealership—is now

---

* "Cocaine Mitch" he is good with and even puts on T-shirts. "Moscow Mitch," though, is crossing the line. Gotcha.

trying to foster a new economy. Ashland's economy needs a jolt, and there has been hope for the last decade that some company would realize the city's potential and come in to save the day.

Enter Braidy Industries. In 2016 Braidy announced it would build a new $1.7 billion aluminum rolling mill in the area. Due to the growing demand for aluminum from automakers switching from steel to aluminum bodies, Braidy said the market was prime for it to become the American standard for aluminum manufacturing. The company would be based in Boyd County, with the signature mill in next-door Greenup County. Braidy's CEO, Craig Bouchard, said the mill would immediately generate a thousand construction jobs and another six hundred full-time workers, with an average salary of $70,000 a year—twice the average pay of the region.

Braidy's vision, said Bouchard, was to "rebuild northeast Kentucky and, in fact, all of Appalachia." It was an exciting pronouncement that boosted the morale of Boyd County instantaneously. Kentucky governor Matt Bevin even decided to invest $15 million of state taxpayer money into Braidy, a highly unusual practice that he said would become an investment boon for the state when the mill took off. For years, people had hoped another industry would come in and re-create Ashland's glory days of old. It looked like those prayers had finally been answered.

Unfortunately, it hasn't been that easy. Braidy found it difficult to attract the kind of financing needed for such a massive operation, and production delays ensued.

The Russians saw an opportunity. Knowing the importance of the enterprise to the Senate majority leader's home state, Rusal, a mammoth aluminum producer controlled by one of President Vladimir Putin's closest allies, oligarch Oleg Deripaska, inquired about investing in Braidy. The Russian company wasn't an obvious choice to finance an American company. For one thing, Deripaska was one of the oligarchs the US Treasury slapped with economic sanctions in 2018 because of his role in supporting Russia's worldwide "malign activity." The move to sanction Deripaska and other oligarchs was in response to, among other things, Russia's interference in the 2016 presidential election in order to benefit the Trump campaign. In addition, according to a statement from the US Treasury Department, Deripaska "has been accused of threatening the lives of business rivals, illegally wiretapping a government official, and taking part in extortion and racketeering." A US embassy cable published online by Wikileaks described Deripaska as "among the 2–3 oligarchs Putin turns to on a regular basis." Not exactly an ideal business partner.

The nesting dolls were beginning to reveal themselves. Braidy was desperate, so in January 2019 two corporations in need came together for mutual benefit. Bouchard traveled to Europe for what he called a "meet and greet" with Rusal executives—a meeting currently under investigation as having possibly violated the US sanctions. They told Bouchard that if "we get the sanctions" on Rusal lifted, the company would be interested in a potential investment. There had been an aggressive lobbying campaign to lift the sanctions, and the previous month a deal had been reached in which Deripaska agreed to reduce his ownership stake in Rusal from 70 to 45 percent, in exchange for the sanctions being withdrawn. This does not appear to have been a significant sacrifice for Deripaska, as his shares in the company were distributed primarily to his allies and close associates. However, the deal was no guarantee; the announcement had created a bipartisan push in the Senate to block the lifting of the sanctions. McConnell, however, worked hard to defeat the attempted strike down of the sanctions deal. Eleven Senate Republicans broke rank to vote with the Democrats. But once Mitch McConnell strong-armed several GOP colleagues who were on the fence, the vote fell three short of the number needed to override what would have been a certain presidential veto, and the measure failed to advance to passage. Less than three months later, Brouchard has his Russian money and two of McConnell's former staffers quickly went to work lobbying to defend Braidy and the Russian investment.

Shortly thereafter, Rusal invested $200 million in Braidy Industries in exchange for a 40 percent stake in the company. Deripaska was able to finally help Russia achieve a long-coveted goal: Rusal had broken into the American economic market in a key industry, and had done so in the Senate majority leader's home state, no less. It was a massive win for the oligarch—and for Vladimir Putin, who now had the president of the United States and the leader of the US Senate going to bat for him publicly. All it took was a $200 million lifeline tossed to a Kentucky company. The much-needed capital saved the aluminum rolling mill project, which had been teetering on the brink of going under.

Mitch had dipped his toe in Russian-associated dollars before. Len Blavatnik, an oligarch with ties to the Kremlin who holds major stakes in two American companies, donated more than $3.5 million to Mitch McConnell's SuperPAC during the period between 2015 and 2017.* For Mitch, undoing the sanctions on Rusal—a company in which Blavatnik also has an investment—likely means more donations will flow his way. Mitch McConnell has repeatedly earned his title Moscow Mitch.

It's hard to remember now, but not so long ago Mitch McConnell was one of the fiercest anti-Russian hawks in the Senate. He spoke repeatedly about the dangers of Russian influence, not only during the days of the Soviet Union but also throughout the Obama presidency. At one point, he chided the Democratic leader for attempting to "reset relations" with Russia and allowing them to "expand their influence" around the world. He went as far as to scold Democrats that "the Russians are not our friends." Now that Mitch McConnell is gone, replaced by a senator who welcomes our foe with open arms (and pockets)—not just to the world stage but also to his home state.

Former senator Alan Simpson, a Republican from Wyoming, said that most senators were uncomfortable fund-raising because it felt unethical. Simpson said McConnell was different. The Kentucky senator's eyes would "shine like diamonds" when it came time to ask for donations. Now those eyes are shining like Russian rubles.

Greenup County

"I Really Believe That If We Give Them Time, They Can Come Through"

We turn up the road toward Greenup County, site of the Braidy campus, where, in 2018, ground was broken amid much fanfare. Politicians from

* We can all agree that this is a big, steaming pile of borscht.

all levels of the government attended, and a public relations campaign pushed the magnitude of Braidy's entry into the local economy. The message was that this wasn't just a new business but a transformational moment for an area that desperately needed it. Braidy said the plant would begin construction in 2018 and be completed by mid-2020.

It is now late 2019, and as we drive by the site of the announcement, it sits empty, with no evidence of progress. Even after all the special treatment that Braidy Industries received, from the state's $15 million investment, to the $200 million pledged by fairy godfather Rusal, the facility is still on hold.

Braidy executives now say the new plan is for the plant to be up and running sometime in 2021—but that's assuming, of course, they are able to procure the rest of their funding. In addition to the questionable outside investments, the company has bought time by engaging in accounting tricks such as loaning its CEO money to buy more stock in the company—a tactic that conveys Bouchard's confidence in the investment, but not that of others. Braidy still maintains a unified front publicly and insists that construction is just around the corner. But at this point, locals are becoming skeptical, and Greenup County, where the miracle investment was supposed to transform the area, is getting worried. No one seems to be drinking the vodka.

One of our first impressions upon entering the county is that support and hope do still exist. A local gas station sign reads "Welcome Braidy" in big block letters and the Braidy name remains on buildings all over town. But when we try to talk to local leaders about Braidy and get their views on the status of the investment, we have little luck in finding people willing to speak. No one wants to talk on the record anywhere, either positively or negatively. We call multiple people, but when I mention Braidy, they say they aren't interested in speaking and quickly hang up. It's as if the whole area is worried about getting on the wrong side of the potential new company in charge.

Online, locals seem bolder. Some community members have turned to outright sarcasm, mocking Braidy Industries on social media. The Facebook page for a nonprofit grassroots community organization called Build Ashland has become a sometimes-scorched-earth commentary on the perceived hoodwinking. "How many years are we going on now?" complains one user. Other posters feel cheated by the prospect of good-paying jobs, with one commenting, "I've said from the beginning that this was a scam and still hold to it." The page administrator eventually disabled comments on one post because they were "becoming redundant and the absolute opposite of constructive dialogue."*

What was once a source of great hope has begun to leave scars, and they are getting worse every day. The area truly needs this to work. Braidy has received more than eleven thousand job applications for a plant still two years away from completion, maybe more. The company partnered up early with the local community college to establish a two-year-degree program to train workers specifically to work at Braidy, and nearly eighty students enrolled, seeing it as a worthwhile investment in an exciting new career. With the plant opening delayed until 2021, many of them have been left in the lurch, with no firm date for when, or even if, their educational investment might pay off.

We spoke with Cullen Callihan, a young journeyman heating, ventilating, and air-conditioning installer who's still holding out optimism for the plant. "I really believe that if we give them time, they can come through," he believes. "This is almost a two-billion-dollar project; it just doesn't happen quickly. They need some time because they need a lot of investors."

Still, Cullen knows not everybody feels like he does. He tells me his job keeps him busy with new construction, both residential and industrial, so things aren't all bad. But, he acknowledges, people are getting worried for their futures. "People are not really willing to sit and wait it out, so they might be going up to another place, like Ohio, to find work. We're used to downturns, so the community will be okay. When Braidy was announced, it gave us a lot of hope, but if it gets delayed again . . ." He pauses a moment. "People might really start to get anxious and worried."

Ultimately, if Braidy is ever able to open the aluminum mill and produce all the good-paying jobs it has promised the area, the fact that the money came from the Russians won't matter to the people here. It is a sign of the economic desperation in these parts that the prospect of working for a company with Russian ownership—something that

* Facebook isn't the best place to find constructive dialogue. It's a place to find out which of your friends are wrapped up in pyramid schemes.

once would have been inconceivable—is embraced now. On this point, I completely understand. After all, $70,000-a-year jobs don't grow on trees in eastern Kentucky, and whether it comes from a Russian billionaire or a faceless American corporation, money is money. Personally, I root for the new venture's success. The economic climate of this area needs flagship businesses such as Braidy to help lift it out of its malaise.

But it is amazing how quickly Moscow Mitch* and other GOP politicians have gone from being the flag-waving Apollo Creed to the dead-eyed Ivan Drago. Ironically, Braidy CEO Craig Bouchard once wrote a book titled *America for Sale: How the Foreign Pack Circled and Devoured Esmark,* in which he said, "[If] Putin harbors a nasty wish to throw a wrench into the works of the US economy, then he now has acquired the means to do so." On the topic of critical industries such as industrial steel, Bouchard made clear that we must be careful when we trust a country overseen by a dictator such as Vladimir Putin: "The bottom line is that we believe it is risky business to trust Russian oligarchs."

Well, at least he used to believe it was risky business. When it's your company, maybe Putin's oligarchs make more sense. Will the deal with the Russian dictator's pal be worth it for Boyd and Greenup counties? Only time will tell. For now, the 40 percent Russian lot still sits empty.

Lewis County

"I Don't Even Care About Your Background, as Long as You Will Work"

As you drive along the flat, open farmland of Lewis County, it would be easy to drift off into a daze (I almost did), but then, at the corner of Lions Club Road and Highway 9, a sign of life arises from the fields to jolt you to life. You can't miss the tall, shiny aluminum silo of Rip's Farm

---

* I am not going to tell you to go ahead and buy a Moscow Mitch T-shirt. However, the only thing that enrages him more is this book, and you have already bought that, so go ahead and do it.

Center in tiny Tollesboro, the go-to spot for feed, seed, fertilizer, and chemicals for the many farmers in the area. It also doubles as proof of humanity here in Lewis County.

We're scheduled to meet one of the store's founders, Jim Meadows, but his wife, Jennifer, tells us that since it's three o'clock, he's already left to finish his farming for the day. I don't blame him. We are late, and the man has a schedule, so I would have left too. She says if we want to talk to Jim, we have to go a mile down the highway and meet him in the fields. She calls ahead and gives us the cryptic markers we'll need to find him: a brick entryway, an old picnic shelter, and a barn on which someone has painted a girl wearing a blue bonnet. They aren't great descriptors, but on this road filled with farm after farm of soybeans, the blue bonnet barn is the best we will get.*

After pulling into Jim's field, we see him barreling toward us in a massive red combine, the farm equivalent of a Sherman tank. The harvester blades calm to a spinning stop as he climbs down out of the driver's seat.

Meadows is the portrait of a seasoned farmer: tanned skin from near-constant sun exposure; a shock of white hair, every strand bending gently with the changing direction of the wind; and wearing a blue-and-white plaid flannel shirt. Jim has farmed his land in Lewis County for years, but these days it's become increasingly tough to find even the most basic number of employees to keep his farm running. The reason is all too common across the Bluegrass State: drug use and the opioid crisis. In fact, on the day we meet Jim, he's just returned from a trip to Cincinnati, two hours north, to pick up one of his farm vehicles from an impound lot; some drug users stole it just to get a few more miles down the highway before abandoning it, leaving behind drug paraphernalia on the seats and floorboards.

---

* These types of directions are common in rural Kentucky. Here are some we received in a different county: "Just go take the highway about four or five miles until you see this big tree hanging over mailboxes next to an old billboard on the left. There will be a green fence on your right. Follow to the end of that fence, and you'll see an old gas station that's closed now. Hostetler Road is past that gas station, on the right." It's like Kentucky sudoku.

"Our biggest struggle is not only keeping employees," Jim tells me, "it's finding employees who want to have a job in the first place."

The problem has gotten so bad that Jim doesn't even worry about high standards in hiring. "Five or six years ago, you'd get a new employee and go get a drug test, but I don't even do drug tests anymore. I'm to the point that I don't even care about your background as long as you'll work." Jim's standards are lower than Conway Twitty's bass range.

Jim speculates that the reason for his difficulties in finding workers corresponds with low-income government housing that entered the county a few years back. He thinks now it's much easier for some residents to go "on the check" rather than finding meaningful work. He argues that in Lewis County there isn't much incentive for some to find a good job because doing so means suddenly making enough money to not qualify for low-income housing and benefits. Thus, for many, it is quite literally more profitable *not* to work than to have a decent job.

Jim's position may sound harsh, but the problem is not easily dealt with by policy makers. Many Republicans want to dramatically cut all public assistance in order to give recipients incentive to go to work, but doing so would harm the most vulnerable among us—children, the elderly, the mentally ill, veterans, to give four examples—by taking away benefits that sustain their lives. The Trump administration's recent proposed tightening of qualifications for food stamps will have a dramatic impact on this area, and a secondary, often unconsidered, impact on local business. But, then, Democrats offer few solutions for curbing abuse of these programs and the economic reality that some create reverse incentives for citizens to remain out of the workforce completely. Since it seems neither side truly wants to confront its own respective negative reality, the debate continues, with little meaningful progress made.

Although Jim is a lifelong Democrat (he votes the way his father did, he says), he isn't sure he can support someone running against Mitch McConnell. If Mitch loses, Jim fears, a freshman senator would take office "at the bottom rung of the ladder," and thus be woefully unable to garner the support Kentucky needs from the federal government.

"I don't know, now, whether he is doing a job well done," Jim says, "but I don't know what that bottom-rung senator is going to get."

When I ask him to name some of the things McConnell has done for Lewis County, he pauses and chuckles. He can't come up with one. It's a common theme, concern for what happens if we lose Mitch, but no evidence of what Kentucky has gained sending him back to Washington again and again. McConnell has done an amazing job at convincing Kentuckians they need him, even if they aren't sure why. I mention to Jim that maybe a new Democratic senator would be seen as having accomplished something special by knocking off McConnell deep in Trump country, and thus the Democratic Party would do whatever it could to help him or her succeed, potentially benefiting the area. Jim smiles and shrugs, but it's clear he's not buying what I am selling.

When it comes to helping Kentucky, Emperor McConnell has no clothes. But as of yet, Kentuckians seem hesitant to call him to task and are still willing to accept his naked body.*

Mason County

Mitch Doesn't Love the Kids

Maysville is a quintessential "river town"; the Ohio River has long been a focal point in the county. Downtown's cobblestone streets are lined with restaurants and pub-style bars, and over at the Gateway Museum Center on Sutton Street you'll find one of the world's finest miniatures collections, its tiny staged rooms filled with elaborately hand-constructed beds, decked-out tables, and framed paintings. It's also where the greatest people in Kentucky live, at least according to my coauthor, Chris Tomlin, who grew up there. He may be biased.

Like many towns in this area, Maysville's heyday was dominated by tobacco, as it hosted the second-largest burley tobacco market in the world, with eighteen warehouses and millions in sales. It's the kind of town where, at one time, students wouldn't show up for school because

* I warned Matt about putting the image of a naked Mitch McConnell in your head, but it's there now, so we might as well all try and press on together.

they were at home on the farm, helping their fathers hang tobacco, and it wasn't counted as an absence.

Chris didn't hang a lot of tobacco, but he loves his hometown, so I will let him take it from here:

The year was 1992. I was a freshman in high school. The youth group I belonged to at the First Christian Church of Maysville was on a trip to Washington, DC. Many of us had never been there before, and the group, which ranged in age from sixth graders to high school seniors, had arrived by bus and was staying in a youth hostel near the National Mall. We hit all the DC hot spots,* of course: the Lincoln Memorial, the Jefferson Memorial, and some of the Smithsonian. Our chaperones had arranged for us to meet with our two sitting senators, Wendell Ford and Mitch McConnell. In retrospect, it was pretty fantastic for a visiting church group; for a bunch of kids, it didn't have the gravity it probably should have, but we knew it was Capitol Hill, the place where laws were made. Maybe we would even see the president! (We did not see the president.)

Our first stop was Wendell Ford's office. The Democratic senator couldn't have been kinder or more thoughtful. At that point in my life, I hadn't had that much exposure to politicians, but we all liked him a lot. He invited all twenty of us into his office and began to describe his day-to-day life in Washington: how he attended meetings, spoke with people back home in Kentucky, and helped to make decisions that would improve our lives. To a fifteen-year-old, he seemed like the president in a movie: wise, caring, willing to listen. We all asked Senator Ford questions, and he took the time to answer each one. He showed us the many photos mounted on his walls and told us about the people in them, and where they were taken. We were quizzed about Maysville and why we liked it. We stayed for nearly an hour and a half, and to this day, Wendell Ford remains my own personal gold standard of what a politician should be, especially with a bunch of dumb kids.

Then we headed down the hall to meet Mitch McConnell in the Capitol Rotunda. We waited as the meeting time passed, and our group

---

* And by "hit all the DC hot spots," I mean got through them quickly because dinner was at TGI Fridays, and we don't have those in Maysville.

grew restless. After twenty fidgety minutes passed, here came McConnell, flanked by aides, approaching us quickly. He looked at us as if he had never spoken to anyone under fifty, and awkwardly asked us if we were having a good time on our trip. He didn't take questions, and the large, circular room with its high canopy was so loud with tourists that I am not even sure what he actually said. He finished the whole encounter in just a couple of minutes, and ended it by saying that he wished he could talk to us more, but he didn't have much time, and hoped that we enjoyed the rest of our trip while dashing away.

It ended as quickly as it began. Our illustrious meeting with Senator Mitch McConnell was a nervous, nebbishy interaction with a person who didn't seem to have the time to be bothered. It was so awkward, I cringe to this day thinking about it. One of our chaperones turned to me, shrugged, and said with a laugh, "Well, I guess that's it."

Afterward, the group was slightly bummed as we moved through the rotunda and into a hallway, where we were approached by another senator, a late-fortyish man in a gray suit who took note of our caravan and stopped us.

"Are you guys having a look around? Everyone having a good time?" he asked.

The more vocal kids in our group responded to him, and so he asked what we'd seen since we'd been in Washington. He genuinely wanted to know where we were from and rubbed his chin as he tried to recall the cities in Kentucky he'd visited. He told us about his committee meeting and what to make sure we saw while we were in the building. He was casual, charismatic, and chatty, shaking hands with all of us, having no idea he was picking up the slack for a closed-off McConnell, who couldn't be bothered for the time. He was just being kind to some random people he saw walking down the hall, and we all agreed he was our favorite senator of all time, even though most of us had no idea who he was before he spoke to us.

That man was Delaware senator Joe Biden. Great dude.

Robertson County

Slow Down, Chris

It's still Chris. Since I have the computer and it's my neighboring county, I thought I would nail down for you all things Robertson County, but here's the deal: it's the least-populated county in the state, with about two thousand people, and it's the second smallest in land mass overall. To top it off, only about 750 of its residents even vote, so there's no big issue to spotlight and no real political trends. If you're hungry, I'd direct you to the Pizza-N-More in Mt. Olivet, where you can get a pretty good pizza (N-More, if you are so inclined), or camp at Blue Lick State Park, where one of the last battles of the Revolutionary War occurred in 1782. It was, in fact, right here in front of Blue Lick where I fought one of my own battles in 1995—one that still irks me to this very day.

It was foggy, and there was no one on the road. It's a flat, straight stretch, and I was in my shiny, hot, blue Ford Taurus station wagon. Close your eyes, and you can picture the beauty.

The citing officer walked up to the driver's-side window and knocked on it with one knuckle.

"You in a hurry? Goin' pretty fast there. Maybe you should slow it down a little bit."

Police scare me, and so I just mumbled something about loving America and our troops to try to curry favor. He took my license back to the cruiser, and I hoped for the best. I imagined he was going to punch the numbers into his driver's license computer and see that I was a good Kentuckian, a sound driver, *and* I even volunteer at a local summer camp. That would all be in his police computer. Then he would return and merely issue a polite warning to this heavenly nineteen-year-old kid in a station wagon* on his way home from spending spring break *with his parents*. I'd thank him and tell him I was really sorry, he'd see I was earnest, we'd have a moment where he'd be like, "I'm

---

* Wasn't driving a Ford Taurus station wagon in college humiliation enough?

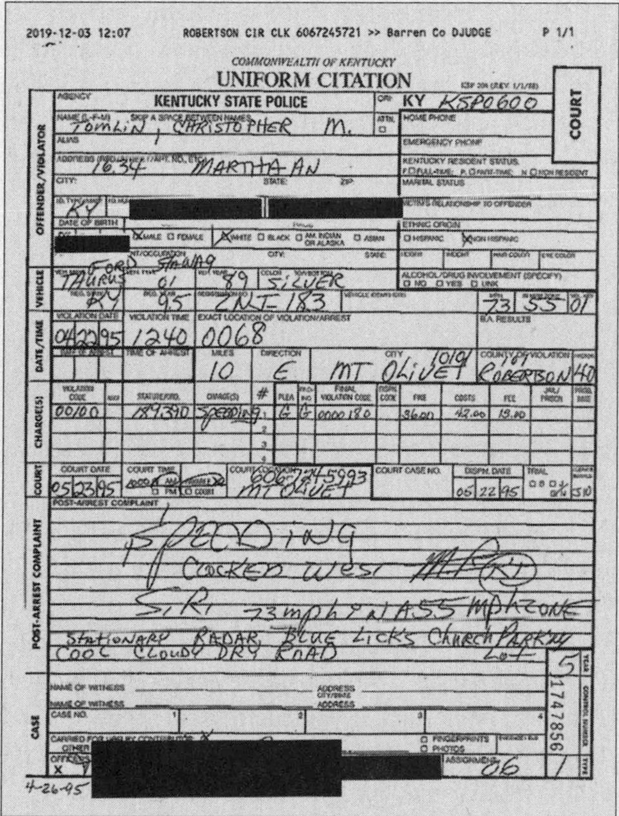

2019-12-03 12:07 ROBERTSON CIR CLK 6067245721 >> Barren Co DJUDGE P 1/1

COMMONWEALTH OF KENTUCKY

UNIFORM CITATION

COURT

OFFENDER/VIOLATOR

AGENCY: KENTUCKY STATE POLICE
ORI: KY KSP0600
NAME (L-F-M): TOMLIN, CHRISTOPHER M.
HOME PHONE
ALIAS
EMERGENCY PHONE
ADDRESS: 1634 MARTHA AN
KENTUCKY RESIDENT STATUS: F. FULL-TIME P. PART-TIME N. NON RESIDENT
CITY: STATE: ZIP:
MARITAL STATUS
KY
RELATIONSHIP TO OFFENDER
DATE OF BIRTH
SEX: X MALE ☐ FEMALE
RACE: X WHITE ☐ BLACK ☐ AM. INDIAN OR ALASKA ☐ ASIAN
ETHNIC ORIGIN: ☐ HISPANIC X NON HISPANIC
EMPLOYMENT/OCCUPATION
CITY
STATE
HEIGHT WEIGHT HAIR COLOR EYE COLOR

VEHICLE

FORD STAWAG
TAURUS 01 89 SILVER
ALCOHOL/DRUG INVOLVEMENT (SPECIFY): ☐ NO ☐ YES ☐ UNK
KY 95 ZNJ-183
73 55 01

DATE/TIME

VIOLATION DATE: 04 22 95
VIOLATION TIME: 1240
EXACT LOCATION OF VIOLATION/ARREST: 0068
B.A. RESULTS
DATE OF ARREST
TIME OF ARREST
MILES: 10
DIRECTION: E
CITY: MT OLIVET 1019
COUNTY OF VIOLATION: ROBERTSON 40

CHARGE(S)

VIOLATION CODE		STATUTE/ORD.	CHARGE(S)	#	PLEA		FINAL VIOLATION CODE	DISPN. CODE	FINE	COSTS	FEE	JAIL/PRISON	PROB. DATE
00100		189390	Speeding	1	G	G	0000180		36.00	42.00	13.00		
				2									
				3									

COURT

COURT DATE: 05 23 95
COURT TIME
COURT LOCATION: 606-724-5993 MT OLIVET
COURT CASE NO.
DISPN. DATE: 05 22 95
TRIAL

POST-ARREST COMPLAINT

SPEEDING
CLOCKED WEST
S.R. 73mph IN A 55 mph ZONE
STATIONARY RADAR, BLUE LICKS CHURCH PARKING LOT
COOL CLOUDY DRY ROAD

5
1747856 1

CASE

NAME OF WITNESS
ADDRESS
NAME OF WITNESS
ADDRESS
CASE NO.
CARRIED FOR JURY CONTRIBUTION
OTHER
☐ FINGERPRINTS
☐ PHOTOS
OFFICER X
ASSIGNED 06
4-26-95

serious," and I'd be all, "Yes, sir, I know, it won't happen again." He'd teach an otherwise good teenager a lesson, and I would drive away, thankful I'd dodged a bullet.

Instead, he came back with an expensive ticket and points on my license that for all I know are still there or on my permanent record.*

Mitch McConnell had been a sitting US senator for more than ten

* This is Matt. My grandmother used to always scare me when I was young by referring repeatedly to my "permanent record," telling me that if I did something bad, it would stay with me forever. As I got older, I assumed she was lying, and no such thing exists. On this journey, I have now learned, Mitch McConnell and the Russians have all of our permanent records.

years at this point. He could have tried to help me with this speeding ticket, and he didn't. Sure, maybe he didn't know. And yeah, maybe it isn't appropriate for a senator to intervene in local traffic court. But that's no excuse. So I had to sit, seething, in a Robertson County traffic school. Where were you, Mitch McConnell? Where were you when a blue-blooded Kentuckian needed you most?

Fleming County

"Mitch McConnell Doesn't Care About Black Kentucky"

The next morning, we start our day at the Dairy Queen in Flemingsburg. The DQ is a must-visit spot in many towns in eastern Kentucky because of the magical combination of soft-serve Blizzards and old men discussing current events. The first person I see is my mom's best friend, Georgianna Sparks, who lives here and greets me with a hug, saying, "The town is so excited you came." I am here to do a remote broadcast of my radio show, but to be honest, more than half the crowd looks to be here not for me, but for the delicious breakfast.*

This particular Dairy Queen franchise, owned and operated by John Sims, Fleming County's Democratic state representative, is a central part of the community. While it offers the traditional DQ fare, it also serves up off-menu items such as fried chicken and batter-dipped fish that the Sims family has prepared and sold for decades. The room is full of the colors blue and red: blue for the Kentucky Wildcats,† and red found on three "Make America Great Again" caps—an accurate representation of Kentucky's current obsessions.

My Tracker has shown up again, this time wearing a sad expression all over his face. He tells me he's about had it with the job. The

---

* Only in Kentucky is your breakfast place the same as your ice cream place.

† In Kentucky blue is for the Cats, not the Democrats.

McConnell folks continue sending him all over the state to trail me, and he doesn't really understand what the purpose of all this is. He asks for my advice and says he is worried if he quits, it will ruin a good opportunity. I chuckle to myself at the absurdity of the moment. The guy hired to bring me down is now seeking my counsel on how to make his job suck less. It's kind of hilarious.

But then I look at him again and try to put myself in his shoes. Here's a twenty-two-year-old kid from out of state who thought an opportunity to work on behalf of the US Senate majority leader would be exciting and a good first step for his career in politics. I am sure he hoped he would be part of an exciting campaign and be on the inside with one of the most powerful people in Washington. Instead he is here, at a DQ in Flemingsburg, after driving across Kentucky by himself, filming me with a room full of our supporters glaring at him like he is the creepiest dude in America. I do feel bad for him. A man can't properly enjoy his biscuits and gravy when he is being scowled at like that. I have joked about his presence on my radio show, but I am going to stop because he says it makes him feel awkward. For some reason I care more about his well-being than McConnell does. I think he is lonely, and I kind of want to become his friend just to try cheering him up. I am sure I am being a softie and should be more skeptical of his presence, but I genuinely feel bad for the guy.* He asks if I can do a favor for him next week and I say yes without even asking what it is. I am way too trusting.

We leave and head out to Taste Buds,† a small diner outside the city, to meet Randy Taylor, a sixty-three-year-old local minister and high school basketball referee. He's an encyclopedia of local knowledge, rattling off the names of former high school basketball players and greeting nearly everyone who walks past our table while telling us their family history. He's lived here his entire life, so he knows his way around, and as we eat lunch, it is hard to get more than two or three

---

* I have come around on him too. It's a shitty job, made even more so because you are doing it for Mitch Freakin' McConnell.

† The logo for Taste Buds is literally a giant picture of a tongue sectioned off to illustrate where each taste sensation is savored on it. It's a bold move for a logo and kind of gross, to be honest.

words out before we are interrupted by someone wanting to greet him. He is clearly the kind of man who commands respect from all ages.

Randy is also African American, a rarity in much of these parts because, like most counties in Kentucky, Fleming County is predominantly white; the black population in the area is only 3 percent. According to Randy, race relations in Fleming County have improved greatly over the years, but it wasn't always that way. He gestures around the room.

"It used to be that this place—right here—is a place we couldn't come," he says of the restaurant, which at the time was known as the Whip and Sip. "And it was like that until the late seventies. I mean, there would be a fight if blacks showed up here during that time. So we stayed away."

Randy explains that the division when he was younger could be traced to a generation of white people who had grown up apart from and with little knowledge of the lifestyles of African Americans. The bigotry diminished over the years, he believes, because the subsequent generation of white and African American kids grew up integrated, growing up together attending the same schools, and playing sports with one another. Their commonalities overcame any prejudice.

"I had my class reunion three months ago, and we're just a big family," he says, smiling. "We just are who we are. We're just people."

But Randy worries that things have regressed a bit in the last few years. He points to the election of Donald Trump as the moment that seemed to give some of his neighbors license to show an ugly side of themselves that they previously may have kept hidden. "It had a little effect," he says. "Some people have gotten a little bold with the rebel flag, you know, and the N-word. We hadn't seen that in a while." Randy said moments like this led him to visit a local school to discuss slurs being used by white kids against their black classmates. He says the students welcomed him, but in order for change to occur, stereotypes have to be overcome, and respect has to be given.

"So many of our young black kids are already perceived as what they are before someone sees who they are," Randy observes. "How they dress, the music they listen to, you know? Sometimes I think black kids are judged on their culture rather than their person."

I switch the topic to Mitch McConnell, and Randy becomes more animated. I ask him if he believes McConnell cares about African Americans in the state. He rolls his eyes and says, "Are you serious right now? Mitch McConnell doesn't care about black Kentucky; Mitch McConnell only cares about how full his pockets get. He'll use the black communities, but you never see him out in one."

The minister's comments are even more direct when it comes to Mitch's relationship with Trump. "When Trump says something racist, McConnell defends him," Randy says. "Mitch says, 'Oh, he didn't *mean* to say that,' or 'Oh, he isn't racist.' Sure."

Randy believes the senator has no interest in the black community and never will. He shows disrespect to African Americans through his disinterest toward them, something Randy says leaves African Americans with no interest in supporting him. "If you don't like me, that's fine, but I'll still sit here and talk to you because that's who I am, it's how I was raised. I'm a person, and you're a person. If I respect you, you should respect me. He doesn't. It's that simple."

Nicholas County

The Savior of Big Tobacco

Nicholas County is dotted by lot after lot of rolling farms, each apparently with a long history of ownership by the same family tracing back generations. It is the kind of place where a farmer will post a road sign out front bearing the family name in big block letters, so you can differentiate it from the other fifty farms on the road that look exactly the same.* The county seat is Carlisle, which is really only a few blocks clumped together and called a town, but it has a homey, cozy feel to it on this fall afternoon. The colors on the buildings vary based on the era they were last tended to and, by the looks of many of them, for some of

* Another convention along these farm roads is to place a full Bible verse about every forty feet. Often these have multiple lines and can be difficult to read quickly. This doesn't feel safe to me.

these buildings it's been quite a while. I stop by the cute local Carlisle Market where I surprisingly see a pint of vegan ice cream. Look how modern Nicholas County is! I buy a pint to be kind to the sweet owners but then hand it to a kid on the street. It is vegan ice cream, after all.

We pop into the local chamber of commerce, where we're greeted by Jerry Johnson. He immediately looks familiar to me, probably because his perky face is on a poster staring directly at me announcing Jerry as this year's Carlisle–Nicholas County Citizen of the Year! I am a little starstruck, but Jerry graciously and humbly waves it off, saying it was just "my turn" to win. The Nicholas County Chamber of Commerce doubles as a historical museum for the county, featuring most prominently its most famous native, author Barbara Kingsolver. Before she gave the world *The Poisonwood Bible*, her eighth book, in 1998, Kingsolver was raised here by her father, a prominent county doctor. As Jerry tells us her life's biography, he is beaming with pride. The way he tells it, Nicholas County is the center of the universe, and Barbara is its brightest star.

We ask about the current economy and Jerry's mood changes. This area is struggling, as the declining US market for tobacco has had a disproportionately large impact here. The northeast of Kentucky—Nicholas, Fleming, Mason, Lewis, and Robertson Counties—were once high-producing tobacco counties, bustling and prosperous for farmers who'd grow their own tobacco, take it to market, and receive top dollar for their product. It's not like that anymore.

"Carlisle had one of the largest tobacco warehouses in the state at one time," Jerry tells us. "People would bring loads into town to sell it here. Of course, now tobacco is decreasing. Several farmers here are trying to branch out into tomatoes, or hemp, but . . . I think the tobacco is getting to be difficult."

During most of the twentieth century, being a tobacco small farmer in Kentucky was a very profitable occupation. Tobacco companies had federal quotas requiring a percentage of their purchases to come from individual small farmers, and the price of the lucrative product helped thousands of Kentuckians maintain a local family farm. Around twenty years ago, however, things changed, and the area hasn't recovered.

There is no more important figure in understanding that change than Mitch McConnell. More than any other legislator, Kentucky's senior senator has shaped the American tobacco industry. Mitch's history with tobacco is long, tortured, and, not surprisingly, littered with choices favoring the Big Tobacco companies over the small tobacco farmers. Throughout the first twenty years of his Senate career, McConnell's allegiance to Big Tobacco might have been his most consistent position. In exchange for around $650,000 in campaign donations, not to mention the millions of dollars given by tobacco companies to the Republican Party and the University of Louisville's McConnell Center.* McConnell gave undying loyalty to whatever position Big Tobacco held. Andy Schindler, a Big Tobacco lobbyist, once called Mitch McConnell a "special friend" to tobacco, and his actions confirmed this repeatedly.

In 1998, after scientific studies and congressional hearings proved once and for all that Big Tobacco had lied to the public for decades about nicotine addiction and the adverse health effects of smoking, John McCain and other senators introduced legislation to try to reduce teen smoking and hold tobacco companies accountable for the harm their products caused. As Big Tobacco's most powerful ally, McConnell went to work tirelessly lobbying his colleagues to defeat many of the bills. Memos obtained by the *Lexington Herald-Leader* newspaper revealed in 2006 that he not only delivered, word for word, speeches that had been written for him by tobacco companies (guess which side *they* took?) but also pressured Republican colleagues to vote against the legislation. They'd be rewarded, he promised, with money for their upcoming campaigns. During this time, McConnell asked Big Tobacco for $200,000 in soft money contributions to the Republican Party—a request so large that, according to the *Herald-Leader*, tobacco company employees emailed one another expressing their suspicions that Mitch was shaking them down.

---

* Donations to the McConnell Center at the University of Louisville represent an unknown source of contributions from groups all over the world. Because it isn't required to disclose publicly the identity of donors or the amounts given, who knows how many potential conflicts of interest have never been investigated?

Big Tobacco still gave and was more than amply compensated for its investment. McConnell parroted the tobacco companies' arguments denying the dangers of secondhand smoke, in the face of substantial scientific evidence to the contrary. And when ill and dying smokers and ex-smokers began suing tobacco companies for having systematically covered up the health hazards posed by their products, Senator Mitch came to their rescue. McConnell collaborated with Big Tobacco's attorneys to help draft the bill he filed to shield the manufacturers from litigation and prevent sick ex-smokers from being compensated. Like a trusty old pack of cigarettes, Mitch was in Big Tobacco's back pocket, and remained there until the bitter end.

In the years since, the tobacco economy for small farmers in America has collapsed, and once-thriving tobacco markets in places such as Nicholas County have fallen by the wayside. Mitch McConnell has done nothing to try to help these areas usher in new economic development, and locals say they can't remember when he was last here for anything but a private fund-raiser.

While it looks as if Nicholas County and its economy have seen better days, Jerry Johnson remains optimistic. He thinks Nicholas County's best days are still to be written, and despite the difficulties, he wants to help usher in whatever is around the corner. "The way I see it, wherever you're planted, you need to bloom," he says, beaming. No wonder he's Citizen of the Year.

Bracken County

Leaving Small Farmers Behind

We head north across broad fields of farmland to Bracken County, the former home of a high-school-aged George Clooney. Yes, that's right: the two-time Oscar-winning actor-producer-director, and one of the most famous Hollywood celebrities in the world, once trod this very ground, from Brooksville to Augusta, in his youth. Who better to reflect on the county than its onetime Augusta High School basketball star? We reached out to Clooney, a well-known progressive, ready to hear his insights on Bracken County and Mitch McConnell, the plague of his home state.

Unfortunately, George Clooney passed.

But, hey, that's okay! Clooney is a very busy man. I am sure there is another *Ocean's* movie or perhaps an *Up in the Air* sequel (criminally underrated) on the horizon. I am not offended.* I get it. But when you can't get Hollywood superstar George Clooney, you get the next best thing: LuAnn Asbury and her husband, Bill Carroll, superstars in their own right.† Bill has worked his three-hundred-acre family farm since the 1970s, while LuAnn is a former school principal who worked just down the AA Highway in nearby Mason County. He's the portrait of the older rural farmer: slow-spoken, wise, and graying; she still has the bright countenance and thoughtfulness that those who love working with schoolchildren keep with them forever.

Bill grew tobacco until 2004, when the Fair and Equitable Tobacco Reform Act (which was neither fair nor equitable but is known in Kentucky as simply "the tobacco buyout") was passed, and, as he promised when he accepted that agreement, he hasn't raised any since. He believes that with the tobacco decline, Bracken County has lost a big piece of its agricultural history.

"Tobacco educated our kids and paid for our farms; it was the only way of life around here for a long time," Bill tells me. "And since the tobacco buyout has taken place, these farmers around here that still raise tobacco do not receive the price they did previously."

LuAnn adds, "So many of the people around here have had to sell their farms and move elsewhere. But practically every farm in this county, somebody raised tobacco on it, and these weren't people who were just raising an acre; they were raising a hundred acres."‡

---

* I am "not offended" either. Just hurt.

† Between the three of them, they have won two Oscars.

‡ The numbers are stark. In 2005, there were 996 tobacco farms in Bracken County. Now there are 66.

The 2004 tobacco buyout is one of the most controversial pieces of federal legislation in Kentucky history.* It ended the federal government's market quota and price support loan programs that had been in place to protect the American small tobacco farmer since 1938. It marked the official deregulation of the US tobacco market, which is a less disagreeable way of saying that the policy allowed American tobacco companies to no longer buy their tobacco in the United States. Not surprisingly, Mitch McConnell was one of the advocates of the change, as it was a priority of (say it with me now) Big Tobacco. More tobacco was available overseas at cheaper prices and, with the health effects having been exposed, McConnell argued it wasn't politically palpable for Americans to continue subsidizing a crop that was killing them. Mitch was probably right; but because tobacco would be much cheaper from foreign manufacturers, the buyout also meant the end of the viability of small Kentucky tobacco farms. The goal of the buyout was to help temper the inevitable pain that was to come and ease the transition as farmers lost the primary means of revenue they had relied on for generations.

Years before, Democratic senator Wendell Ford had proposed a similar buyout, and the debates between him and McConnell on the issue in the 1990s grew very bitter. Ford knew his time in the Senate was ending, and he wanted to see a plan with two components: (1) give onetime bulk payments to farmers to stop growing based on their average tobacco sales over a multiyear period, and (2) set aside money to help transition farmers into other crops or professions to ease the economic impact. In 2003, Ford, despite having retired from government, joined with Kentucky's Republican governor, Ernie Fletcher, and every other elected Kentucky official—except Mitch—to advocate for these components again, finding considerable support among his old colleagues in the Senate. Big Tobacco disliked both ideas due to cost, however, and had McConnell propose a different plan, consisting of (1) a onetime payment based on 2002 tobacco sales (the worst year of the modern era for tobacco) and (2) no transition money.

---

* This would have been a great place for us to draw the parallels between this situation and George Clooney's 2007 film about toxicity in agriculture, *Michael Clayton*. But you'll just have to imagine it. Thanks again, George.

McConnell made the Big Tobacco plan his top priority and it was passed, ignoring all the components of the Ford plan designed to help farmers. The tobacco manufacturers were happy, as it saved them hundreds of millions of dollars in payments and allowed them to cut ties with the small farmers who had relied on them. On the losing end, naturally, was the little guy. The small tobacco farmer received about a third less money and no safety net for the future. With a single piece of legislation, McConnell ended the small Kentucky tobacco economy forever and replaced it with absolutely nothing.

When I ask Bill about McConnell's role in the 2004 buyout, he thinks for a moment before answering.

"Well," he says with his drawl, "a lot of people felt like the buyout could have been better if Mitch McConnell had done a few more things. He could've pushed the tobacco companies for more money."

McConnell claimed later that he approved the buyout legislation only because it was the best deal he could get passed. It's a dishonest and disingenuous claim. In 1998 he killed multiple attempts for stronger regulation against Big Tobacco by making it a priority to defeat the provisions. He took up for Big Tobacco when all of America was against it, utilizing his political capital to bury multiple important regulations to help the consumer. This time, protecting small Kentucky farmers simply wasn't worth the same effort. I ask Bill and LuAnn if they think Mitch McConnell has done right by the Kentucky tobacco farmer. He answers definitively and confidently.

"No, he certainly has not."

Montgomery County

Business Up Front, Party in the Back

Nearly every county in this state has an annual festival and each one is a big deal to the people there. These events come in a close fourth behind basketball, bourbon, and horse racing on Kentucky's priority list, and you could literally spend every weekend from April to November traveling the state and getting your festival on. The biggest and most anticipated of these in the entire state is the Mt. Sterling Court Days, in Montgomery County. It's a huge event with history dating back to 1794, when the Kentucky General Assembly decreed that each county should meet once a month to hold "court." Knowing that all the citizens of the county would descend upon the courthouse on that day, traders would show up as well to make a little money. That system has since been abandoned, but in Mt. Sterling, the hoopla of those court days of yore is still celebrated each October. Here you'll find not only miles of vendors from around the state selling their wares, but also food trucks, bluegrass pickers, a Court Days express minitrain offering free rides to children, large bouncy houses, and even the Court Days Mullet Contest (with a trophy reading "Business Up Front, Party in the Back" awarded to the contestant with the "best" mullet, if such a distinction exists), all of which make it the biggest party in the state.

Court days used to also be a haven for tobacco goods, befitting Montgomery County's role as a major tobacco producer. Danny Razor,* a chatty and knowledgeable Montgomery Countian with a terrific, manly moustache that would make actor Sam Elliott envious—at least a little bit—has a unique perspective on the crisis facing tobacco farmers. Not only is he a farmer himself but he also once worked for the USDA (United States Department of Agriculture). He was part of the team charged with administering McConnell's tobacco buyout program at the county level.

Each farmer was given a check to provide short-term relief but also signaled the end of a way of life for many in the county. Razor tells us every farmer seemed to have a different take on the buyout. Some wanted to continue doing what they'd done for years and were very disappointed. Some, even bitter. But other farmers, such as those who were close to retirement anyway or who accepted the reality that growing tobacco would no longer be viable in the United States, welcomed the buyout as a clean break—money to either pad

---

* Danny missed his calling; with a name like that, Danny would have made a great professional wrestler or character on *Sons of Anarchy*.

their impending golden years or provide a foundation while they considered their options for another way to earn a living. "It fit them pretty good," he tells me. "It was an influx of money that probably tainted their judgment."

Razor was proud of his life's work but does seem to have a sense of remorse regarding the product. "The hard part of all of it is just getting back to the health issue," he confides, "and how that would end up—it's so taboo now, smoking." So taboo that even Mitch McConnell, the tobacco industry's most awesome BFF, recently helped get a bill passed to raise the smoking age to twenty-one nationally and implement other restrictions to curb youth tobacco use. When I first heard the news, I was surprised. Maybe even a little shocked. Had Big Tobacco's most devoted advocate somehow developed a heart in his final years? Was Mitch changing and seeing the light on the damage done by a product he once claimed had little negative health impact?

Of course not. Mitch was still doing Big Tobacco's bidding, just in a different way. As it turns out, the tobacco companies *supported* McConnell's bill because it gave them a perfect trade-off. In exchange for the public relations coup of appearing to demonstrate corporate responsibility by curbing youth smoking, the bill left future regulation to the states, taking it out of the federal government's hands. As tobacco companies know well, the states are not nearly as flush with funds and personnel, which will make it significantly easier for them to manipulate future legislation (read: defang proposed regulations) without attracting critical national media attention. What's more, it costs far less in campaign contributions to influence state races than it does for national contests. That means more lobbying influence bang for the buck. In short, it's a win-win for Big Tobacco. And all it took was raising the smoking age three years to put everyone off their scent. Mitch McConnell did it again for Big Tobacco, as he always has.

It's been sixteen years since the tobacco buyout of 2004, and the area once blanketed with tobacco farms has seen a massive cultural change. Some places, like Montgomery County, have discovered new crops to farm and economic development to help make the sea change easier and have seen a gradual rise after the initial shock. Others, like

Bracken and Nicholas, are having a more difficult time, and the sting of 2004 lingers. But thanks to Mitch McConnell, Big Tobacco is the one party that has survived the fall better than anyone. Unlike the Kentucky farmer, they had friends in high places.

Bath County

The Most Anti-Mitch County of All

Only one county has voted against McConnell all six times he has run for office. Bath County, named for the medicinal springs found in the area, is a tiny mountain enclave that holds the title of being the most consistent anti-Mitch area anywhere, an honor many in this community wear proudly.

Owingsville is Bath County's largest town. It is decorated for fall with cornstalks tied to all the streetlights on Main Street, each wrapped in an orange ribbon. It's a cheery place where people still vote Democratic, even though on some issues their positions are different from that of the national party. This area is pro-life and pro-gun, but the mass flipping from blue to red that has happened in similar rural counties hasn't taken hold here like in the rest of the state. It's rural. It's conservative. But it's still anti-Mitch. I have no idea what the hell is going on in Bath County, but I like it.

"I think the general view around here used to be that Mitch was with the tobacco farmers," says Jacky Watson, the local property valuation administrator, "but now I think a lot of farmers feel like he sold them out. They feel like he should have defended tobacco." The same sentiment is expressed to me in a slightly different way when, as we walk through town, a car pulls up with two burly young guys in the front. The passenger rolls down the window.

"*Matt Jones!* What about them Cats, boy! What are you doing in Bath County?"

I answer that I am here working on the book, and he responds bluntly, "Well, go kick Mitch's ass! You and Rocky are the only ones that can do it. Ain't no use thinkin' about it too hard."*

Fair enough. This is clearly a place where the pockets of local anti-Mitch fervor run deep. But there's a whole different part of Bath County where Mitch McConnell is not only irrelevant but many don't even know his name.

Bath County has a large Amish community, which began in the mid-2000s or so when a mass migration of Amish into the area started, mostly by word of mouth. A few early-modern pioneers had come to Bath County, where they found abundant land, thanks to the shuttering of tobacco farms. They sent word back to their former neighbors that opportunity existed for settlement, and since then, approximately 1,500 Amish have made their way to the county, and their impact has been large.

We go to visit the area for ourselves, taking twisty, winding Mill Creek Road to Jacob Girod's property. When we arrive at Jacob's farm, the sun is setting behind the house as he and his brother Ervin wait on the front porch. We are late (we got lost, and the whole "no cell phone service" thing made it difficult) but the Girods don't seem to mind. Both are dressed in traditional Amish work clothes—suspenders, wide-brimmed hats—and have thick chinstrap beards, even though neither looks to be over twenty-five years old. The Girod family came from southern Indiana several years ago, one of the first groups of Amish to settle in the area. They were ready for a change of land, and were convinced by a non-Amish farmer who'd been a friend of their father's that Bath County was the place. The family built the house we're sitting in front of from foundation to finishing touches in six weeks.

"When we first came here, we had fifteen acres of tobacco," says Ervin. "It was Dad, the six of us boys and two sisters, and the first thing we did was start on tobacco. We'd do tobacco every day, from the time we woke up until the time we went to bed." Since then, as in the rest of

---

* The "rolled-down-window shoutout" happens to Matt at least once per county. It usually includes "What are you doing *here*?" followed by a "Go, Cats!" The shouters are almost uniformly burly.

the state, tobacco has slowly dissipated for them as a cash crop, forcing the Girods to find other crops to supplement.

The Girods aren't sure exactly how many Amish families have settled in the area, but they estimate that more than fifty large groups have concentrated in three central places around the county. When we ask why Bath County, the answer comes down to the soil, which they say is near perfect.

"It's pretty rich," Ervin tells me, his voice lilting with Dutch-tinged inflection. "Do you see that field over there? The soil is solid black. When you plow it, it just falls apart. It's wonderful ground. I wouldn't trade this ground for nothin'."

Overall, the Girods have found the community to be welcoming, but life isn't totally easy. An extended member of their family ended up in jail recently in a highly publicized local case. In 2017 a federal judge sentenced Samuel Girod to six years in prison for producing and selling an herbal skin cream without the government's permission. Girod marketed his creams as being able to cure skin disorders, sinus infections, and even cancer. He sold them throughout the Midwest for twenty years. However, he never took the basic steps necessary to receive FDA approval for his products. Even though his ingredients were natural, he never conducted any scientific studies to support his curative claims and, as such, the judge and jury determined he was in violation of federal law.

The case drew national attention and three years later, Samuel is still in prison. Girod's case raised important questions about the relation between religion and federal law, as he claims his freedom of religion gives him immunity from needing to have his creams approved by the FDA. Putting an Amish farmer in prison for selling homemade cream may seem harsh to many, but allowing him to evade any government regulation by just claiming religious freedom would potentially open up massive loopholes that could be exploited in the future by less scrupulous actors.

It's a fascinating issue, but one that neither Ervin nor Jacob is much interested in discussing. Their lives are much more peaceful, focused solely on their farm. They obviously don't watch the news and follow politics only peripherally. The brothers tell me they usually vote in Bath

County's general elections for local races, but they don't follow national politics at all.* In fact, when I ask them what they think about Donald Trump, Ervin gives a refreshing answer that makes me envy him greatly. "Well, I don't know." He takes a beat. "He is the president, but I don't know much about him. Is he doing his job or not?"

Morgan County

The Tornado That Changed Everything

"West Liberty used to be a booming little town," says local resident Jerry Barker, sitting at a table at the town's new McDonald's. "I used to manage grocery stores, and back in the eighties, it was just booming. Crowded, had lots of stores, the prison came and brought a lot of businesses in. Then the tornado devastated all of it."

Early in the evening of March 2, 2012, West Liberty was hit by a massive tornado that caused extensive damage, especially its downtown area. Wind gusts of 140 miles per hour ripped apart multiple buildings. Six people were killed, and at least seventy-five were injured. It was one of the worst weather disasters in Kentucky's recent history, and it touched down in the middle of the Appalachian Mountains, where, ordinarily, tornadoes are an afterthought. Few warning systems are in place, and safety precautions are rare. No one expects a devastating tornado in the middle of the mountains. It is the kind of thing that just doesn't happen, until it did.

After the tornado, I brought *KSR* to West Liberty to heighten awareness of the devastation the area was going through, and to try to raise a bit of money for the recovery. We held a radio telethon in the middle of downtown to raise funds. University of Kentucky men's basketball coach John Calipari flew in to help lift the town's spirits, and it was a rare day of happiness in a county that was still reeling from so much grief and loss. Over the course of two hours, our listeners donated

* In their world, snowflakes are *actual snowflakes*. How refreshing.

more than $50,000 for the recovery efforts, money that was used by the city to clean up downtown buildings. It was a special moment in the history of our show and maybe the first time I realized just how powerful a force for good our forty-plus affiliate radio network truly could be.

In returning to West Liberty seven years later, I can see some things in the area have improved, but much still needs help. The tornado roared down Main Street, demolishing a carpet store, an insurance agency, and several buildings that used to host the town's most popular flea market. Walking around the town now, there are few remnants of that devastating day. The buildings have been mostly reconstructed, and unless you know where to look, the line of the tornado's path, once so prominent and eye opening, has faded into the background.

A few months prior to the disaster, John Calipari and the Kentucky basketball team designed a tour to celebrate the school's national championship and show off the national title trophy to fans in small towns across the state. I went along for the ride, and we spent a lot of time in the mountains. Calipari told me that seeing the towns and hollers where UK basketball was so important up close was a transformative experience. I gave him a little history of each area, and seeing the UK basketball coach's effect on average Kentuckians was really quite sweet. A few months later, as we walked in downtown West Liberty and looked at a badly damaged building, he patted me on the shoulder and said, "You really love this area. I hope you will try to make it better."

Walking a similar path in West Liberty today, I toss those words around in my mind. I have thought for a long time that the best thing I can do for this state is what I am doing now: radio. I am one of the few avowed progressives in America that speaks daily to primarily Donald Trump voters. Three-fourths of my listening audience voted for Trump. We disagree strongly about him and have differences on some political issues (although less than the partisan media would have you believe). Yet they still listen to me, even when I talk about politics, because of our shared affinity for Kentucky basketball and because I think they know I respect them. In a world where people look down on rural America, doubly so for rural Appalachians, I try to be an advocate for the area and a voice for them on a broader scale. It's not an act of charity—the radio show and covering UK sports has been good business—but

I have tried to set an example that you can come from the mountains, be true to yourself, enjoy success, and give back to the area you love in the process.

But now I wonder if it is time for a next step. My frustration with McConnell is well known. But my experiences in Washington with DC liberals have illustrated what a lost cause the Democratic Party is for my people. I found Chuck Schumer to be personally pleasant and charming, and a much better alternative than Mitch McConnell. But the reality is that the party that he leads has no clue about places like West Liberty, and since they aren't on their political radar, no plan for helping their people.

Here's a question: name me one Democratic national political figure or media member who currently represents rural America. Can you think of one who lives in a small town? Can you think of a notable Democrat with a southern accent? The reality is that this area, which was once the blue-collar base of the Democratic Party, is now just written off as Trump country and cynically viewed as a lost cause. No effort is made to understand the people's lives or even win their vote. The Democrats can't win Kentucky because Kentuckians and those from similar states don't have a seat at the table with them. General Colin Powell, who served as secretary of state in the George W. Bush administration, once said that Republicans wouldn't make inroads with African Americans until they turned on the television and saw people like them represented by the party. Well, now, fifteen years later, a rural Kentuckian would have a hard time seeing anyone in the Democratic Party who represents him or her either.

Mitch McConnell came to West Liberty in the days after the tornado and toured the town. He expressed his sympathy, wished them luck, and took off, not returning since. When I ask people from the area what help he has provided in the recovery, no one can point to anything that has been done. Long ago it became clear that waiting for Mitch to help places like West Liberty was a lost cause. But now, if I am honest, that describes the Democrats, too. Maybe it's worth trying to change that, although with Trump on the ballot, it may be a suicide mission.

As I head out of town, I pass a man coming out of a vape shop. He gives me a friendly wave and grin that is the common greeting for most passing strangers on the road in the mountains. I notice he is wearing a tight-fitting, bright-red T-shirt bearing the slogan "Trump: 2020. You Can't Stop It!"* It feels like a message he is personally sending to me.

Menifee County

Winning Is All That Matters

"Mamaw's not here to show people around right now."

So I'm told by a man who pulls up as I stand out in front of the Swamp Valley Antique Shop—at least that's what I'm guessing; the letter *T* in *antique* and *S* in *shop* appear to have dropped off the sign long ago. Swamp Valley, I'm told via a nearby sign, is located "halfway between Lizzord Ridge and Possum Hollow"—information that simultaneously made it both less and more clear where I was. I wanted to look inside but with Mamaw gone, I instead head down the road to the Frenchburg Mall, which hosts a flea-market-style collection of goods including samurai swords, loose brassieres, Christmas ornaments, and decorative engraved knives (one, dedicated to John F. Kennedy, reads "An American Tragedy"; another, dedicated to O. J. Simpson, is less affectionately engraved with "Keep the Juice in the can"). It's a uniquely Menifee County type of place, the kind you'll find in a county where trees outnumber people ten thousand to one.

Menifee County is tiny. Most rural counties in Kentucky like Menifee are about as Republican as you can get; in fact, there is a reverse correlation in Kentucky between the number of inhabitants in a county and its likelihood to vote Republican. But somehow Menifee remained an outlier; it voted Democrat consistently until 2016, when Donald Trump came along and changed everything. Case in point: in 2014, Menifee was one of just ten counties to vote against Mitch McConnell. Two years later, Donald Trump won there by twenty-five points. In the 2018 state rep election between Andy Barr and now-senatorial candidate

* Like most Trump slogans, it doubles as a semi-veiled threat.

Amy McGrath, Barr won by *twenty-nine* percentage points, the biggest margin anyone can remember for a Republican in the county's history. Nowhere else in Kentucky has the "Donald Trump Effect" changed the political landscape more dramatically than in Menifee County.

We sat down with seventy-six-year-old James Lawson, a lifelong Democratic resident of Menifee, to understand why. Lawson chooses his words carefully before he speaks, saying he needs to think before going too far. He's the old guard around here, one of the leaders of the county's eroding Democratic Party. He says things in Menifee used to make sense to him. It was a poor county, heavily dependent on governmental assistance programs, and it would vote consistently for candidates who would maintain or expand those programs intended to help the area. That's not necessarily the case these days.

With a sigh, he says, "I just don't understand Menifee County at this point in my life. The way I see it right now, it's a pretty good place to live, pretty good people, but we're a poor county, one of the smaller ones in the state. Per capita, people probably use as many federal programs as any county anywhere—Medicare, Social Security, welfare—but it turned just as red as can be."

Lawson is troubled by his county—and others like it—which continually seems to vote for candidates who are against their own interests. He says it simply doesn't make sense and gives me a story to illustrate the point:

"There was this young guy up at the store—they serve breakfast and things like that, and he was talking pretty right wing. I'm seventy-six years old, and I've known the guy ever since he was young. His mother was on disability; she had one of those heart valves that was prone to go bad, you know, and *he's* been on all those [government] programs. Then when he got married, before you could turn around, he had four children. And he got all his prenatal and postnatal stuff paid for. But he doesn't know how he got it, and that's just the way so many people are."

Kentucky receives the second-highest amount of federal money per capita of any state in the country, and yet its citizenry has begun repeatedly voting for the party that tries to slowly take it away. In fact, the counties that are flipping from blue to red the fastest are also the counties, like Menifee, that take the greatest percentage of government assistance. It is a dichotomy that is hard for many older Democrats to understand.

I think the explanation is twofold. First, the reality is that the Republican Party has masterfully manipulated the system into presenting politics as simply a bipolar choice for people. The rise of right-wing talk radio, and later Fox News, Breitbart News Network, and their ilk, has transformed all of politics into a two-dimensional morality question. Whose side are you on, ours or theirs? Theirs is amoral and evil. Ours is patriotic and wholesome. Just as on my sports radio show, when I say the Kentucky Wildcats are great and the Louisville Cardinals are terrible, people love it, and listenership goes up. The same is true with politics, although, unfortunately, the stakes are a lot greater than a college basketball game. There are no more shades of gray. You are on one of two sides, and "winning" is of the utmost importance.

So why side with the GOP? I think they do it because the Democratic Party has completely abandoned rural America in both words and deed. Social justice, minority rights, environmentalism, gun control, and so forth—all extremely important issues in their own right—have now become the entirety of the Democratic Party platform. Discussions about the working class or rural America in general just aren't a part of most national Democratic Party debates. And when rural America *is* talked about, it is usually in a condescending manner or to mock and scorn. Religion, patriotism, and other values that matter to rural Americans are often secondary issues in liberal circles, and many Kentuckians feel they aren't an important part of Democratic platforms. I don't think the reason why is due to hatred but is a function of ignorance. There simply aren't many working-class or rural Middle America Democrats representing the party at the highest level of politics or in national media. Don't get me wrong, Democrats still represent working-class interests far more than their Republican counterparts. But the party is now centered on the two coasts and in large urban areas, making it hard to know how rural America feels when they aren't even a party to the discussions.

So then when voters are told that there is a "culture war" for the "heart and soul of America," and there are only two choices, they choose the one speaking to them directly. Democrats too often don't even try. Charismatic, fake scoundrels like Donald Trump and his media enablers at least pay lip service to the value and importance of rural America and its beliefs. Thus, these voters accept as necessary parasitic leaders such as Mitch McConnell, who actively work against their interest because he is on their "team," warts and all. If given the choice between a Democratic establishment that either mocks or ignores them and a party that appeals to them directly, they will choose the devil that validates their importance every time.

The point is pounded home to me as I leave town, when I see a giant banner beside the road that has Trump's head photoshopped onto the body of Sylvester Stallone's John Rambo, shirtless and bandannaed, holding a large rocket launcher. In giant red letters the sign reads "TRUMP," beneath which is the line "No man, no woman, no commie can stump him."

Lee County

"Mitch's Stance Is Whatever Makes Him Look Good"

Beattyville, in Lee County, is a small town with not a lot going on. Well, at least not until recently, when whispers started going around that the county's landscape was about to change. Apparently, Lee County has become so attractive to outdoor types that a new set of summer homes have been built (it's whispered that there may even be a few millionaires in the mix). No sushi bars or Whole Foods have popped up yet, but it's got the town buzzing, and why not? This place is so deep in the mountains and beautiful, it was only a matter of time before them damned bourgeoisie found out.

We are here to meet with Dedra Brandenburg, codirector of the Three Forks Historical Center, about the town's famous Woolly Worm Festival, a three-day celebration of Lee County life based on its most favored little creature. According to Dedra, the woolly worm (which is slang for a woolly bear caterpillar around these parts) is one of the many folksy tools historically used to predict the weather around these parts, as much prognosticator as pest. Each fall, the woolly worms in the area can be analyzed to tell how long winter will be. The darker the woolly worm's middle regions, the colder the coming winter. In addition, the number of foggy mornings in August you have will equal the number of snows as well (a "snow" being classified as any amount of snow you can track a rabbit in).* And if you break open a persimmon and find a seed shaped like a shovel, you're going to be shoveling snow as well.† It's all very scientific, and I love every minute of her explanation, as you might imagine.

Blessed with this knowledge, we head back on the highway looking for some woolly worms hanging out on persimmons, and instead come across a roadside peddler selling fruit and hot takes of his own. I duck under his tent out of the rain and ask him if I can buy an apple.

"Sour or sweet?" he asks succinctly. He has the thick, tangled beard of a lumberjack, faded jeans, and an old, worn-out hat over his head. He is passing the time carving an apple with his sharp, large knife. He is a man who, it is very clear, does not suffer fools gladly.

"Sweet," I say, and he silently points to a bushel with the blade of his knife. He doesn't charge me, which is good of him, but also makes me wonder about his business plan.

It's a hell of an apple. As I take a bite, I strike up a conversation. I ask him about the county, the people, and the politics of the area. He responds bluntly, "What do you need to know? I'll tell you anything you need." His only requirement is that I don't print his name, which isn't ideal for the book, but considering that he is standing here in the rain, holding a massive knife, and giving me free apples, it seems like a small price to pay for a safe and interesting conversation.

The peddler doesn't believe the Democrats are serious about beating Mitch McConnell again, saying, "If the Democratic Party wants rid of him so bad and they can run any person they want to run, there's probably somebody out there that can beat him, someone who would

---

* I don't know how to track a rabbit so I would be a poor Lee County meteorologist.

† False. No matter how big that seed is I will leave the snow be, hoping it melts, and instead fall and hurt myself.

win in a landslide—but it ain't Amy McGrath. So why did they choose her?"

The man insinuates that national-level Democrats don't make beating Mitch a priority because wealthy interests control both parties. If the senator is so unpopular—and he is—then why should it be so hard to beat him? He doesn't think Democrats even truly try.

He continues. "You ever watch professional wrestling? These two big guys go up, and they talk about how they hate each other, right? When it's over, they go to the same bar, they have a drink, they stay at the same hotel, and they're the best of friends. It's the same thing."

Maybe he does know me, because I am a sucker for this analogy. First of all, I love wrestling, but also the more I get immersed in politics, the more I see that most political games we see on television are just a big show. Politicians and media types scream at each other when the camera lights are on, and then smile and laugh it off when it's over. Many politicians are full of bluster and aren't nearly as passionate about issues as they appear to be. They are playing a role for the cameras to get attention and gain votes. It is somewhat frustrating to me, as these wrestling personas get Americans riled up and hateful toward one another, but often those making the arguments don't believe what they are saying. It's just a show.

My new acquaintance pauses, takes a bite of an apple, and starts in on McConnell.

"He stands on a conservative platform, and he does nothing conservative," he tells me. "He helped bankrupt coal. He's a yes-man. If Hillary Clinton was president right now, you wouldn't hear Mitch McConnell say anything about the law, anything about the border. He'll ride the coattail of anyone he can. Now it's Trump. Mitch's stance is whatever makes him look good, whatever pays the most."

On this, he is undoubtedly correct. McConnell is very intelligent. He is probably the greatest political mastermind of the modern era, having accumulated a level of legislative power not seen since Lyndon Johnson. But in so doing, he has sold out all of his principles to follow the prevailing political winds of the day. When he first ran for county judge-executive in Louisville in 1977, the thirty-five-year-old was prochoice, a strong believer in civil rights, collective bargaining for state employees, and a liberal judicial interpretation of the Constitution. All those policies represented the mainstream of the moderate wing of the Republican Party at the time, the so-called Rockefeller Republicans. But as that ideology fell out of favor, Mitch quickly flipped on every issue.

Even more recently, McConnell was one of the Senate's biggest advocates of free trade. Then Donald Trump came along and made tariffs the centerpiece of his economic policy. Faced with confronting a more popular president, Mitch quickly abandoned his central economic philosophy and became a protectionist. On foreign policy, he advocated his entire career for the bipartisan post–World War II notion of using US power for the world's good to promote democracy. Then Trump's isolationism became the flavor of the day for the GOP, leading to pullouts from Syria, alliances with foes such as Russia and North Korea, and publicly trashing our NATO allies. McConnell merely shrugged in response to all those major policy shifts, refusing to utter a word against his Republican president. McConnell was once a conservative idealist but decided long ago that ideas were irrelevant, so long as political wins can be gained. The only consistent political principle of Mitch McConnell is that he doesn't have one.

My new Lee County friend likes Trump, and for that reason alone, he will hold his nose and vote for McConnell. "Right now, as long as the Republicans hold the majority, Mitch is going to ride that Trump shirttail and play conservative for a while. I'm going to vote for Mitch this time because of that."

He knows the senator is fake. He knows he's full of it. He knows he can't be trusted. But Mitch is for Trump, so he is going to vote for him anyway. In ten seconds, my apple-peddling friend has summarized better than any natural political pundit ever could why beating Mitch in Kentucky is so difficult.*

---

* This was a consistent theme this entire trip. For someone as outgoing and loud as Matt, he never likes to tell people he might run for office. I think it's because he doesn't want anyone to think he is a politician. This could be a hindrance in the actual race.

Owsley County

Fastest Internet in the State

Booneville, Kentucky—population 127—is the most sparsely populated county seat in the state, and likely in the entire nation. It's a real blink-and-you'll-miss-it situation. The Owsley County Courthouse occupies the middle of town, but honestly, Booneville is so small, it's all pretty much the middle. The tiny courthouse holds the entire county government: the circuit clerk, the county clerk, the police department, and everything in between. It would seem cramped except it actually fits the rest of Booneville, which is basically composed of four churches, the board of education, and the Farmers State Bank and Farm Bureau Insurance. (In every single downtown we've seen, banks and insurance branches are always the most well-kept buildings, likely because they have the money.) Booneville's most interesting sight today is a lazy hound dog cuddled up next to a napping spotted billy goat—just two animal buddies chilling out on the side of a public street on a Thursday.*

Ask most people in Kentucky what they know about Owsley County and, unfortunately, they will probably mention the poverty level; it has the lowest median household income of any county in Kentucky and is one of the five poorest counties in America. Driving into town on Highway 11, it's hard not to notice the dilapidated houses, buildings with whole sides knocked out of them, collapsing pink roofs, and front yards cluttered with broken-down forgotten automobiles. Many people here are struggling to get by, and, on the surface, it looks depressing.

But underneath this exterior is an area with rich history and the potential to become a beacon for eastern Kentucky on how to grow a new economy. Take, for instance, Charles Long. I met Charles two years ago, when he was crowned the oldest mayor in America. Long was first

---

* I must note here that I used to write a series of articles for *National Geographic Kids* on "Animal Friends," and I find such cross-animal friendships adorable. You would too.

elected mayor of Booneville in 1959 and served the office for sixty consecutive years until his death in 2019, only a couple of months shy of his hundredth birthday. When I came to town to meet him, he was beaming with joy. He wore a large red hat that said, "Mayor: Booneville," and when I asked him about his service, he said:

"When I got in office, Booneville didn't have nothin.' They had a wheelbarrow, some hand tools, and outside toilets. We have made it a lot better since then."

It is a lot better. In a place plagued by inadequate infrastructure for generations, Owsley County has become a leader in one important area. Thanks to incredible foresight from some county leaders a decade ago and the use of a New Deal–era policy that dates back to President Franklin D. Roosevelt, it has one of the fastest Internet systems in the entire country, which is utterly amazing considering the location. Nearly eighty years ago, a local co-op was created by city and county officials to bring electricity and phone service to the county, after private companies refused to build the infrastructure due to cost. Ten years ago, officials said they could use the same co-op to bolster the Internet service as well. They partnered with a private telecom company and utilized the money from Obama's federal stimulus package to create a faster, state-of-the-art Internet system that could cover the entire county.

We walk into the Action Team and Teleworks Hub, a community center–esque building with multiple offices inside, to see this Internet put to use. Due to its speed, international companies are now using Owsley County and nearby Lee County as hubs for customer service calls from around the world. In one room, a young man with a headset sits in front of an Xbox and fields customer service calls from gamers around the country. In another, Apple field assistants are on call to help with iPhone problems from all over America. Teleworks has provided hundreds of jobs for this tiny county, and the number continues to grow. Individuals of all ages take the time to train online and the quick Internet allows them to work from wherever they want: here, at their own stations, or even from home. It's been an economic lifesaver and has revolutionized the county's economy. I love the idea that the next time you call Apple assuming your help is coming from a large service center in a major city, you might, in fact, be calling a trailer park in Owsley County.

Owsley County has shown how a small federal investment in infrastructure can completely change a region. Most expect Owsley County to soon climb out of the basement of the state's poverty ratings, and when it does, it will be the fast Internet access that will be the primary reason. On average, eastern Kentucky has the slowest Internet service in the country except in Owsley County and Lee County. And it is not a coincidence that those places are seeing the makings of a viable future economy. If such a dramatic change can occur via the work of one small local electric co-op in the poorest county in Kentucky, imagine what the federal government focusing its resources could do if the region's senior senator cared enough to try.

Rowan County

Fiddling Our Stories

Rowan County is the home of Kim Davis, the fundamentalist right-wing county clerk who took the national stage in 2015 after she refused to grant marriage licenses to same sex couples due to her personal religious beliefs that marriage should be only between a man and a woman.* Because of Davis's actions, Rowan County became the focal point for the gay marriage debate, and the county filled with demagogues seeking to exploit the moment and grandstand, such as former Arkansas governor and GOP presidential candidate Mike Huckabee. It was a national spectacle, but around here, it was just a big hassle. Rowan County, in fact, is a lovely place with a wonderful university and a friendly population. The national attention skewed this area's image nationally in a way that pleased no one. Incidentally, Kim Davis was soundly defeated in the next election in the primary.

---

* Who better to judge the sanctity of marriage than someone who has been married four times and divorced three.

I head to Morehead State University to watch my friend Professor Jesse Wells chat with young musicians about their futures. I call him "Professor" because that's what he is: a teaching professor about Appalachian music. But it's also the nickname bluegrass artists use when they need the perfect fiddle* to round out a song (as in, "Call in the Professor for this one!"). Jesse Wells is an amazing musician. He can literally play anything and is the assistant director and archivist for the university's Kentucky Center for Traditional Music. He is also the fiddle player for Tyler Childers, one of the hottest "real" country musical artists in America (and maybe my personal favorite current musician). Having a band member of a rising country music star as your professor has to be a pretty amazing setup for Morehead students. In this area, where Childers's music is so beloved, it is the local musical equivalent of having Draymond Green coaching basketball at the San Francisco YMCA.

As we sneak quietly into his classroom, the lesson's already begun. We slide into desks in the back row and listen. Jesse is asking his students to articulate the role they hope music will play in the rest of their futures. A boy in camouflage shorts tells the class in his thick mountain accent that he gets frustrated playing music sometimes, but the good moments make the bad ones worth it, which Jesse says he understands. A girl with blond bangs talks about how music brings her family closer together, while a soft-spoken young woman named Sara-Kate longs to be a songwriter and express herself to the world.

Jesse, rubbing his dark-goateed chin, honestly doesn't look a whole lot older than the students as he kindly listens and nods. He ponders their responses and then offers his musical advice. "You have to be patient and let things happen," he says. "Being musically talented is important, but it's about being a good person more than anything else—showing up and being kind to the people you meet. If you get along with people, music supersedes any hard feelings."

As class ends, I join Jesse outside and we walk the halls, the open

* The difference between a violinist and a fiddler is like the difference between a house dog and a wolf; the latter is more feral and exciting.

rooms filled with the sounds of students practicing instruments. Jesse explains why bluegrass and Kentucky music are just plain different from everything else.

"I grew up playing bluegrass and old-time string band and square dance music." (His father, Jamie Wells, is also a longtime local bluegrass legend.) "Of course, that's not commercial music; you're not out there playing for huge audiences. It's a very community-based music, with a deep history in the mountains and reaching back to our ancestors in Europe and Africa. For me, that's my connection. It goes way beyond my generation, my parents' generation—it reaches back to Northern Ireland." For eastern Kentuckians, this music became the best way to document their lives, stories, and heritage to a world that had little interest in their plight.

"It's talking about day-to-day life for these people," he explains. "As the world expands and information expands, music is one of the things we can still connect to. For me, that's what it is. This music has been here in eastern Kentucky since Kentucky's been Kentucky. And it still is. Kentucky music is one thing that connects our culture, present and past."

Jesse's performances with Childers, from nearby Johnson County, promote the soundtrack of a new, younger mountain generation, one struggling to embrace an uncertain future. Listening to Childers's and Wells's music, you hear the yearning of an area and the desperation it can sometimes bring. On "Nose on the Grindstone," one of Childers's early recordings, he sings in a voice both mournful and angry:

Daddy worked like a mule mining Pike County coal.
He fucked up his back, he couldn't work anymore.
He said, "One of these days, you'll get out of these hills.
Keep your nose on the grindstone and out of the pills."

Tyler, Jesse, and the rest of the band (known as the Food Stamps) are immensely popular in the mountains. Jesse believes the music they play is eternal. "Tyler's music is the old fiddle music from this region, and there are people playing it now in Seattle and Portland, New York

City, Chicago," he says of Kentucky music's increasing reach. "They've learned the music from archival recordings and now there are more people playing it elsewhere in super-urban areas, but then they come visit here, and they still feel a deep connection here to the place and the people."

For Jesse, that's what the music is about: an expression of a way of life and providing a connection. Connecting people to common experiences, connecting Kentuckians to their past, connecting people outside of the state to the unique heritage in eastern Kentucky. This variety of bluegrass and country music *is* eastern Kentucky. It's the soundtrack of a region.

"For the songwriting, the storytelling part of our music," says Jesse, "I don't think there's a stronger place anywhere than these mountains."

Estill County

Kickin' It on the Creek

It's time for me to admit something to you folks:

I am tired of talking about Mitch McConnell.

Not so tired that I am ready to abandon this trip, with only twenty-five or so counties left to go. But tired enough that I need a break. *Move, Mitch, get out the way!* So it was with great anticipation that I began my drive down this curvy dirt road through a holler in Estill County to the Kickin' It on the Creek Music Festival.

Kickin' It on the Creek is unlike any music event you've ever been to. It is 100 percent eastern Kentucky and might be my favorite getaway in the entire state. Held on the remote two-hundred-acre property of Byron Roberts, an Estill County local legend, it is three days of musical heaven that has become a celebration of mountain life and the chance to have (as one concertgoer says to me) "the best sorta-clean fun anywhere in these hills."

In 2015, Roberts threw a twenty-first birthday party for his son that doubled as a CD benefit for Tyler Childers to help raise money for the release of his first album. It was very successful and drew a large crowd to his home, making Roberts ask himself, Why not create a grassroots music festival right here on my property, in these dark woods around Little Ross Creek? He invited some bands he knew to play, spread the news via word of mouth throughout the county, and had a weekend campout concert that everyone agreed was a special time. The next year it grew bigger, and now he has more than a thousand people, mostly still locals from the area, make their way to his holler annually for a concert that may be the toughest ticket in the state.*

Even though Childers has become a national star, he returns to play Roberts's farm every year and brings with him a who's-who lineup of forty local musicians, bluegrass bands, and friends of the festival. Most of them camp out and hang with the locals; there's no going back to some fancy hotel. It's a musical party for them as well. All the money collected goes toward paying the acts, and the rest is donated to the community. Roberts does it only for the sheer joy of the weekend. I had heard great things about the festival for the last two years, and this year, when Byron reached out to me and sent me an invite, I had to go. He knew I loved Childers's music, and wanted me to come see the event for myself. I couldn't wait.

The drive to Roberts's farm takes you deep into the backwoods of Estill County. It's two miles off any named road, and the traffic becomes heavy on the one-lane narrow road. The sun is setting as I pull up among a sea of pickup trucks and greet Byron Roberts, who immediately runs over and gives me a big hug. He has his usual look of a dark beard with grayish streaks, whatever music T-shirt he has picked out (today it's the local band The Wooks), and a Country Boy Brewing hat. As I walk up, Roberts says, "Welcome to my home!" We have never met, but he treats me like an old, lost friend, patting me on the shoulder and telling me every possible fact about the event.

Byron drives me on his golf cart through the mass of people that have taken up residence on every inch of his property and up to his house. Roberts doesn't live on a giant mega-lot. It's a small farm with

* The size has grown slightly, but the event remains largely locals, unless you know a guy who knows a guy.

a modest house and a massive stage erected right in the front yard. It's unlike anything I have ever seen, and as Byron takes me to his front porch, I marvel at his creation. We take a seat in rocking chairs looking out over a throng of people waiting for the next act. It's a surreal scene, a hillbilly Bonnaroo, but in a man's front yard and with attendance limited to a thousand people, all of whom seem to be close friends.

Roberts begins to describe his feelings. "Matt, I have always loved the music. This place is so special to me, and these hills are so special, and I just wanted to do something for these people. And since then, it's just grown, and there's just so much love here. You can feel it. They love you, Matt, even if they don't know you. It's the best of these mountains, and I love every minute of it."

I see immediately what Byron means as I walk out into the crowd. The bluegrass band Town Mountain is tearing up the stage, and everyone seems to be in the moment, swaying to the music. I look around, and it is as representative a cross section of my home area as you can imagine. Every age, from college students to grandparents, all dancing in harmony and smiling. Hugs abound as people greet strangers like they are old friends. It's a beautiful sight.

I take a walk along the vendor area, and it is a celebration of mountain culture, arts, crafts, and jewelry made from everything—from "Estill County wood" to "spoons of every era."* There are food trucks in the back, including one for a place called Hillbilly Hibachi, that is legendary for driving around the mountains and bringing country-Asian fusion to a different town every day. Person after person comes up to me, introduces himself/herself, and says some form of "You gonna run? I am for you if you do!" This isn't a pro-Mitch crowd, as demonstrated by one older gentleman who says, "I don't have any money to give you, but if you run, I will put some of my Breathitt County voodoo on him!" I don't know what that means but having been in Breathitt County, I'm pretty sure Mitch should be worried.

---

* You pick the spoon based on the year the person you are buying it for was born. The spoon is then turned immediately, right in front of you, into a ring for your finger. It sounds ridiculous, but it's kind of awesome.

I expect a similar interaction when a middle-aged man with glasses walks directly up to me with purpose. He is wearing a T-shirt, cargo shorts, and Birkenstocks, and hands me a small bumper sticker that says, "Who the hell is Jeff Cox?" I look at it with puzzlement as he tells me, "I am Jeff Cox, but now you will remember that, which you wouldn't have otherwise." He is right—I still do!

Around the back walking paths of the holler, the attendees are all camping out, playing music of their own or simply fellowshipping with their neighbors. I get a sense of why this is so special to people around here. Byron Roberts told me on the phone, "We are just a bunch of hillbillies having fun," but it's more than that. It's a proud reclamation of hillbilly culture, the much-mocked lifestyle that is so misunderstood outside this region. Whereas the rest of the world stereotypes eastern Kentucky as full of hate-filled, Trump-loving bigots, Kickin' It on the Creek shows the friendly, caring, talented core of mountain life. The folks here are proud people who have lived hard lives in some of the most difficult circumstances and terrain in the country. But they love it here and celebrate their home, community, and culture with pride. The title of a short film on the concert best encapsulates the feeling: *Let the Mountains Ring Forever.*

It's a little past midnight and I have to head back home, so I walk to Byron's house to say goodbye. He begs me to stay and camp: "Tyler is playing tomorrow night; you don't want to miss that, Matt!" I tell him I can't, as I have more counties to visit, and he pulls me to the side, looking me directly in the eyes.

"We are proud of you, brother," Roberts says sincerely, emotion in his voice. "I love how you support these mountains, and we love how you have success and are proud of this place. I just want you to know, if you run, you definitely have the mountain people of Kentucky standing beside you. Go kick McConnell's ass, and we will be with you every minute."

CHAPTER 9

God, Guns & Babies

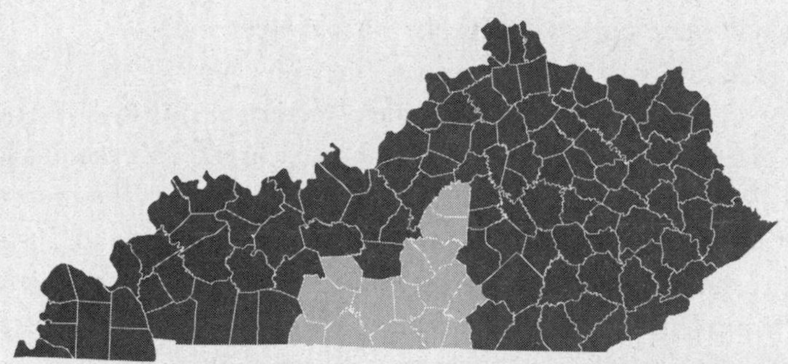

With only a few weeks left before my decision, it is time to dive deep into south-central Kentucky. This is hard GOP country. After spending a week in the mountains, feeling the support and words of encouragement, this area will likely give me a healthy reality check. South-central Kentucky is the kind of place Democrats used to win but now aren't even competitive in. Understanding why is key to defeating Mitch McConnell.

Warren County

"Money Is Speech"

Do you know anyone who drives a Corvette? I don't, but I believe they fall into one of three main stereotypes: (1) a fifty-one-year-old man who doesn't have the energy or opportunity for an affair but does have the money to buy a Corvette; (2) a sixty-one-year-old man who has extra space in his garage, where he keeps his Corvette covered like King Tut except for the occasional Sunday afternoons he takes it out for a drive, imagining he's turning heads (he's not); (3) a seventy-one-year-old man whose favorite day each year is the local Fourth of July parade when he can meet the fifty other people in the ten-county radius who also own Corvettes, and they get their collective moment in the sun. I know that's not everyone, but it feels like a healthy percentage.

If you are one of those people, then Bowling Green, in Warren County is a must-visit for you. Besides Western Kentucky University,* the city's primary attraction is the National Corvette Museum, a large dome-like building that is heaven for Corvette lovers. The museum's exterior is a bright, colorful mix of modern technology and '50s soda shop décor. It looks like Disney's Space Mountain if it were disguised as a Sonic Drive-In. It is located here because it's five minutes away from the General Motors Bowling Green Assembly Plant, where every Corvette in the nation has been manufactured since 1981.

In the early-morning darkness on February 12, 2014, a sinkhole opened up underneath the museum, swallowing eight cars from the museum floor, including a classic 1962 model. (There's a video online showing security camera footage of it happening, and if you want to go watch that now, I'll wait. It's awesome.) There is no sign of the sinkhole now, as the interior of the National Corvette Museum is as clean, crisp, and streamlined as a new Corvette itself. With its shiny black floors and polished chrome, it looks like the future as conceived back in 1953, the year the sleek, sexy sports cars first rolled off the assembly line. In the lobby sits the latest Corvette model, and the museum displays the story of every incarnation of the car.

Before we exit, we pass a wall bearing the names of financial donors who have given to the facility, which operates as a nonprofit. Only those who have donated generously enough to qualify for what is called the Spire Society are listed by name. They are separated into tiers:

---

* *Sports Illustrated* called WKU's mascot Big Red, a round, furry blob of awesomeness, the eighth best in football history. They are wrong. It's #1.

Foundation, $25,000 to $99,999;
Heritage, $250,000 to $499,999;
Pinnacle, $500,000 to $999,999; and
Summit, $1 million and above.

Those are some hefty gifts. We counted 160 people who have given to one of the tiers and have been inducted into the Spire Society. Even more amazing, there are six members of the Summit group who have given the Corvette Museum at least $1 million. Think about that for a second: 160 people have such disposable income that they are fine donating *at least* $25,000 (some much more) of their charitable dollars to a private company's foundation, solely to preserve the memory of cars whose base-level cost is around $60,000. Yep, I'll get you next time, American Heart Association. Hey, Red Cross, I gave at the office. The charity that touches my heart is the National Corvette Museum.

I will be honest, though. I would rather these obscenely wealthy donors put their dollars toward preserving the cars of the American dream than to the disgusting institutional morass that is the current political campaign finance system.

If you are looking for the biggest reason politics has gotten so out of whack in the last twenty years, look no further than the money. Thanks to *Citizens United v. Federal Election Commission*, the 2010 Supreme Court ruling declaring that corporations are people, our campaign system is now flooded with unlimited dark money that has taken politics completely away from the average citizen and made it the play toy of only the wealthy. The person most responsible for this change? The one individual who has, since the 1990s, made it his sole goal to get rid of all barriers to unlimited political bribery?

Who else but Mitch McConnell.

Back in the simpler times of the early 2000s, the worst forms of political corruption occurred on the individual level. Mitch McConnell or some other senator would hold a fund-raising dinner where donors paid something like $2,500 for the pleasure of his company (but can you really put a value on such an exhilarating experience?). Mitch would make a quick speech, shake a few hands, scare a few babies, and the night would be over. It was corrupt and peddling influence, but it was on a somewhat transparent, smaller level.

Mitch made sure all that would dramatically change. In the early days of his political career, he actually supported campaign finance reform. As with every issue, it wasn't because of his strong political or moral belief about donations but because of his realpolitik analysis. He knew labor unions were more effective at raising cash in bulk from their members and, if given unlimited donation ability, Democrats would benefit most, so reform was needed. Fast-forward fifteen years and labor unions have lost power, limiting the ability to raise institutional Democratic money. Now Mitch sees an opening and proclaims, "Money is speech!" "Corporations are people!" "The First Amendment applies to both." The politics changed, and then, predictably, so did Mitch's principles. Rinse and repeat.

In late 1999 one of the classic Senate floor debates of all time occurred between McConnell and John McCain on this very issue. Mitch argued that there was no need for McCain and Wisconsin senator Russell Feingold's Bipartisan Campaign Reform Act because (get this) *there was no proof of corruption in politics.** I'll continue after your laughter subsides. McConnell demanded to know who McCain thought was so corrupt that they needed to be regulated. The Arizona senator was too polite to state the obvious: that McConnell was the prime example of the corruption he was trying to prevent. Finally, after McConnell kept prodding, McCain said, "I was in the Republican caucus when a certain senator stood up and said it's okay for you to vote against the tobacco bill because the tobacco companies will run ads in our favor. I yield the floor," said McCain, dropping the mic. Every senator in the chamber knew exactly what McCain was referring to and whom he was targeting. Nobody objected, and McConnell went silent.

Eventually, in 2002, the McCain-Feingold Act, as the bill is also known, passed and became the law of the land. McConnell later said that the day the bill passed was the "worst day of my political life." It is worth remembering that Mitch's political nadir was in March 2002,

---

* An absurd statement that should have gotten McConnell voted out of office at that moment.

barely a year after terrorists took more than three thousand American lives flying hijacked planes into Manhattan's Twin Towers, the Pentagon, and a Pennsylvania field. His priorities were never clearer.

McConnell set out on a mission to challenge the bill legally, and, four years later, when the Supreme Court became more conservative after Justice Sandra Day O'Connor retired from the bench and was replaced by Justice Samuel Alito, he attacked. In a 5–4 decision, *Citizens United* struck down spending limits on individual donors, corporations, and all interest groups during elections as being in violation of the First Amendment so long as they were done by outside SuperPACs. This new political action committee spending would be unregulated and mostly untraceable, and now the dominant form of campaign fund-raising. For McConnell, it was a perfect result. Now all the corporate donations could be given directly to PACs supporting him and with no spending limits. He and the rest of the GOP would have unlimited resources, and because it was done via a First Amendment argument, no piece of legislation in the future could ever change it. The court decision also had the secondary impact of opening the door to foreign election interference, as countries could funnel donations to campaigns through organizations such as the National Rifle Association, and there would be very little the government could do about it. The battle was over. Mitch won; democracy lost.

Citizens United had one of the most dramatic effects on American electoral democracy of any Supreme Court case in history. Mitch McConnell ensured for the wealthiest Americans that money is now First Amendment–protected speech, giving them the absolute freedom to hijack the political process. And they do, bombarding our political elections with their deluge of advertisements. Seen through that lens, the fact that a few choose instead to ignore politics and celebrate old Corvettes is actually quite encouraging.

Allen County

The Dollar General Takeover

In the parking lot of the Fred Hale Shopping Center on Old Gallatin Road in Scottsville are a number of fine Allen County businesses, including White Plains Barber Shop, Allen County Vapes, the Discount Tobacco Center, and H&R Block. This slightly run-down set of stores looks like your average small shopping center except for one singularly unique factor: the tall sign bearing the strip mall's name has a black-and-white drawing of a dog on its hind legs, wearing a hat and smoking a pipe. At its base is an elaborate granite gravestone marking the memorial for the original owner of the shopping center. That owner? A local dog, Miss Dynamite.

Yes, a dog once owned this property. The October 4, 1973, edition of the *Corbin-Times Tribune* explains more:

> **Wealthy Dog Dies Yesterday**
>
> Scottsville, KY (AP)—Miss Dynamite, a dog who was the legal owner of a Scottsville shopping center and had her own bank checking account, is dead at 15.
>
> The little black and white dog, an Amertoy, had traveled to many parts of the country with her owner, Fred Hale, a retired executive of a soft drink bottling company. The breed is a cross between a chihuahua and toy terrier.
>
> She had received mail from several famous personalities, including former President Lyndon B. Johnson, several governors, bandleader Lawrence Welk, and astronaut John Glenn.
>
> She had also received letters of proposals on behalf of other dogs.
>
> When her owner opened a shopping center at

> Scottsville, he filed papers making Miss Dynamite the legal owner but provided that the property would revert to him upon her death.

Forty-five years later, the monument and gravestone still stand. It reads:

MISS DYNAMITE NEVER SAW A STRANGER IN ALL HER TRAVELS. SHE ONLY STAYED AT THE BEST HOTELS AND WAS NEVER REFUSED ADMITTANCE THOUGH SIGNS READ "NO PETS ALLOWED." HER HOSTS OFTEN SAID MISS DYNAMITE HAD MORE INTELLIGENCE THAN SOME GUESTS WHOM THEY HAVE REGISTERED. MISS DYNAMITE ENJOYED HER PERSONAL BANK ACCOUNT, AND SHE "PAW SIGNED" CHECKS FOR BILLS DUE IN THE SHOPPING CENTER.

The beautiful memorial on her grave is cleaned annually though it is currently obscured by a sign promising a "Two-for-One Deal" at the vape store. I am sure she would be proud.*

Miss Dynamite's shopping center is unique not just because of her posthumous presence, but also because of what is *not* to be found there.

Unlike nearly every other square inch of rural Kentucky, there is *no* Dollar General store anywhere within sight. I have been amazed traveling around this state at how many Dollar Generals have invaded the commonwealth. They're everywhere we go, that plain yellow sign popping up on the horizon every few miles. The more isolated the place, the more Dollar Generals. The chain began right here in Scottsville with one store, operated by a local owner. But since then, it has grown like kudzu, leaving a trail of boarded-up mom-and-pop stores in its wake.

If you have been in one Dollar General store, you have been in all of them; giant, rectangular, metal buildings made of siding and steel, with whatever sale of the day is available on the sidewalk out front. Inside the one we went to in Allen County every product imaginable is available. Here we have exercise kettlebells across the aisle from Elmer's

* Proud would not, however, describe the tenant handing a rent check to a dog.

Glue-All. A pair of fuzzy, striped children's tiger slippers sits on a shelf above the dog food and below some picture frames. Vitamins, hair coloring, mini-donuts, flannel pajamas, phone chargers, Legos, leggings, frozen pizza, butterfly shrimp, and stuffed peppers. Cheap goods at low prices all in one location. Its one-stop-shopping business model clearly works.

And because it works, Dollar General is now expanding faster than any other retailer in America. The chain added nearly a thousand stores in 2019 alone and plans to continue growing over the next five years. Dollar General has created a unique business strategy: building stores in the middle of areas that are often rural and isolated and are not serviced by Walmart, Target, or any similar big-box-type retailer. The cost of the land and the building is cheap and as the only game in town, the market is open. It's worked like a charm.

Unfortunately, Dollar General's presence does not necessarily improve an area's economy. After one has moved in, the first casualty tends to be the locally owned small grocery stores. They don't stand a chance. Dollar General purchases most of its products overseas, taking advantage of cheap labor. When the company does buy within the United States, it does so in bulk from other large businesses and receives discounts that nonchain stores such as Glen's (you remember: home of the Ziploc bag full of gumdrops) in Whitley County do not. Dollar General is able to keep its prices so low they could do the limbo. The little individual stores can't hope to compete, and over time the little man is bled dry. Rural Kentucky is littered with abandoned mom-and-pop groceries and gas stations that went out of business in the last decade, often with a Dollar General right around the corner. This insatiable, predatory brand seeks to destroy all in its way.

There's more. Once Dollar General crushes the local stores, its presence hurts future innovation. Larger supermarkets such as Kroger and Walmart see the cluster of Dollar Generals in a rural, sparsely populated area and decide to avoid the fray, leaving the market entirely to the new kid in town. With more than fifteen thousand stores in forty-four states, Dollar General controls the rural city, and, as other grocery stores weaken or die off, it becomes the only food seller in the area. Now town residents have fewer options not only in where to shop for food but also in what they can buy. Sure, Dollar General stores are filled with Oreos and Ding Dongs, but they don't carry much by way of fruits and vegetables. This creates "food deserts," where fresh or healthy foods are difficult to find, if available at all. The processed Dollar General choices become the food selection of choice, and the health of the community suffers.

Dollar General left tiny Scottsville long ago, moving its headquarters to Nashville. A distribution center remains, but as we drive to it this afternoon, we see little movement. Dollar General has a folksy, old-timey name, and when it first opens, it seems like a gift to a community. However, every yellow Dollar General sign we pass represents the loss of local business ownership and profits that will immediately be shipped out of the area, hurting the local economy a little more every day.

There is no single policy that led to the Dollar General takeover, but Mitch McConnell's favored economic system certainly paved the way. His preference, and exhaustive work, on trade benefits for China and other developing nations opened the door for an influx of the very kind of cheap foreign products that Dollar General relies on to price out local stores. His opposition to overseeing the business practices of corporate behemoths ensured that the government would rarely enforce antitrust policy to protect rural America. Because Dollar General also counts on squeezing out more profits by paying low wages, and McConnell refuses to raise the minimum wage, many folks in small towns simply can't afford to shop anywhere but the local Dollar General.

The world of Miss Dynamite and the Fred Hale Shopping Center is disappearing. Mitch McConnell's vision of rural America, a Dollar General on every corner, is the new reality.

Simpson County

Criminal Justice Reform: Simpson County Style

Having eaten up thousands of miles of Kentucky road, we come to our first fork in the road on the outskirts of Franklin, in Simpson County.

Not a metaphorical fork; an actual fork. Twenty-one-feet high, made of metal and painted silver, the large sculpture is literally in the middle of nowhere. No map or GPS even registers the street it's on; to get there, you have to have a local drive you, as one did for us.

The 2018 senior welding class at Franklin-Simpson High School apparently had some jokesters in it and decided to erect its big fork sculpture here as a bit of a lark, and now it has somehow become the area's go-to tourist attraction.* When I ask why it's out this far, one local answers, "Well, that's where there was a fork in the road." Touché.

In the county's largest town of Franklin, population 8,408, we stop by the Simpson County Detention Center to see Eric Vaughn, the Simpson County jailer. Vaughn is a young man, country to the core. He looks to have a big chaw under his lip. With a thick southern accent, he speaks with confidence and authority, the stereotypical demeanor of a warden who would be a real asshole in a prison movie. I feel comfortable saying that, because he is actually the exact opposite.

As Vaughn explains it, he is a bit of a maverick in the world of correctional facilities. Frustrated with the ineffective prison system in Kentucky (one of the most overcrowded in the United States), Vaughn decided to try a new path. He was tired of seeing the same prisoners in and out repeatedly and wanted to eliminate the revolving door of recidivism by developing a program that was less punitive and more rehabilitative, and could better the community in the process.

With the help of deputies Ashley Penn and Brent Deweese, he created Second Chance Offender Rehabilitation and Education, or SCORE—Vaughn seems to take great personal pride in the catchy acronym—which is designed to allow residents to begin a path toward a more productive life while still incarcerated. (Yes, Vaughn calls all the inmates residents, in the belief that it helps validate their status as human beings and not just prisoners.) Each resident completes an MRT (moral reconation therapy) course that determines their ability to follow societal norms. Based on their performance, they attend classes to enhance their general decision-making skills, and, if they didn't

* In my day, the welding classes gave back by carving the Van Halen logo into everything they could get their hands on. Technology has clearly improved.

graduate high school, work toward a general equivalency diploma, or GED. Upon completing both, they are placed in an actual paying job with one of the various industries in the area. There they learn a skill and earn a salary they can use to help family, pay child support, or build a foundation for success when they are finally released. The participants work regular hours as a company's employee, all while still serving their time.

Donny Kendrick, a resident who is going through the SCORE program, agrees to speak with us. He has only a few minutes, as he is being promoted to the supervisory team at his job at a nearby factory today and can't be late.

"I've been locked up for a long time," he says, "this time in particular for fleeing and evading. In the past, I'd get out and go right back to the same old thing. I'd go to work for a little bit, and wouldn't hardly be making no money, and I'd just get out and just go back to what I know."

This time, he says, when he gets out, it will be different. He has learned a new skill and loves working at the factory and away from the jail. He's saved $11,000 in a bank account and tells me he is excited that he will be able to finally send money home to get presents for his children this Christmas.

Vaughn says Kendrick's story is common: the detention center has an extraordinary 87 percent success rate of ending recidivism for SCORE graduates. He believes that treating the residents with respect and dignity is a major factor in the project's success. "When I took office," he reflects, "we had to have a culture change in this building. My thought process was, to every one of my deputies, you're going to treat them like human beings. You're not going to judge them; they've already been judged. Your job is to make sure they're safe and secure, their needs are met. Because you don't ever know if it'll be your sister or your brother, or your mother or your dad that comes in. If someone else were handling them, you'd want someone to treat them the same way."

It also clearly is appreciated. I see a card on Vaughn's bookshelf, and I ask if I can open it. Inside, in addition to about two hundred signatures, it reads: "We appreciate your kindness in supporting us with a special breakfast. It's great knowing that someone is thinking of us in times like these. Thanks for everything, from your guys at the

Community Center." The card is from his residents; Vaughn has to be one of the only jailers in Kentucky getting thank-you cards from the county's locked-up criminals.

Vaughn says they had to act locally because the federal and state governments have no idea how serious the prison overcrowding situation is or how to properly handle criminal justice reform. He notes that private prisons, for which Mitch McConnell has advocated and from which he has received huge donations, are absolute disasters. The training is shoddy, and they lead to inhumane and dangerous atmospheres. "Politicians talk about all this stuff, but they don't know how it really is," he says. Then Vaughn adds, "If Mitch McConnell wants to help law enforcement and lower crime, he needs to come sit in that chair and listen. He needs to help us out, instead of us having to do this on our own."

Prisons treating their inmates as humans and moving them toward a better path. Prisoners writing to thank their jailer for how they are being treated! The nineteenth-century Russian novelist Fyodor Dostoevsky, who spent four years in a Siberian prison camp, wrote in his semiautobiographical novel *The House of the Dead; or, Prison Life in Siberia*, "The degree of civilization in a society can be judged by entering its prisons." If so, Simpson County may be Kentucky's Mesopotamia.

Russell County

Fruit of the Loom Leaves Town

Jamestown, in Russell County, is full of "lake people." By that I mean people who live for boating season to come around—they're the type of people who buy signs for their homes which read "Life is better at the lake" or "Don't bother me, I'm on lake time." It isn't so much that they love the lake as they like to talk about the lake, and if you have a lake near you, then you know exactly who I am talking about. Many congregate here in Russell County because it sits on Lake Cumberland, making Jamestown a quintessential lake town. Here you'll find the Anchor

Inn, Anchor Liquors, Bill's Boat Barn, Captain Jake's Snack Shack, and fellow Captain Hock's Boat Storage. Russell County is a lake place for lake people, and you will feel that vibe from the moment you cross the county line.

In most counties, we learned about the area by talking to average citizens, but here we decided to use a different strategy. We called ahead and asked to meet with the "leaders" of Russell County. A group was assembled to meet in the back room of a local State Farm branch, and they came in ready, with lots of bones to pick. The demographics were typical of what we'd tended to see in rural Kentucky. Most participants were white, easily over fifty years old, and many of them carried themselves in the traditional county old-guy stance: sitting straight up in their chairs, arms folded, semi-scowl on their face. At the head of the table sat the only woman present, Lou Ann Flanagan, of the Kentucky Education Association. She'd assembled the group and urged everyone to have something from the snack spread and to speak freely. We were ready to hear their issues.

Most of the complaints are common throughout the state (they hate Governor Matt Bevin, don't like the national Democrats, etc.), but there are a couple of new ones that are definitively local—one man thinks the town should lease a dock from the county to build floating cabins on the lake ("People like to float," he says)—but the experience in general is typical. Then one man in a sweater vest and a blue oxford cloth shirt pipes up.

"'Course, Fruit of the Loom shut down. Six hundred and two people working there when they shut down. You know, at one time, there were three thousand at peak."

The room all nods in agreement. A man in the corner, wearing a black captain's hat, nods. "Almost one person in each family in this county lost a job," he says.

"One of the largest manufacturing facilities that Fruit of the Loom had," another man interjects rather authoritatively. "And when NAFTA went in, they went out."

Fruit of the Loom. In south-central Kentucky, no event has been more defining than the construction, and closing down, of the four Fruit of the Loom factories all located within this sixty-mile radius. At its peak, more than eight thousand employees worked for the garment manufacturer in this tri-county area, and the factories became the predominant economic engine of local life in Russell, Green, and Taylor Counties. Then, beginning in the late nineties, they slowly and systematically disappeared. First, the Greensburg plant closed in 1995, then Campbellsville in 1998, and then Jamestown in 2014, taking with them the vitality of a region that has never regained its footing.

Longtime Russell County judge-executive Gary Robertson was at a fund-raising event at the Governor's Mansion in Frankfort the day he got the call that the Jamestown plant was pulling out.

"My stomach turned upside down," he tells me. "It was a gut-wrenching feeling, to be honest with you. They didn't give us any time to prepare, they didn't give us any heads-up. We lost all those jobs in one strike of the hammer. In three months' time, they phased out, and they were gone by the end of the year."

There had been no warning. Even though the other plants had closed years before, the Jamestown plant had actually expanded, with the city reworking its water treatment system to provide the greater water capacity the plant needed. Robertson wrote a letter to owner Warren Buffett, the celebrated business magnate and investment "Oracle of Omaha," asking for an explanation. He got no response.

The explanation, however, is simple: NAFTA, the North American Free Trade Agreement that opened up the trade relationship among the United States, Canada, and Mexico, treating our neighbors to the north and the south essentially as if they were two big states. Passed in 1994, trade barriers were all but eliminated, and these countries were able to enjoy all the benefits of the US economy but without its legal oversight on matters such as wages, pollution, and workers' rights. Companies realized quickly that relocating jobs to Mexico meant exponentially cheaper labor costs, so turning their backs on their American factories was a no-brainer. "There is no job that can't be transplanted to Mexico," labor leaders warned at the time. They were right.

The policy was a bipartisan effort of President Bill Clinton and the Republican Congress, with which he was desperate to make a deal. GOP leaders, including Senator Mitch McConnell, helped push through the bill, which was a massive win for US corporations. Mitch said at the time, "NAFTA is so obviously the right thing to do, particularly in this global economy, that I am surprised it is in trouble." He shepherded it through the turmoil, thus dooming the American textile industry in perpetuity.

However, the blinking warning lights of what was to come were there to see at the time for anyone who was looking. Kentucky Democratic senator Wendell Ford broke with Clinton and refused to support NAFTA because of the effect it would have on his home state. Stalwart Republican congressman Hal Rogers, who represented eastern Kentucky, foresaw the disaster that would come down on his constituents like a flood and sweep away their livelihoods. "NAFTA threatens jobs in eastern Kentucky," he said, "jobs we simply can't afford to lose." Rogers voted against it, and the citizens in his and other districts suffered mightily after its passage. Even though they were members of different parties, Ford and Rogers were both deeply connected with their working-class constituents, which helped them have a feel for NAFTA's likely real-world effects, something far too few members of Congress shared.

After NAFTA, Fruit of the Loom and similar manufacturing facilities were destined to leave. Driving through Russell County, you can see the impact to this day. Even though the proximity to the lake gives the county some natural advantages, the loss of industry simply cannot be replaced quickly. As with coal and tobacco, McConnell's advocacy for NAFTA was promotion of a bill destined to hurt his constituents forever. He did so without question or without a backup plan for their futures. And, as with coal and tobacco, the areas he left behind are still suffering.

The negative legacy of NAFTA is now much more widely accepted by members of both parties. Leaders as diverse as Donald Trump and Bernie Sanders have criticized it, and in 2019, Democrats joined with Trump in renegotiating its provisions. Mitch McConnell was left out of the process, for good reason. As one labor leader said of him at the time of NAFTA's approval, when it comes to protecting the American worker, the senator from Kentucky is "a lost cause."

Green County

It Won't Be the Same Again

We head west into aptly named Green County, and the moment we cross the county line, we get stuck behind a tractor. Here's the thing. I am not a patient person. So there is little that frustrates me more on the road than driving behind a tractor at a snail's pace down a two-lane country road. I understand that this isn't a problem many of you can relate to. But in Kentucky, if you are on a two-lane highway and get behind a giant tractor blocking two-thirds of the lane, life becomes hell. These traveling behemoths creep along at around six miles per hour and they are very difficult to pass. There are, psychologically, four stages of getting stuck behind a tractor: *Anger*, as you stick your head out the window to see around it, which is impossible; *Impatience*, as you realize there's no way on earth of knowing how far it's going or how long you'll be in this situation; *Questioning*, as you start eyeing your Google Maps to see the minutes being added to your arrival time; and, finally, *Resignation*, as you succumb to the conclusion that you are behind this tractor as long as he chooses you to be. It's my personal hell.

After two miles (or twenty minutes) of tractor drafting, we finally hit Greensburg, allowing me to see the 135-year-old courthouse that locals say is the oldest courthouse west of the Allegheny Mountains.* It is showing its age a bit but looks good for 135. There is very little going on around the town, so we stop at the local McDonald's and head to the "old guy" table to chat with a couple of men eating lunch. They don't seem to enjoy the interruption. One is wearing a hat that reads "Donkey" on it, and when I ask why, he says, "Because my name is Donkey." I ask Donkey where everyone in the town is and he replies, "Ain't a lot of people around. Nothing has been the same since Fruit of the Loom left here and Campbellsville. It won't be the same again. That's just how it is."

---

* See, I told you. I don't know what it is about those Allegheny Mountains.

Everything changed in Green County the day the corporate bigwig flew in from the city on a helicopter and gave the news.* Mary Huntsman Taylor, a Green County native who worked as a librarian at nearby Campbellsville University, tells us, "I was driving into work when I heard it on the radio. A guy from New York—he had a very strong accent—flew in on a helicopter and landed in one of the parking lots behind the plant. All the radio people were there, the TV stations were there, and he steps up and announces, 'I'm here to announce that we're shutting our plant here down and moving our operations to Honduras.'"

The news came as a shock to the tiny community, but some employees saw it coming. Jennifer Simpson Judd and her husband, Andy, both worked at the plant, as did Andy's mother, who had at one point been recruited to take a trip abroad. "My mother was in quality control, and they took her to Honduras along with some other people from the Greensburg plant to train people at the Honduras plant," Andy says. "And then, after they'd done that for a few months, it was 'We're closing this plant down.' Essentially, they were training people to take our jobs."

Both Andy and Jennifer were transferred from the closing Greenburg plant to a nearby plant in Taylor County, which later also shut down. Jennifer says she at least found a silver lining through the workforce retraining programs. "I feel like I was lucky and benefited a little from NAFTA," she says. "When the Taylor County factory shut down, I was seven months pregnant, and I went back and got my degree—now I'm an engineer at our local hospital."

However, most of the workers at the plant weren't so lucky. When the Green County plant shut down, the average worker was probably in his or her late thirties or forties, with a family. "Most of those people didn't think they could go to college," Mary says. "They would say they were too old to learn something new."

Fruit of the Loom was not just a job, it was a community builder. The plant paid its employees very well. Some of the factory workers at the time made salaries that would now be equivalent to sixty dollars

* Few Kentucky stories that begin with a corporate bigwig flying in on a helicopter end well.

an hour or more. The town's entire economy was so tied to Fruit of the Loom that when the plant had its annual closures for vacation, the other businesses in town scheduled off those days as well. According to Jennifer, gas stations and smaller businesses began to close. "There were people who'd go eat at the same restaurants every day, and those restaurants counted on the influx of factory workers, and suddenly those crowds weren't coming down for lunch anymore."

Green and Taylor Counties were Fruit of the Loom company counties, and when they left, recovery was nearly impossible.

No one can recall seeing Mitch McConnell come to the area at the time (Why would he? His NAFTA bill sent the factory packing), and most remember him only for his public advocacy for the bill that destroyed the local economy. "I'll be honest, I never voted for Mitch McConnell after that," Andy says.

Marion County

Will Hemp Save the Day?

We are almost to the end of the journey and I feel like I haven't talked enough about bourbon. In Kentucky, bourbon has become an important economic engine for the state, exploding worldwide over the last decade. We are the experts here, and, technically, Kentucky is the only place where a drink that calls itself bourbon is allowed to originate.* We take it seriously. We know the right lists to get on for a rare bottle of Pappy Van Winkle—that is, if we don't already have a friend who has a bottle he'll share. We have giant shelves with fifteen to twenty bottles of different bourbon in our homes and are happy to sample them with you. We love it. This isn't just some cutesy novelty we cling to.†

---

* We know there are those who don't follow this rule. We hate those people.

† Except for mint juleps. The one thing we will continually be folksy about and push on you are mint juleps during Derby season, which is a great joke to us because no Kentuckian worth his or her salt really likes those.

No place better embodies the Kentucky bourbon experience than the Maker's Mark distillery in Loretto, in Marion County. Picture what you think a bourbon distillery would look like, and Maker's Mark does. It sits on a perfectly manicured lawn accented by little bridges and barn-style wooden buildings painted black with crisp red shutters. Here you can dip your own bottle in the signature red wax that seals every Maker's Mark product, smell the frankly not-great odor of the giant fermenting vats, and buy all the Kentucky-priced bourbon you out-of-towners can handle. It's a magical place, part of the Kentucky Bourbon Trail, and thanks to the soaring demand for the product (from both America and Asia), a key stop for hundreds of thousands of tourists each year.

Kentucky is hoping the same explosion it has seen in bourbon will follow for another locally produced product. Thanks to a change to the Farm Bill in 2018, commercially produced hemp can now be grown across the United States. And Kentucky, with its perfectly suited soil, hopes to become the industry standard for the product. Bold claims have been made by public officials about the crop's viability, and Mitch McConnell has taken a victory lap around the state, telling anyone who will listen that it was his work that granted Kentucky its potential future economic miracle. Of course, he doesn't mention that he singlehandedly blocked the bill's passage for the decade prior or that he set up a system that vastly favors the large corporate farmers over our individual farmers. But hey, that's Mitch.

We make our way to Craig Lee's farm outside Lebanon to learn a little about hemp. Craig is a wild character. Even though he's never met either of us, he greets us as if we're old friends. With a strong handshake, a slap on the shoulder, and a mischievous grin, he's the kind of guy who always looks like he is up to something. He's been waiting for us out in front of his house, wearing a beat-up old button-down and tinted glasses. He laughs easily and hard with a big, hoarse, infectious laugh that usually ends in a cough. Before we can even say hello, he's talking a mile a minute. His pace is so furious that for the first twenty minutes, I can't follow his verbal barrage and have no idea what he is saying. Craig weaves a crazy, meandering tale that intersects multiple stories, including running for local magistrate, former governor Louis

B. Nunn, Kentucky marijuana advocate Gatewood Galbraith, Kentucky state senator Jimmy Higdon, cannabidiol (CBD) oil measurements, and hugging and picking Mitch McConnell up and holding him in the air.* He is animated, funny, and constantly nudging us with his elbow, as if life's a joke that he knows we share with him.

Despite his enthusiasm, Lee hasn't had a great day. He harvested an entire hemp crop this year only to discover that it clocked in at 0.89 in THC content (tetrahydrocannabinol, the main active ingredient in cannabis), which exempts it from being classified as usable hemp and, in fact, makes it a non-potent form of marijuana—a total loss for Lee. Too strong for hemp, too weak for marijuana, it is unusable. When federal agricultural officials got the measurement, by law they had to burn the entire crop. A year of work up in flames.

"I didn't know it was 0.89 until after I'd harvested it," he tells us. "So, it's all lost. I can't tell the percentage of THC as I'm growing it; I don't have a microscope." Lee would like to see the legal limit increased from 0.3 percent THC to 1 percent, as he feels then the CBD would be more potent and more attractive to the industry, which is beginning to boom. For reference, Lee explains that 8 to 10 percent THC is "getting-high"-level smokable marijuana. No one would want to smoke anything around 1 percent, he says, but it could make a world of difference to the local hemp grower.

The THC problem is just one of myriad issues currently facing small hemp farmers trying to achieve success in the new industry. Mitch McConnell wrote the new hemp laws in such a way to set up a system that helps massive corporate growers but makes it nearly impossible for local farmers to turn a profit. Whether it's the strict THC guidelines that hurt Lee (the USDA estimates 20 percent of all hemp will have to be wastefully burned for not meeting the strict requirements), or requiring that Kentucky farmers sell only to corporate middleman processors (as opposed to CBD manufacturers or to consumers directly), cutting into their profits, or creating regulatory systems that

---

* About one potential candidate for local public office, Lee says that if the woman had won, people everywhere would be "throwing up in the streets." That would have been bad.

are profitable only on a mass scale, the small farmer has almost no margin of error in place.

"Right now, it's bad for the small farmer," Craig says of the companies coming in to dominate the industry. "Right now, at this very minute, this is killing the small hemp farmer and we are just trying to get started."

Still, Lee holds out a small hope that Mitch McConnell will do right by the farmers. He says Congress, the USDA, and the DEA (Drug Enforcement Administration) are fighting about these issues, and the only person who can actually fix them so that growing hemp works for the small farmer is Kentucky's senior senator. "I can't do anything about these bureaucracies," Lee notes. "I am just a little guy. So, we take it back to Mitch McConnell and company and say, 'We need your help.' Then we just hope." I ask Lee if he is optimistic Mitch will listen, and he just shrugs. He wants to believe, but clearly knows better.

Craig tells us goodbye, hollering more hemp statistics and far-fetched stories at us as we pull away. He's great entertainment and I genuinely hate to leave.

We pull onto Woodyville Road to head home, and ten minutes later my phone rings. It's Craig. "I want to thank you guys for coming by," he says before exclaiming loudly, "and one more thing I forgot to tell you: Mitch McConnell looks like a turtle!"

Edmonson County

Telling Stories

It's a new morning in Edmonson County, where we find ourselves in tiny Brownsville, a place so small you can lap around the town in one and a half minutes and see everything there is to see. I will give you the quick tour. There is Stacy's on Main (a boutique), Kerr's Flowers & Gifts, and Berties Ice Cream (it's Bertie good, if you ask me!).*

* I have to stop letting Matt try out his footnote ideas.

Edmonson County's small size has made it tough for us to figure out what to do here. Thus far, the best lead has been a comment on a town Facebook page: "Me and Colleen just seen a huge UFO in Edmonson Co. at 6:05 am . . . Did anyone else see that shit?"

In lieu of investigating flying saucers or chatting with Stacy, Kerr, or Bertie, we called Kyle White. Kyle is the county's property valuation administrator, a position that puts him in daily contact with all types of people in the area. Kyle tell us if we want a real treat we should head over to the courthouse in the middle of town, and he will assemble a couple of locals who have some things to say.

Kyle meets and introduces us to two verified characters. The first is Johnny Vincent, a tall, elderly man with giant, meathook-size hands. He is intimidating, with his arms crossed wearing a matching black baseball cap and hooded sweatshirt. Our second guest hasn't arrived yet but has the courthouse buzzing. Secretaries and colleagues pop their heads into the office to ask, "Is Natty here yet?" and "Let me know when Natty gets here, I want to see him."

Five minutes later we hear a boisterous cacophony of excited greetings from the staff outside the office and our ballyhooed guest gingerly shuffles in. The curiously named Natty Bumppo is old, white-bearded, and frail, with a brass-handled wooden cane that he delicately rests on his inner thigh as he lowers himself into a chair opposite me. He has a spryness to him that belies his age—he wears a wide-brimmed, beige panama hat and a worn but comfortable-looking gray plaid suit with a bright-orange-and-mustard velveteen tie that matches a pocket square peeking out of his front suit pocket. He looks like Santa Claus reimagined as a character from *Guys and Dolls*, and his grin upticks at one side in a mischievous smirk, as if he knows something we don't. I have a feeling he does.

Natty's birth name is John Dean. But in the 1970s, sharing a name with the defrocked White House counsel whose riveting testimony during the Watergate hearings helped bring down the presidency of Richard Nixon wasn't exactly ideal for an attorney. "I'd walk into a courtroom," he recalls, "and the judge would say, 'John Dean, I thought you were disbarred,' or 'John Dean, I thought you were in jail.'" He eventually got tired of the mix-ups and decided to change his name legally to Natty Bumppo, the Native American protagonist in James Fenimore Cooper's five-novel series *The Leatherstocking Tales*, which he has never read.* He has no explanation for the name choice other than it "sounded good." Bumppo was at one time the county attorney here, but he wasn't well liked by the more mainstream legal community because he refused to prosecute bootleggers. "I just thought it was unconstitutional," he explains. "I thought it was a liberty people should have in all counties." So, he never charged any of them, upsetting the local authorities—in retribution, the Fiscal Court (county legislature) moved his office to a tiny broom closet beneath the stairs, which had been used to store the courthouse's Christmas decorations.

Natty says he's a registered Republican. "But that's so I have the right to vote," he clarifies. "If you're not a Republican in Edmonson County, you don't have the right to vote." He's joking. Maybe.

We ask if politics around these parts was rough back in the day, and Johnny laughs, saying, "I am telling you the truth, it was wild in town here. 'Course, we had a pool hall, and we had a restaurant and everything, and they counted the votes there at the courthouse. And I'm telling you, you didn't want to get too out of line, because there would be fistfighting, and if they wanted to win, they'd keep their absentee ballots hidden until they saw how close the election was going to be. If their man was behind, they'd start pulling all those absentees out."

Natty jumps in: "I've heard when they remodeled this old part of the courthouse, they found some more of them old absentee ballots in the cracks." Both men cackle again with laughter.

Each story dovetails into the next, as they recount a series of characters straight out of a Faulkner novel. There's Congressman Big Doc, who once got into a fistfight on the floor of Congress, and it was such a big deal, "he got his picture all the way on the front page of the Cleveland paper." And Erastus Selleng, a mail carrier who delivered mail by horseback and decided to only read one book his entire life front to

* Changing your name to a book character without reading it nearly happened to me before my wife thankfully talked me out of filing papers to become Lord Voldemort.

back: the dictionary. Bill Taters down the road had thirty fox hounds, and Junior Ashley had three daughters and named them all Carla.

To hear these men tell it, the world begins and ends at the Edmonson County line. Before we say goodbye, we thank the two for their time and tell them they were a hoot. On the way out the door, Chris shakes Johnny Vincent's hand and asks him half skeptically if all these stories we heard today were true.

He gives us a big toothy grin and says, "I wouldn't know how to tell a false one."

We return to Bowling Green, our home base for this segment of our trip. I do my radio show at a restaurant, and when it's over, the Tracker—who is in the audience, as usual—comes up to chat. He needs to do some storytelling as well. In a whispering voice, he says, "Look, Matt. My bosses are getting on me because I don't have enough video of you they can use for ads. I don't just want to tape you when you aren't looking, because that's not cool, and taping you on the radio is stupid. Can I come to your show this week, and we just set up a second where you walk to your car, and I'll ask you a bunch of questions? I will just run up to you, ask you about the wall or something and then you can go. Can we do that? Just to make them happy?" This must be the favor he'd alluded to last week, in Flemingsburg.

I love it. The Tracker has completely won me over. He is now essentially asking if I am cool working together to give Mitch McConnell the stupid footage he needs, in exchange for my personal privacy. I laugh at the absurdity of the situation and tell him, "Of course." Before I get into my car, I smile at him and say, "I'm going to get you to vote for me before this is through."

He smiles and replies, "Yeah, maybe."

Metcalfe County

"I Have the Full Ability to Own Any Weapon I Want"

We pass through Edmonton, primarily so I can get a bottle of Ski, the carbonated soda beloved in this area. Ski tastes like a tart Mountain Dew with a lot more sugar. It's hard to drink in bulk. It will make your heart beat faster than Mitch McConnell's when Elaine Chao reads him *Robert's Rules of Order* over his nightly bath. You can literally taste the calories. You can only really find it in this small area of Kentucky and Tennessee. It originated in nearby Chattanooga, a few hours south, but has been appropriated all over this region as the drink of choice. If you listen to country music, you might have heard Ski referenced in the 1990 hit "Dumas Walker" by the bluegrass-country group the Kentucky Headhunters, who won a Grammy Award for the album, *Pickin' on Nashville,* on which it appeared:

> *Let's all go down to Dumas Walker*
> *We'll have a slaw burger, fries, and a bottle of Ski*
> *Bring it on out to my baby and me.*

Reading the lyrics now, it doesn't seem like a Grammy-worthy song, but I won't say that too loudly around here. The Headhunters are from Metcalfe County and still occasionally make the trip back to play for the locals. They are huge here and play on the local radio as we come upon the town of Summer Shade. Even though it sounds like a modern retirement community, it's actually a tiny dot on the map, and is the location of Summer Shade Guns, a small cabin-style gun store. Summer Shade Guns is the type of place that would fit neatly into whatever gun store stereotype is currently in your head. It sits unassumingly next to the highway, sharing a lot with a small house and a gun range to the side, which is full of tires, a plastic deer,* and several hanging metal targets.

We walk in the shop and find owner Josh England, who looks to be

* That poor, poor plastic deer.

in his early thirties, wearing a baseball cap and camouflage T-shirt. As we talk, he keeps one eye on the news channel above. In a very rare turn of events on this trip, it's not Fox News, which seems to be on every other public television in the state.

"How can I help you boys?" he greets us unassumingly.

We tell him we don't know much about guns, and Josh says he is happy to help. He begins by telling us about the AR-15 rifle—specifically, how he believes it is misunderstood, as the *AR* doesn't stand for "assault rifle," as the current groupthink might believe. It stands for Armalite, the company that designed it. The AR-15 is semiautomatic; the AK-47, which we've all seen in a million action movies mowing down villainous enemy soldiers, can be fully automatic and was designed by a Russian general, Mikhail Kalashnikov. The difference, he explains, is that a semiautomatic fires one round (one bullet) with each pull of the trigger, while an automatic continues to spray bullets as long as the trigger is depressed. But he's quick to label neither an assault rifle.

"Any weapon on this earth can be used as an assault weapon, no matter what it is," Josh says. "A baseball bat, anything. Once you use it to assault someone, it's become an assault weapon. The government is just throwing that out there to make people that don't know much about firearms lose their minds. I have the full ability to own any weapon I want, and I agree that I should have any weapon that I want. I'm a firm believer that if I wanted to go out and buy a fully automatic BMG"—a Browning Machine Gun—"that shoots a bullet about the size of this handle here, I should have that right without having to pay a three-hundred-dollar stamp and having to wait a full year to get a background check. It's not the majority of people that buy them for purposes of murder."

It's an extreme view, but one that is more common than you think, and Josh expresses it without shame. He takes us outside to teach Eli—our twenty-two-year-old research assistant wearing a Christmas sweater who has little to no gun experience—how to load and fire a pistol at the metal targets. A couple of minutes of tutoring, and five sharp, popping blasts later, and the sight on the pistol is so accurate that he hits the target three times. It makes Eli's adrenaline surge.*

* Mental note: don't cross Eli!

One of the most interesting things about Josh is that while you'd expect him to be a Republican (because, guns), he's not. He's a registered independent. While he believes Trump is the best president in years, he also says he would have voted for Bill Clinton. He generally has good things to say about Republicans until, like many others, it comes to Mitch McConnell, whom he thinks has been in office for way too long. "Our president only gets eight years max, why do [senators] get fifty?" England asks.

It's a valid question. Thirty-six years is too long for any senator, and Mitch McConnell is a walking example of the need for term limits. But if it weren't for his length in office, England might actually like Mitch, at least when it comes to guns. McConnell has made the gun issue a central part of his campaign strategy over the years. Even though those who know him say he couldn't care less about guns, he knows his constituents do care, thus leading him to use the issue as a wedge in nearly every election. He is against nearly all gun control legislation and rarely even allows bills to be brought up for a vote. As reward, he was named the NRA's 2014 "Defender of Freedom" and has taken more than $1.2 million in donations from the group.

McConnell has repeatedly refused to advance any gun control legislation after each of our nation's many mass school shootings, making it clear time and time again that no action will be taken. Not even after the deadliest mass shooting by an individual in US history: the 2017 Las Vegas Mandalay Bay Hotel massacre in which a man fired 1,100 rounds into a country music festival, killing fifty-eight people. In the aftermath of the horrific tragedy, McConnell was asked about gun policy. He told the reporter his "priority is on tax reform." No matter the human toll, McConnell's primary concern is always reducing taxes for the rich.

While putting away his guns and saying goodbye, Josh asks about our book. We tell him it's about McConnell. He says that when it comes to Mitch, "although he's on Trump's side, he's sneaky, and I don't care for him."

Monroe County

A Wall with Respect

We had to make a quick trip back to Lexington so I could handle a few political responsibilities. Specifically, sit down and determine what the game plan would be if I ran in a primary against Amy McGrath. I had long thought about utilizing a unique strategy of daily advertising that wasn't *really* advertising. Just me . . . on camera . . . every morning . . . from a different place in the state talking directly to the voters. Because I am used to live radio, scripted readings have never felt authentic to me. But this would be different. If McGrath was going to take me off my own television show, I would make every ad into a show, airing every night with the goal of using spontaneity and candor to get attention. McGrath and McConnell could have their scripted, $1 million productions. I would run a punk rock campaign, trying to entertain and inform along the way. It was different and unusual, but, without their resources, likely my only chance.

The next morning after hosting my radio show from the Lexington studio, I met the Tracker outside. We agreed to stage him "bombarding" me with questions as I left the building for my car. I walked outside normally with my cohost Ryan Lemond and then he ran up to me in a flurry, barking, "Matt Jones! Do you think Donald Trump should be impeached?" He was surprisingly aggressive, much more so than usual, and it caught me off-guard. I couldn't help but laugh, causing Ryan to giggle, and then the Tracker to follow suit. All three of us realized how absurd this moment really was. I was staging a video for Mitch McConnell's gratification all so that the Tracker could keep his job. If we were successful, we could all go our merry ways, continuing to travel the state separately in this wasteful political farce. It was ridiculous.

I regained my composure and went back inside for take two. This time I acted distracted, and he rushed toward me, screaming, "Matt Jones! Do you think Donald Trump should be impeached?! Do you believe in *Roe v. Wade*?! Are you for the wall?!" Conventional wisdom says you are supposed to say nothing in these scenarios and act like it doesn't bother you. But I made a perturbed face to try to play it up for the camera to give him some good video. He asked the questions quickly, presumably giving insight to the issues on which Mitch thought I was most vulnerable. I got into my car, the Tracker turned off his phone, and I rolled down the window and offered to buy him lunch. He asked for a rain check (he had to return the video) and we went our merry ways. My most unlikely, budding friendship.

Afterward, Chris and I drove toward Monroe County, which sits on top of a region known as the Pennyroyal Plateau. On this overcast afternoon, we take a walk around downtown Tompkinsville and meet the sisters who co-own Family Circle Clothing and Shoes, two talkative ladies whose shop is full of browsers on this "Terrific Tuesday" sale. They welcome us and put on quite a sales pitch. Chris even bought a nice sequined scrunchie for his young daughter. He is the last of the big spenders.

The people of Tompkinsville are unabashedly Republican, and they don't mind telling you one bit. Billy Joe Williams, who owns the local body shop, is leaning against the door of his pickup truck. He is an older man, but still a bruiser, and as we speak a gigantic bonfire of brush burns behind him in a field. He has been introduced to us because we said we were looking for someone who truly loves Mitch McConnell. Not just votes for him but *loves* him. That man, locals tell us, is Billy Joe Williams.

"Mitch McConnell stands for the conservative side of things," he tells us in his rich, booming voice. "And if you're in Monroe County, you'll know that we're very conservative people, this is a very conservative county. He has been, I think, very good for the state of Kentucky, and I would be for Mitch McConnell again if he runs."

Williams says he likes that Mitch has reached the top of the Senate, and it's important to have someone with a conservative voice in that lofty perch. Like most of his party (and most in this county) he's very pro-gun and pro-life, and he thinks McConnell has been a stalwart on these issues. But without prompting, he also tells me he feels that Mitch and the party should loosen its grip a bit on immigration.

"I think the Republicans have taken a little too stern of a stand," he says thoughtfully, "because we can't line all the Hispanics up and march them back down south like we did the Cherokee Indians. You can't do the Hispanic people like that. There needs to be some kind of way to give Hispanic people who have been here for a certain time some type of legal status."

Interesting. I didn't expect that. A man who loves McConnell, is pro-Trump, yet wants to see a softer tone on immigration. People are complex. As I'm trying to process this, Billy Joe goes on to say that he still believes Donald Trump is right, and America needs the wall.

"I don't see anything else that might work," he tells me, as ashes from the bonfire float down over us like snow. "I would like to see so many miles of wall put up every year. It's not something we can just throw a trillion dollars at; it's something that's going to have to be systematic and done in an orderly fashion. You can't put a soldier every one hundred feet. I *guess* you could, but I think a wall would be much more efficient than a bunch of soldiers on the border. That doesn't look good; that's distasteful."

So: wall classy, soldiers distasteful. Okay. Williams does seem like a good man and I appreciate his empathy for the Hispanics here. Yet he has become convinced by the current political rhetoric that a wall is needed for this country's protection.

It is fascinating to me how quickly "the wall" has been elevated in the national political conversation. Until Trump, no one serious was advocating for a border wall. It was the fantasy of the extreme xenophobes on right-wing message boards. The wall is a really stupid idea and a complete waste of money. It will do almost nothing to curb illegal immigration, as the vast majority of illegal immigrants initially come here legally and just don't leave, something a wall will do nothing to prevent. McConnell knows this fact and yet continues to push the wasteful project, showcasing how barren his political conscience truly is. One of those twerps was Stephen Miller, a campaign advisor, and he, along with the Trump campaign's CEO, Steve Bannon, made the wall his signature issue. When he brought it up at rallies, the simplicity of the idea drew cheers, and it has given the president a signature issue he can rely on to excite his supporters.

When asked about his stance on immigration, McConnell is famous for pointing to his wife, Elaine Chao, and reminding everyone that he's married to a legal immigrant. That's nice. But Chao was from a wealthy Chinese family that, since her immigration to the United States when she was eight years old, has helped make Mitch McConnell tremendously wealthy. She did not face the hardship that the workers who sweat and toil in harsh conditions do on a daily basis just to help their families make their lives marginally better. Yet, Mitch will continue to cite her, and then project support for an unnecessary, wasteful wall because it plays better in today's Trump-centric GOP political environment. For Mitch, it's principle be damned. Say whatever you want about Hispanic laborers; we have judges to confirm.

Barren County

"If There Is a Heartbeat, There Is Life"

I have made the drive south on I-65 between Louisville and Nashville approximately five hundred times and every time I have passed, and been amused, by the sign for Dinosaur World, located, appropriately enough, in Barren County's Cave City. At exit 53 (once voted Best Interstate Exit by *Southern Living* magazine, an award whose qualifications I would love to know), a giant, orange-striped Tyrannosaurus rex stares directly into your eyes as you go by. I have often thought to myself, "Why would anyone stop there?" Today I decided to find out.

Dinosaur World itself is a park with more than a hundred fiberglass, steel, and concrete dinosaurs planted along a trail to resemble a real-life Jurassic Park. I am sure if you have kids, are a Jeff Goldblum fanatic, or are on mushrooms, it's a tremendous place to visit.* All the dinosaurs are of the weathered pastel variety, and as you pass by, you can smack their hollowed-out metal bodies for fun. Random dinosaur roars thunder in the background, and most of the trash has been cleaned up. It's like a *Mystery Science Theater 3000* movie come to life but in the form

* I am currently all three.

of an amusement park with some added chipped paint. Perfectly fine, but I decided it wouldn't be the best place to ask around about Mitch McConnell (dinosaurs stick up for their own kind), so we head down the road to Glasgow, to visit my good friend Judge Gabe Pendleton.

I know Glasgow well, thanks to Judge Gabe. Every year, I play in the Glasgow Member-Guest Golf Tournament and have gotten into fights during the tournament only twice in the last five years.* Barren County is a fairly Republican area, where ultraconservative religious values are the norm, and that is why we decided to speak to Bridget Kehrt Groce, a radio personality for Christian Family Radio in Glasgow. Groce's station provides area listeners with round-the-clock faith-based programming and prior to that, she was the former executive director of Crossroads Life Center, a pregnancy resource center that encourages pro-life ideals.

For Groce, the abortion issue is her most important priority. "If I say I'm pro-life, that means I'm pro-*life*," she says. "It doesn't mean I'm pro-life because you make the decisions I want you to. I seek out people that I know are very pro-abortion, meaning, 'I want a woman to be able to have an abortion, it's her body, it's her right.' And I pursue them, and I say, 'Even though I disagree on the outcome, I'd love to have some educated discussion with you, because I want to know why you stand on this issue where you do.'"

Groce is more cheerful than the usual pro-life advocate you see in the media. She admits that trying to convince women that abortion is not the best option for them is her number one goal. Her pro-life stance is influenced heavily by her faith, and she sees herself as a resource she can offer to women struggling with a tough decision.

"My faith is invigorating, it's inspiring," she says. "In a crisis pregnancy center, you have women who don't feel supported for whatever

* One time Matt fought a doctor and once a banker. One was about college basketball and another was about whether a golf ball was out of bounds. This is also the part of the state where that one doctor attacked his neighbor Rand Paul over mulch. Something about the professionals in this area causes them to be quite testy over insignificant things.

reason—they're in a critical cycle—and it was invigorating for me to be able to step in."

Toi Dixon Carter, a stay-at-home mother with eight children, six of which are fostered or adopted, also lives in Barren County. She is similarly strongly pro-life, but for a different reason. "I take the stance that, scientifically, if there is a heartbeat, there is life," she explains. "I also hold the stance that taking life, no matter what the reason, is never the first option. Experience-wise, I can say that all of my children whose parents chose life, in even crappy scenarios, are still glad to be alive."

For Carter, religion is only part of the reason why her pro-life beliefs are so strong. "I think if you would have asked me when I was fifteen, I would have said religion and science were equal in my mind," she says. "However, asking me today, I'd say the science behind it is clear enough that, religion put aside, it would not matter."

Carter says she doesn't agree with the current marketing of the term "pro-choice." "I think there's good intention in it," she explains, "and I have heard them say to me, 'I don't want them to take the right away from a woman, I want her to be able to choose.' I have respect for that statement, but we're discussing a situation where there's another individual involved."

This is the question these women and many in the pro-life movement in general focus on. What is life, and when does it begin? For those who dedicate their existence to the pro-life cause, the answer is absolute and not debatable.

Mitch McConnell's position on abortion has flipped multiple times based on the prevailing political winds of the day. He began his career in Jefferson County as a strong pro-choice advocate, actively seeking the support of pro-choice groups in his first county campaign, and remained pro-choice throughout his time in office in the county. When he decided to run for Senate, however, he read the political tea leaves of the state and flipped his stance, relying on the fact that few would know his prior beliefs. But the moment he took on the mantle of the pro-life cause, he went all in, writing in a *Louisville Courier-Journal* op-ed that "the sanctity of life is under attack" and urging his Senate colleagues to "join me in sending a clear message that our country respects and values life." His interest in the abortion issue is solely as a political weapon, attacking any candidate who is pro-choice, no matter where they fall on the spectrum, as being immoral and having no respect for human life. He has made abortion a central issue in nearly every campaign—never addressing, needless to say, the audacity of the fact that he, like Donald Trump, held a different opinion until politics made his personal convictions untenable.

I am firmly convinced that the current stalemate of America's abortion debate is exactly how Mitch McConnell wants it to be. He knows the Supreme Court, even with its current conservative majority, is unlikely to overturn *Roe v. Wade.* (I believe Chief Justice John Roberts and the newest justice, Brett Kavanaugh, will limit *Roe* but not overturn it. The reason why is a topic for another day.) And I don't believe Mitch McConnell wants the court to reverse *Roe.* Three in four Americans favor it being upheld, and if *Roe* were ever overturned, Republicans would face a massive political backlash, especially in swing states where the pro-choice position remains popular. Instead, he loves wielding it as a red-meat campaign issue to rally the troops and get out the vote, particularly in his home state. Even though the current decision has been in place for nearly fifty years, and many GOP-appointed Supreme Court justices have had a chance to strike it down, it remains settled law. It's a perfect McConnell scenario. He can use abortion as a political weapon but suffer none of the consequences of the policy proposals he advocates. The cynical Mitch couldn't ask for a better result.

For many Kentuckians, abortion is the most important issue in determining their role. Unlike McConnell, most of the pro-life voters in this state don't come to their position through political strategizing, but through their own moral convictions. Even though there is only one operating abortion clinic in the entire state of Kentucky, those convictions drive their voting record. The fervor in the abortion rights debate, especially in Kentucky, is on their side. McConnell knows it, and he is glad to exploit it.

That fact alone makes defeating him very difficult.

Washington County

"They Portray Us as Baby Killers. . . . How Ignorant Is That?"

What if I told you that in the very same county where Jacob Beam, great-grandfather of Jim Beam, sold his very first bottle of bourbon, you can't go into a store and buy one in his honor? Well, it's true. Washington County, unofficially called "the doughnut hole of the Bourbon Trail," is one of Kentucky's thirty-eight remaining dry counties, a phenomenon that must seem bizarre to most Americans but is common here. Eight states still have such laws on the books, but really only four—Kentucky, Arkansas, Oklahoma, and Tennessee—have multiple locations where alcohol is banned. The Bluegrass State tops the list, with more counties here prohibiting the sale of alcohol than any other state.*

Not only is Washington County dry, it also has a unique geographic religious divide. Ask anyone around here, and he or she will tell you the same thing: Catholics live in the southern and western parts of the county, while Baptists and Protestants have all the rest.† It isn't a hard-and-fast rule, but it's just how it has worked out. Houses, schools, and businesses have developed in this divide, and even the local funeral homes take their sides, with one serving predominantly Catholic families, while the other handles Baptist services. One local man assures us, "We do all still go to each other's funerals, of course." That's good. Unity in death.

But neither alcohol nor denomination is the true dividing line in Washington County. For many, it's abortion—and *that's* a line much tougher to cross. In a county with at least forty-seven churches, and the number of registered Democrats just edging out their Republican neighbors, this single issue is the overriding factor that keeps Washington County voters pulling the lever for Mitch McConnell.

---

* The irony, of course, is that the kind of place that bans alcohol is the exact type of place where you most need a drink.

† Guilt, however, is countywide.

"How can you be a one-issue voter in 2019?" Julia Spalding, the president of Washington County's Democratic Women's Club, says in frustration. "They fail to take into consideration the totality of what goes on in our world. We have a large number of farmers and people who are *really* hurting, and they continue to vote against their best interests."

Spalding adds that several members of the club have come to her upset after folks in their own county took personal shots at them based on their pro-choice beliefs. "They portray us as baby killers, or whatever, because of our stance on a woman's right to choose," she says. "How ignorant is that?"

Spalding, though, makes it clear that no one has had the audacity to say such a thing to her, and if they did she knows how she would handle it. "People know better than to come to me with words like that, or at least I hope they do. We would have a really good conversation."

It's a conversation that unfortunately seems to be occurring more often. The "baby killer" phenomenon has grown in recent years, with the phrase used often in the state against anyone who claims to be pro-choice.

During the 2019 governor's race, the phrase was weaponized often against Attorney General Andy Beshear. It is used because it works. Pro-life Republicans know that regardless of their other sins, being pro-life is the great cleansing that washes away all the bad things they do.

Spalding thinks that many blindly faithful pro-lifers adopt a hard-line position without considering the issue fully. "I don't know a person on earth who is 'for' abortion. No one wants that," she says. "What we *are* for is a woman's right to choose. You don't get to choose what a woman does in the privacy of her home or what is between a woman and her God."

Spalding has strong feelings about Mitch McConnell, as you might imagine. "I think a lot of people don't like him. He comes across as a Grinch at the highest level—just a mean man, you know? But they feel, for some reason, he does an incredible job. I just don't get it. I've heard people say, 'I don't like Mitch, but he brings home the bacon.' I just don't know what that bacon has been for us."

I find the abortion issue complex morally, and on a personal level I struggle with my beliefs. But on a policy level, the conclusion is easier for me. I have no role to play in the determination of a woman's medical and personal decision on how to deal with her own body. Abortion is a difficult issue, but one I believe is best left to a woman, her doctor, and her God. They don't need my input.

Such a position is the minority, however, in this state. I have to ask myself, Am I ready to have good Christians—the ones I grew up with, the ones who listen to me on the radio, the ones I even went to church with—watch me be labeled, or worse, potentially label me themselves, a baby killer? Because, despite the fact that his moral convictions are based solely on which side will ensure him power, Mitch will make sure to demonize me and distort my genuinely difficult moral quandary for all Kentuckians into a simple statement.

Matt Jones: *baby killer*. If I run against him, Mitch McConnell will repeat the phrase so often he will ensure that for many the label will always apply to me.

Cumberland County

"You Almost Aren't a Real Person"

It's a quiet Sunday as we make our drive toward Cumberland County. Shells of old barns sit out in fields like forgotten elephant skeletons, beams exposed but wood panels long gone. Along the road sits a billboard that reads, in all capital letters, "YOU NEED JESUS." A local antique shop called Charlie's Treasures 'n' Stuff quantifies itself in the practical and expectation-managing slogan "Not everything's a treasure."

Burkesville, the county's largest town, is nearly completely deserted on this Lord's Day—the barbershop, hair salon, flower shop, and county courthouse sit darkened and desolate in the middle of town, and I look around for signs of life, seeing almost none.

Then I look up.

Overlooking the town is a towering, worn-down resort hotel hanging on the edge of a cliff. From any spot in this community, it would be hard not to notice the huge one-and-a-half-story letters spelling out its name: "Alpine Wotel."

Surely that's a mistake. I assume they mean the "Alpine *M*otel." Maybe some punk kids went up there and flipped the letter. Regardless, we have to go find out, so we head up the mountain's winding roads to check it out.

It's the Alpine Wotel, all right, and it's from a bygone generation. The resort was built in 1951 as a pit stop for motorists heading to or from Chicago, Cincinnati, or Indianapolis. At that time, Kentucky Route 61 was the lone north/south road for the journey in this part of Kentucky and with no hotels in the area except the Alpine, a business was born. It looks as if it might have been swank back in the day, but roughly seventy years later, things have changed.

The sign out front reads "Let Our Altitude Change Your Attitude," but the moldy exterior projects the vibe of "Screw it, let's get out of here." And although it looks abandoned, the half-inflated green alien balloon in the window of the gift shop suggests someone has been here recently. The door is unlocked, so we slowly creep past a hallway vending machine selling only two items (C3, which is a box of raisins,* or B1, microwaveable popcorn). The place appears deserted—and maybe haunted—until a cook appears from the restaurant. Her frown never leaves as she, without speaking or even nodding, points us toward the main office. Shocked this place is actually a functioning hotel, we drift toward the entrance and bump into this sign hanging outside the door:

CAUTION! THIS RESORT IS
POLITICALLY INCORRECT. WE SAY

1. Merry Christmas
2. Respect our men in blue
3. Honor our veterans
4. God bless America

* I can't imagine how old these raisins are, but if the dollar-bill slot wasn't broken, I was willing to discover.

5. Free speech forever
6. Profiling makes sense
7. Etc-etc-etc-etc-etc.

Yeah, you read number six right. I had the same thought. Tiptoeing inside what could be the setting for the opening scene of a bad horror movie, we find a friendly older couple in their seventies, Bill and Lynn Bost, who own what used to be the Alpine Motel. The Bosts, originally from Fort Lauderdale, fell in love with the place on a visit and when they heard it was for sale, they jumped at the opportunity to leave their lives as Florida retirees and move to Burkesville. They changed the sign from "Motel" to "Wotel" to get attention (I guess that worked), and now they are here. I ask them about the off-putting door sign.

"We are Trump fans," Lynn says bluntly.*

Well, then. I mention number six and inquire if they think the profiling line might be offensive to some who might be here to stay the night. Seems a bit *wacist* if you ask me.

"It means I don't want anyone up here who's a drunk or whatever," Bill tells me from behind the counter while messing with multiple stacks of casino chips he says are his "accounting system." I note that "drunks" aren't usually a profiled class and minority ethnic groups might feel he is taking a direct shot at them.

"They might think that. But if you were in a different generation, maybe you wouldn't think that's what it means," he says, dismissing my point. Well, then, I hope only seventy-year-olds visit.

We leave the Wotel before he profiles us and head off to see the rest of Cumberland County. It's the home of Judge David Williams, the former Republican Kentucky State Senate president for twelve years. Williams's story is fascinating. For more than a decade, he was the most powerful Republican in Kentucky not named Mitch McConnell, holding the same job Mitch does, only on the state level. Working primarily with Democratic governors and a Democratic majority House,

* One of the most eye-opening things about this trip has been how many people say offensive things and then very self-awaredly point to themselves and just say, tongue-in-cheek, "Trump fan," as if to say "*Hey, what're ya gonna do?*"

Williams had the reputation of a feared, hard-nosed political figure. His nickname was "the Bully of Burkesville," for his refusal to budge while pursuing his agenda. A writer for the Louisville alternative paper *LEO Weekly* once described him as "Napoleonic," "apoplectic," and "hell-bent for revenge" against his political adversaries.* I will be more blunt. He had the reputation of being an asshole.

But now things are different. After running for governor and losing handily, Williams stepped down from his state senate seat. He accepted an appointment as a local judge in Cumberland County and set about changing his life. He reaffirmed his religious faith, becoming involved more significantly in his local church. What's more, according to Williams, he also found himself "unexpectedly single" after his longtime marriage ended, and his day-to-day existence became quieter and more solitary. He was no longer the big-shot state lawmaker. He was just David from Burkesville.

Williams tells me that getting out of the political arena was humbling. "When I was in office, people would say to me, 'Who are you? You are Senator Williams.' The challenge was that what you are becomes who you are. All of a sudden, all your jokes are funny. Everything you say is smart. You don't ever drive or do anything on your own. You almost aren't a real person. My life was not normal."

Williams says that while his postpolitical life is more solitary and sometimes lonelier, it is a more fulfilling existence. He realizes the Kentucky Senate, where he had once been such a central figure, goes on without him, noting, "The graveyards are full of indispensable people." Listening to him talk, I sense there are times he misses the action of his old duties in Frankfort, but he also realizes that the job had turned him into a person he did not want to become and does not want to be again.

Leading the Kentucky State Senate had been Williams's entire purpose, and in so doing, his personal relationships and friendships suffered. He warns me that if I run, the same will happen to me. It already has. During this decision-making process, my personal relationships

* Fun fact: that *LEO* article was written by Mark Nicholas, who now runs Amy McGrath's campaign. You may remember that he worked behind the scenes to get Matt fired from the television show. Hypocrisy runs amok.

have suffered, so I can only imagine what would happen if I actually get in the race.

Williams says that while in office, he became almost entirely a political being. It's a description often used for Mitch McConnell, and I ask Williams about the man he worked with extensively during his time as Senate president. His description of Mitch is similar to the one he used for himself.

"Mitch has no other life besides politics. He is completely dedicated to his political life. If you are willing to do that, to have it be your whole life, then you can do it and be very successful. But soon you can't have your normal life from before. No church, friends, sports, or even really time with your children. You don't appear as a normal person. Mitch is good with that. Not everyone else can be."

Clinton County

Guys Around Here Just Vote Republican

Clinton County is the most isolated of all the Kentucky counties; however, the county seat of Albany has just about everything a person could ask for. Lil Joe's Deli & Hand Dipped Ice Cream serves up a $5.25 special that includes a pepper-turkey sandwich, chips, and a drink.* The Klassic Shop keeps the trendy ladies of the county up with all the latest styles.† And Homer Lowhorn Bait Shop will get you outfitted for a day out on Dale Hollow Lake before dinner at King of Kings Pizza, where their people and the dough are, as their sign reads, "Alive and Lifted Up."

Albany also has a whole lot of churches, and we're driving the streets on this Sunday afternoon, looking for an evening service to attend. We are referred to one of the largest in the county, right off the highway

* Prices in Kentucky are already cheap, but in the rural areas, they are insane. I have yet to spend more than $10 on any meal, and as our waistlines can attest, we have eaten well.

† Namely through items such as koats, kardigans, and kapri pants.

outside town. As we drive up, we see people gathering at the impressive recreation center next door and decide to walk inside to take a look.

There is a flurry of movement everywhere: a dozen women are in a kitchen, busily putting supplies together; kids, still in their church clothes, are sprinting around playing a perpetual game of tag; and two men stand alone, chatting inside the door, doing nothing but observing while the women and children work and play. We introduce ourselves and ask about all the fuss, and they tell us the church is preparing to deliver two thousand meals to needy people around Clinton, an impressive accomplishment in a county this small.

I commend them on their community service and ask more about their denomination and church. It's a polite question born out of a sincere desire to see if the church would be worth visiting later in the evening. It's clear, however, they don't want us. One man says, "Before we go any further, do you have any credentials?" I note that I don't carry radio credentials around the state, and I tell him about this book and our visit to every county. He looks at me skeptically, so I try to break the ice by asking if we would be welcome at the evening service tonight.

He rolls his eyes and says sarcastically, "Oh, sure. Yeah, why don't you do that?"*

Knowing when we aren't wanted, we exit and head out of town on Wolf River Dock Road. For the first time on our trip, I'm left with a sour taste in my mouth, but it's forgotten when I look up and see an intriguing sight. Just off the road, back about a hundred yards, sits a house surrounded by scrap metal: old, giant tractor hubcaps, empty hot water heaters, broken-down ancient automobiles, and two hundred or so bags of walnuts, all described with a handwritten "Junk" sign along the road.

Two men walk out of the faded wooden home to greet us. One is much older, white haired, rail thin, wind worn, and wearing an old button-down shirt. He smokes a long cigarette that he holds gingerly between his fingers. Alongside him is a younger fella with a scraggly beard and an insulated brown Carhartt jumpsuit. They welcome us

* I guess that night's sermon was on the book of Exodus.

sociably (much more so than the people at the church, even though we're strangers just intruding onto their land), and we ask about the sign.

"We just tinker with things here," the unshaven young man tells me.

"*I* tinker with 'em," the old man interrupts.

"He tinkers," repeats the younger man. "We just do what we can to get by. I just help him do whatever he wants me to do; that's pretty much what I do, anyway."

The young man is Jordan, and he was born and raised right up the road here in Clinton County. He says the two of them do whatever they can to make money. Their current strategy involves using the nine hundred pounds of walnuts that they have found in the area. Once they hull them, they'll take the nuts to the Mennonite man up the road who, they say, pays $15 for every hundred pounds of hulled walnuts they deliver. It seems like awfully hard work for such a small payoff, but the two men just shrug; it's what they do to get by.

Jordan tells me he is on the Passport Health plan, a benefit he received thanks to the Affordable Care Act. "About a year ago," he recounts, "I wound up in the hospital, pretty bad sick, and they just signed me up at the doctor's office, because they know how I live. I'm not one of those people who cares about money, as long as I'm getting by." I ask if he's glad to have insurance. "Lord, yes," he says, grinning.

It's clear that Jordan is a bit of a rascal. He is charming in a devilish way, but then he begins to disclose his life story. He kicks the dirt and says nonchalantly that he's been in jail thirty-four times—yes, thirty-four times, and he's only twenty-nine—but nothing drug related. He's been off drugs for a long time and acts as if his arrest record isn't odd at all.

I ask Jordan if, like most of the county, he's a Republican. "Lord, yes," he replies. "We're all Republican." He knows a few Democrats, but they're not from here. He hunkers down to level with us. "You've got to think about the Republican views on things, guys. I mean, around here we fish and hunt for a living, and we work hard to take care of ourselves and each other, too. You know, Democrats a lot of times are hollering about wanting to take our guns and this and that. We kill a lot of our food. As far as that goes, it seems like Republicans lean more toward the farming communities and things like that."

Jordan admits he's voted for a Democrat before, but he can't remember which one. He also wants to make clear to me that there are some Republicans he doesn't like, and he won't vote for just any of them. "It's kinda like pickup trucks and women, guys: there's good and bad of all of 'em."

Jordan says he thinks he has voted for Mitch McConnell in the past but doesn't recall why or when. However, he is much more confident about the president. He voted for Donald Trump solely because he didn't like Hillary Clinton. It's a common refrain around the state: "I voted for Trump just because I couldn't vote for Hillary." While Trump has some strong admirers, many of his voters aren't enamored with him as much as they were anti-Hillary. She has almost no fans in this area. But, I ask why, if Jordan likes his Obamacare insurance, he votes for people trying to take it away, and he says he didn't know that's what Trump and McConnell were trying to do.

Jordan is just Republican because, as he says, that's what "guys around here do." Most men in these parts, they own guns, they drive trucks, they love Jesus, they help their neighbor, and they vote Republican. It's just how it is. Being a Democrat, well, honestly, it's looked at as a little bit strange, like being weak or too sensitive. Being a Republican is being a man. The fact that the Republican Party wants to take away their health care, gives tax cuts to the corporations taking their jobs, and is made up of millionaire politicians who don't care about them—

Well, boys, everything ain't perfect.

Adair County

"I Don't Drink, Smoke, or Chew, but How Is It Between Me and You?"

Hardscratch General Store has everything. Its selection is diverse, bringing together shoppers with needs ranging from candles, to sunglasses, to homemade Reese's peanut butter cake. The citizens of the tiny town stop in and chat beneath antiquated tin signs endorsing Red Man chewing tobacco or touting that this is "John Deere Country."*

As I roam the store, I receive a phone call. One of my advisors says excitedly, "Three national shows are vying to have you announce you are running on their air." I smile and remind the advisor that I am not yet running, and if I do, I will do the launch in Kentucky to differentiate myself from Amy McGrath, who made the mistake (in my opinion) of announcing on MSNBC's *Morning Joe* and not in the Bluegrass State. The advisor on the other end says, "Well, sure, but you have to go on these shows too." I say I will deal with that when the time comes and hang up to browse the unbelievable selection of Vienna sausages.

Since Clinton County's largest church left us feeling unwelcome, we were still searching in Adair County for our church spot. You can't do a book on Kentucky without attending a church service, and with most services beginning between six and seven o'clock, we are running out of time. We decide to stop at whatever church we see next on these country roads, and that is Cavalry Temple Church. We are about twenty minutes late, but we slip into our chairs just as Pastor Troy McWhorter's sermon begins. I can immediately see Troy is a fiery one, and the fact that he still has his blazer on means he is just getting going.

The sanctuary is bright, welcoming, and surprisingly full of people on this cold night. A drum set and some guitars are set up to the right of the pulpit for the music we have missed; Bibles sit at the end of each row, and the congregation is made up of everyone from old farmers to young couples with children. A man walks over to our seats and whispers below the preacher's tones, "Welcome! We are so glad you are here!" It's instantly comforting, and a 180-degree change from the response in Clinton County.†

The pastor has projected a Bible verse onto the large screen behind him: a passage from Matthew 5:22 from the New Testament, which reads: "But I tell you that anyone who is angry with a brother or sister will be subject to judgment."

---

* Hillary did not win the popular vote in John Deere Country.

† And we didn't even have to present our credentials!

Troy, with authority, belts out, "I tell you that the worst thing that can happen is people who take on the mantle of Christianity but don't act like Christians!" The congregation answers out loud. This is one of those churches where the sermon is actually a dialogue between the pastor and the worshipers. When the pastor makes a point, he expects the parishioners to respond, and if they don't, he will make it again. These calls range from the outspoken "Praise thy name!" to the more casual and encouraging "C'mon, now," to the ubiquitous *"Amen!"* The declarations surround us, and everyone participates. I have been around this kind of preaching and this kind of service my entire life, so I am used to it.

Our twenty-two-year-old assistant Eli is from Louisville, and, truthfully, he looks a little freaked. This kind of service is almost an art form, as the rhythmic back-and-forth between preacher and congregation creates a mesmerizing singsong effect that resembles a performance. It's a unique way of delivering a religious message, one seen only in rural southern or African American churches.

McWhorter's Kentucky accent shines through most distinctly as he reads a Bible verse saying that God (*"Gawwwwwwhd"*) will judge those of us who project out anger toward others. I try not to let the fact that he is yelling this message distract from the point. Christianity is about loving thy neighbor and feeling no anger toward your fellow man. I think how different this is from the actions of Donald Trump, but my goal is to not let the disappointment I feel when Christians defend his actions ruin the moment. McWhorter's words are rambling and energetic, but his message is clear: you can claim to follow all the biblical rules and be a good person all you want, but if you aren't kind to others, none of it matters. He sums it up with perfect Kentucky flair:

"I don't drink, smoke, or chew, but how is it between me and you?"

That phrase has now entered my regular vernacular.* As Troy continues, his voice grows more spirited, his hands flailing wildly, and when he whips off his suit coat and hands it to a congregation member sitting off to the side, it's clear the message is coming to its crescendo.

"Sure, you can be *surface-level good,*" he proclaims, "but what's

* I wish Matt had decided this before his Chuck Schumer meeting.

gonna happen when the rubber meets the road and times are hard? Will you be good then?!?"

McWhorter has the churchgoers in the palms of his hands, and they begin calling back loudly and multiple times. He steps back, and like a truly great performer (I don't mean this as an insult, for a great sermon or speech is actually a performance), he lets the moment sit and soaks it in.*

McWhorter transitions to a different part of the message, and with forty-five minutes of preaching taken in and many miles still to go, we decide to slip out. I thank those around us, all of whom make it a point to invite us to return, and we head out the back door into the chilly night. As the doors of the church close slowly behind us, and McWhorter's hoarse voice fades, I realize that what I came to see in Adair County had been affirmed. My dismay at the fact that public religious hypocrites who take on the mantle of Christianity but act against most of its teachings continue to be celebrated by national religious leaders remains. But on the ground, in actual real life, things are still as I remembered. People welcome strangers with open arms, preach about the need to treat your fellow man with respect, and come together as a community to perform acts greater than themselves. Not all of us Christians are Jerry Falwell Jr., and sometimes we need to be reminded of that.

---

* As an aside, my favorite point in the sermon was when McWhorter mentioned they were about to put more outdoor lights in the parking lot, to which a blond woman with a Bible in her lap three rows in front of me exclaimed loudly (and without accompaniment)—and with more enthusiasm than any response all night—"*Praise God!*" It was her highlight of the sermon and seemingly the answer to her specific prayer.

Taylor County

To Grandma's House We Go

I'm dreading our final stop in this region of the state. Not because I have anything against Campbellsville. I actually really like the place. Like Jamestown and Greensburg, it's a quiet town that hasn't quite fully recovered from the departure of Fruit of the Loom, which employed 20 percent of the county. We see few people downtown, but that is mostly because all the businesses have moved out to the highway. I do an annual radio show out there at Mr. Gatti's Pizza that always draws a big crowd of friendly folks excited about the combination of UK sports opinions and the half-price lunchtime pizza buffet.*

My trepidation about this trip to Campbellsville is solely personal. As I entered the final couple of weeks before making my Senate decision, I knew it was important I go to Taylor County. As a child, I spent a good amount of time here visiting my paternal grandmother. My mom, the wonderful person that she is, made sure I stayed in touch, driving me across the state to see her. Even though I haven't been there in at least twenty-five years, I can retrace the path by memory, and do so on this day.

As I made the winding turns to Ray Street, through the back of a low-income housing community where my grandmother lived for a number of years, I noticed it looked the same as it did in 1988; the same small housing unit next to identical replicas of it, each with a shared backyard and an abandoned lot across the street. Someone else lives in the unit now, so I discreetly walk toward the back and see a clothesline with three T-shirts hanging out to dry and a broken-down basketball hoop hanging by a thread against the wall. My grandma had a small hoop back here for me. I wonder if it's the same one.

Growing up, I enjoyed visiting my grandma. She was a sweet lady

* Matt's show *is* better with a pizza buffet.

who let me do things I wasn't allowed to do at home. My most vivid memory is watching professional wrestling with her, huddled around the TV for *WCW Saturday Night*, both of us seemingly blissfully unaware that the matches we found so thrilling were all fake. She loved Sting, Lex Luger, and the good guys. I loved Ric Flair, the Four Horsemen, and the bad guys. It was always a happy time.

My memories of my father aren't nearly as positive. I lost contact with him at a young age. My parents divorced when I was five. He visited sporadically over the next few years, and I spent a few days here and there with him and his new wife in Clay City, Kentucky. I knew little about his life except that he was once an attorney. He wasn't really a father in any sense of the word; he was a visitor whose presence neither added to, nor subtracted from, my daily life. If he was there, fine. If he wasn't, that was fine too.

Then one day he called to say he was moving out of the country, and he would talk to me when he could. He didn't try contacting me again for the next ten years. Once, when I was in college, he somehow got my dorm phone number and called me on a Friday night. He was in Lexington and wanted to meet up the next day to reconnect after a decade gone. I told him I wasn't really interested in seeing him at this time, especially after having been gone without so much as even a call for so long. He proceeded to curse me out and ask if I was on drugs. I hung up on him. Ten years later, he wrote me once on Facebook, asking if there was ever a way we could reconnect. I didn't respond. It wasn't out of anger; I truly hold no animosity toward him. But at this point, he is a stranger, and bringing that baggage into my world isn't of interest to me, no matter his intentions.

However, if I choose to run for office, his presence will no longer be tucked away in my memory. After the divorce, my father spent some time in prison. One night, while driving drunk through rural Kentucky, he lost control of his car and hit two men changing a tire on the side of the road, killing them both. Growing up, I knew little of the incident. I knew it happened, and I knew he was in jail, but the gravity of the situation never really weighed upon me. My mother protected me and made sure my life was normal and not disrupted. By this time, my stepfather had taken over the role of father, and so my dad being in jail just meant that I saw him even less than before. It was just another disappointment in a long line of them. Just my father being my father.

That is how my memory of him has remained. His presence in my life has been peripheral, part of my story, but not of true consequence. His only lasting impact was on my decision to go out of state for law school after I learned from a friend that they studied a Kentucky Supreme Court opinion about my father's case in an ethics class at UK Law School. But everything will change if I run for office. I have already had a couple of media members ask me off the record about his story, and there is no doubt that I will be saddled with his baggage if I choose to run against McConnell. Mitch is vicious, and any opening will be exploited in the pursuit of victory. At best, I will have to deal with multiple stories of his transgressions, which could influence the way people view me. At worst, the sins of the father I barely knew will be visited upon the son, and my life will never be the same.

I think of this legacy as I walk around outside my grandmother's house. She died a few years back at the age of ninety-nine—coincidentally, while I was in Washington preparing for my meeting with the DCCC about a potential congressional run. I was scheduled to be out of town during her funeral and decided not to change my arrangements—solely so I wouldn't have to see my dad. It was a painful decision, but one I thought best and one I hoped she would understand.

I drive out to visit my aunt Sue, a wonderful woman who is the only person on my dad's side of the family with whom I remain in contact. She gives me a big hug and tears up at the sight of me. I ask her about some of the details about my dad's current state in life, not so much because I want to know but because I need to.

Aunt Sue obliges. He lives on the West Coast with a new wife, and she says he is doing well. I guess I am glad to hear it. She says she wishes my father and I could reconnect but understands if we don't. I don't respond but just tell her that I love her and how thankful I am for the kindness she has shown to my mother and me my entire life. I leave and tell her she will always be in my heart.

I don't know my father beyond a handful of random characteristics. He was very intelligent, a star debater, loved to read, and liked soul singer Sam Cooke. He also had a bad temper, was prone to self-destructive behavior, and abandoned his son without remorse. As with everyone, I guess there is good and bad.

CHAPTER 10

The Decision

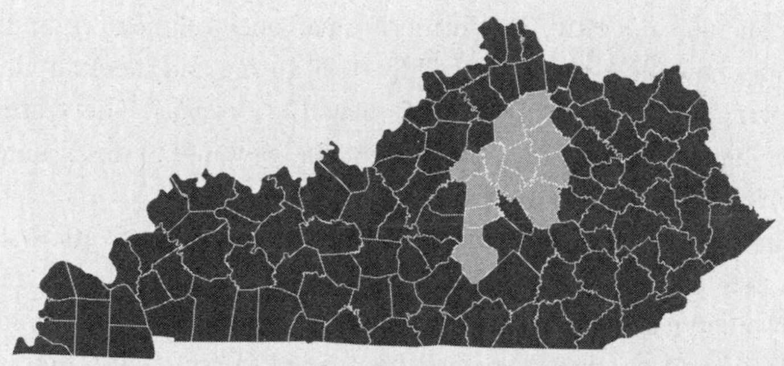

It's ten days until the governor's election in Kentucky, and politics is on the state's mind. Incumbent Republican Matt Bevin is historically unpopular but still a favorite to win. Many see this as a test for the Democratic Party's short-term viability in the state. If Bevin, who accused public school teachers of being responsible for sexual abuse while they were on strike, protesting for their pensions, can't be beaten, then how can McConnell, or anyone else?

My plan is to decide on my future one week after the November 5 election. I keep flipping my decision back and forth by the day; the indecision is maddening. This has been on my mind for two full years, and the pressure of making the correct choice is weighing heavily on me. I hope to find clarity during our final week on the road.

Mercer County

Beijing Mitch

It is starting to rain as we pull up to Shaker Village of Pleasant Hill. This was once one of the three largest Shaker communities in the country between 1805 and 1910. The formerly small once-religious community is empty now; its big, blocky, solidly built dorms and meeting houses look straight out of Arthur Miller's play *The Crucible*. There are few people here besides us; unsurprisingly, the best day to do an outdoor tour of Shaker Village is not when it's pouring rain.

The Shakers are a puritanical religious sect defined more so by what they gave up than what they gained. The group followed an Englishwoman named Ann Lee, who claimed to be the Second Coming of Christ. They were called Shakers because of the members' animated, almost possessed-by-God movements during their services, a feature of their worship that sometimes attracted ridicule. They were a wholly unique group. On the one hand, they were almost puritanical in their behavior, celibate, and avoiding all sin in their community. But in other ways, they were quite progressive, allowing women to preach and pray as leaders of the church, a revolutionary idea that Shakers embraced long before other denominations. There is one Shaker community (consisting of two people in Maine) left in America (that whole celibacy thing tends to undermine growth), and most, like Shaker Village here, are now odes to the past.

Down the road from where the Shakers used to roam is Harrodsburg, home to a Corning International Corp. manufacturing plant. If you own a cell phone, then you have in your hand a product that likely has its ancestry in Mercer County. Virtually all iPhone screens are made here in this massive, beige factory with large, dark windows and a pair of twin *Willy Wonka*–esque spiral smokestacks poking out of the top. The parking lot is full of day laborers hard at work on the lines inside.

Corning's success is, in large part, due to its symbiotic relationship with China, where it operates in nine separate locations. The Chinese presence in Kentucky has grown immensely in recent years and that growth is tied to Mitch McConnell's radical shift in his stance toward the Chinese government.

Early in his political career, McConnell was one of Congress's most vociferous critics of China. He spoke often about the human rights abuses in the Communist country and was one of only eight Republicans to sign on to a letter written by archconservative senator Jesse Helms, which condemned President Ronald Reagan for filling foreign policy posts with those he considered "too soft" on China. McConnell criticized China repeatedly for the 1989 massacre of hundreds if not thousands of student demonstrators in Tiananmen Square, Beijing, and expressed disappointment in President George H. W. Bush when he sent a delegation to meet with Chinese officials shortly afterward. Mitch said it sent "the wrong message at the wrong time. What must those students and citizens who put their life on the line in Tiananmen Square think when they see [the US] toasting Prime Minister Qian Qichen?"

Everything changed when Mitch met Elaine Chao, his future wife. Beginning in 1989, McConnell began attending fund-raisers at which Chao was a prominent figure, and his views on the nation changed dramatically.* He regularly began receiving enormous campaign donations from Chinese interests. The country he had condemned just a couple of years before had suddenly become one of his biggest resources.

Chao's family is of Chinese descent and runs an American shipping company with strong ties to their homeland. They are connected to the most powerful economic interests in the country. Most of their business dealings are with the Chinese. The *New York Times* once described Elaine Chao's family and business interests this way: "In China, the Chaos are no ordinary family. . . . Over the years, Ms. Chao has repeatedly used her connections and celebrity status in China to boost the profile of the company, which benefits handsomely from the expansive industrial policies in Beijing that are at the heart of diplomatic tensions with the United States. . . ."

As soon as McConnell and Chao began their relationship, Mitch

---

* My buddy's views on *The Notebook* changed after he found love. Mitch's changed on China. Love conquers all.

started receiving nearly as much in donations from Chinese interests as he did from Big Tobacco. In the two years leading up to his 1996 reelection bid, McConnell received PAC contributions from nineteen of the top twenty contributors to the US-China Business Council, an organization comprised of American companies whose aim is promoting trade between the two countries. According to the *Times,* members of Chao's extended family members have given at least $1 million to McConnell's PACs or campaign funds. That family money appears to have had a quick effect on Mitch.

After McConnell left the Senate Foreign Relations Committee, he took a post on the Senate Appropriations Committee, where he could influence how US tax dollars were spent. McConnell started pushing for trade benefits for China, including most-favored-nation status, which gave the country favorable tariff status and allowed it to become a member of the World Trade Organization. McConnell's push for Chinese trade benefits helped Chao's family's company explode. James Chao, Elaine's father, was allowed to start building his ships in Chinese state-owned shipyards, and over the next few years, more of Chao's ships were ordered and built. After the Chinese status was changed, his company grew exponentially and the family fortune ballooned. In 2008 James gave a gift of between $5 million and $25 million to McConnell and Chao in memory of his late wife, making Mitch a very rich man.

McConnell also flipped his stance on human rights; whereas he once demanded changes from the Chinese regarding their behavior, he now argued the United States should push human rights reforms after economic reforms. He said not bestowing trade benefits was "a stupid way to punish the Chinese government" and argued that if the United States did not grant China the trade benefits, the only wounded party would be "the forces of change in China." He said, "Political reforms are going to come behind the economic reforms, and I believe it's going to come in an evolutionary way. It's going to evolve to the point where you wake up one day and you can't find a Communist with a flashlight" in China. That was more than twenty-five years ago, and as Communist president Xi Jinping stands as leader for life, it's clear that McConnell's predictions were spectacularly off the mark.

The senator's advocating for Chinese trade and membership in the

WTO has been a tremendous success for China's economy on every level. Prior to its joining, the US trade deficit with China was $83 billion. In 2018 it reached a record $420 billion, with Chinese interests taking over more and more parts of the American economy. Soon after McConnell met Chao, Chinese economic interests flourished, and Mitch has been rewarded handsomely in return.

Other Kentucky officials in both parties saw this for what it was, with Democrat Wendell Ford and Republican Jim Bunning fighting McConnell almost every step of the way. Bunning, the junior senator from Kentucky, accused his colleague of "putting profits ahead of people" when it came to China. McConnell's judgment, he contended, was clouded by campaign donations. "If there is one thing that we have learned about Communist China, it is that they only act responsibly when threatened with economic and trade sanctions," Bunning stated. "Now that we are about to give them permanent normal trade relations, we have lost one of our most effective instruments for keeping China in line."

From the moment McConnell met Chao, a war chest of Chinese money has lined Mitch's pockets, both personally and politically. The man who started as one of the most aggressive China hawks in Congress has now given up the fight and has turned the country into his own personal ATM. The fact is, Mitch sold out.

Boyle County

"It's My Kitchen, and I'll Fry If I Want To"

So reads a wooden placard hanging at the bar at Red Rooster Café in Danville, where we're seated at the bar for lunch. Punny signs line the walls, including, "Mind your own biscuits and life will be gravy," and "If you want breakfast in bed, sleep in the kitchen." It's the sassiest of the countless diners we've visited in the past three months, and only one KISS MY GRITS sign from being perfect.*

* Kentucky's three major exports are coal, bourbon, and diner sass.

The Red Rooster is run by Angela Curtsinger, who cooks in the kitchen with her daughter Jessica (her granddaughter Reana works shifts as well). In the mornings, the Red Rooster is teeming with Boyle County's movers and shakers, and server Dawn Wise is always ready; she knows the guests' regular meals here so well that she has the table set before they come in each morning. "The politicians tend to ask for a private room off to the side there," she says.

She tells us she hears a lot of political debate in the Red Rooster, which is fitting for the area. Boyle County is the home of Centre College, a liberal arts school that is considered one of the best in the state. The college's presence brings in a lot of students, professors, and administrative staff, which creates a small liberal community in Boyle, which has traditionally been one of the most conservative counties in the state. A divide exists between the city of Danville and the county, both culturally and politically, yet the relationship is also quite tight-knit. People find a way to deal with their differences, and it's why people from Boyle County and Danville are so proud of their home—and will talk your ear off about it, even if you didn't ask.*

Civil debate has always been a feature of this area. In the late eighteenth century, Kentucky's leaders traveled to Danville's Grayson's Tavern every week to deliberate the political issues of the day. Senators, congressmen, and judges engaged in the Danville Political Club's weekly discussions, and it served as the centerpiece for the earliest Kentucky governmental debates. Many of the most important early Kentucky decisions were made here, from separating from Virginia, to drafting the provisions of the Kentucky Constitution. All occurred in that very tavern.

It's a spirit that still lives on in Boyle County residents such as Matt Walter and John Russell. Both are in their early forties; Matt's a small-town lawyer, and John works at an independent insurance agency here in Danville. The two have known each other for about thirty-five years; as kids, they called themselves the Twin Towers of their recreational

---

* Boyle County people won't stop talking about Boyle County. Look, we get it. You have a great high school football team, bakery, and hospital. Yes, we'll put it in the book. There it is.

basketball league. (John jokes they each stood about five foot six in the third grade.) Both drew their political inspirations from their parents: John's father was brash, outgoing, and conservative, while Matt says his mother was "a social worker, an outspoken liberal, and a bleeding heart."

The two men belong to different parties and believe strongly in their views, but they remain great friends and find commonalities in practical political matters when they talk it out.

"We really find common ground in our conversations," Matt says. "If we're on the golf course talking about current events, we tend toward the things we agree on rather than the things we disagree on."

"I try not to let anybody's political views define the way I think of them," John says. "It's who you are. It's a free country, and if you have strong opinions about something, let it be known. If someone's going to bash you because of your political opinions, do you want to subject yourself to that person anyway?"

Matt agrees. "I would just say 'Own it.' It's no different from liking ketchup* but not mustard. It's a character trait; it doesn't mean you're a horrible person, it doesn't mean the other people are horrible. It's a preference, and, at the end of the day, I think in the two-party system, as divided as we are, nobody agrees with every issue their party takes a stance on."

It's refreshing to hear both men, one a Democrat and one a Republican, proving that the rhetoric on television and especially on social media—which is often so filled with hate and suggests America is constantly "in crisis"—isn't reflected in daily life. In most of life, friends are friends and politics doesn't change that.

Both men volunteer to me, unprovoked, that this incivility and hyperpartisanship can largely be laid at the feet of Mitch McConnell. "We're both adamant that the 'Party of No' that has developed due to Mitch McConnell is counterproductive to getting anything done governmentally," says Matt. "I think we both yearn for the days when Speaker of the House Tip O'Neill and Ronald Reagan could work together and pull the country out of crisis."

That was certainly not the relationship McConnell chose to have with

* Unless that ketchup is Hunt's. That stuff is trash.

President Obama. He blocked more judicial nominees under Obama than in the entire history of the country before then. When he took over leadership of the Senate in 2015, he ignored all of his legislative priorities. McConnell's war on Obama was personal. He wanted to cut the president off at the knees and exert dominance over him. He once stated, "We have a new president with an approval rating in the seventy percent area. We do not take him on frontally. We find issues where we can win, and we begin to take him down one issue at a time. We create an inventory of losses, so it's Obama lost on this, Obama lost on that." For Mitch it was never about what was best for the country. It was always about ruining Obama. Political destruction is his primary passion.

Thankfully, most of our country is like John and Matt, not like Mitch McConnell. The vast majority of Americans would like our government to function and work for the average citizen. They wish leaders would bicker less and come together to get things done more. Then the rest of the population could focus their debates on the most important thing in life.

"We probably argue about Kentucky basketball more than anything else," Matt says.

Casey County

The Bread of Life

From the outside, the Bread of Life Café looks like a regular restaurant. It sits along US-127 in rural Casey County, just across the street from acres and acres of harvested farmland. The restaurant has an expansive parking lot in front, and a large, white porch lined with comfortable rocking chairs if you just want to sit for a piece. The sign on the front of the building, just under the restaurant's name, displays the Bible verse John 6:35:

"I am the Bread of Life; he that comes to me shall never hunger, and he that believes in me shall never thirst."

Inside the front door is a "trading post" full of candy, candles, and books. The young girl working the counter is chatty, and the dining room sits just beyond the archway ahead. The entire place gives off the vibe of an authentic old country home, a legitimate, real-life Cracker Barrel without the cheesiness. A long, outfitted dinner bar stretches out in the middle of the main room, serving up all the southern delicacies you could possibly want: fried chicken, green beans, mashed potatoes, fried catfish, okra. It's the real deal, and it's delicious.

I will detour from any spot within fifty miles for the buffet, but the real magic of Bread of Life lies in its owners. Jerry and Sandy Tucker were married in 1963. They knew they wanted a big family but struggled to have children, so in 1969 the couple adopted their first child, Jeremy.

"We adopted him, and it was a blessing," Jerry tells us, "and, like hotcakes, kids kept coming for us to adopt. We ended up adopting about thirty-three children over a period of many years."*

Jerry says the number thirty-three so casually, but it's an unbelievable answer. Not to Jerry, however.

"I don't think God gave us time to think about it," Sandy once said. "We took every child God sent us—one person's pain is another person's joy. We just get joy out of it."

Many of the children they adopted have either a mental or physical disability or were part of a sibling group that the adoption process would have separated. They stayed here and raised all the children in Casey County, with many of them helping out around the restaurant.

In 1991 they expanded their care and began Born Free Ministries, established to care for babies whose mothers were incarcerated in the Louisville prison. Jerry says they'd take in as many as twenty-three newborns at a time, nurturing them until their mothers were released. The total number of children who have been helped is now close to seven hundred.†

The Bread of Life Café became the next step. It started as a Christian

---

* You know you have adopted a lot of children when you aren't 100 percent certain how many you have adopted.

† If you're beginning to feel like a terrible person, it's not just you. Anyone would standing next to the Tuckers.

bookstore that Sandy, always one for a new idea, thought should be transitioned into a restaurant. They started serving soup and sandwiches at lunchtime as a way to raise a little bit of extra money for the ministry, and, like their family, it simply kept growing. In 2001 the Tuckers cut the ribbon on their full-size restaurant, just five miles south of Liberty on Highway 127. It seats 150 people, and it's full from open to close. Except on Sundays, of course, when they take the day off.

In 2007, however, Sandy died after a lengthy battle with cancer, and Jerry says things simply haven't been the same. But her memory lives on in a restaurant that is not only beloved by the community, but has also become an economic force for the area.

"Counting the restaurant, the trading post, the school, and the home, we have a hundred forty-four employees," Jerry said proudly. "We're the fourth-largest employer in the county."

I'm often asked why, after attending Duke Law School, I came back to Kentucky. People also wonder why someone would stop being an attorney with a major law firm to talk about sports on the radio. And others are perplexed why I would leave a sports media company I created to run for US Senate. The answer to all three of these questions lies in people like the Tuckers. They are the Kentucky I love, putting people before profits and trying to better the world one day at a time in Casey County. They're all the things that are right about America, and specifically right about rural Kentucky. It is for people like them that I continue to gravitate closer to the people of my home state.

As I sit and enjoy my mishmash of Bread of Life food (I went with the fried chicken, white beans, sauerkraut, and fried apples), a couple who has been sitting a few tables over comes by to say hello. They are both around my parents' age, and they thank me for coming to Casey County. They say they miss my television show and think it "wasn't right what they did to take you off." The wife asks if I am going to run, and I say I am not sure but have to decide soon. But I remark that if I do run, it will be hard for me in places like Casey County, one of the most heavily Republican areas in the state. The man stops and puts his hand on my shoulder.

"The people who started this place. That's what service is. Matt, just remember them and always be for the people. If you do that, nothing anyone can say will do you harm."

Jessamine County

Thirty-Six Years Is Too Long for Anyone

Twenty years ago Jessamine County was quite rural. Now, however, the sprawl of Nicholasville Road in nearby Lexington has brought commercialization here en masse. Locals, though, have a lot of pride and want you to know Nicholasville isn't just another Starbucks location on Highway 27. The 2014 Kentucky Derby winner California Chrome lives here;* they have a PGA Tour golf tournament at local championship course Keene Trace; Ohio State University Buckeyes basketball coach Chris Holtmann is from here (scoop: one of his favorites to be the new UK coach when Calipari retires); and the most underrated food in central Kentucky is over at the Dixie Café in Keene.

This neck of the woods has also been well represented for thirty years by Republican state representative Tom Buford, and people here seem to quantifiably love the guy. He's already been brought up twice since we rolled into Jessamine County. In the downtown clothing shop Embroidery Fox,† we encounter husband-and-wife owners George and Maleia Kinder. Maleia recognizes us from *Hey Kentucky!*, and the blue-eyed, smiling George hesitantly says he does too. He is a kind, friendly man, the type of guy who acts like he knows you from television when he clearly doesn't. George is a Democrat and Maleia a Republican, so they differ on many issues—but one on which they agree is the need for term limits, even on those they love, like Tom Buford.

"Tom Buford is doing a good job, and he's been in there for a long time, and I'd vote for him until the day I die," George says. "If I need anything, I can just call him. I love the guy, and it's not anything against him, but I think he should have term limits too."

His tone is more condemning with Mitch McConnell, however.

---

* You can see him hanging out at all the local watering holes.

† Sacramento Kings and former UK star De'Aaron Fox's little-known nickname. He specializes in draining threes and bedazzling jeans.

"Look, Mitch has been in there too long," he tells me. "I think he could lose focus on the people that are in this community. He's such a Washington guy. He's a big guy, and for Kentucky, it's nice to have somebody at the right hand of the throne, but I'm for term limits for everybody."

"He's been there too long"—the complaint about McConnell that I have heard on the lips of every type of person, from Republican to Democrat, young to old, rural to urban. No matter the demographic, there is a universal belief that politicians shouldn't be able to serve in office forever.

"I think, get elected three times to a four-year term, so that'll give you twelve years,"* George says, as if he's given this some thought before. "Give it your best effort for twelve years, and then somebody else needs to give it their best shot for twelve years. I don't agree with lifetime politicians. I just don't. I don't think that's good for the country. We need to have a different set of eyes on our economy every once in a while."

Let's look at this objectively. McConnell has been in office for thirty-six years. *Thirty-six years!* That's longer than Katy Perry has been alive. When he was first elected to the US Senate, the first *Police Academy* was one of our nation's top films. The most talked-about drama on television was *Cagney & Lacey.* (I bet most of you don't even know who was Cagney and who was Lacey.)† No person deserves to be in office that long, especially someone as destructive and generally unpleasant as the Kentucky Turtle.

For comparison's sake, here are a few things less old than Mitch McConnell's senatorial career:

The first Air Jordans
Nintendo
WrestleMania
The Goonies, Back to the Future, and *Fletch*
The reign of Egyptian pharaoh Rahotep

---

* A Senate term is *six* years, but George is rolling, and I am *not* going to make him stop.

† Both were no-nonsense women cops.

Mary-Kate *and* Ashley Olsen
Ming Ming, the fourth-oldest panda that ever lived

Only two senators in Washington have served longer than McConnell, and they are (even older men) Chuck Grassley and Patrick Leahy. By the end of his current term, McConnell will have served as a senator longer than all but sixteen in the history of the United States.

In other words, in a position dominated by old, white men, Mitch McConnell is one of the oldest and whitest of them all. He isn't an idealist. He isn't a moralist. He isn't even a deal maker. He's just a cynical, vitriolic power grabber.

Thomas Jefferson was in favor of term limits and believed that people who hold office for too long begin to see a position less as a public service and more as a job for personal enrichment. As if foretelling the reign of the distinguished gentleman from Kentucky, he wrote: "Whenever a man has cast a longing eye on [offices], a rottenness begins in his conduct."

Scott County

Chasing Amy

The number of people in Scott County varies dramatically based on the time of day. With every shift change at the Toyota Motor Manufacturing Kentucky factory, Scott County sees an influx of workers unmatched by any other workplace in the state. The massive auto plant off Cherry Blossom Way is bigger than many towns we have visited, with its buildings together equaling the size of 169 football fields. Inside, you can't tell if it's day or night—but that doesn't matter, because it's always up and running.

The Scott County facility is Toyota's largest in the world, employing around ten thousand people, or 20 percent of the county's population. Its presence has made Scott County the fastest-growing county in the state. On this trip, we have talked to people who live as far away as

Paintsville (two hours away) who commute each day to work for Toyota. It's the type of job that has become ever rarer in America: blue-collar factory work with high wages and great benefits. Toyota is a coveted place to work in this area, and almost everyone in Scott County knows multiple people who have spent their lives working there.

We head into downtown Georgetown and walk to the Upbeat Café to determine our game plan. The barista behind the counter starts asking us questions about why we are in town. She is very curious why two strangers would be writing a book about her hometown, but we tell her "not to worry," we are writing about everybody's hometown in Kentucky. An older gentleman sits on the couch, watching us chat. As we step away from the counter, he gets up and shuffles over to the barista.

"Who'd they say they were with?" the old man asks loudly. The woman tells him we're working on a book and were just asking some questions, and he responds with increasing volume, "Did they say they were *Democrats*? I was hoping they didn't say Democrats, because the Democrats are all insane, every damn last one of them! If they'd said they were Democrats, I was gonna throw up."*

Scott County actually happens to be the home of Amy McGrath, the one major candidate left that we haven't yet talked to for this book (besides McConnell, which was a lost cause). Since the day last March that she promised me she would "stay in touch" to talk about the race and converse about our decisions, she has texted me twice: once at four thirty in the morning on the day she announced her candidacy, and once when she mistakenly consoled me for my father's death. We requested multiple times to interview her for the book and so far, our attempts have been futile. She is clearly ignoring us.

Chris and I discuss our options. In the old days, we'd have done some "gotcha" journalism and just shown up at a campaign stop or some event in Scott County. Catching people when they least expect it is a good journalistic tactic, but since I am still considering entering the race, it would probably be looked at unfavorably by the public as a

* Which is decidedly not what one wants in a coffee shop.

whole. Chris and I debate other methods,* but at some point, we reach the same conclusion. She isn't interested in talking to us and doesn't value my opinion. She misled me about her intentions to enter the race. Her campaign manager worked behind the scenes to get me fired from my job. I have many reasons to be upset.

But there are things more consequential than my individual frustrations. We should have a common goal of taking down Mitch McConnell, and I do think her perspective as to why she entered the race is a valuable one. I had friendly and productive conversations with Mike Broihier and Charles Booker, and there is no reason the same couldn't have been true with her. I get why she might be skeptical. But my offer is genuine. It would be nice if we could set aside whatever differences we may have and work toward the common goal of defeating Mitch. That is much more important than either of our own individual aspirations. If after all that has happened I can do it, surely she can too.

Woodford County

The Politics of Personal Destruction

With its centralized location in the Bluegrass State, you can enter Woodford County a number of different ways, but I highly recommend my favorite route down Versailles Road, past the Lexington Bluegrass Airport and the Keeneland racetrack (along with California's Del Mar and New York's Saratoga, one of the three best places to watch a horse race in America). There, on your right, sits one of the most unique visuals anywhere in the state.

The Kentucky Castle is a real-life to-scale replica of a medieval castle located right here in the Bluegrass. It is huge, an honest-to-God stone *castle*, with an outer protective wall, four big turrets, a giant, magnificent

---

* I suggested parachuting into her yard, but Matt made some good points about the legal implications of such a decision.

front gate, and ornate fountains—the works. It is a legitimate, could-probably-protect-you-if-things-suddenly-went-bad level castle. The only thing missing is a moat. It was built by real estate developer Rex Martin in 1969 after a trip to Europe on which his wife, Caroline, was entranced by the castles across the Continent. She wanted one of her own, so the contractor built it on fifty acres in Woodford County.

A few years later, Rex and Caroline divorced.* The castle was abandoned and sat empty for thirty years, simply an odd marvel on Highway 60.† But it has been revitalized and was recently remodeled and opened as a luxury hotel with a high-end restaurant. Philadelphia Eagles quarterback Carson Wentz even proposed to his girlfriend there, which is exactly the kind of random fact that makes big news in Woodford County.‡

I pass by it on my way to speak with James Kay, the Woodford County judge-executive. He is a friend who has previously been a target of the McConnell intimidation machine. In 2013 Woodford County state representative Carl Rollins stepped down, forcing a special election. The local Democrats nominated then thirty-one-year-old Kay. It was an off year, with few other races, but McConnell and other Republicans believed this tiny state representative matchup could be seen as a proxy for the political battleground statewide. So Darth Vader went to work.

"As soon as I was nominated and the race was announced, McConnell had the Republican Party hire ten new staffers just to work on this race," Kay tells me. "It was the middle of the year in an off-election cycle, so this was the only election going on, basically, in the country. So immediately they started researching me and my background. I had a tracker following me around, trying to record anything I said and anything I was doing in public."

I tell Kay I can relate, although the relationship with my Tracker is a

---

* This is why I never built a castle. You just can't please people.

† And a good way to surprise visitors from out of town. No one is truly prepared to see a castle appear across the street from a Super America.

‡ His Super Bowl LII rival Tom Brady of the New England Patriots got engaged during a particularly romantic part of the UGG footwear factory tour.

little different. (Example: he tells me that his bosses were pleased with the video of me that we staged together.) Kay says the normal research took a different turn as he began noticing a light-blue car parking in different places on his street. A car with someone inside.

"I noticed him parked on the street, and I immediately knew there was something off, so I actually approached the guy, and he was sitting in his front seat. And I said, 'What are you doing out here?' And he said, 'I'm a private investigator, and I'm looking into you for running for the House.' I said, 'I'll be honest with you: the neighbors are getting uncomfortable, and my family is really uncomfortable, and I'm going to contact the police and say you're harassing me if you don't get out of here.'"

Kay says the PI visits stopped after that, but soon pictures started popping up on Facebook of Kay in college, painting him as, in his words, "a womanizer and a party animal and a 'bro.' There was a ton of dark money—no one really knew where it came from. It was an eye-opening experience to see the levels they'll go to try to destroy you personally and professionally just to win."

It's a line of attack that I feel is likely to be aimed at me as well.* Kay says that, thankfully, the small Woodford County community had watched him grow up and, as such, saw the attacks as just political garbage. But Kay had seen the machine behind the curtain. "The old McConnell line is 'If you throw a pebble at me, I'm going to throw a boulder at you.'" It's a common mantra for Team Mitch, repeated often by McConnell staffers. "But the reality of it is he's much more of a calculating, cold-hearted person, because I have never referenced him, never said anything bad about Mitch McConnell in my life, and he and his minions immediately did the only thing they knew how to do."

I reach out to Dr. Daniel Mongiardo, a central Kentucky physician and former state senator who ran for the US Senate against Republican Jim Bunning in 2004. Mongiardo was the target of some of the worst of

---

* Matt's Facebook feed is mostly just him posting a picture at some event—let's say the musical *The Book of Mormon*. There are comments about how fun it looks, someone calling him a liberal, and then a hundred back-and-forth angry comments about Trump. It's delightful.

Mitch's dirty politics. While Mongiardo, the son of Italian immigrants, had little name recognition when he ran in 2004, McConnell believed that his message could resonate with Kentuckians. Mitch decided to spend resources to take down Mongiardo, arming the Bunning campaign with all the nastiness of a McConnell Senate race itself.

Republicans began attacking the doctor personally, specifically targeting the fact that he was a single man in his forties and implying he was gay. Republican legislators pushed insinuations about his sexuality, with one state senator calling him a "limp wrist" and another saying, "I'm not sure the word *man* even applies to him." The coded attacks forced Mongiardo to deny the claim to reporters, but the damage was already done in this conservative state. Mongiardo has said in the past that he is convinced Mitch McConnell's political machine orchestrated the entire attack plan. The rumors had a cumulative effect and ended up working. Jim Bunning won by one percentage point.

I contact Mongiardo to try to interview him for this book, but he declines politely, saying, "I'm in a different place now." He understandably doesn't want to relive the hardest times of his life or the pain inflicted on him by Senator Mitch's mudslinging machine, especially now that he has a family. Although he was defeated at the ballot box by Bunning, the slanderous personal assaults were all McConnell, and he doesn't want them repeated.

I continue to come back to the threat to me on that Kentucky Chamber of Commerce stage. "We won't *try* to destroy you, we *will* destroy you." It wasn't an exaggeration. It was a goal and a statement of fact. The politics of Mitch McConnell are the politics of hate and personal destruction. It's the drive of a soulless political being. The only question is who is next.

Madison County

Free College the Right Way

We are standing just off campus at Berea College, a small liberal arts institution with a unique place in Kentucky higher education. As the sun is beginning to set on what's been a very busy afternoon, Berea is bustling with students and locals moving about the town square. Berea's downtown is plucked from the Massachusetts coastline, with white buildings and quaint boutiques centered around the town hub. The Boone Tavern Hotel and Restaurant—a pristine, colonial-revival-style white mansion in the center square—has a full room of diners and guests in its cozy confines for the evening.

At the Berea Coffee & Tea Company, a comfortable, dimly lit coffee shop just down the street from the tavern, nearly every table is filled with a college student, brow furrowed, studying hard—there's no fooling around or idle gossip. This is a school that takes academics seriously, and distraction is not easy to come by. That's by design, as Berea has a no-tuition model that is unique to almost anywhere else in America. Accepted students to Berea pay no tuition but are required to hold jobs on campus to help defray costs. All of the town of Berea's facilities, from the student center, to the Boone Tavern restaurant, to the shops that sell brooms and butter churns, are operated by students, which allows the school to remain tuition free. Admissions standards require that virtually all the students at Berea College come from economically underprivileged areas. Most are from the surrounding areas of Kentucky and other parts of Appalachia. The only cost is a modest fee for room and board, and as a result, 49 percent of students graduate debt free. For the rest, the average debt is less than $6,000.

It's relatively simple living: food comes from the nearby Berea College Farm, which supplies all the campus food services, cafés, and area restaurants. The average household income of a Berea college student's family is under $30,000. A whopping 96 percent of students qualify for federal Pell grants. It's a haven for students from nearby urban and Appalachian areas to get a quality education. Berea is consistently rated one of the best small colleges in the South, and *Money* magazine named it the most affordable school in the country. It's no joke—it's practically a real-life, free college.

"I've heard stories where people googled 'free school,' and Berea popped up," student Pedro Herrera tells me from behind a laptop at one of the coffee shop tables, grinning. "A lot of times, they don't believe it. That's the first thing I hear is, 'This is a scam.'"

It's not a scam, as Pedro can attest. Born in Tierra Blanca, Mexico, Pedro's family moved to Somerset, Kentucky, when he was six years old. The son of an auto body shop owner and a caterer who specializes in authentic Mexican food, Pedro is considered a DACA student (Deferred Action for Childhood Arrivals), also known in the current colloquial as a "dreamer," which means he doesn't have citizenship status.

"Because I'm not considered a citizen, that automatically disqualified me from getting any KEES [Kentucky Educational Excellence Scholarship] or government aid, or anything like that," Pedro says. "I come from a low-income family—my parents together probably make about thirty thousand dollars a year together, so pretty low. In high school and middle school, my family and I, we lived day to day, trying to make ends meet. Berea just said, 'Man, come here, and we'll cover you.'"

Pedro is graduating in a few weeks. As we speak with him, he's finishing his last paper to complete his degree, and he tells me that the community of people fostered by the college creates a real bond among them. "A lot of times, students come to Berea from a low-income background, and Berea gives us the ability to become comfortable. We don't have to worry about when our next meal is going to be or where we're going to sleep. It provides all our basic needs, and that allows us to focus on our studies. Yesterday our [graduation] speaker said that Berea might be the only college where students debate over who came in the poorest."

Unfortunately, there aren't many Bereas, and thus higher education often requires students to take out massive amounts of debt. The student debt crisis is slowly crippling our nation's graduates, and the problem is only getting worse. *Forbes* magazine estimates total student loan debt in 2019 at $1.56 trillion, with 44.7 million people still owing money. The expenses are much higher than even when I went to college twenty years ago, inflated by skyrocketing tuition costs and fewer financial aid options.* The long-term effect for students, and the economy as a whole, is too much working income tied up in debt payments, stifling opportunity and innovation.

Mitch McConnell's concern for those saddled with student debt is nonexistent. In contrast to the tremendous burdens he often complains are put on the nation's millionaires, when it comes to young people in college, his feelings are quite different. During a speech in Buckner, Kentucky, McConnell was asked his thoughts about forgiving student debt:

"I think it's outrageous that it costs as much as it does, but I don't think the federal government ought to be in the business of forgiving, in effect, obligations owed . . . so I rule out forgiving obligations that have been voluntarily incurred."

Of course. Mitch approved $16.8 trillion in Wall Street bailouts just during the 2008 financial crisis alone. That is more than ten times the total amount of student loan debt in America. For Mitch McConnell, helping relieve student debt is outrageous, helping Wall Street is business as usual.

In 2014 a bill was introduced to allow people to refinance their student loans at lower rates. It was a modest proposal, but one that would have saved debt-riddled young workers millions. Mitch responded again by only playing politics: "The Senate Democrats' bill isn't really about students at all. It's really all about Senate Democrats. They want an issue to campaign on to save their own hides this November," he scoffed.

Ultimately, whether the policy would have helped students was irrelevant. No matter the wisdom of any legislation, for Mitch, the calculus is always clear. If a bill might help Democrats politically, you can guarantee Mitch McConnell will be dead set against it.

---

* A word of advice to any thirteen-year-olds reading this: open a 529 plan account for your future children now.

Clark County

The Obstructionist in Chief

The bluegrass area of central Kentucky is some of the most beautiful in America. With its sprawling horse farms, majestic animals, and regal homes, it gives off the aura of refined culture mixed with plenty of old money. Then there is the city of Winchester, in Clark County. If central Kentucky is the Griswolds, Clark County is Cousin Eddie, a little rowdier, less mannered, and a bit rougher around the edges. This is an area that likes to call itself "Sinchester," and chances are high wherever you are in the county, you are likely within a hundred yards of a cockfight at any moment. As an old high school coach once said to me, "When you invite Winchester to the party, you know when they have arrived."*

Clark County and its largest town, Winchester, are synonymous with Ale-8-One (it's meant to sound like "a late one" with emphasis in all the weirdest places), a ginger-ale-style soda that comes in tiny green bottles that you can occasionally find littered here and there along the county's roadways. Out-of-towners shouldn't be surprised if they've never heard of it; it's the very definition of "regional," but it's the pride of the area. Its taste can be best described as mostly sweet and a little bitter with a punchy bite, which would also be a great way to describe Clark Countians themselves.

Ale-8 is sold at every location around here, including Clark County High School, where retired social studies and politics teacher Ann Humble taught in the public school system for thirty-seven years. She tells me that although she's a Democrat, she always tried to teach as nonpartisan as possible. "Whenever I was presenting something to the class," she says, "I would say, 'Okay, these are the facts. And there are lots of opinions out there about these facts; you need to form your own opinion.'"

---

* Clark Countians allege that beer cheese was invented here. This county literally looked at cheese and decided it needed more beer.

Humble is a Democrat but was respected for allowing her students to hear and understand all sides of the issues. It did, however, lead to a strange set of encounters with the Senate majority leader. On multiple occasions Mitch McConnell tried to come and speak to her students, even though Ann had no prior relationship with him.

"When he came to Winchester, he always wanted to come speak to my class," she recalls. "I don't know why. I suspect—though I'm not positive—it's because Clark County has a very high percentage of Republicans and political donors, and I taught most of them, so it may be a way to influence the children of some of these donor parents."

Humble says Mitch's office called numerous times to try to get him in front of her class, and the more she ignored the calls, the more they persisted. Sometimes she even pretended to be the maid, taking a message. "Eventually I said, 'I am sorry, I've heard you've called my house before, and I'm really sorry about this, but if he wants to come to my class, this is testing time, and it just doesn't work. Maybe some future day he could come.'

"Do you know what he did?" Her eyes widen, and she shakes her head in disbelief. "He went to the superintendent and said, 'I would like to speak to Ann Humble's class, but it seems it's "testing time," and she doesn't think that she can allow me to come because it's going to affect the testing.' So, the superintendent called me and said, 'I just got a call from Senator McConnell, and it's such a great honor that he wants to come speak to your class.'"

The guest visit was exactly what you'd expect from Mr. Charisma, Mitch McConnell. "So I reserved the library so he could stand in front of them and pace," Ann says. "So many kids were just flabbergasted at how he started this speech. He knows that these kids are advanced placement seniors. He started with 'Let me explain to you the structure of the US government.' And he went through the legislative, executive, and judicial branch, just like they had never heard of it. And they were looking at me like, 'Huh?'"

It's an odd story, but I kind of love it. On the surface, it seems farfetched. Why would McConnell be so concerned about a single high school class that he would demand to speak in front of it? Why did it get stuck in his craw so bad? Ann insists that the only reason she didn't jump at the offer was that testing was going on, but I think her personal feelings had to play at least some small part. Humble says her major frustration with McConnell is his obstructionism, especially in the realm of judges. On that issue, Mitch has no equal.

For instance, take Kentucky Supreme Court deputy chief justice Lisabeth Tabor Hughes, appointed to the bench in 2007. Six years later, President Obama nominated Hughes to the United States Court of Appeals for the Sixth Circuit. Hughes was rated "unanimously well qualified" by the American Bar Association and would have been an uncontroversial nominee by any reasonable standard. But for Mitch McConnell, the only standard that mattered was who was nominating the judge. Refusing to allow Barack Obama to have a nominee in Kentucky for any reason, Mitch closed the door on considering Hughes's nomination. A spokesman stated that "Leader McConnell tried to work with the White House to fill this vacancy, including submitting a qualified Kentuckian for consideration. Rather than work with him to fill this vacancy, they submitted Justice Hughes without even notifying Leader McConnell. He will not support action on this nomination."

That's code for "President Obama didn't want to nominate the conservative Federalist Society jurist McConnell preferred, so obstructionist Mitch will block consideration of it out of spite." The reality was that no nominee Obama put forth would have passed McConnell's "standards," and he much preferred doing exactly what he did: leave the vacancy open, wait for a Republican to become president, and then fill it as quickly as possible with someone loyal to him.

McConnell's actions were rewarded when President Trump made Amul Thapar, a McConnell loyalist, his first appointment to the US Court of Appeals. In that respect, Justice Tabor Hughes suffered the same fate as Merrick Garland, the Obama Supreme Court pick that Mitch refused to even give a hearing. Just after Justice Antonin Scalia died, in 2016, McConnell immediately made clear he would not operate in good faith and debate the nomination of whomever the White House put forth. His citation of the "Biden Rule" was completely fabricated, and an ex post facto justification for Mitch's win-at-any-cost brand of politics. The laughability of his rationale was proven when speculation about Justice Ruth Bader Ginsberg's health caused some to question whether McConnell would invoke the rule if she stepped down in 2020. Mitch has made it clear on multiple occasions that he won't follow his own precedent. Of course.

The result of all this obstructionism? Trump and McConnell have transformed the federal courts. One in four judges on the federal appellate bench at this time are Trump appointees, a rate unmatched in US history. McConnell's refusal to confirm judges during the final Obama years has led multiple positions that used to be held by Democratic appointees to be replaced by Trump picks. The federal judiciary is being transformed, and Mitch McConnell's destruction of the judicial nomination process has been rewarded.

It's a terrible result for democracy, separation of powers, and an independent judiciary. But it's a great result for Mitch McConnell and his party's power, which for him is all that has ever mattered.

Bourbon County

Politics as Potato Chips

Daniel Boone once allegedly said "Heaven must be a Kentucky kind of place." He was likely talking about the area around Cumberland Gap, but it just as easily could have been Bourbon County. The fourteen-mile stretch of road along Highways 27 and 68—connecting Lexington with Paris, the county seat of Bourbon County—is the most beautiful Sunday drive in the state. "Paris Pike," as it is known in Bourbon County, is home to perfectly manicured horse farms divided by colored wooden fences or waist-high rock walls. Horses gallop through the fields with unbridled joy; wobbly colts learn to walk alongside encouraging mothers. It's all very stunning. The people who own these farms are very, *very* rich. Like, loaded. The horse world is the playground of Kentucky's aristocratic elite, so the least they can do is give us this beautiful little drive.

The horse industry is one of the state's most visible exports, and its signature moment, the Kentucky Derby, brings more visitors and attention to the commonwealth than any other event. Horse racing is a vital component of the economic engine of the state, and it gives millions of Kentuckians joy, and quite a few, employment.

Fittingly, the sport of kings is also one of the biggest supporters of Mitch McConnell.* Mitch consistently finagles large checks from the horse industry and counts those in it as some of his most loyal supporters. Thoroughbred owners fork out almost the *yearly* median salary in the state to help McConnell, who, in turn, helps push for tax breaks on ownership and income that save the industry millions.

The horse industry is but one example of McConnell's big-money strategy that has turned Congress into the largest fund-raising organization in the world. The days when Washington focused primarily on legislating are long gone. Big money wins elections, so campaigns never end. According to former Florida Republican congressman David Jolly, the expectation now is that elected officials will spend more time raising money than legislating. Democrat Tom Daschle, who once held McConnell's post as the head of the Senate, says that senators have to spend at least two-thirds of their time raising money to be successful.

I saw this process firsthand when visiting Washington at the DCCC and DSCC offices over the last four years. In both buildings, rooms are set aside for legislators to come in and do what's known as "call time," the mind-numbing process of phoning strangers and begging for money. Elected officials sit in a tiny cubicle with a computer screen and, script in hand, call the wealthiest people in the United States (or in McConnell's case, Russia) in the hopes that these millionaires and billionaires will help bankroll their next campaign. This undignified act of "dialing for dollars" is dutifully fulfilled by all our senators and representatives, often taking up much of their days. In all my visits to DC, the call-time rooms were always occupied.

It's clear why a principled person might be a bit ashamed by all of this, but McConnell revels in political greed. His push for unlimited money in our elections has now created a flood of nearly $1 billion in dark money that controls modern democracy. This money comes from

* Although unlike the great horses, no one is paying Mitch McConnell's stud fee.

tax-exempt groups such as "social welfare" organizations that sound charitable but are anything but. These "social welfare" organizations include groups such as the NRA and Karl Rove's "American Crossroads," and they are allowed to raise and spend unlimited amounts of money for these "social welfare" purposes, of which campaigns are considered a part. Because the money doesn't have to be reported, there really isn't a good way to know exactly how much money gets funneled into these dark operations or even where it comes from. We know that Russia has used some of these groups to funnel huge amounts of money into US elections and it is safe to assume others have, or will, too. Mitch McConnell believes more money in politics is better and he has gotten his wish, even if it is hostile foreign money meant to sabotage democracy.

Complaints about the influx of money in politics have little effect on McConnell. When he has been confronted with the outrageous dollar figures spent during our election cycles, Mitch often has a simplistic reply. "Where did this notion get going that we were spending too much in campaigns?" McConnell has said. "Compared to what? Americans spent more on potato chips than they did on politics."

Well, most Americans do.* The kind of Americans that spend more on potato chips than politics are not McConnell's donors. His donors are multimillionaires who spend more on politics than the average Kentuckian spends on anything. They have corrupted the political process by making sure a disproportionate wealthy few will have an oversize impact on our elections and the information we receive.

Or to put it another way, the campaign finance system that Mitch McConnell has created for America has ensured that we will elect people just like Mitch McConnell.

---

* Mitch hasn't yet cracked "Big Potato Chip."

Anderson County

"Mitch Will Say That He Supports Troops in Front of the Cameras, but Actions Speak Louder Than Words"

I like Anderson County, as it is a piece of the country lifestyle fairly close to the city of Lexington. People here still sound like me. In case you didn't know (and how could you), I have an average mountain accent. Around Kentucky, people wouldn't necessarily agree with that statement; they think I sound normal or maybe even a little citified. But get outside the Bluegrass State and chances are you would notice it. It's especially prominent when I turn words that end in *-ight* to *-iiiiiite*, or make words that end in *-eel*, like *steel*, into multisyllable words like *ste-uhl*. The accents in Kentucky ramp up from mine, however.

One accent, however, that we don't get a lot of is the one we run into at Tastefully Delicious, an artisan food and gift shop on Main Street in downtown Lawrenceburg, the county seat of Anderson County. There, a white-haired, goateed Eric Silverman begins chatting with us, and his thick Long Island accent is striking. He's loud and very northeastern—a stark difference from every shop owner we've met so far. He admits that when he and his family migrated south to Anderson County fifteen years ago, his accent and mannerisms made it hard to win over the natives.

"When we first came out here, we opened up a little shoe store, and it took a while," Eric says, "because people were nervous. They'd say, 'You're not from around here.' So I said, 'What does that mean?' And they said, 'Well, I'm going to go to Shoe Carnival,' that's what that meant.*

"My landlord gave me only four months; he thought I'd be out by then."

Silverman, his wife, Gail, and their home-schooled son, Justin, came here when Justin received a scholarship to nearby Georgetown

* To be fair, "I am going to Shoe Carnival" is my go-to exit line as well.

College. The cultural change was an eye opener for Eric. "New York was really hustle-bustle, you don't help your neighbor, stuff like that," he explains. "It's really just look out for yourself. I was in Lexington, and I had to get across, and it wasn't at a light, and people saw you try to edge out, and they actually stopped. This was a four-lane street, and everybody stopped and let you go across. That would never ever happen in New York."

Anderson County is very Republican, and its close proximity to Lexington and Louisville means that GOP politicians make it a regular stop when in the area. While we're driving around the county, we pull into the American Legion parking lot—the spot where, just two years ago, protestors managed to infiltrate one of McConnell's speaking events. Frustrated that he never makes himself publicly accessible, they asked him hard questions at the rare town hall he usually tries to avoid. He dodged protestor questions and finally responded, "Winners make policy, and the losers go home."*

Fine, Mr. Winner. Since you were at the American Legion, let's talk a little veterans policy.† In just one year, McConnell led the effort to kill the Wounded Veteran Job Security Act, the Veterans Retraining Act, the Veterans Business Center Act, the Homeless Veterans Reintegration Program Reauthorization Act, and the Disabled Veterans Home Improvement and Structural Alteration Grant Increase Act. All were designed to provide support for veterans and create a stimulus for the economy. All were also proposed by Obama and thus a nonstarter for McConnell, regardless of their merits.

In 2014, McConnell continued to ignore any Obama administration aid for veterans by derailing a *$21 billion* bill that would have provided funds for veterans to help with health care, education, unemployment, retirement, and training. The bill was a response to the scandals around treatment problems at Veterans Affairs hospitals and attempted to alleviate an intense backlog of care. McConnell blocked the bill, and two

---

* A charmer, that McConnell.

† Matt has reached the point in this trip where he is addressing Mitch McConnell out loud directly as if he is in the room. Sometimes I have to pretend to be him just to make it stop.

hundred thousand veterans had their unemployment benefits cut off. Instead of solving the crisis, Mitch wanted to make Obama-era treatment of veterans a 2016 campaign issue. Party over country always, even when the welfare of our nation's veterans is at stake.

Mitch McConnell's response was to accuse Democrats of engaging in election-year politics by trying to expand and improve health care for millions of veterans. How *dare* they! The American Legion disagreed. National Commander Daniel Dellinger called the stunt "political gamesmanship." But, unlike McConnell, who blamed Democrats for playing games, Dellinger said, "There was a right way and a wrong way to vote today, and the senators [who voted no] voted the wrong way. That's inexcusable. I don't know how anyone who voted no today can look a veteran in the eye and justify that vote."

The "political gamesmanship" was so egregious that veterans groups launched a $300,000 ad campaign to highlight McConnell's "Intransigence on Veterans Care." Charles Erwin, a veteran from Mayfield, Kentucky, said in a television ad, "Senator McConnell, I did my duty. But after thirty years in Washington, you failed to do yours." McConnell has never explained any justification for derailing the bill beyond not wanting to help the Democrats in an election year, and he has yet to even muster up the courage to deal directly with the issue.

Anderson County High School teacher and retired US Marine Fred Cox, who was deployed in Saudi Arabia, Kuwait, and the Persian Gulf, says that McConnell and the GOP "seem to master the art of supporting the troops when it is beneficial to them to say so, but they don't really seem to deliver when it's time. They've never met a farm subsidy they didn't love or a bank bailout that wasn't sweet."

As with the countless other issues we have encountered, when Mitch McConnell has the ability to help our nation's veterans, he engages only in a political calculus. If the act will help Democrats seem supportive of veterans, he's against it. No questions asked. As Cox says, "Mitch will say that he supports troops in front of the cameras, but actions speak louder than words. And his actions are *screaming*."

Harrison County

"Thank God We're Not Mississippi"

It's time to roll into Cynthiana, a small town that sits as a gateway between bluegrass horse country and the suburban sprawl of northern Kentucky. I spent part of my early childhood in Cynthiana, from ages two to four. I don't remember much about it except that I broke my leg once and would nap on the front pew of the Cynthiana Baptist Church. On the way into town, I pass the church and Bell's Outdoor Sports & Pawn, which continues the tradition of Kentucky multifaceted stores with a sign that reads in bold letters:

GUNS
LIVE BAIT
ARCHERY
CASH LOANS

I can't imagine a scenario where you would need all of those at the same time, unless you were either entering a survival contest or committing a federal crime. But if any of those is on your list, you have Bell's.*

Things have changed since my earliest days limping in a cast through Cynthiana. Downtown is taking on a hipster vibe with a massive *Walking Dead* mural on the side of a building (one of the TV show's creators is from here), the upscale Burley Market and Café, a martial arts dojo called Sin thé Shaolin, and a cheese store with a sign in front that just says "Cheese Store."† They are all nice, but when I am in town, I will always go to Biancke's (pronounced "Byyy-*ank*-eees") Restaurant, which opened here in 1894. Its paneled wood and dark-green walls give it an old hunting-club feel, and it is lined with composite pictures from

---

* Make sure you pay back that loan.

† We hope you forgive us for assuming they sell cheese at the Cheese Store. We didn't go in.

every class at the old Cynthiana High School. Every generation of Cynthianan has eaten here, and on this evening, we see a cross section of residents: a family with children, an old married couple, and a group of coworkers celebrating something exciting at a long table in the back.

We sit down with Greg Coulson, a young Harrison County attorney who stopped by on his way home from work. He is friendly and easygoing, but when the topic turns to McConnell, he has strong opinions. He thinks Mitch has hurt his Harrison County home and that the senator hasn't produced results as promised.

"What we've seen from Mitch over the last thirty-six years is this real top-down approach where there's this mythical fairy tale that if you cut taxes at the top, it'll reach its way down to the bottom, and it hasn't here," Greg tells us. "Harrison County is an area where you can see Mitch has really abandoned rural Kentucky. We don't have any millionaires here, we don't have CEOs here. What we do have is people who work for a living."

Greg notes that McConnell's run in the Senate has completely flipped the tax structure to favor the wealthy without pumping the promised investment back into the working classes in rural counties. The top 1 percent of Americans now own 41 percent of the nation's wealth, but McConnell has engineered multiple tax breaks for them, only exacerbating inequality. The inequality difference in the United States is now the highest in our history—higher than every European country and on a par with nations such as Russia and Iran.

The clearest indicator of McConnell's priorities for the superwealthy over Kentuckians was his vote on a 2008 tax amendment. It would have restored the tax rate for those making more than $1 million to pre-2001 levels (which were still the lowest in history) and then used the savings to fund Head Start programs, child care, and school construction projects, many of which would have been earmarked specifically for rural Kentucky. McConnell voted no and lambasted the amendment in public statements.

"You have Mitch McConnell representing a rural, poor state," Greg says, exasperated. "We're very low on the per capita income, and we generally live more rurally than the rest of the country. Yet we have a senator who's been there for thirty-six years who constantly pushes policies that favor urban areas and the rich. None of that money is coming back to our schools, none of that money is coming back to build roads. These aren't pie-in-the-sky social issues, they're programs—basic requirements of functional government.

"Everybody says, 'It's been so great to have Mitch McConnell as majority leader, because he really brings the pork home to Kentucky,'" Coulson continues. "Where is it? Where is it, guys? Instead, we're here in Kentucky saying, 'Thank God we're not Mississippi.'"

New York City

Free Matt Jones

I left Harrison County and flew to New York to visit my girlfriend and try to get away. Election Day had arrived and all of Kentucky wanted to see if a Democrat could actually win in the state and defeat Matt Bevin, who had become a very unpopular governor. I kept insisting publicly that whatever happened in the governor's race was of little consequence for my decision. If the mainstream Democrat Andy Beshear lost, that didn't necessarily mean that I, an unconventional outsider, would lose. Similarly, if he won, that didn't automatically mean it was a good time for me personally to jump into the race. In reality, however, I knew that wasn't the case. If Matt Bevin, one of the most unpopular political figures in modern Kentucky politics, was still able to be re-elected simply because he was a Republican, then, really, there was no use for any Democrat to run in the Trump era. Kentucky would be a lost cause.

I passed the time on election night by going to Madison Square Garden and watching Kentucky take on Michigan State. It was a matchup of the top two teams in the college basketball rankings and, for most Kentuckians, the more important of the two big events of the day. Kentucky fans, as always, flooded the Garden, and while I was walking on the court prior to the game, it felt as if Lexington had moved to the big city. I checked my phone furiously for results, and as they trickled in, the result became clear. Looking up in the crowd, I saw fellow Kentuckians who pumped their fists at me, happy that Matt Bevin was out of the Governor's Mansion.

Even before the nine thirty tip-off, my phone began to blow up. Messages came from everywhere:

"You gotta run!"

"It's set up for you now! Go beat the bastard!"

"First Bevin, now McConnell! It's your time, Matt!"

The Beshear win revved up talk about the 2020 Senate race. On social media, all the national political pundits were discussing Beshear's victory not as a referendum on an extremely unpopular governor (which it was) but as either a referendum on Trump (which it most certainly wasn't) or a signal that Mitch McConnell could be beaten. The latter became the predominant talking point, and as the Cats and Spartans tipped off, I checked my email to find twelve messages from political operatives requesting meetings. Things were clearly about to take off, so I turned off my phone and watched the Cats put a beatdown on Tom Izzo's team.*

The next morning started normally. I woke up, shuffled into my girlfriend's living room, where I was remotely broadcasting that morning's *KSR* show. It was a cold day, and I peered out the window to make sure no trackers had taken up residence on the street below. We began talking about the game. The combination of a big Kentucky win and a Bevin cleansing had the callers in an unusually good mood. The show proceeded typically until I was interrupted by a text message from a reporter asking if I had a comment on the new complaint filed against me with the Federal Election Commission, or FEC, the regulatory agency that enforces campaign finance law. My heart fluttered, and I took the show's final call, from a soldier serving in Afghanistan, thanking me for bringing a little piece of his Kentucky home to him thousands of miles away. It would be my last time on the air for the near future.

The chairman of the Kentucky Republican Party, no doubt at the direction of Mitch McConnell, had filed a complaint alleging that my

---

* Spoiler alert: 69–62. Tyrese Maxey played great.

radio show and this very book were violations of federal election law because they counted as "contributions" to my political campaign. As the basis for the allegation, the complaint pointed to the fact that I had created an "exploratory committee," which was being used to raise money for a potential run. He claimed that publicity from the radio show and our travels for the book were illegal contributions by my bosses and by Simon & Schuster, the book's publisher, intended solely to further my potential run.

It was an absurd argument, one so laughable that I couldn't believe its audacity. My "exploratory committee" was simply a way for me to raise a small amount of money (less than $10,000) for polling and staff help while I figured out what I was going to do. I did it for reasons of transparency, but it had apparently put me in the purview of Mitch's manipulation of the federal government.* I never mentioned the exploratory committee on the radio and raised no funds based on being on the air. As for the book, virtually every single candidate (or potential candidate) writes a book. Including Mitch. It was ridiculous to say I was breaking election law if they were not. First, I lost my television show for thinking about running, now I was losing my radio show for driving around the state.

The game plan quickly became clear: the FEC currently had only three members, one short of a quorum. Thus, the commission was unable to hear any complaints, and any that were filed would simply sit in limbo. The person in charge of approving new members? You guessed it: Mitch McConnell. He had refused to approve any more, and many believed he planned to leave the commission bare until after the 2020 election, thus essentially leaving it as a free-for-all. This bogus complaint, however, would put my employers on notice, setting them up for potentially significant penalties if the conduct was found to be a violation. There was no way iHeartRadio, the company that broadcasts my show, could risk letting me stay on the air until the matter was settled, and

* He should have done what everyone else does. Don't file with the FEC and take all the hidden money while you still can. Politics never rewards the right moral decisions.

because the commission wasn't hearing any complaints, it couldn't be settled in the near future. Thus, I would be taken off the air, regardless of the complaint's merits.

It was underhanded. It was devious. It felt like . . . Mitch. And it worked. After consulting with their attorneys, my iHeart bosses let me know I couldn't continue on the air until I made my decision about the election, and if I did run, they would have to take me off permanently. It was a devastating blow to me personally. I loved the show, and I recognized the prospect that Mitch would play dirty with everything on the table, including my employment. What made it even more absurd was the fact that McConnell is the one man who has done more to flood our elections with money and corporate greed than any other. The man has spent his career fighting against campaign finance reform, and now campaign finance law and "election fairness" was being invoked to strike his blow. The hypocrisy was staggering.

McConnell is worth millions of dollars himself, raises hundreds of millions from God-knows-who, and literally has an unlimited supply of right-wing media outlets to put out any propaganda he chooses. Yet my two-hour radio show and book travels were somehow disrupting our electoral system unfairly. And I wasn't even a candidate yet! He is the worst.

I went online and wrote a message saying I would no longer be on the show and would make a decision about whether I was going to run very soon. Instead of waiting to see the response (there's nothing less relaxing than reading Twitter comments), I turned off the computer and went to bed. With no show, I didn't have an early wake-up call, so I settled in with my copy of *Night Boat to Tangier* and drifted off to sleep.

I knew something was going on when I woke up to seventy-five text messages. Unbeknownst to me, outrage had erupted in Kentucky after my removal from the show. The fans of *Kentucky Sports Radio* rose up and collectively expressed their anger at McConnell. All is fair in love, war, and politics, but this was a sports show, and one that they dearly loved. *KSR* is part of life's daily fabric for many Kentuckians around the state. No matter where you are, you can walk into a local business and find it playing in the background as people go about their day. This bogus complaint had taken that away for no reason except petty politics, and folks were mad.*

Calls came in to the radio show throughout the morning, and my cohosts, Ryan, Drew, and Shannon, suggested that listeners tag #FreeMattJones on Twitter. The tag quickly went viral, and within one hour, it was the number one trending topic in the country,† a position it held throughout the day and into the night. I was flooded with messages from friends, family, supporters—and even dozens of Republicans—angry about what had happened. Many of the GOP county judge-executives we had met on our travels wrote me and said they would be calling McConnell and expressing their discontent. Mitch's Twitter handles were inundated with complaints, and national news outlets began covering the story and reaching out for interviews. A local T-shirt company created a #FreeMattJones shirt that our fans wore in support around the state. Someone even paid for an electric billboard in Lexington on the city's busiest street to broadcast the "#FreeMattJones" hashtag. It had spiraled out of control and was becoming a theme for my supporters: "Senate Majority Leader Has Sports Radio Host Removed from His Show."

I spoke to a source with ties to McConnell's world and asked him why this was happening. "Matt, they are really pissed about the book. They don't like that you are going around Kentucky and going after him, and they want to stop the book. They thought this might keep Simon & Schuster from publishing it. They didn't realize that the focus would be on the radio show. It has completely backfired, and they know it."

It was an uncharacteristically stupid move by Mitch and his team.

---

* He should have foreseen this, but the last time Mitch listened to the radio he got freaked out by Orson Welles's *War of the Worlds* broadcast.

† My favorite part of all this occurred then, when people found the #FreeMattJones hashtag and didn't know who he was, and said things like, "I am not sure why we should #FreeMattJones. We don't know what he did, and he might be dangerous!"

He had violated my lifelong theory "Never punch down, only punch up." Losing my show turned me into a martyr, rallying my supporters and giving me a platform I never would have had otherwise. Not a good outcome for the Tactical Turtle.

The biggest impediment to me entering the race was whether I could attract the national attention and spotlight necessary to raise enough money to compete with Amy McGrath's war chest in the primary. Now I had been given both a launching point and a narrative I could run with in the race: Mitch the bully, trying to take away people's livelihoods in pursuit of political power. It felt personal to people, and it felt wrong. And it was perfect for a campaign: "Mitch took my job! Now I will take his!"

My advisors called me repeatedly, urging me to seize this moment. One text read, "Matt, you couldn't have asked for anything better! Now is the time to get in. Let's announce this weekend on one of the Sunday-morning shows!" My plan had been to take a week after the governor's race and come to peace with whatever decision I was going to make. But that was before what I like to call Mitch's glitch, and now seemed to be the time to take the leap if I was going to do it. The national spotlight was on me, and the pressure was only ratcheting up. People smelled blood in the water, and thanks to a ridiculous FEC complaint I had what I didn't have before: a potential path to victory. It was overwhelming.

I boarded a flight back home to Kentucky. It couldn't be put off any longer. I had to make a decision.

Fayette County

I Will Be Taking My Talents to . . .

Lexington is essentially the home base for the state of Kentucky. Technically, Frankfort is the capital and Louisville the largest city, but when it comes to the heart and soul of Kentucky, it lies in the middle of Fayette County. Every major industry important to the state's economy has a foothold here: coal, bourbon, horse racing, tobacco, farming, and automobiles are all either centralized here or have important components in the city. The state's main university is located downtown—along with the mecca of college basketball, the twenty-two-thousand-seat Rupp Arena—and given the commonwealth's love for the Cats, the "trip to the big city" for most of the state means going to Lexington.

It has also been my base for the past twenty-plus years. Even though I have lived elsewhere at times, my education, my business, and my friendships have always been centered in Lexington. So, it made perfect sense to me that we would end our tour in the city that in many ways is the pulse of the state.

Politically speaking, Lexington is as close to a swing district as you will find in Kentucky. It is progressive enough that it had a very popular openly gay Democratic mayor, yet conservative enough that it is represented in Congress by the Trump-loving Republican Andy Barr. The city is generally very content, there is little unrest, and the economy is consistently good enough that work is relatively easy to find. It's a perfect college town.

With my removal from radio still stinging, I decided to go off the grid for a few days. I had all the information I needed to make a decision. Andy Beshear proved that a Democrat could still win in Kentucky if the circumstances were correct. After his victory, national progressive groups were reaching out in bulk, offering support if I entered the race. When Chuck Schumer agreed to lift his unofficial embargo on my candidacy, some top-level staffers—including highly respected campaign managers—became interested in meeting. Recruiting a quality staff was no longer going to be an issue. My internal polling on the race versus McConnell showed that I would be an underdog, but an underdog with a path to victory. My head-to-head numbers against him were closer than any other candidate's (5 to 7 points), and many more people were "willing to consider" voting for me over other Democrats. If I wanted a case for getting into the election, there certainly was one to be made.

Of course, the negatives were still there too. The state loves Donald Trump. He will be on the ballot in 2020 and get 60 percent of the vote, making it more difficult for Kentucky Democrats to win down-ballot races. McConnell will clearly play unbelievably dirty, and running puts not only my life, but those of my family, girlfriend, and friends all directly into the national public eye. It isn't an exaggeration to say this could be the second-biggest race in America besides the presidential race in 2020. So it's not unrealistic to think that foreign countries might try to interfere with the proceedings. The amount of spying or hacking that could occur toward me is impossible to predict.

There is also the issue of the Democratic primary, where the national establishment and a massive war chest of cash are all waiting for me to declare so they can attack me personally and knock me out before I even get a chance to take on the Grim Reaper. Even if I have one stone to throw, this election will take two.

I took a trip to my alma mater, Transylvania University, just off Fourth Street and Broadway in the downtown area, to walk around. The campus has changed quite a bit since I attended; much more modern and new buildings have replaced virtually all that existed then. Transy was where I found my political voice, publicly advocating for a number of issues, including convincing the college administration to designate Martin Luther King's birthday as a school holiday, an issue that was surprisingly controversial at the time.*

As I walked into the building where I took all my political science classes, I could hear in my head the voice of my favorite professor at the school, Dr. Don Dugi. I once told him I might one day want to run for office in DC, and he said he thought that was a *terrible* idea. "Jones, these people in Washington play a different game from everyone else. It's ruthless. That's not you. The people who succeed there care only about themselves and will stab anyone in the back for power. You don't want that life."

Part of me thinks he is right. Look at Mitch McConnell. He is, by all accounts, one of the greatest politicians of modern times, becoming, through cunning and political acumen, the most powerful legislator in the United States since Lyndon Johnson. But he is also universally

---

* At the time, Transy was one of only a handful of schools in America that didn't recognize it.

reviled and disliked even by those he helps. He is said to have virtually no friends or close personal relationships. Is that what I really want?

Then I think of the messages of support and hope I have been flooded with for the past few months. In every county, I have heard the same message: "Matt, you have to run. You can win, and we will get behind you and help you!" I am sure every candidate hears some version of this, and it can easily create a distorted reality. But it is also effective and exhilarating. You truly begin to believe there is a movement for you, whether there is one or not. Still, I can't run in order to make others happy. If my heart isn't in it, then it wouldn't be the right thing to do.

I feel guilty for where my mind is taking me. Selfishly, I think it isn't worth the personal sacrifice required to take on this monster. But I also know Mitch needs to be defeated. I decide to call Rocky Adkins in Elliott County and get advice on what to do. We both have agreed not to run against each other, so if he is running, my decision is made. It would make it easy. Rock can win and I won't feel the burden of letting down so many people.

After exchanging pleasantries, Rocky leads off the conversation. "Matt, I have thought about it, and if you want in, and your heart is in it, have at it. I don't think it's for me." Damn it. Rocky beat me to the punch!

"That's what I was going to say to you!" I tell him. "Look, one of us needs to do this. You have more experience. Why not go for it?" He chuckles and says he doesn't really want the hassle or to have to deal with what it would mean for his family. I respond that I understand but feel guilty about the conclusion. People all over the state want one of us to get in; if we don't, aren't we letting them down?

Rocky replies, "Matt, my dad is an old codger, but he has a lot of wisdom. When I talked to him about this the other day, I said, 'Dad, a lot of folks want me to run against Mitch. What do you think?' He looked at me and said, 'Well, if they want you to run so damn much, tell *their* ass to run!'"

I laugh out loud. But he was right. Nobody else will have to stand in the ring and go face-to-face with the twin bulls of the Democratic Party and Mitch McConnell except the person running. If I'm not 100 percent ready to step into that arena and devote my every waking moment to it, I'm going to have to say no, even though part of me still wants the fight.

Two days later, I went on my radio show and announced my decision. The *KSR* sports fans were mostly pleased (particularly those who care more about who John Calipari is recruiting than they do about whatever happens in the Senate), preferring that their favorite sports show continue over me leaving for a political race. Lots of people called and wrote in with support—including my mom, who made a rare phone call to show her support. Her words of encouragement made me cry like a baby.

There was a lot of anger as well, especially on social media, as Democrats from around the country expressed their frustration that McConnell's reelection campaign just got easier. Some criticized me for "hurting McGrath" (presumably by the story coming out about her campaign getting me fired from my television show), while others simply called me selfish or weak. It was disappointing, but thanks to Rocky's dad, I had my retort to them.

I left the studio with mixed emotions. On the one hand, there was a great burden off my shoulders. A decision I had wrestled with for nearly two years was over, for better or worse, and there was relief. But I knew I would eventually have regrets. As I watched the campaign unfold, I was sure I would become frustrated with the decisions the other candidates made, and I would wish I was in the fight. It wouldn't be healthy, but it was probably inevitable.

The next day, my cohost Drew Franklin called me. Mitch McConnell's Tracker had showed up at our radio show and told Drew he wanted to speak with me when I had a minute. Drew got his number, and when I called, I was surprised by what he said:

"Matt, I wanted to let you know I quit my job. I found out they were going to do the FEC complaint a couple of days before it got released, and I tried to talk them out of it. I told them it was dirty, and it would backfire. I also said you guys didn't deserve it, but they don't get it and didn't listen. So, I put in my notice, and I quit. I don't want to be a part of this political race anymore, and I think I might go back home."

I was taken aback. I knew the Tracker wasn't happy with his job, but I didn't expect him to quit, certainly not at this point. Then he went further:

"I also just wanted to thank you. I followed you guys around the state this entire time, and you were always nice to me everywhere I went, even when you had no reason to be. I watched you guys interact with fans in all these small towns, and I could tell you guys really cared about the people. And then I would listen to my bosses talk about what their plans were to come after you, and . . . I just couldn't do it anymore. I am glad you are not running. It's not worth it."

I was left silent. I had grown to like the Tracker and felt sorry for him, but I couldn't have imagined this result. I told him I thanked him more than he could know. I said, "You have a bright future and are a good guy. You protected me and my girlfriend when you didn't have to. If you ever need anything, just ask."

"One request," he said. "How about one of those 'Free Matt Jones' shirts?"

EPILOGUE

FRANKLIN COUNTY

It's a New Day in Kentucky

"It's a new day in Kentucky, and time for a change!"

For the first time in a long time, Democrats in Kentucky have something to smile about. They are gathered en masse at the state capitol in Frankfort today to celebrate the inauguration of the brand-new Democratic governor. Andy Beshear's win over Matt Bevin sent shockwaves across the nation but was mostly met with a big sigh of relief in Kentucky. Finally, the state was rid of Matt Bevin and his brand of destructive politics that had divided Kentucky for so long.

It's a brisk, cold morning, but that hasn't stopped the victors from turning out large for the inaugural parade to the capitol. Food trucks hand out warm dishes on paper plates. When you are a Democrat in Kentucky, you take what you can get, and the smiles beaming throughout the large crowd showcase the happiness felt after four difficult years on the sidelines. People line the sidewalks of Capital Avenue, dressed in winter coats to cheer on the new boss and celebrate the changing of the guard in Kentucky.

I grab a free cup of hot chocolate from a tent nearby and make my way up the sidewalk. The inauguration parade includes people from each county in the state, so, as I watch the procession, constant reminders of our trip pass by.

There is the Hart County band playing a beautiful chorus of "America the Beautiful" through their shining brass horns, reminding me of Nichole Nimmo's tale of tears the day the ACA repeal was voted down, when she knew she would have the health care needed for her family.

Behind them is the Livingston County band, probably happy that they are marching on a well-tended street in the state's capital, rather than passing over their terrifying, cobbled-together bridge that divides their county in two. Their uniforms look sharp, and I can tell by their faces that they are excited for this big moment in the sun.

The Muhlenberg County Mustang Marching band is next, and the drums seem particularly powerful in their set. Our trip there opened my eyes to the way our nation systematically turns its back on our nation's coal miners, making it extremely difficult for them to get the care they need for the devastation caused on their bodies by the plague of black lung disease.

Looking a little rowdy is the Floyd Central Jaguar band (you can take the boy out of the mountains, but you can't take the mountains out of the boy), clad in blue and laughing as they march down the avenue. Their smiles take me back to the kindness of a boisterous group of Bible-studying seniors who welcomed us in for a barbershop Bible study, no questions asked.

Everywhere I look, something triggers a memory. We shake the hand of Kentucky Supreme Court Justice Lisabeth Tabor Hughes, who should be a judge on the Sixth Circuit Court of Appeals but became collateral damage of Mitch McConnell's war on Barack Obama's judicial nominations. We get her attention enough to ask her if we can interview her for the book, but she smiles and waves us off. Some things are better left forgotten.

Russell County judge executive Gary Robertson stands on the street, looking quite cold in his snug earmuffs. He is here representing a county still trying to overcome the hit of losing Fruit of the Loom, its biggest employer, with no warning. The community still hasn't totally recovered, but he is here, likely looking to promote his beloved hometown and help create a new future.

We hear a shout from the distance and see a smiling Lyon County judge executive Wade White, who taught us firsthand about the out-of-control Asian carp situation by taking us bowfishing under the stars and giving me my finest moment as an outdoorsman. He is a Republican and a Mitch McConnell supporter, but more important he has become a friend, and I root for his success in ending the leaping slimy fish plague that has taken over his county.

My goal when I left ten weeks ago was to determine what effect Mitch McConnell has had on the state of Kentucky. I knew he was the most destructive figure in modern American politics, but I wanted to understand what his leadership had done to my home state. The conclusion is now clear.

Time and time again, Mitch McConnell has consistently turned his back on the people of Kentucky, either voting against their interests or ignoring them altogether. Even though the state has been blessed with his supposed unprecedented aggregation of power and influence, it's citizens have been rewarded with nothing but heartache and wasted opportunity. McConnell has systematically supported policies that hurt Kentuckians disproportionately, from attempting to repeal the ACA to passing unprecedented tax cuts for the wealthiest Americans. Whenever there is a choice for Mitch between helping the state that elected him or the billionaire corporate Wall Street class that funds him, he chooses the latter—every time. The effect on the ground of those policies can be seen in the communities devastated by the loss of industry, individuals praying to have their most basic needs met, and teachers sacrificing to educate their children. McConnell has not only refused to use his power to help Kentucky, he has instead chosen policies that will specifically hurt them, bleeding his state dry of its resources and ensuring that its citizens have no voice in Washington to fight for their needs.

But this trip has taught me much more than just about Mitch McConnell. I have seen up-close how much of Kentucky, and America, feels left behind by modern politics in general, and how ill-suited our current system is to responding to their needs. Whether it's the laid-off coal miner in Pike County, the former tobacco farmer in Nicholas County, the flood victim in Pendleton County, the migrant worker in Todd County, the couple without insurance in Hart County, the Taco Bell employee in Jefferson County, or the small grocery store owner in Whitley County, a vast segment of America is completely ignored by politicians, media, and much of what passes as our current national conversation. Kentuckians are forgotten by a mainstream culture that devalues their importance and gives them almost no representation. The national parties don't even ask their opinion before selecting the candidates they believe best represent them, thus making them feel that there is no way for their voices to be heard. Even while having the most powerful leader in all the land on their side, Kentucky's economy, culture, and way of life have been completely transformed, with little care about what the future may hold for its citizens. Mitch's stock only rises, but Kentucky's remains stuck in place.

However, despite these difficulties I am also reminded about how many amazing Kentuckians are still fighting the good fight on the local level, trying to make their fellow citizens' lives better. From men like Wes Addington in Letcher County, who tirelessly works with little fanfare to protect the rights of sick coal miners; to Jenny Urie, the teacher in Owen County who uses her own money to allow her students to have reading material; to Kat Moses, the young woman in Pulaski County who worked to allow her fellow rural LGBTQ community to have pride in the fact that they are not alone. They are the part of Kentucky that makes it special—regular, average citizens who realize that the best values of the state are shown in helping others, especially those in need.

There could be no better result for Kentucky, or America, than for Mitch McConnell to be defeated and removed from office. He has been a singular destructive force for our state and our nation. However, I can't say that I am confident that is likely. Mitch McConnell is a political force in this state, and whether it's because of social issues, longevity, or fear, his power will be difficult to overcome.

But it is not impossible. People in Kentucky don't like Mitch McConnell and would love to have another valid option. But for that to occur, we have to focus on what really matters to people, the bread and butter issues that affect their daily lives. That means showing the impact of Mitch McConnell's leadership and policies not on a theoretical level, but in the real world, with the people hurt by his leadership. Political leaders and media need to do what Chris and I have done, get out into the communities across America and talk to those who feel left behind by modern America. There is no love for Mitch McConnell in

Kentucky, but until they feel others genuinely care and will fight for them, they will choose the devil they know over the ones they don't.

For thirty-six years Mitch McConnell has exacted his own will upon this state, without regard or consideration for the people we've met over the past few months. These are good people who need him, people who deserve better, and people who have been increasingly ignored at the hands of a senator whose only ambition is to amass power. That power isn't used to help. It's used to crush. But I'm encouraged by the people I've met on this trip. I've seen their resilience and their hope. I want change for them, and I'm heartened that a shift is beginning. It may be slow, and it may be a long road, but it's a beginning.

As I pull into my driveway and turn off my headlights, I sit for a moment in my darkened car. After 9,300 miles on the road, I'm left with one thought—we can do better than this. And, though it may be tough, it is up to us to show a new and brighter way.

ACKNOWLEDGMENTS

This has been an amazing experience for which we will forever be grateful. We would like to start by thanking our unbelievable researchers and assistants, without whom we could have never completed this project. Matt Young came to us highly recommended as an elite researcher and intellect. He surpassed that recommendation at every turn, and the depth of this book reflects his work. Eli Farrar began with us as an assistant and became our key resource, helping us in every way imaginable and using his creative and practical vision to improve the book every day. Maggie Davis is our longtime coworker, whose skills far exceed her young age. She was instrumental in helping us connect to the many wonderful people we met in this book. Each of these people came to us as resources, and we are proud to now call each of them friends.

We would also like to thank Simon & Schuster, who took a chance on two first-time authors and gave them the ability to pursue their dreams. Specifically, Jonathan Karp, who helped create the vision for this book and the freedom to shape it in the way we wanted. Thanks to our editor, Amar Deol, who has been an amazing confidant and helped walk us through this journey. This book would not have been possible without his expert guidance. A special thanks to our copy editor, the mysterious Phil Bashe, whom we have never met (but have a picture of in our head) but who improved this book exponentially. Thank you also to the Simon & Schuster staff, including Kimberly Goldstein, Gabby Robles, Caitlyn Reuss, Stephen Bedford, Jonathan Evans, Paul Dippolito, and Lisa Erwin for their help and support.

MATT: I would like to thank my mother, who has always believed in me and been my #1 fan. I love you more than you know, and you will always be my hero. Thanks to my father, Larry, the kindest human I will ever know. I'd like to thank my brilliant girlfriend, Rachel, for her love, understanding, and advice during this difficult process. You will one day write a book much better than this one, and I can't wait to read it. Thanks to all my wonderful friends for their support and guidance, and specifically my coworkers Ryan, Drew, and Shannon, who picked up the slack while I was gone and kept our radio show humming. Thanks to my agent, David Larabell, for helping make this book happen and teaching a first-time author how to navigate this difficult process. A special thanks to the fans of *KSR* and the people of Kentucky. It is for you guys that I worked so hard to make this book as good as it could be. And finally, thanks to Chris. I could never imagine having done this project with anyone else. Only you know what this was truly like, and I appreciate you helping me through these times more than you will ever know. You are an amazing author (we can say that now!), but a much better friend.

CHRIS: I can never thank enough the friends, family, and loved ones who have consistently encouraged me through this experience. The amazing love and positivity I felt from them at all hours of the day during this process has been invaluable and, truly, will never be forgotten. I'd like to thank my incredible wife, Laura, for her unfailing guidance, faith, confidence, and love; my son and daughter, Quentin and Ari, who made each of my returns through the front door of our home a celebration of happiness, joy, and reinvigoration; my brother, Scott, who has been there for me every day of our lives; and my late parents, John and Ann Tomlin, who always believed that, someday, I'd complete a book. I finally did, Mom and Dad. And I know you were present for all of it. To all of you, from the bottom of my heart, thank you. And, of course, I would like to thank Matt Jones; there's never been a better sounding board, travel companion, coworker, roommate, confidant, or compatriot—and no adventure grander than taking on this endeavor with a lifelong friend.

NOTES

CHAPTER 1: THE RISE OF MITCH

12 *Huddleston thought little of:* Michael York, "McConnell, Huddleston Senate Battle Heats Up," *Lexington (KY) Herald-Leader*, August 6, 1983, A1.

13 *He did little campaigning:* Ed Bean, "Huddleston Sees Negative Battle from McConnell," *Lexington (KY) Herald-Leader,* January 23, 1984, A1.

13 *spent not even $1 million:* Mark R. Chellgren, Associated Press, "McConnell Begins Campaign to Take Huddleston's Seat," *Lexington (KY) Herald-Leader*, January 18, 1984, B2.

13 *"Dope on Dee":* Diana Taylor, "At Fancy Farm, Politicians Pay Tribute," *Lexington (KY) Herald-Leader*, August 5, 1984, A1.

13 *The rise of Ailes:* Alec MacGillis, *The Cynic: The Political Education of Mitch McConnell* (New York: Simon & Schuster, 2014).

13 *He began campaigning harder:* Diana Taylor Osborne, "Senate Candidates to Debate Tonight," *Lexington (KY) Herald-Leader*, October 8, 1984, C1.

14 *around five thousand votes:* Kentucky State Board of Elections, "General Election Nov 6, 1984 | United States Senator," https://elect.ky.gov/SiteCollection Documents/Election%20Results/1980-1989/1984/84ussenate5.txt.

14 *Ailes took credit for the upset:* MacGillis, *The Cynic*.

14 *In the years following:* "Huddleston, Who Lost Senate Seat to McConnell, Dies," *Madisonville (KY) Messenger*, October 17, 2018, A2.

14 *never even saw him coming:* York, "McConnell, Huddleston Senate Battle Heats Up."

20 *millions of dollars:* Open Secrets Center for Responsive Politics, "Kentuckians for Strong Leadership, 2018 PAC Summary," n.d., https://www.opensecrets .org/pacs/lookup2.php?cycle=2018&strID=C00543256.

26 *Along with the transfer:* Jim Warren, "Fort Knox Is in Line to Lose Its Tanks—Armor in Kentucky Would Go to Georgia Pentagon Calls for Realignment of Military Bases," *Lexington (KY) Herald-Leader*, May 14, 2005, A1.

26 *Mitch McConnell promised repeatedly:* Ibid.

27 *He loudly took credit:* "Senate Candidates Push for Hardin Vote—Both Men Praise BRAC, "*News-Enterprise* (Elizabethtown, KY), October 29, 2008, https://www.thenewsenterprise.com/news/senate-candidates-push-for-hardin-vote/article_f45b71e2-9e48-5c0e-a0fd-812ce16cf91f.html.

27 *had nearly occurred in 1989:* Associated Press, "Measure Bans Moving Fort Knox Brigade," *Lexington (KY) Herald-Leader*, November 4, 1989, C2.

27 *Three thousand soldiers in the Third:* Marty Finley, "Campaigns Weigh in on Military Cuts—Potential Losses at Fort Knox Factor into Senate Race," *News-Enterprise* (Elizabethtown, KY), July 30, 2014, https://www.thenewsenterprise.com/news/local/campaigns-weigh-in-on-military-cuts/article_31a0a6b4-bd08-5368-a0ee-75bd9b3fd992.html.

27 *Even in his role:* Marty Finley, "Campaigns Weigh In on Military Cuts—Potential Losses at Fort Knox Factor into Senate Race," *News-Enterprise* (Elizabethtown, KY), July 30, 2014, local news sec.

28 *Abraham Lincoln Birthplace National:* National Park Service. "Abraham Lincoln Birthplace," n.d., https://www.nps.gov/abli/index.htm.

30 *On January 4th, 2019:* Matthew Daly, "Dems Pass Funding Plan Without Wall, Trump Digs In," *Chicago Sun-Times*, January 4, 2019, news sec.

30 *Browning wrote in a 2018 essay:* Christopher R. Browning, "The Suffocation of Democracy," *New York Review of Books*, October 25, 2018, https://www.nybooks.com/articles/2018/10/25/suffocation-of-democracy.

30 *British journalist William Howard:* James B. Conroy, *Lincoln's White House: The People's House in Wartime* (Lanham, MD: Rowman & Littlefield, 2016).

32 *wrote our state song:* My Old Kentucky Home State Park, "My Old Kentucky Home Is One of the Most Iconic 19th-Century Homes in America," n.d., https://www.visitmyoldkyhome.com/history-overview.

33 *Ellis was ambushed and shot:* Matthew Glowicki, "Who Killed Bardstown Officer Jason Ellis? 5 Years Later, Nobody Knows," *Louisville (KY) Courier-Journal*, May 22, 2018, https://www.courier-journal.com/story/news/crime/2018/05/22/bardstown-police-officer-jason-ellis-ambush-murder-investigation-mystery/612709002.

33 *Their assailant was never:* Travis Ragsdale, "Sunday Marks 5 Years Since Netherland Family Murders in Bardstown," WDRB online, last modified April 17, 2019, https://www.wdrb.com/news/sunday-marks-years-since-netherland-family-murders-in-bardstown/article_69bed6c4-6145-11e9-8600-9bdf5e1c006c.html.

33 *her car was discovered:* Fallon Glick, "New Lead Detective Takes Over Disappearance of Crystal Rogers," WDRB online, last modified August 27, 2019, https://www.wdrb.com/news/new-lead-detective-takes-over-disappearance-of-crystal-rogers/article_6f805470-c932-11e9-ac9d-270ee3dc06c6.html.

33 *on his property:* Katrina Helmer, "Bardstown Family Mourns Tommy Ballard on What Would Have Been His Birthday," WDRB online, last modified January 7, 2019, https://www.wdrb.com/news/bardstown-family-mourns

-tommy-ballard-on-what-would-have-been/article_a451e082-12d6-11e9-a517-9bd75cabdddc.html.

36 *Donald Trump won with 74:* Kentucky State Board of Elections, "Official 2016 General Election Results," n.d., https://elect.ky.gov/results/2010-2019/Documents/2016%20General%20Election%20Results.pdf.

37 *uninsured rate in Kentucky plummeted:* Jessica C. Barnett and Edward R Berchick, "Health Insurance Coverage in the United States: 2016 Current Population Reports," United States Census Bureau, September 2017, https://www.census.gov/content/dam/Census/library/publications/2017/demo/p60-260.pdf.

37 *would denote a bipartisanship:* Carl Hulse and Adam Nagourney, "Senate G.O.P. Leader Finds Weapon in Unity," *New York Times*, March 16, 2010, https://www.nytimes.com/2010/03/17/us/politics/17mcconnell.html.

37 *absent from Obama's presidency:* Dan Witters, "Kentucky, Arkansas Post Largest Drops in Uninsured Rates," Gallup online, last modified February 8, 2017, https://news.gallup.com/poll/203501/kentucky-arkansas-post-largest-drops-uninsured-rates.aspx.

38 "*root and branch*": Adam Cancryn, "McConnell's Straight Repeal Strategy Collides with Reality," *Politico*, July 18, 2017, https://www.politico.com/story/2017/07/18/mitch-mcconnell-obamacare-repeal-240676.

CHAPTER 2: THE WESTERN FRONT

47 *had embarrassed him a year earlier*: Mrs. Tyler Thompson, "Listen to Senator Mitch McConnell on Kentucky Sports Radio," *Kentucky Sports Radio,* October 8, 2014, https://kentuckysportsradio.com/main/listen-to-senator-mitch-mcconnell-on-kentucky-sports-radio.

49 *wading through ankle-deep sludge:* Associated Press, "Ky. Worker Testifies About Radiation," *Akron (OH) Beacon Journal,* September 21, 1999, A8.

49 *wiping green salt off:* John Warrick, "In Harm's Way, but in the Dark," *Washington Post*, August 8, 1999, A1.

49 *"Today we know the truth":* Ibid.

49 *Powder on the floor:* John Warrick, "A Deathly Postscript Comes Back to Life; After Being Rejected, Warnings of Paducah Atomic Worker Now Hailed as Heroism," *Washington Post*, August 11, 1999, A1.

49 *I have fingernails coming:* Michael Collins, "At Paducah Federal Plant, Workers Fear Toxic Betrayal," *Kentucky Post* (Covington, Ky.), August 14, 1999, 1K.

50 *The US Department of Energy:* Associated Press, "Widow Says New Tests Show Husband Died from Radiation," *Lexington (KY) Herald-Leader* (KY), June 18, 1985, B2.

50 *Joe's widow, Clara, was livid:* Ibid.

50 *No effort was spared:* Warrick, "A Deathly Postscript Comes Back to Life."

51 *"Drum Mountain":* GAO/RCED-00-96, "Nuclear Waste Cleanup DOE's Paducah Plan Faces Uncertainties and Excludes Costly Cleanup Activities," United States General Accounting Office (GAO), April 1, 2000, https://www.gao.gov/assets/240/230269.pdf.

51 *The Department of Energy inspector:* Ibid.

51 *Deep Water Horizon exploded:* United States Coast Guard, "On Scene Coordinator Report Deepwater Horizon Oil Spill," September 2011, https://homeport.uscg.mil/Lists/Content/Attachments/119/DeepwaterHorizonReport%20-31Aug2011%20-CD_2.pdf.

51 *black radioactive ooze seeping:* Associated Press, "Radioactive Ooze Found Outside Plant," August 29, 1999.

51 *wells of at least a hundred:* Susan Thomas, "People Complaining of Illnesses Live Near Smaller U.S. Plants, Too," *USA Today*, September 22, 1998.

51 *Well, there's no doubt we've:* Associated Press, "Paper Reports Old Maps Show Trail of Plutonium Outside Paducah Plant," *Evansville (IN) Courier*, October 2, 2000, B9.

51 *agreed to pay for those:* Thomas, "People Complaining of Illnesses."

51 *"In the past, I believe":* Warrick, "A Deathly Postscript Comes Back to Life."

52 *The bill provided $150,000:* United States Congress, "Title 42—The Public Health and Welfare Chapter 84—Department of Energy Subchapter Xvi—Energy Employees Occupational Illness Compensation Program," 2000, https://www.cdc.gov/niosh/ocas/pdfs/theact/eeoicpaall.pdf.

52 *To date, the plan has cost:* United States Department of Labor, "Office of Workers' Compensation Programs (OWCP) EEOICP Program Statistics," n.d., https://www.dol.gov/owcp/energy/regs/compliance/statistics/WebPages/PADUCAH_GDP.htm.

52 *Those individuals received no:* United States Congress, "Title 42."

52 *"west of I-65" reelection strategy:* Keith Lawrence, "McConnell: Bush Plans to Focus on Western Kentucky," *Owensboro (KY) Messenger-Inquirer*, May 19, 2000, 2.

52 *In 1988, just as McConnell:* Associated Press, "Congress Considering Buying Paducah Land," *Evansville (IN) Courier & Press*, July 11, 2005, B5.

52 *influence with the George H. W. Bush:* "Finalists to Be Interviewed for Economic Development Job," *Lexington (KY) Herald-Leader*, October 5, 1990, C2.

52 *get a new plant built:* Bill Straub, "Western Kentucky Vital in Senate Race," *Kentucky Post* (Covington, Ky.), October 30, 1990, 6K.

52 *even brought Dan Quayle:* Associated Press, "Politics—Quayle's Planned Visit Draws Criticism from Sloane," *Kentucky Post* (Covington, Ky.), October 5, 1990, 7K.

52 *McConnell turned around McCracken:* Kentucky State Board of Elections, "General Election Nov 6, 1990 | United States Senator," https://elect.ky.gov/SiteCollectionDocuments/Election%20Results/1990-1999/1990/90ussenate.txt.

53 *The dam broke in 1999*: Warrick, "In Harm's Way."

53 *McConnell and Kentucky's other:* GAO/RCED-00-96, "Nuclear Waste Cleanup."

55 *then completely collapse:* Pat Thomann, "Old Ledbetter Bridge Collapses," Kentucky Publishing Inc Newspaper Group, n.d., http://www.ky-news.com/old-ledbetter-bridge-collapses-cms-8067.

58 *Highway 64 would be expanded:* Kentucky Transportation Cabinet, "Kentucky's Fy 2016—Fy 2022 Highway Plan 'Connections to the Future,'" June 17, 2016, https://fivco.org/wp-content/uploads/2016/08/3-2016HighwayPlan.pdf.

64 *Asian carp population began multiplying:* "Asian Carp Overview," National Parks Service online, last modified June 24, 2019, https://www.nps.gov/miss/learn/nature/ascarpover.htm.

68 *led to the fort's abandonment:* Kathryn M. Fraser, "Fort Jefferson: George Rogers Clark's Fort at the Mouth of the Ohio River, 1780–1781," *Register of the Kentucky Historical Society* 81, no. 1 (1983): 1–24.

75 *McConnell's and Chao's offices coordinated:* Tanya Snyder, "Emails Reveal Coordination between Chao, McConnell Offices," *Politico,* February 19, 2019, https://www.politico.com/story/2019/02/19/mitch-mcconnell-elaine-chao-relationship-1163655.

75 *It has the third-fewest:* Kentucky Atlas and Gazetteer, "Hickman County, Kentucky," n.d., https://www.kyatlas.com/21105.html.

76 *Trumps tariffs have hurt:* Maya Rodriguez Valladares, "Trump's Trade Wars Are Hurting Midwest Farmers, Banks, and State Coffers," *Forbes*, last modified August 12, 2019, https://www.forbes.com/sites/mayrarodriguezvalladares/2019/08/12/trumps-trade-wars-are-hurting-midwest-farmers-banks-and-state-coffers/#378c308c5140.

76 *subsidies being offered to farmers:* Mike Dorning, "Trump's $28 Billion Trade War Bailout Is Overpaying Farmers," Bloomberg, December 4, 2019, https://www.bloomberg.com/news/articles/2019-12-04/trump-s-28-billion-trade-war-bailout-is-overpaying-many-farmers.

77 *soybean exports to China:* Jonas Ekblom and Chris Prentice, "Factbox: From Phone Makers to Farmers, the Toll of Trump's Trade Wars," Reuters, last modified August 23, 2019, https://www.reuters.com/article/us-usa-trade-china-costs-factbox/factbox-from-phone-makers-to-farmers-the-toll-of-trumps-trade-wars-idUSKCN1VE00B.

77 *Total agricultural exports:* Alan Rappeport, "Farmers' Frustration with Trump Grows as U.S. Escalates China Fight," August 27, 2019, *New York Times*, https://www.nytimes.com/2019/08/27/us/politics/trump-farmers-china-trade.html.

77 *Bankruptcies on agricultural loans:* John Newton and Allison Wilton, "Farm Loan Delinquencies and Bankruptcies Are Rising," American Farm Bureau Federation, last modified July 31, 2019, https://www.fb.org/market-intel/farm-loan-delinquencies-and-bankruptcies-are-rising.

77 *Family farms have been:* Alana Semuels, " 'They're Trying to Wipe Us off the Map': Small American Farmers Are Nearing Extinction," *Time*, November 27, 2019, https://time.com/5736789/small-american-farmers-debt-crisis-extinction/?fbclid=IwAR2HnDS0KvCqF7bHa6Fov3F3r4XkHWNBDvo55xNPGTuAXGKuvHO8YTYd17c.

86 *Kota was elected in 2018:* Derek Operle, "Meet Princeton's Young Mayor," *Paducah (KY) Sun*, December 30, 2018, https://www.paducahsun.com/news/local/meet-princeton-s-young-mayor/article_2f3780bc-5f6c-5295-b0f5-4de621c6f008.html.

89 *Two students were killed:* Holly Yan, Anne Claire Stapleton, and Paul P. Murphy, "Kentucky School Shooting: 2 Students Killed, 18 Injured," CNN, last modified January 24, 2018, https://www.cnn.com/2018/01/23/us/kentucky-high-school-shooting/index.html.

92 *Congress passed the Dickey Amendment:* Christine Jamieson, "Gun Violence Research: History of the Federal Funding Freeze," American Psychological Association, n.d., https://www.apa.org/science/about/psa/2013/02/gun-violence.

CHAPTER 3: SUBURBIA

98 *fourth elected* dog *mayor:* Brian Wiechert, "Rabbit Hash Has a New Dog Mayor," WLWY online, last modified January 4, 2017, https://www.wlwt.com/article/rabbit-hash-has-a-new-dog-mayor/8264863#.

98 *Bezos is now one:* "Bloomberg Billionaires Index #2 Jeff Bezos," Bloomberg, n.d., https://www.bloomberg.com/billionaires/profiles/jeffrey-p-bezos.

98 *number of billionaires:* Luisa Kroll, Matthew Miller, and Tatiana Serafin, "The World's Billionaires," *Forbes*, last modified March 11, 2009, https://www.forbes.com/2009/03/11/worlds-richest-people-billionaires-2009-billionaires-intro.html#569df3ad3847.

98 *jumped to more than*: Rupert Neate, "Number of Billionaires Worldwide Surged to 2,754 in 2017," *Guardian* (US edition), May 15, 2018, https://www.theguardian.com/business/2018/may/15/number-of-billionaires-worldwide-wealth-x-census.

98 *percentage of our nation's wealth:* Emmanuel Saez and Gabriel Zucman, "Wealth inequality in the United States since 1913: Evidence from capitalized income tax data," *Quarterly Journal of Economics* 131, no. 2 (2016): 519–78.

98 *Under his watch, tax:* Robert Bellafiore and Madison Mauro, "The Top 1 Percent's Tax Rates over Time," Tax Foundation online, last modified March 5, 2019, https://taxfoundation.org/top-1-percent-tax-rate.

98 *capital gains:* Tax Policy Center, "Briefing Book | How Are Capital Gains Taxed?", n.d., https://www.taxpolicycenter.org/briefing-book/how-are-capital-gains-taxed.

98 *Inheritances:* Julie Garber, "Federal Estate Tax Exemptions 1997 Through

2019," *The Balance,* last modified July 25, 2019, https://www.thebalance.com/exemption-from-federal-estate-taxes-3505630.

98 *Alternative minimum tax:* Tax Policy Center, "Briefing Book | Who pays the AMT?", n.d., https://www.taxpolicycenter.org/briefing-book/who-pays-amt.

98 *The cuts have been so extreme:* Aimee Picchi, "America's Richest 400 Families Now Pay a Lower Tax Rate Than the Middle Class," CBS News, last modified October 17, 2019, https://www.cbsnews.com/news/americas-richest-400-families-pay-a-lower-tax-rate-than-the-middle-class.

99 *used for stock buybacks:* Bob Pisani, "Stock Buybacks Hit a Record $1.1 Trillion, and the Year's Not Over," CNBC, last modified December 18, 2018, https://www.cnbc.com/2018/12/18/stock-buybacks-hit-a-record-1point1-trillion-and-the-years-not-over.html.

99 *claiming it will trickle:* William G. Gale and Andrew A. Samwick, "Effects of Income Tax Changes on Economic Growth," Economic Studies, available at https://www.brookings.edu/wpcontent/uploads/2016/06/09_Effects_Income_Tax_Changes_Economic_Growth_Gale_Sa mwick.pdf.

99 *expiring in just a few years:* Tax Policy Center, "Briefing Book | How Did the Tax Cuts and Jobs Act Change Personal Taxes?", n.d., https://www.taxpolicycenter.org/briefing-book/how-did-tax-cuts-and-jobs-act-change-personal-taxes.

99 *cuts to programs Kentuckians rely* Ryland Barton, "Kentucky Residents Fear Consequences of Obamacare Repeal." NPR, last modified March 1, 2017, https://www.npr.org/2017/03/01/517988156/kentucky-residents-fear-consequences-of-obamacare-repeal.

99 *Medicare, and Medicaid:* Nicole Goodkind, "Mitch McConnell Calls for Social Security, Medicare, Medicaid Cuts After Passing Tax Cuts, Massive Defense Spending," *Newsweek,* October 16, 2018, https://www.newsweek.com/deficit-budget-tax-plan-social-security-medicaid-medicare-entitlement-1172941.

99 *cut benefits for his Whole Foods workers:* Bob Bryan, "Amazon-Owned Whole Foods' Decision to Drop Health Benefits for Hundreds of Part-Time Workers Reveals How Promises to Workers like CEO Jeff Bezos' Recent Pledge Are Worthless," *Business Insider,* last modified September 13, 2019. https://www.businessinsider.com/whole-foods-healthcare-amazon-ceo-jeff-bezos-promises-business-roundtable-2019-9.

99 *average wage against inflation*: Sarah A. Donovan and David H. Bradley, "Real Wage Trends, 1979 to 2018," Congressional Research Service, last modified July 23, 2019, https://fas.org/sgp/crs/misc/R45090.pdf.

100 *share of wealth is dwindling:* Center on Budget and Policy Priorities, "Policy Basics: Non-Defense Discretionary Programs," July 12, 2019, https://www.cbpp.org/research/federal-budget/policy-basics-non-defense-discretionary-programs.

101 two hundred thousand *rumble along:* James Pilcher, "Yes, the Brent Spence Bridge Is 'Even Worse' than Before," *Cincinnati Enquirer,* February 14, 2017, https://www.cincinnati.com/story/news/your-watchdog/2017/02/14/brent-spence-accident-rates-traffic-counts-climb-bridge-national-spotlight/97643112/.

101 *estimated 3 percent of the US:* Ohio Department of Transportation in Conjunction with the Kentucky Transportation Cabinet. "BRENT SPENCE BRIDGE PROJECT OPTIONS ANALYSIS," September 2013, http://www.dot.state.oh.us/news/Documents/2013-10-01%20BSB_Options_Analysis%20FINAL.pdf.

101 *windshield, was completely shattered*: Amanda Van Benschoten, "Falling Concrete from Brent Spence Misses Tailgaters," *Cincinnati Enquirer*, September 14, 2014, https://www.cincinnati.com/story/news/local/2014/09/14/bengals-fan-car-totaled/15644057.

102 *horrendous, the accidents are dangerous:* Ally Marotti, "Four Were in Car That Fell 25 Ft off Brent Spence," *Cincinnati Enquirer*, August 5, 2014, https://www.cincinnati.com/story/news/traffic/2014/08/05/brent-spence-bridge-crash-update/13627677.

102 *emergency and national security projects:* "President-elect Trump: Emergency & National Security Projects," https://www.documentcloud.org/documents/3409546-Emergency-NatSec50Projects-121416-1-Reduced.html.

102 *reducing wages of construction workers:* "McConnell Campaigns for Low Wages," International Brotherhood of Electrical Workers online, last modified June 30, 2014, http://ibew.org/articles/14daily/1406/140630_america.htm.

102 *future, he punted:* John London, "Bridge-Building Takes Center Stage During Mitch McConnell's NKY Visit," WLWT online, last modified March 28, 2018, https://www.wlwt.com/article/bridge-building-takes-center-stage-during-mitch-mcconnells-nky-visit/19617804.

103 *the top eighty suburban:* Sean Rossman, "The Suburbs Turned on Republicans and Trump. The Midterm Election Results Prove It," *USA Today*, November 9, 2018, https://www.usatoday.com/story/news/politics/elections/2018/11/08/midterms-suburbs-republicans-democrats-trump/1921590002.

109 *Tourism, Arts and Heritage:* Kentucky Tourism, Arts and Heritage Cabinet, "Notice of Breach of Tax Incentive Agreement," July 18, 2017, https://ffrf.org/images/FFRFArkRecords_7.21.2017.pdf.

109 *$18 million in tax incentives:* Tom Loftus, "Ark Park Tax Incentives Worth up to $18M Approved," *Louisville (KY) Courier-Journal*, April 26, 2016, https://www.courier-journal.com/story/news/politics/ky-governor/2016/04/26/ark-park-tax-incentives-worth-up-18m-approved/83540204.

111 *"the Flood"*: " 'There Isn't Much Left of Falmouth,' " *Cincinnati Post*, March 3, 1997, 8A.

111 *95 percent of Falmouth:* Rick Van Sant, "62 Ft. and Rising: Flooding Worst in Generation," *Cincinnati Post*, March 4, 1997, 1A.

112 *eligible for a buyout*: John C. K. Fisher, "Abolishing Part of Falmouth Is Best Flood Plan, Officials Say," *Kentucky Post* (Covington, KY), March 20, 1997, 3K.

112 *213 residents applied:* "Flood Aid Divvied Up—Worst-Hit Homes OK'd for Buyouts," *Kentucky Post* (Covington, KY), May 28, 1997, 2K.

122 *Even Congressman John:* Phillip M. Bailey, "Yarmuth: Amy McGrath's Early Errors Show a Primary Challenge 'Might Be Helpful,' " *Louisville (KY) Courier-Journal*, July 11, 2019. https://www.courier-journal.com/story/news/politics/2019/07/11/amy-mcgrath-stumbles-spark-call-democratic-primary-challengers/1702660001.

123 *McGrath's advisors contacted my:* Daniel Desrochers, "Jones Says McGrath's Campaign Got Him Pulled from TV Show. But Did She Get Him Fired?" *Lexington (KY) Herald-Leader*, August 19, 2019, https://www.kentucky.com/news/politics-government/article234143142.html.

123 *political news website the* Intercept: Ryan Grim and Akela Lacy, "Amy McGrath's Senate Campaign Manager Helped Get Her Potential Primary Opponent Fired," *Intercept,* last modified August 18, 2019, https://theintercept.com/2019/08/18/amy-mcgrath-matt-jones-kentucky-senate-race.

125 *Wendell Berry:* Amanda Petrusich, "Going Home with Wendell Berry," *Atlantic*, July 14, 2019, https://www.newyorker.com/culture/the-new-yorker-interview/going-home-with-wendell-berry.

127 *"I am not a scientist"*: Amanda Terkel, "Mitch McConnell Pulls Out the 'I'm Not a Scientist' Dodge on Climate Change," *Huffington Post*, October 3, 2014, https://www.huffpost.com/entry/mitch-mcconnell-climate-change_n_5926548.

127 *mercury emission regulations:* Bill S J Res 20, vote number 2005-225 on September 13, 2005.

127 *Arctic National Wildlife Refuge:* Senate Roll Call Vote 52, 2005.

127 *Clean Water Act:* Senate Roll Call Vote 295, 2015.

128 *coal mine safety regulations:* Senate Roll Call Vote 98, 2012.

128 *national forests:* Bill HR.2107; vote number 1997-242 on September 17, 1997.

128 *global warming concerns into:* S.Amdt.1094 to H.R.1495; vote number 2007-166 on May 15, 2007.

128 *League of Conservation Voters:* League of Conservation Voters, "Scorecard | Mitch McConnell," 2018, http://scorecard.lcv.org/moc/mitch-mcconnell.

130 *guardian of gridlock:* Dana Milbank, "Mitch McConnell, the Man Who Broke America," *Washington Post,* April 7, 2017, https://www.washingtonpost.com/opinions/mitch-mcconnell-the-man-who-broke-america/2017/04/07/8e12f1d8-1bbd-11e7-9887-1a5314b56a08_story.html.

132 *9.1 percent of its county's population:* United States Census Bureau, "2017 Estimates," American Community Survey, 2017.

134 *border security and the wall:* Phillip M. Bailey, "McConnell and Paul Vote on Opposite Sides of Trump's Border Emergency," *Louisville (KY) Courier-Journal*, March 14, 2019, https://www.courier-journal.com/story/news/politics/2019/03/14/mitch-mcconnell-rand-paul-differ-trump-national-emergency-resolution/3161717002.

CHAPTER 4: COAL COUNTRY

142 *Hurricane Creek (pronounced "hurr-uh-cun"):* Tony Oppegard, "45 Years Ago, 38 Miners Were Sacrificed for Coal," *Lexington (KY) Herald-Leader*, December 29, 2015, https://www.kentucky.com/opinion/op-ed/article5213 7230.html.

142 *safety violations within three:* Ben A. Franklin, "Mine Where 38 Died Had Record of Safety Risks: Re-check Was Overdue," *New York Times*, January 1, 1971, 1.

146 *currently at a twenty-five-year high:* D. J. Blackley, C. N. Halldin, and A. S. Laney, "Continued Increase in Prevalence of Coal Workers' Pneumoconiosis in the United States, 1970–2017," *American Journal of Public Health* 108, no. 9 (2018): 1220–22.

146 *donated more than $7 million:* "Murray Energy (PAC) Summary," Open Secrets/Center for Responsive Politics, https://www.opensecrets.org/pacs /lookup2.php?cycle=2020&strID=C00410985. See also: "Murray Energy (organizations) Summary," Open Secrets/Center for Responsive Politics, https://www.opensecrets.org/orgs/totals.php?id=D000022123&cycle =2020.

147 *$330,000 to McConnell himself:* Tom Loftus, "Mitch McConnell's Top 50 Donors [UPDATED]," *Louisville (KY) Courier-Journal*, February 8 2016, https://www.courier-journal.com/story/news/politics/mitch-mcconnell/2016 /02/08/mitch-mcconnells-top-50-donors-updated/79996856/.

147 *"sleeping with your boss"*: John Cheves, "When McConnell's Pull Fails, His Labor Secretary Wife Fills In," *Lexington (KY) Herald-Leader*, October 20, 2006, *https://www.kentucky.com/news/special-reports/article44409960.html.*

149 *American Mines Act:* Alex Thomas, "Manchin, Capito Push Lawmakers to Fund Miners' Pensions, Health Care," *West Virginia Metro News*, November 21, 2019, http://wvmetronews.com/2019/11/21/manchin-capito-push-law makers-to-fund-miners-pensions-health-care.

149 *Mitch McConnell refused to call:* Joe Manchin, "Manchin, Brown, Casey, Kaine Fight for Retired Coal Miners Who Will Lose Their Healthcare by the End of the Year," press release, June 7, 2019, https://www.manchin.senate.gov/news room/press-releases/manchin-brown-casey-kaine-fight-for-retired-coal-miners -who-will-lose-their-healthcare-by-the-end-of-the-year-.

149 *Manchin was particularly furious:* Joe Manchin, "Manchin Condemns Mitch McConnell for Blocking Votes on Miners' Healthcare and Pensions," press release, June 27, 2019, https://www.manchin.senate.gov/newsroom/press -releases/manchin-condemns-mitch-mcconnell-for-blocking-votes-on-miners -healthcare-and-pensions.

149 *spoke with a number of legislators:* Rick Childress, "Miners Went to McConnell Hoping for His Endorsement. They Left with Mixed Feelings," *Lexington (KY) Herald-Leader*, July 24, 2019, https://www.kentucky.com/news/politics-gov ernment/national-politics/article233016257.html.

154 *Hunt rose from his seat:* Hey Kentucky!, "Martin County Water Crisis," YouTube, January 31, 2018, https://www.youtube.com/watch?v=gnx5i6AeMr8.

154 *nearby seventy-two-acre impoundment:* Alec MacGillis, *The Cynic: The Political Education of Mitch McConnell* (New York: Simon & Schuster, 2014).

154 Exxon Valdez *oil spill:* Ibid.

154 *contaminated the drinking water:* Ibid.

155 *From there, things moved quickly:* Lee Mueller, "Chao Seeking Inspector General's Review of Slurry Spill Investigation—Mine Agency's Engineer Complained of Problems," *Lexington (KY) Herald-Leader*, April 21, 2001, A1.

155 *anticipated hundreds of thousands of dollars:* MacGillis, *The Cynic.*

155 *federal fines totaling only* $5,600*:* Rita Price, "Still Buried in Sludge: Four Years After More Than 300 Million Gallons of Coal Slurry Inundated Part of Martin County, Ky., People There Feel as Bad Off as Ever," *Columbus (OH) Dispatch*, October 10, 2004, 1A.

155 *McConnell was the driving force:* MacGillis, *The Cynic*

155 *coal industry donations*: "Coal Mining - Summary," Open Secrets/Center for Responsive Politics, https://www.opensecrets.org/industries/indus.php?ind=e1210.

159 *Hazard hotel brought a lawsuit:* "Eastern Kentucky Man Sues Hampton Inn, Accuses Boss of Trying to Force Exorcism on Him," WKYT online, last modified March 28, 2019, https://www.wkyt.com/content/news/Eastern-Kentucky-man-sues-Hampton-Inn-accuses-boss-of-trying-to-force-exorcism-on-him-507789871.html.

161 *went to the train tracks and stood:* "Miners Block Train Tracks to Protest Bankrupt Coal Company," Associated Press State Wire: Kentucky (KY), July 30, 2019.

161 *Their resistance ignited an organized:* Sydney Boles, "Inside the Harlan County Coal Miner Protest," *Rolling Stone*, September 3, 2019, https://www.rollingstone.com/politics/politics-features/harlan-county-coal-miner-blockade-879324.

163 *ended the protest on September:* Chris Kenning, "Laid-off Kentucky Coal Miners End Their Railroad Protest but Still Seek Their Back Pay," *Louisville (KY) Courier-Journal*, September 26, 2019, https://www.courier-journal.com/story/news/2019/09/26/eastern-kentucky-coal-miners-end-blackjewel-railroad-blockade-protest/3775735002.

165 *Hillary Clinton proclaimed proudly*: "Full Rush Transcript, Hillary Clinton Part One, Democratic Presidential Town Hall," CNN, last modified March 13, 2016, http://cnnpressroom.blogs.cnn.com/2016/03/13/full-rush-transcript-hillary-clinton-partcnn-tv-one-democratic-presidential-town-hall.

166 *"Bloody Breathitt" County:* T. R. C. Hutton, *Bloody Breathitt: Politics and Violence in the Appalachian South* (Lexington: University Press of Kentucky, 2013).

167 *in 1903 and reported:* "The Disgrace of Kentucky," *New York Times*, June 18, 1903, 8.

169 *RECLAIM Act:* Eric Dixon, "Where's McConnell on Boost for Coal Country?," *Lexington (KY) Herald-Leader*, September 18, 2016, 5C.

169 *Even though Rogers was:* James Higdon, "The Obama Idea to Save Coal Country," *Politico Magazine*, June 3, 2017, https://www.politico.com/magazine/story/2017/03/the-obama-administration-idea-to-save-coal-country-214885.

169 *Obama's bill but to refile it:* "Bipartisan RECLAIM Act of 2017 Introduced for 115th Congress," Congressman Hal Rogers Press Release, March 27, 2017, https://halrogers.house.gov/press-releases?ID=BFABA136-F679-406F-A27E-57D365E0A46A.

169 *gone to receive a vote in the Senate:* S.728—115th Congress (2017–2018)

170 *Wolfe County:* Robert Wood Johnson Foundation. "County Health Rankings and Roadmaps | Kentucky, Wolfe County," https://www.countyhealthrankings.org/app/kentucky/2018/rankings/wolfe/county/outcomes/overall/snapshot.

171 *problem get worse over the years:* United States Centers for Disease Control and Prevention, "Vulnerable Counties and Jurisdictions Experiencing or At-Risk of Outbreaks," n.d., https://www.cdc.gov/pwid/vulnerable-counties-data.html.

171 *prescriptions for opioids in Wolfe:* "U.S. County Prescribing Rates, 2017," Centers for Disease Control and Prevention, last modified July 31, 2017, https://www.cdc.gov/drugoverdose/maps/rxcounty2017.html.

172 *improvements to its downtown*: Matt Young, "Revitalization Effort Kindles Hope in Campton; Aim Is to Attract Residents, Tourists," *Lexington (KY) Herald-Leader*, August 18, 2014, A3.

172 *campaign donations from Big Pharma:* Open Secrets/Center for Responsive Politics. "Pharmaceuticals / Health Products: Money to Congress," n.d., https://www.opensecrets.org/industries/summary.php?ind=h04&recipdetail=S&sortorder=A&cycle=All.

172 *companies to market directly to consumers:* Susan Kelly, "U.S. Doctor Group Calls for Ban on Drug Advertising to Consumers," Reuters, November 17, 2015, *https://www.reuters.com/article/us-pharmaceuticals-advertising/u-s-doctor-group-calls-for-ban-on-drug-advertising-to-consumers-idUSKCN0T62WT20151117.*

172 *held up a near-unanimous bipartisan bill:* Colby Itkowitz, "The Health 202: Some experts think McConnell is playing politics with the opioid crisis," *Washington Post*, July 26, 2018.

182 *repeatedly tried to take NEA*: Mary Ann Roser, "Delegation Wants to Curb Arts Agency's Power—State's Congressmen Upset by Content of Some Federally Funded Exhibits," *Lexington (KY) Herald-Leader,* July 29, 1990, B1.

183 *as a senior he helped its 1982:* Staff, "Morehead to Honor 1982-83 NCAA Tournament Team," WKYT (Lexington, KY), February 1, 2018, https://www

.wkyt.com/content/sports/Morehead-to-honor-1982-83-NCAA-tournament-team-472182243.html.

184 *Coal employment is now less:* "Kentucky Quarterly Coal Report," Kentucky Energy and Environment Cabinet, August 15, 2019, https://eec.ky.gov/Energy/News-Publications/Quarterly%20Coal%20Reports/2019-Q2.pdf.

184 *less than six thousand:* Federal Reserve Bank of St. Louis, "All Employees: Mining: Coal Mining in Kentucky," n.d., https://fred.stlouisfed.org/series/SMU21000001021210001A.

CHAPTER 5: MITCH'S BASE

194 *stared directly at the sun:* Chris, Cillizza. "Yes, Donald Trump Really Did Look into the Sky during the Solar Eclipse." CNN, August 22, 2017, https://www.cnn.com/2017/08/21/politics/trump-solar-eclipse/index.html.

201 *improvements to the Henderson Riverfront:* Scripps Newspapers. "Senators visit Henderson/McConnell applauds riverfront upgrades," *Evansville (IN) Courier & Press*, p. 4A.

205 *not help the American farmer:* David G. Tuerck and William Burke, *NFAP Policy Brief: An Analysis of Tariff Costs and Regulatory Savings Under Trump Administration Policies* (Arlington, VA: National Foundation for American Policy, September 2019), https://Nfap.Com/Wp-Content/Uploads/2019/09/Tariffs-And-Regulations.Nfap-Policy-Brief.September-2019.Pdf.

205 *happening already in South American countries:* Karl Plume and Hallie Gu, "After Trade Talks in U.S., China Ramps Up Brazilian Soy Purchases," Reuters, last modified October 18, 2019, Reuters.com/article/us-usa-trade-china-soybeans/after-trade-talks-in-us-china-ramps-up-brazilian-soy-purchases-idUSKBN1WX1AG.

213 *requires miners to jump:* United States Department of Labor, "Division of Coal Mine Workers' Compensation (DCMWC) Step-by-Step Guide to Filing for Benefits," n.d., https://www.dol.gov/owcp/dcmwc/guidefilingbenefits.htm.

214 *through government safety regulations:* United States Department for Health and Human Services, "Criteria for a Recommended Standard | Occupational Exposure to Respirable Coal Mine Dust," September 1995, https://www.cdc.gov/niosh/docs/95-106/pdfs/95-106.pdf?id=10.26616/NIOSHPUB95106.

217 *only one abortion clinic:* Deborah Yetter, "With Future of Kentucky's Abortion Clinic at Stake, Battle Shifts to Federal Appeals Court," *Louisville (KY) Courier-Journal*, August 8, 2019, https://www.courier-journal.com/story/news/politics/elections/kentucky/2019/08/08/battle-over-kentucky-abortion-clinic-rules-shift-to-federal-appeals-court/1946352001.

221 *Her opponent was an older:* Doreen Dennis, "Daniels, Townsend Compete for Seat on Madisonville Council," SurfKY News, October 21, 2016, https://surfky.com/index.php/hopkins/hopkins-county-news/113551-daniels-townsend-compete-for-seat-on-madisonville-council.

224 *systematically eliminated long-standing Senate:* Robert Reich, "How McConnell Is Killing the Senate," *American Prospect*, April 16, 2019, https://prospect.org/power/mcconnell-killing-senate.

224 *party's political gain:* Dana Milbank, "Mitch McConnell, the Man Who Broke America," *Washington Post,* April 7, 2017, https://www.washingtonpost.com/opinions/mitch-mcconnell-the-man-who-broke-america/2017/04/07/8e12f1d8-1bbd-11e7-9887-1a5314b56a08_story.html.

224 *the confirmation of Judges:* Norm Ornstein, "The Senate Shreds Its Norms," *Atlantic*, September 7, 2018, https://www.theatlantic.com/ideas/archive/2018/09/senate-kavanaugh/569596/.

225 *One-third of all coal:* Evan Gorman, "Union Co. Leads State's Coal Production, Receives Biggest Share of Excess Coal Severance Tax Revenues," WFIE online, last modified August 5, 2019, https://www.14news.com/2019/08/06/union-co-leads-states-coal-production-receives-biggest-share-excess-coal-severance-tax-revenues.

CHAPTER 6: RETURNING HOME

247 *Bill Clinton once visited:* James E. Castro, "Special Report: President Clinton Visits Appalachia," Appalachian Regional Commission, https://www.arc.gov/magazine/articles.asp?ARTICLE_ID=97&F_ISSUE_ID=13&F_CATEGORY_ID=.

254 *On the day of the event:* Bill Estep, "Pride and Protest. First LGBTQ Festival in Southern Kentucky Points up Different Views," *Lexington (KY) Herald-Leader*, October 6, 2019. https://www.kentucky.com/news/state/kentucky/article235851652.html.

255 *ask Moses about Mitch McConnell:* Charles Lane, "A More Appropriate Target for the LGBTQ Discrimination Case: Mitch McConnell," *Washington Post*, October 14, 2019, https://www.washingtonpost.com/opinions/a-more-appropriate-target-for-the-lgbtq-discrimination-case-mitch-mcconnell/2019/10/14/16be3d02-ee8f-11e9-8693-f487e46784aa_story.html.

255 *He is against gay marriage:* D. John Sauer, "Brief of 57 Members of U.S. Congress as Amici Curiae in Support of Respondents," Amici Briefings, United States Supreme Court Case Numbers 14-556, 15-562, 14-571, and 14-574, n.d.

257 *number of citizens:* 2016 Kentucky Health Issues Poll, "Uninsured Rate for Kentucky Adults at 12 percent; Public Insurance Declines," February 2017, https://www.healthy-ky.org/res/images/resources/KHIP-insurance-FINAL_1.pdf.

257 *2013 and 2016 the number of uninsured:* Jessica C. Barnett and Edward R. Berchick. "Health Insurance Coverage in the United States: 2016 Current Population Reports," United States Census Bureau, September 2017, https://www.census.gov/content/dam/Census/library/publications/2017/demo/p60-260.pdf.

258 *receive a primary election challenge:* Alec MacGillis, *The Cynic: The Political Education of Mitch McConnell* (New York: Simon & Schuster, 2014).

258 *"win" for President Obama:* Hulse and Nagourney, "Senate G.O.P. Leader Finds Weapon in Unity."

260 *and other similar rural medical facilities:* United States Government Accountability Office, "GAO-18-634 RURAL HOSPITAL CLOSURES | Number and Characteristics of Affected Hospitals and Contributing Factors," August 2018, https://www.gao.gov/assets/700/694123.pdf.

260 *remaining financially solvent:* Richard C. Lindrooth et al., "Understanding the Relationship Between Medicaid Expansions and Hospital Closures," *Health Affairs* 37, no. 1 (2018): 111–20.

260 *most will end up closing:* Joan Alker, Jack Hoadley, and Mark Holmes, *Health Insurance Coverage in Small Towns and Rural America: The Role of Medicaid Expansion* (Washington, DC: Georgetown University Center for Children and Families and the University of North Carolina NC Rural Health Research Program, September 2018), https://ccf.georgetown.edu/wp-content/uploads/2018/09/FINALHealthInsuranceCoverage_Rural_2018.pdf.

261 *Insurance providers are some:* Open Secrets/Center for Responsive Politics. "Insurance—All Senators—All Cycles," n.d., https://www.opensecrets.org/industries/summary.php?ind=F09&recipdetail=S&sortorder=A&cycle=All.

261 *more money from insurance providers:* Open Secrets/Center for Responsive Politics. "Health Services/HMOs—All Senators—All Cycles," n.d., https://www.opensecrets.org/industries/summary.php?ind=H03&recipdetail=S&sortorder=A&cycle=All.

261 *insurance industry spent $102:* Rick Unger, "Busted! Health Insurers Secretly Spent Huge to Defeat Health Care Reform While Pretending to Support Obamacare," *Forbes*, June 25, 2012, https://www.forbes.com/sites/rickungar/2012/06/25/busted-health-insurers-secretly-spent-huge-to-defeat-health-care-reform-while-pretending-to-support-obamacare/#77b6a05d4248.

261 *half million Kentuckians would lose:* Deborah Yetter, "Talk of Obamacare Repeal Alarms Kentuckians," *Louisville (KY) Courier-Journal*, January 30, 2017, https://www.courier-journal.com/story/news/politics/2017/01/30/talk-obamacare-repeal-alarms-kentuckians/97038598.

261 *"If you get sick in America":* Brian Montopoli, "Alan Grayson 'Die Quickly' Comment Prompts Uproar," CBS News, September 30, 2009, https://www.cbsnews.com/news/alan-grayson-die-quickly-comment-prompts-uproar/.

262 *premise goes something like:* Mary Meehan, "Two Clear Visions = One Clinic—Doctor and Woman Share Philosophy to Help Town in Need," *Lexington (KY) Herald-Leader*, September 24, 2000, C1.

263 *fishing on their lunch breaks:* Katie Rollins, "Paint Lick News: Meeting Planned for Village Fest," *Richmond (KY) Register*, August 15, 2019, https://www.richmondregister.com/community/meeting-planned-for-villagefest/article_881c7f71-50a6-58b4-ad6d-176066c1bea6.html.

263 *Thankfully, the Affordable Care Act:* Jim Warren, "Closed Garrard Clinic Will Reopen in August: Founder Will Work Under New Management," *Lexington (KY) Herald-Leader*, May 2, 2014, 3A.

264 *temporary health funding for areas:* Jason Cherkis and Zach Carter, "Mitch McConnell's 30-Year Senate Legacy Leaves Kentucky in the Lurch," *Huffington Post*, July 11, 2013, https://www.huffpost.com/entry/mitch-mcconnell-profile_n_3550173.

269 *wrote his senior thesis:* Staff report, "12 Things to Know About Mitch McConnell," *Christian Science Monitor*, November 30, 2014, https://www.csmonitor.com/USA/Politics/DC-Decoder/2014/1130/12-things-to-know-about-Mitch-McConnell.

269 *Harry Reid leered at his:* Kathleen Hennessey, "Congress Calls on Henry Clay in Budget Debate," *Los Angeles Times*, April 8, 2011, https://www.latimes.com/world/la-xpm-2011-apr-08-la-na-shutdown-clay-20110408-story.html.

274 *Two Corinthians 3:17:* Jessica Taylor, "Citing 'Two Corinthians,' Trump Struggles to Make the Sale to Evangelicals." NPR, last modified January 18, 2016, https://www.npr.org/2016/01/18/463528847/citing-two-corinthians-trump-struggles-to-make-the-sale-to-evangelicals.

275 *editorial in the publication Christianity Today:* Mark Galli, "Trump Should Be Removed from Office," *Christianity Today,* December 19, 2019, https://www.christianitytoday.com/ct/2019/december-web-only/trump-should-be-removed-from-office.html.

CHAPTER 7: "WE NEVER EXISTED"

289 *Three-fourths of its black populace*: Michael L. Jones, "American Cities Are Still Grappling with the Legacy of a Louisville Zoning Case After More Than a Century," *Insider Louisville,* January 16, 2019, https://insiderlouisville.com/economy/american-cities-are-still-grappling-with-the-legacy-of-a-louisville-zoning-case-after-more-than-a-century.

290 *In his autobiography:* Muhammad Ali and Richard Durham, *The Greatest: My Own Story*, repr. ed. (New York: Random House, 1975; Los Angeles: Graymalkin Media, 2015).

290 *city passed an ordinance prohibiting:* U.S. Reports, "Buchanan v. Warley, 245 U.S. 60 (1917)," http://cdn.loc.gov/service/ll/usrep/usrep245/usrep245060/usrep245060.pdf.

290 *even under the "separate but equal":* Ibid.

290 *Home Owners' Loan Corporation (HOLC):* The Louisville/Jefferson County Information Consortium, "Redlining Louisville," December 14, 2017, https://www.lojic.org/redlining-louisville-news.

290 *work of Harland Bartholomew:* Joshua Poe, "Redlining Louisville: Racial Capitalism and Real Estate," The Louisville/Jefferson County Information

Consortium, December 14, 2017, https://lojic.maps.arcgis.com/apps/Map Series/index.html?appid=e4d29907953c4094a17cb9ea8f8f89de.

291 *May 27, 1968, on the corner:* Staff Report. "Guard Ordered to Riot Duty as West End Looting Flare," *Louisville (KY) Courier-Journal*, May 28, 1968, A1.

292 *were pelted with rocks:* Reginald Stuart, "Louisville: Underlying Issue Remains Race," *New York Times*, November 6, 1977, https://timesmachine.nytimes.com/timesmachine/1977/11/06/167920722.html?pageNumber=197.

292 *Mitch McConnell began his political career:* MacGillis, *The Cynic*.

292 *incumbent county judge-executive:* John David Dyche, "The Rise of Mitch McConnell," *Louisville (KY) Courier-Journal*, October 30, 2007.

CHAPTER 8: MOSCOW MITCH

298 *"It's an effort to smear me:* Sarah Ladd, "Over the Top" McConnell Still Mad about #MoscowMitch, Calls Attention to 2020 Election," *USA Today*, September 4, 2019, https://www.usatoday.com/story/news/politics/2019/09/04/mcconnell-moscow-mitch-over-top-smear-and-unbelievable/2207022001/.

299 *Braidy's vision, said Bouchard:* Morgan Watkins, "Braidy Industries Breaks Ground on Bevin-Backed, $1.5B Aluminum Mill," *Louisville (KY) Courier-Journal* online, June 1, 2018, https://www.courier- journal.com/story/news/politics/2018/06/01/braidy-industries-breaks-ground-aluminum- mill-eastern-kentucky/646290002.

299 *Matt Bevin even decided to invest:* Ronnie Ellis, CNHI News Service, "15 Million to Braidy Explained," *Daily Independent* (Ashland, KY), May 26, 2017, https://www.dailyindependent.com/news/million-to-braidy-explained/article_62c74312- 425f-11e7-b6aa-f70296e698fe.html.

299 *move to sanction Deripaska:* "US punishes key Putin allies over worldwide 'malign activity,' " BBC News, April 6, 2018, https://www.bbc.com/news/world-us-canada-43672190.

299 *statement from the US Treasury:* U.S. Department of the Treasury, "Treasury Designates Russian Oligarchs, Officials, and Entities in Response to World-wide Malign Activity," April 6, 2018, https://home.treasury.gov/news/press-releases/sm0338.

300 *A US embassy cable:* Simon Shuster and Vera Bergengruen, "A Kremlin-Linked Firm Invested Millions in Kentucky. Were They After More Than Money?," *Time*, last modified August 13, 2019, https://time.com/5651345/rusal-investment-braidy-kentucky.

300 *"meet and greet" with Rusal:* Ron Wyden, "Letter to Mr. Craig Brouhard," United States Senate Committee on Finance, October 8, 2019. https://www.finance.senate.gov/imo/media/doc/100819%20Wyden%20Letter%20to%20Craig%20Bouchard%20Braidy%20Industries.pdf

300 *shares in the company were distributed:* Polina Devitt and Arshad Mohammed, "Questions Linger over Deripaska's Rusal Influence after U.S. Deal," Reuters, February 9, 2019, https://www.reuters.com/article/us-usa-russia-sanctions-rusal-analysis/questions-linger-over-deripaskas-rusal-influence-after-us-deal-idUSKCN1PT0K9.

300 *Mitch McConnell strong-armed several GOP:* Kenneth P. Vogel, "Republicans Break Ranks over Move to Lift Sanctions on Russian Oligarch's Firms," *New York Times*, January 15, 2019, https://www.nytimes.com/2019/01/15/us/politics/republicans-sanctions-russian-oligarchs.html.

300 *two of McConnell's former staffers:* Natasha Bertrand and Theodoric Meyer, "Ex-McConnell Staffers Lobbied on Russian-Backed Kentucky Project," *Politico,* last modified July 31, 2019, https://www.politico.com/story/2019/07/31/mcconnell-staffers-lobbied-russian-backed-kentucky-project-1442550.

300 *Rusal invested $200 million:* Chris Otts, "Braidy Industries CEO Craig Bouchard Says Kentucky's Most-Anticipated Aluminum Plant Will Be Built," WDRB online, last modified November 11, 2019, https://www.wdrb.com/in-depth/braidy-industries-ceo-craig-bouchard-says-kentucky-s-most-anticipated/article_bfdb6448-04d1-11ea-990b-c3d75bca8000.html.

301 *donated more than $3.5 million:* Dana Milbank, "McConnell's New Posture Toward Moscow," *Washington Post*, August 2, 2019, https://www.washingtonpost.com/opinions/mcconnells-new-posture-toward-moscow/2019/08/02/a3b5a080-b53f-11e9-951e-de024209545d_story.html.

301 *fiercest anti-Russian hawks:* James Carroll, "Bunning Has Begun Process for Another Senate Run in 2010," *Louisville (KY) Courier-Journal*, December 5, 2004.

301 *"shine like diamonds":* John Cheves, "Senator's Pet Issue: Money and the Power It Buys," *Lexington (KY) Herald-Leader*, October 15, 2006, https://www.kentucky.com/news/special-reports/article44409951.html.

302 *procure the rest of their funding:* Chris Otts, "Braidy Industries Still Lacks Financing for Eastern Ky. Aluminum Mill, Filing Shows," WDRB online, last modified July 16, 2019, https://www.wdrb.com/in-depth/braidy-industries-still-lacks-financing-for-eastern-ky-aluminum-mill/article_7a087dd2-a7d6-11e9-870e-37955752433a.html.

302 *loaning its CEO money:* Otts, "Braidy Industries CEO Craig Bouchard Says."

303 *more than eleven thousand job applications:* Ibid.

303 *two-year degree program:* Ibid.

304 *America for Sale:* Craig T. Bouchard and James V. Koch, *America for Sale: How the Foreign Pack Circled and Devoured Esmark* (Santa Barbara, CA: ABC-CLIO, 2009).

317 *choices favoring the Big Tobacco:* Cheves, "Senator's Pet Issue."

317 *exchange for around $650,000:* Open Secrets/Center for Responsive Politics, "Tobacco—All Senators—All Cycles," n.d., https://www.opensecrets.org/industries/summary.php?ind=A02&recipdetail=S&sortorder=A&cycle=All.

317 *University of Louisville's McConnell Center:* Tom Dreisbach, "Tobacco's 'Special Friend': What Internal Documents Say About Mitch McConnell," NPR, last modified June 17, 2019, https://www.npr.org/2019/06/17/730496066/tobaccos-special-friend-what-internal-documents-say-about-mitch-mcconnell.

317 *Big Tobacco's most powerful ally:* Cheves, "Senator's Pet Issue."

318 *shield the manufacturers from litigation:* Ibid.

320 *Wendell Ford had proposed a similar:* Suein L. Hwang, "Tobacco Companies Say Deal Would Cut Cigarette Use 43 Percent," *Wall Street Journal*, October 10, 1997, https://www.wsj.com/articles/SB876440444197153500.

320 *advocate for these components again:* Nancy Zuckerbrod, "Ford Urges Farm Leaders to Back Company's Plan," *Kentucky Post* (Covington, KY), August 9, 2003, K3.

320 *McConnell propose a different plan:* James Carroll, "Senators Propose $13 Billion Buyout of U.S. Tobacco Program," *Louisville (KY) Courier-Journal*, July 31, 2003.

321 *about a third less money:* Cecil H. Yancy Jr., "Tobacco Buyout Takes Center Stage," *Southeast Farm Press*, July 2, 2003, https://www.farmprogress.com/tobacco-buyout-takes-center-stage-0.

323 *industry's most awesome BFF*: Tom Driesbach, "Tobacco's 'Special Friend': What Internal Documents Say About Mitch McConnell," NPR, June 17, 2019, https://www.npr.org/2019/06/17/730496066/tobaccos-special-friend-what-internal-documents-say-about-mitch-mcconnell.

323 *still doing Big Tobacco's bidding:* Angelica LaVito, "Sen. Majority Leader McConnell to Introduce Bill to Raise the Minimum Age to Buy Tobacco to 21," CNBC, last modified April 18, 2019, https://www.cnbc.com/2019/04/18/mcconnell-to-introduce-bill-for-a-minimum-age-to-buy-tobacco-of-21.html.

323 *the tobacco companies* supported*:* Alex Kotch, "McConnell's Tobacco 21 Bill Exposes States to Big Tobacco's Wishlist," *American Prospect*, last modified May 31, 2019, https://prospect.org/justice/mcconnell-s-tobacco-21-bill-exposes-states-big-tobacco-s-wishlist.

323 *a perfect trade-off*: Renuka Rayasam, Rachana Pradhan, and Sarah Owermohle, "McConnell Plan to Hike Smoking Age Could Be Win for Tobacco Companies," *Politico,* last modified April 28, 2019, https://www.politico.com/story/2019/04/28/mitch-mcconnell-smoking-age-tobacco-companies-1376631.

323 *future regulation to the states:* Liz Essley Whyte and Dianna Nanez, "Big Tobacco's Surprising New Campaign to Raise the Smoking Age," Public Integrity, May 23, 2019, https://publicintegrity.org/politics/state-politics/copy-paste-legislate/big-tobaccos-surprising-new-campaign-to-raise-the-smoking-age.

323 *did it again for big tobacco:* Al Cross, "As the Tobacco Industry Transitions into E-Cigarettes, McConnell Transitions from Tobacco Advocate into Health Advocate," Kentucky Health News, last modified June 19, 2019, http://ci.uky

.edu/kentuckyhealthnews/2019/06/19/as-the-tobacco-industry-transitions-into-e-cigarettes-mcconnell-transitions-from-tobacco-advocate-into-health-advocate.

326 *judge sentenced Samuel Girod to six:* Jordan Reimschisel, "How the FDA Made a Felon Out of This Amish Farmer," *Daily Beast*, August 1, 2017, https://www.thedailybeast.com/how-the-fda-made-a-felon-out-of-this-amish-farmer.

331 *second-highest amount of federal money:* Rockefeller Institute of Government, "Giving or Getting? New York's Balance of Payments with the Federal Government," September 2017, https://rockinst.org/issue-area/giving-getting-new-yorks-balance-payments-federal-government-2.

335 *first ran for county judge-executive:* Alec MacGillis, *The Cynic: The Political Education of Mitch McConnell* (New York: Simon & Schuster, 2014).

337 *lowest median household income:* United States Census Bureau, 2017 American Community Survey.

338 *state-of-the-art Internet system:* Callie Rainey, "Two Eastern Kentucky Counties Ahead of Broadband Speeds in America," WYMT online, last modified February 8, 2016, https://www.wymt.com/content/news/Two-Eastern-Kentucky-counties-ahead-of-broadband-speeds-in-America-368070431.html.

CHAPTER 9: GOD, GUNS & BABIES

349 Citizens United v. Federal Election Commission: Supreme Court of the United States, "Citizens United v. Federal Election Commission," January 21, 2010, https://www.supremecourt.gov/opinions/09pdf/08-205.pdf.

349 *unlimited dark money:* Karl Evers-Hillstrom, et al. "A Look at the Impact of Citizens United on Its 9th Anniversary." *Open Secrets | Center for Responsive Politics*, 21 Jan. 2019, *https://www.opensecrets.org/news/2019/01/citizens-united/*.

349 *made it his sole goal:* Alec MacGillis, *The Cynic: The Political Education of Mitch McConnell* (New York: Simon & Schuster, 2014).

350 *He knew labor unions:* "Editorial: Union Busting," *Louisville (KY) Courier-Journal*, April 19, 2003.

350 *Democrats would benefit most:* T. Klumpp, H. M. Mialon, and M.A. Williams, "The business of American democracy: Citizens United, independent spending, and elections," *The Journal of Law and Economics* 59(1), 2016, 1–43.

350 *exactly what McCain was referring:* Alison Mitchell, "Republicans Pillory McCain in Debate over Soft Money," *New York Times*, October 15, 1999, https://www.nytimes.com/1999/10/15/us/republicans-pillory-mccain-in-debate-over-soft-money.html.

350 *"worst day of my political life"*: Katrina vanden Heuvel "Mitch McCconnell's 47 Percent Moment," *Washington Post*, September 3, 2014, https://www.washingtonpost.com/opinions/katrina-vanden-heuvel-mitch-mcconnells-47

-percent-moment/2014/09/03/24f5fd70-32e6-11e4-8f02-03c644b2d7d0_story.html.

351 *foreign election interference:* Lauren Gambino, "Trump Campaign May Have Broken Law by Seeking Foreign Political Donations," *Guardian* (US edition), June 29, 2016, https://www.theguardian.com/us-news/2016/jun/29/trump-campaign-donations-foreign-politicians.

351 *such as the National Rifle Association:* "The NRA and Russia: How a Tax-Exempt Organization Became Foreign Asset," U.S. Senate Committee on Finance Minority Staff Report, September, 2019, https://www.finance.senate.gov/imo/media/doc/The%20NRA%20%20Russia%20-%20How%20a%20Tax-Exempt%20Organization%20Became%20a%20Foreign%20Asset.pdf.

354 *added nearly a thousand stores:* Nathaniel Meyersohn, "Dollar General Is Opening 1,000 New Stores Next Year," CNN, last modified December 5, 2019, https://www.cnn.com/2019/12/05/business/dollar-general-stores-stock-earnings/index.html.

354 *Dollar General's presence does not:* E. F. Racine, A. Batada, C. A. Solomon, and M. Story, "Availability of Foods and Beverages in Supplemental Nutrition Assistance Program—Authorized Dollar Stores in a Region of North Carolina," *Journal of the Academy of Nutrition and Dietetics* 116(10), 2016, 1613–20.

355 *This creates "food deserts":* Renee E. Walker, Christopher R. Keane, and Jessica G. Burke, "Disparities and Access to Healthy Food in the United States: A Review of Food Deserts Literature," *Health & Place* 16, no. 5 (2010): 876–84.

356 *one of the most overcrowded:* Kentucky Department of Corrections, "Kentucky Department of Corrections 2018 Annual Report," 2018, https://corrections.ky.gov/About/researchandstats/Documents/Annual%20Reports/2018%20Annual%20Report.pdf.

356 *resident completes an MRT:* Todd A. Armstrong, "The Effect of Moral Reconation Therapy on the Recidivism of Youthful Offenders: A Randomized Experiment," *Criminal Justice and Behavior* 30, no. 6 (2003): 668–87.

358 *received huge donations from:* Campaign Legal Center, "Trump Super PAC Received Illegal Donations from Private Prison Company," December 20, 2016, https://campaignlegal.org/press-releases/trump-super-pac-received-illegal-donations-private-prison-company.

358 *are absolute disasters:* Kara Gotsch and Vinay Basti, "Capitalizing on Mass Incarceration: U.S. Growth in Private Prisons," The Sentencing Project, 2018, https://www.sentencingproject.org/wp-content/uploads/2018/07/Capitalizing-on-Mass-Incarceration.pdf.

360 *More than eight thousand employees:* Bill Estep, "Jobs Gone, Fruit of the Loom's Unpaid Property Tax Bill Remains in Russell County," *Lexington (KY) Herald-Leader*, March 21, 2015, http://kentucky.com/news/local/education/shortchanging-our-schools/article44563605.html.

360 *no job that can't be transplanted:* Stewart Jennison, "NAFTA Local Debate on Free Trade Agreement Mirrors Heated National Controversy—NAFTA The

Arguments At a Glance," *Owensboro (KY) Messenger-Inquirer*, October 17, 1993, 1D.

361 *so obviously the right thing:* John C. K. Fisher, "McConnell Worried NAFTA Will Fail," *Kentucky Post* (Covington, KY), November 13, 1993, 8K.

361 *foresaw the disaster that:* Lisa Hoffman, "Ky. Votes 4–2 Against NAFTA," *Kentucky Post*, (Covington, KY), November 18, 1993, 1K.

361 *senator from Kentucky is a lost cause":* Stewart Jennison, "NAFTA Local debate on free trade agreement mirrors heated national controversy NAFTA The Arguments at a Glance," *Owensboro Messenger-Inquirer (KY)*, October 17, 1993, p. 1D.

363 *it was a community builder:* David Streitfeld, "Prime Anchor: An Amazon Warehouse Town Dreams of a Better Life," *New York Times*, December 27, 2019, https://www.nytimes.com/2019/12/27/technology/amazon-kentucky.html.

366 *helps massive corporate growers:* Vincent H. Smith, "Hemp and CBD Now Qualify for One of the Most Lucrative—and Wasteful—Government Subsidies," *Market Watch*, December 20, 2018, https://www.marketwatch.com/story/hemp-and-cbd-now-qualify-for-one-of-the-most-lucrative-and-wasteful-government-subsidies-2018-12-19.

367 *it's bad for the small farmer:* "USDA Estimates 20 Percent of Hemp Grown in 2020 Will Be Hot," *Hemp Wire News*, December 2019, https://www.hempwirenews.com/usda-estimates-20-percent-of-hemp-grown-in-2020-will-be-hot/amp/.

373 *$1.2 million in donations:* Braidy United Against Gun Violence, "WHICH SENATORS HAVE TAKEN THE MOST NRA MONEY?," n.d., https://www.bradyunited.org/act/nra-donations-116th-congress-senators.

373 *priority is on tax reform*: Jordain Carney, "McConnell: 'Premature' to Discuss Gun Control Legislation," *Hill*, October 2, 2017, https://thehill.com/homenews/senate/353672-mcconnell-premature-to-discuss-gun-control-legislation.

376 *come here legally and just don't leave:* Robert Warren, "US Undocumented Population Continued to Fall from 2016 to 2017, and Visa Overstays Significantly Exceeded Illegal Crossings for the Seventh Consecutive Year," Center for Migration Studies, January 16, 2019, https://cmsny.org/publications/essay-2017-undocumented-and-overstays/.

379 *strong pro-choice advocate:* Kelly McEvers and Eric Mennel, "Mitch Part 1: 'Win This Thing,' " NPR's *Embedded*, June 6, 2019, https://www.npr.org/transcripts/728314472.

381 *Eight states still have such:* National Alcoholic Beverage Control Association, "Wet and Dry Counties," n.d., https://www.nabca.org/sites/default/files/assets/publications/white_papers/WetDry%20Counties.pdf.

386 *Louisville alternative paper LEO Weekly:* Mark Nickolas, "Bluegrass Politics: The Burkesville Bully," *LEO Weekly*, last modified March 14, 2006, https://www.leoweekly.com/2006/03/bluegrass-politics-the-burkesville-bully.

CHAPTER 10: THE DECISION

400 *relationship with China:* Corning China, "OPPORTUNITIES IN CHINA," n.d., https://www.corning.com/careers/cn/en/Locations/China.html.

400 *Chinese presence in Kentucky:* "Owens Corning | Milestones," March 31, 2017, https://www.owenscorning.com/owenscorning.com/assets/sustainability/about-us/our-story/Milestones_4-b4968e25a428aebbaa6022423803a8fab9075abdfdd9681346f7e6229c6e1ffd.pdf.

401 *one of only eight Republicans:* John B. Judis, "Sullied Heritage: The Decline of Principled Conservative Hostility to China," *New Republic*, April 23, 2001.

401 *sent "the wrong message":* Jim Mann, "Bush Reportedly Ready to Ease China Sanctions—Democrats Say They'll Retaliate," *San Francisco Chronicle*, December 12, 1989, A1.

401 *McConnell began attending fund-raisers:* Judis, "Sullied Heritage."

401 *most powerful economic interests:* Curtis Ellis, Harry Wu, "Love Is Blind When It Comes to McConnell, China," *Cincinnati Enquirer*, October 4, 2014., A10.

401 *described Elaine Chao's family:* Michael Forsythe et al., "A 'Bridge' to China, and Her Family's Business, in the Trump Cabinet," *New York Times* , June 2, 2019, https://www.nytimes.com/2019/06/02/us/politics/elaine-chao-china.html

402 *nearly as much in donations:* Judis, "Sullied Heritage."

402 *building his ships in Chinese state-owned:* Ibid.

402 *between $5 million and $25 million:* Michela, Tindera, "A $59 Million Will Sheds Light On Shipping Fortune Connected To Elaine Chao And Mitch McConnell," *Forbes*, June 10, 2019, https://www.forbes.com/sites/michelatindera/2019/06/10/million-will-sheds-light-on-shipping-fortune-connected-to-elaine-chao-and-mitch-mcconnell/#e2509622eb2b.

402 *"punish the Chinese government":* Mary Ann Roser, "Kentucky Congressmen Favored Sanctions," *Lexington (KY) Herald-Leader*, July 11, 1991, A3.

402 *only wounded party would be:* Mitch McConnell, "Hong Kong and the Future of China Three Years After the Tiananmen Square Massacre," Heritage Foundation, June 5, 1992, https://www.heritage.org/asia/report/hong-kong-and-the-future-china-three-years-after-the-tiananmen-square-massacre.

402 *"Political reforms are going to come":* Curtis Ellis, "While D.C. sleeps, China plans to replace America - Exclusive: Curtis Ellis talks to expert who questions GOP's Beijing-is-our-friend tack," *WorldNetDaily* (USA), February 6, 2015.

402 *spectacularly off the mark:* Malcom Brabant, "This Dissident Leaked Explosive Documents Depicting China's Brutal Treatment of Uighurs," *PBS NewsHour*, January 10, 2020, https://www.pbs.org/newshour/show/this-dissident-leaked-explosive-documents-depicting-chinas-brutal-treatment-of-uighurs.

403 *trade deficit with China:* United States Census Bureau, "Trade in Goods with China," 2019, https://www.census.gov/foreign-trade/balance/c5700.html.

403 *"putting profits ahead of people":* John Cheves, "Wedded to Free Trade in China," *Lexington (KY) Herald-Leader,* October 20, 2006, A7.

403 *learned about Communist China:* Associated Press, "GOP Senators Split on Trade Vote," *Kentucky Post* (Covington, KY), September 20, 2000, 14A.

403 *Mitch sold out:* Helene Cooper and John Harwood, "The vote on GATT—the rules change: Major shifts in trade are ensured as GATT wins U.S. approval—senate vote on pact to slash tariffs 40 percent should spur global economic activity—politics and the middle class," *Wall Street Journal,* December 2, 1994.

404 *political issues of the day: Thomas Speed, The Political Club, Danville, Kentucky, 1786–1790: Being an Account of an Early Kentucky Society from the Original Papers Recently Found. No. 9.* (John P. Morton, 1894.)

406 *blocked more judicial nominees:* Robert Reich, "Mitch McConnell Is Destroying the Senate—and American Government," *Guardian,* April 6, 2019, https://www.theguardian.com/commentisfree/2019/apr/06/mitch-mcconnell-senate-republicans-donald-trump-judges.

406 *ignored all of his legislative priorities:* Gay S. Sheryl, "McConnell Promised to End Senate Gridlock; Instead, Republicans Are Stuck in Neutral," *New York Times,* August 3, 2019, https://www.nytimes.com/2019/08/03/us/politics/senate-votes-mcconnell.html.

406 *take him on frontally:* Alec MacGillis, *The Cynic: The Political Education of Mitch McConnell* (New York: Simon & Schuster, 2014).

406 *about ruining Obama:* Nicole Goodkind, "Mitch McConnell Described as a Hypocrite for Defending the Filibuster," *Newsweek,* August 22, 2019, https://www.newsweek.com/mitch-mcconnell-filibuster-senate-2020-1455762.

406 *bicker less and come together:* Ella Nilsen, "House Democrats Have Passed Nearly 400 Bills. Trump and Republicans Are Ignoring Them," *Vox,* last modified November 29, 2019, https://www.vox.com/2019/11/29/20977735/how-many-bills-passed-house-democrats-trump.

411 *Only two senators in:* United States Senate, "Longest Serving Senators," n.d., https://www.senate.gov/senators/longest_serving_senators.htm.

416 *implying he was gay:* MacGillis, *The Cynic.*

416 *"limp wrist":* Roger Alford, "Bunning, Mongiardo Rally Their Supporters," *Kentucky Post* (Covington, KY), October 28, 2004, K6.

416 *the word* man *even applies:* Bruce Schreiner, "Mongiardo responds to personal attacks from Republicans," Associated Press, October 29, 2004.

416 *McConnell's political machine orchestrated:* MacGillis, *The Cynic.*

418 Money *magazine named it:* Tim Jordan, "MONEY Ranks Berea College #1 in Affordability," Berea College, July 6, 2017, https://www.berea.edu/news/money-ranks-berea-college-1-affordability/#more-13610.

419 *total amount of student loan debt:* Zach Friedman, "Student Loan Debt Statistics in 2019: A $1.5 Trillion Crisis," *Forbe,* February 25, 2019, https://www.forbes.com/sites/zackfriedman/2019/02/25/student-loan-debt-statistics-2019/#29ec9cea133f.

419 *Buckner, Kentucky:* Tyler Spanyer, "Senate Candidates Talk Student Loans to Court Youth Vote," *Floyd County Times* (Prestonsburg, KY), October 28, 2014.

419 *$16.8 trillion Wall Street bailouts*: Mike Collins, "The Big Bank Bailout," *Forbes*, July 14, 2015, https://www.forbes.com/sites/mikecollins/2015/07/14/the-big-bank-bailout/#773792ca2d83.

419 *isn't really about students:* Erica Werner, "Senate Republicans block student loan bill," Associated Press, June 11, 2014.

422 *justice Lisabeth Tabor Hughes:* Curtis Tate, "Mitch McConnell won't consider Obama judicial nominee from Kentucky," McClatchy Washington Bureau, March 18, 2016.

422 *Appointed to the bench in 2007:* Kentucky Court of Justice, "Deputy Chief Justice Lisabeth T. Hughes," n.d., https://kycourts.gov/courts/supreme/Pages/hughes.aspx.

422 *Refusing to allow Barack Obama:* "Explaining Senate's Blue Slip Process," Targeted News Service (USA), November 29, 2017.

422 *spokesman stated that:* "McConnell Opposes Louisville Judge Nominated to Appeals Court," WFPL online, last modified March 18, 2016, https://wfpl.org/kentucky-supreme-court-judge-nominated-appeals-court.

422 *immediately made clear he would not:* Jonathan Karl, Pierre Thomas, and Martha Raddatz, "Antonin Scalia - Death Of Longest Serving Supreme Court Justice," ABC World News (USA), February 13, 2016.

422 *citation of the "Biden Rule"*: Ledyard King: " 'We'd Fill It:' Mitch McConnell Blocked Obama Supreme Court Pick but Says He'd Help Trump Fill a Vacancy," *USA Today*, May 29, 2019, https://www.usatoday.com/story/news/politics/2019/05/29/mcconnell-blocked-obama-supreme-court-choice-wouldnt-stop-trump/1268883001.

423 *One in four judges:* Rebecca Klar, "Trump Has Officially Appointed One in Four Circuit Court Judges," *Hill*, November 7, 2019, https://thehill.com/homenews/administration/469519-trump-has-officially-appointed-one-in-four-circuit-court-judges.

424 *yearly median salary:* Donation to Bluegrass Victory Committee, "WATER HAY OATS ALLIANCE PAC," June 22, 2018.

424 *time raising money than legislating:* David Jolly, "Peeling Back the Curtain," *Politico*, n.d., https://www.politico.com/f/?id=00000152-5783-daaf-a75b-7fa766540000.

424 *spend at least two-thirds of their time raising money:* Shane Goldmacher, "Former Senate Leader Says Senators Spent Two-Thirds of Time Asking for Money," *National Journal*, January 16, 2014.

425 *unlimited amounts of money for:* Ken Buck, *Drain the Swamp: How Washington Corruption Is Worse Than You Think* (New York: Simon & Schuster, 2017).

425 *Russia has used some of these groups:* Alex Finley, "How Russian Money and Influence Slipped Through Cracks in the US Legal System," *Vox*, last modified

October 25, 2018, https://www.vox.com/policy-and-politics/2018/10/25/18016212/russian-meddling-dark-money-influence-2018-midterm-elections-citizens-united.

425 *Potato chips*: Kelly McEvers, "Mitch Part 2: 'Money Money Money,' " NPR, last modified June 6, 2019, https://www.npr.org/transcripts/729736263.

427 *infiltrate one of McConnell's speaking:* Tom Loftus, "Protesters Have Heated Questions for McConnell," *Louisville (KY) Courier-Journal*, February 21, 2017, https://www.courier-journal.com/story/news/politics/mitch-mcconnell/2017/02/21/protesters-greet-sen-mitch-mcconnell-heated-questions/98188380.

427 *In just one year, McConnell led:* Vernos Branco, "How Often Do Republicans Undermine Veterans? Here's a List," *Las Vegas Sun*, August 13, 2015, https://lasvegassun.com/news/2015/aug/13/every-turn-republicans-undermine-veterans.

427 *Wounded Veteran Job Security Act:* H. R. 2875.

427 *Veterans Retraining Act:* H.R. 1168.

427 *Veterans Business Center Act:* H.R. 1803.

427 *Homeless Veterans Reintegration Program Reauthorization Act:* H.R. 1171.

427 *Disabled Veterans Home Improvement and Structural Alteration Grant Increase Act:* H.R. 1293.

427 *derailing a* $21 billion *bill:* Juana Summers, "Republicans Derail Senate Vets Bill," *Politico,* last modified February 27, 2014, politico.com/story/2014/02/veterans-benefits-senate-republicans-104060.

428 *two hundred thousand veterans had their unemployment benefits:* Arloc Sherman, "Emergency Jobless Benefits Cut-Off Has Hit Nearly 200,000 Veterans and Counting," Center on Budget and Policy Priorities online, February 28, 2014, https://www.cbpp.org/blog/emergency-jobless-benefits-cut-off-has-hit-nearly-200000-veterans-and-counting.

428 *welfare of our nations' veterans:* Jonathan Capehart, "The GOP and Veterans: It's Complicated," *Washington Post*, May 21, 2014, https://www.washingtonpost.com/blogs/post-partisan/wp/2014/05/21/the-gop-and-veterans-its-complicated.

428 *National Commander Daniel Dellinger:* Summers, "Republicans Derail Senate Vets Bill."

428 *launched a $300,000 ad campaign:* Vote Vets, "VoteVets Launches $300,000 Kentucky Ad Buy That Puts Mitch McConnell's Intransigence on Veterans Care into Human Terms," n.d., https://m.votevets.org/press/votevets-launches-300000-kentucky-ad-buy-that-puts-mitch-mcconnells-intransigence-on-veterans-care-into-human-terms.

430 *top 1 percent of Americans now own 41 percent:* Emmanuel Saez and Gabriel Zucman, "Wealth Inequality in the United States Since 1913: Evidence from Capitalized Income Tax Data," *Quarterly Journal of Economics* 131, no. 2 (2016): 519–78.

430 *inequality difference in the United States:* Telford Taylor, "Income Inequality Is

Highest Since Census Started Tracking It, Report Shows," *Washington Post*, September 27, 2019.

430 *higher than every European:* World Bank, "GINI Index (World Bank Estimate)," n.d., https://data.worldbank.org/indicator/SI.POV.GINI?most_recent_value_desc=true&view=map.

430 *savings to fund Head Start programs;* Bill S.Amdt.4218 to S.Con.Res.70 ; vote number 08-S064 on March 13, 2008.

432 *complaint filed against me:* Sarah Ladd, "GOP Complaint Takes Sports Radio Host and Potential Mitch McConnell Challenger Matt Jones off Air," *USA Today*, November 6, 2019, https://www.usatoday.com/story/sports/2019/11/06/matt-jones-mitch-mcconnell-complaint/2514428001/.

INDEX

ABOUT THE AUTHORS

Matt Jones is an attorney and founder of Kentucky Sports Radio, the most popular radio program and website in the state. Jones graduated from the Duke University School of Law and finds himself thankfully removed from the daily practice of law. He lives in Lexington, Kentucky. @KySportsRadio

Chris Tomlin is a writer and humorist whose work has appeared on Kentucky Sports Radio and McSweeney's Internet Tendency, and in the *New York Post*, among other national outlets. He lives with his family in Fort Thomas, Kentucky. @cm_tomlin